Legal Context, Skills and Ethics

PEARSON

We work with leading authors to develop the strongest learning experiences, bringing cutting-edge thinking and best learning practice to a global market. We craft our print and digital resources to do more to help learners not only understand their content, but to see it in action and apply what they learn, whether studying or at work.

Pearson is the world's leading learning company. Our portfolio includes Penguin, Dorling Kindersley, the Financial Times and our educational business, Pearson International. We are also a leading provider of electronic learning programmes and of test development, processing and scoring services to educational institutions, corporations and professional bodies around the world.

We enable our customers to access a wide and expanding range of market-leading content from world-renowned authors and develop their own tailor-made book. You choose the content that meets your needs and Pearson produces a high-quality printed book.

Every day our work helps learning flourish, and wherever learning flourishes, so do people.

To learn more please visit us at: www.pearsoned.co.uk/personalised

Legal Context, Skills and Ethics

David Hodgkinson. LL.B, LL.M, PGCE, Barrister
Course: LL.B
University of Derby

PEARSON

Harlow, England • London • New York • Boston • San Francisco • Toronto • Sydney • Auckland • Singapore • Hong Kong
Tokyo • Seoul • Taipei • New Delhi • Cape Town • Sao Paulo • Mexico City • Madrid • Amsterdam • Munich • Paris • Milan

Pearson Education Limited
Edinburgh Gate
Harlow
Essex CM20 2JE
England

and Associated Companies throughout the world

Visit us on the World Wide Web at:
www.pearson.com/uk

© 2014 published by Pearson Education Limited

All rights reserved. No part of this publication may be reproduced, stored in a retrieval system, or transmitted in any form or by any means, electronic, mechanical, photocopying, recording or otherwise, without either the prior written permission of the publisher or a licence permitting restricted copying in the united Kingdom issued by the Copyright Licensing Agency Ltd, 90 Tottenham Court Road, London W1T 4LP.

ISBN 978-1-78376-257-6

Printed and bound in the UK.

Contents

Advocacy Fred Motson	1
Answering Problem Questions Andy Vi-Ming Kok	31
Career Planning Fred Motson	49
General Study Skills for Law Dave Hodgkinson	95
Mooting Per Laleng	113
Negotiation Fred Motson	135
Writing Law Essays Janette Porteous	159
Finding Cases Rick Canavan	193
Finding Legislation Rick Canavan	223
How to Read Primary Sources of Law Dave Hodgkinson	245
Using Secondary Sources Stephen Bunbury	277
Finding Secondary Sources Stephen Bunbury	293

1
Advocacy

Fred Motson

What is the art of advocacy?

Advocacy is often defined as the art of persuasion. To be more precise, we can say that advocacy is the art of persuading others to accept, or look favourably upon, your cause, opinion or point of view. In this sense, advocacy goes far beyond the courtroom and can be found in almost all areas of life:

- Politicians use advocacy to promote political ideals and policies
- The advertising industry is based on advocating particular products to consumers
- People in business use advocacy to negotiate contracts, to suggest ideas, to try and attract investors, to manage staff and much more
- You yourself will have used advocacy many times in your life, from persuading your friends to do something you want, to the written advocacy in your university applications

Advocacy means much the same in a legal context. While the most obvious example is barristers and solicitor advocates using their advocacy skills to persuade a judge to find in their client's favour, all lawyers need to be able to effectively argue a point and convince others. In everyday legal practice, lawyers may have to deal with and persuade difficult clients, hostile opposition and their own colleagues! However, we shall focus on the specific art of persuading a court and/or jury on behalf of a client.

Why do we describe advocacy as an "art"? Despite the classification of law as "legal science", you will know from your own studies that the law, particularly in a common law system such as in England and Wales, is rarely black and white. Even in cases where the overall result is almost certain, a skilled lawyer may be able to influence the practical outcome considerably – a defendant in a criminal case who pleads guilty may have to accept that he will be sentenced to prison, but effective advocacy might be the difference between 2 years and 10 years behind bars.

Thus advocacy can be of crucial importance. However, it is not possible to "learn" advocacy the same way we can learn contract law or the law of equity. There are three key reasons why we must define advocacy as an art rather than a science:

1. Advocacy is inherently subjective. Just as a particular advertisement may convince you to buy a product, while it merely irritates others, a particular style might be extremely persuasive to some judges, while to others it may actively turn them against the advocate's point of view.

2. Advocacy is an individual skill. While you can study and improve on your advocacy technique, some people are inherently suited to advocacy more than others. This does not mean that someone who has less experience or confidence cannot be a great advocate, but it does mean that you must develop your own personal style.

3. Advocacy is dependent on the circumstances. The best advocate in the world will not win a case if the evidence or the law make success impossible. It is important to learn not only the effectiveness of advocacy, but also its limitations.

What makes a good advocate?

Because of the difficulties in teaching advocacy listed above, there is no definitive answer to the question of what makes a good advocate. Just as a debate over the "best" centre-forward or the "best" rock band can have no final answer, we cannot point to a particular lawyer and say "this is the best advocate in the world, with the most effective style, and with the highest chance of winning any given case". What we can do is select some specific qualities, which are present to at least some extent in all effective advocates.

Communication

Whatever style you develop as an advocate, certain practical qualities are vital. If you cannot communicate your points to the judge, then you cannot persuade him that they are correct. Most obviously, this means that a good advocate must be audible (although not necessarily very loud); must speak at a reasonable pace (slowly enough for the judge to catch all of the argument, quickly enough not to bore the court); and must be able to use emphasis, tone and body language to convey the impression they wish to give. While some people are naturally talented public speakers, "almost anyone can learn to speak in public effectively"[1]. Key communication skills such as making and maintaining eye-contact and speaking clearly are much easier to achieve when you are well-prepared and confident in your arguments.

Confidence

As already discussed, the purpose of advocacy is to persuade another as to the merit of your argument. However, if you do not appear to believe in your own argument, it is very unlikely anyone else will! This means that confidence is very important, as it is human nature to more readily accept something we are told with confidence rather than points raised in a tentative manner. However, a brief note of warning – do not confuse confidence with bluster or arrogance. Confidence is giving the impression that you understand your argument and believe that it offers the most logical conclusion, not that it is the only argument or must be accepted.

Intelligence

Even if an advocate can communicate their points brilliantly, the content of their argument still remains the most important part of any piece of advocacy. Thus intelligence is crucial – not just the narrow

---

[1] D. Pope and D. Hill, *Mooting and Advocacy Skills* (Sweet & Maxwell 2007) p.96

academic knowledge of an area of law (although this is of course very important), but the overall intelligence to condense all the complexities of the case, the evidence and the law into a coherent and logical argument. While an advocate who has just lost a seemingly strong case may not agree, you should always bear in mind that in our common law system judges are drawn from some of the most-respected advocates in the legal system and therefore have the legal knowledge and intelligence to see through a badly-constructed or illogical argument.

Diligence

As mentioned above, advocacy is a very individual pursuit. In the vast majority of trials, you will be the only person representing your client[2] and depending on the case that may mean you are individually responsible for their financial well-being, their employment, their reputation or even their freedom. A good advocate will recognise this responsibility, and ensure that they give everything they can to every case. This means you need the diligence to prepare for the trial as fully as possible and the persistence to argue every reasonable point even under stern questioning from the judge.

Knowledge

When we examined intelligence we said that legal knowledge was not enough on its own to create an effective argument, however it is of course still crucial. The last thing any advocate wants is to be pulled up mid-flow due to a basic legal error, nor do they want to be frantically researching the law when they could be composing a scintillating final speech. What is important is to understand the general principles of law, rather than trying to learn every single case in a particular area.

> *"It is true that questions of law do not often arise in everyday practice, and that most trials turn entirely on the facts. All the same, other things being equal, an advocate who is also a good lawyer – and does not obtrude his law until it is necessary – has an advantage over an advocate who is not."*[3]

Objectivity

Every lawyer comes to expect the inevitable question when they reveal their profession – "how can you represent someone you know is guilty?" The short answer is of course that everyone deserves a fair trial and our legal tradition is founded on the principle of innocence until proof of guilt. However, this question does raise an important point which all advocates must remember: while it is your duty to give your client the best possible representation, you must remain objective at all times. It is equally as dangerous to become convinced your client is in the right, as to become convinced they are in the wrong. In order to convince the court, you must be able to see the case from the point of view of the judge or jury, not just your client's. If you allow personal feelings to intrude in your advocacy, you will make elementary mistakes, such as becoming angry or upset. This will not only impair your advocacy but also reflect poorly on both you and your client. In the words of Baron Bramwell:

> *"A man's rights are to be determined by the Court, not by his attorney or counsel. It is for want of remembering this that foolish people object to lawyers that they will advocate a case against their*

---

[2] In the higher courts it is more common to have a senior and junior counsel for each party. However, even in this case, each advocate will be addressing separate issues on the whole.

[3] J. Munkman, *The Technique of Advocacy* (first published 1951, Universal Law Publishing 2007) p.8

own opinions. A client is entitled to say to his counsel, I want your advocacy, not your judgment; I prefer that of the Court."[4]

Experience

It may seem somewhat premature at this stage in your legal education to discuss the importance of experience, but as with so many skills, the more advocacy you undertake, the more you will improve. You will find that even a handful of attempts at, for example, an opening speech, or examining a witness, will dramatically improve your abilities. In legal practice, experience also assists in handling cases – for example, when to emphasise a point and when to accept the judge has made his mind up and move on.

Ethics

The importance of ethics

Despite the negative perception of lawyers as unscrupulous and unprincipled, legal ethics are in fact at the cornerstone of the legal profession in England and Wales. Nowhere is this more apparent than in the realm of the advocate, who not only owes a duty to his or her client, but also to the court itself. Without a clear ethical code, our court system would soon lose its legitimacy. As the famous legal aphorism states, "not only must Justice be done; it must also be seen to be done"[5].

However legal ethics are not merely for show. The rules and duties which govern advocates perform a number of functions, among them:

- preventing fraud, falsehoods or untruthful assertions by advocates,
- preserving the respect due to the court,
- ensuring that parties to the case, witnesses, court officers and members of the public are treated fairly and politely in court,
- preventing advocates' personal feelings from influencing the outcome of a case,
- avoiding unnecessary expense or waste of the court's time.

So what are legal ethics? Much has been written on this subject, but to take a single definition for our current purposes, we can say legal ethics involves:

"the relationship between morality and Law, the values underpinning the legal system, and the regulation of the legal services market, including the institutions, professional roles and ethics of the judiciary and legal professions."[6]

---

[4] *Johnson v Emerson and Sparrow* (1870-71) L.R. 6 Ex. 329 at 366
[5] This comes from the case of *R v Sussex Justices, Ex parte McCarthy* [1924] 1 KB 256, where Lord Hewart CJ commented "it is not merely of some importance but is of fundamental importance that justice should not only be done, but should manifestly and undoubtedly be seen to be done" (at 259).
[6] Taken from the recommended definition of legal ethics by Professor Andrew Boon, *Legal Ethics at the Initial Stage: A Model Curriculum* (Report for the Law Society of England and Wales, December 2010)

A crucial word in this definition is 'regulation'. From the beginnings of the modern legal profession in the 13th century until recently, lawyers in England and Wales were self-regulated and 'legal ethics' were a set of very general, unwritten principles which had developed out of tradition rather than a cogent list of rules, in a similar way to constitutional conventions in public law. One writer, addressing junior advocates, gave the following advice in 1947:

> "But one who is intended coming to the profession might ask where is this code [of ethics] to be found, and how is to be learnt? The answer to the first question is in the traditions of the profession. The answer to the second is in the Schools of the profession, its ancient craft guilds, called the Inns of Court, where all matters of professional conduct are freely and daily discussed, and where the transgressor is answerable for his misconduct. It is, of course, incapable of being stated or written out in full like a Legal Code."[7]

Despite Hilbery's assertion, today we do indeed have written ethical codes, namely the Code of Conduct of the Bar of England and Wales[8] and the SRA Code of Conduct[9] which regulate barristers and solicitors respectively. These codes contain clear written rules and aim to provide lawyers and clients with an unambiguous guide to appropriate standards of conduct in legal practice.

Key duties of the advocate

Both regulatory codes contain numerous duties which barristers and solicitor-advocates must adhere to when appearing in court. For our current purposes, we will examine a selection of the most important. Please note that to avoid repetition we will focus on the Bar Code of Conduct (hereafter referred to as 'the Code') but similar duties can be found in the SRA Code.[10]

Duties to the court

> **Extract: Code of Conduct of the Bar of England and Wales**
>
> 302. A barrister has an overriding duty to the Court to act with independence in the interests of justice: he must assist the Court in the administration of justice and must not deceive or knowingly or recklessly mislead the Court.

As the extract above makes clear, the foremost duty you will owe as an advocate is to the court. As an "overriding" duty, this will take precedence even over your duty to your client. This means that while it would be beneficial to your client to distort the facts or fail to reveal case authority which harms your case, this would deceive or mislead the Court and is thus not permitted. Other parts of the Code of Conduct include a number of specific duties owed by an advocate to the Court, including:

---

[7] The Hon. Sir Malcolm Hilbery, *Duty and Art in Advocacy* (Stevens and Sons Ltd, 1946) p. 7
[8] Available at http://www.barstandardsboard.org.uk/regulatory-requirements/the-code-of-conduct/
[9] Available at http://www.sra.org.uk/solicitors/code-of-conduct.page
[10] Note one key difference between barristers and solicitors is the so-called 'cab rank rule' – solicitors may decide whether to represent a client, while barristers must take on any client able to pay their fees if they are not too busy, similar to the first taxi at a cab rank.

- Not to assert his or her personal opinion of the facts or the law[11];
- To bring any procedural irregularity to the attention of the Court during the hearing (rather than waiting to use it to support an appeal)[12];
- Not to invent evidence or devise facts to assist the case[13];
- Not to make submissions which in the advocate's opinion are not properly arguable.[14]

Duties to your client

> ### Extract: Code of Conduct of the Bar of England and Wales
> 303. A barrister:
>
> (a) must promote and protect fearlessly and by all proper and lawful means the lay client's best interests and do so without regard to his own interests or to any consequences to himself or to any other person (including any colleague, professional client or other intermediary or another barrister, the barrister's employer or any Authorised Body of which the barrister may be an owner or manager);
>
> (b) owes his primary duty as between the lay client and any other person to the lay client and must not permit any other person to limit his discretion as to how the interests of the lay client can best be served;

Paragraph 303 demonstrates that apart from the overriding duty to the court, an advocate's primary duty must be to his or her lay client[15]. Another extremely important duty is to "preserve the confidentiality of the lay client's affairs" – you cannot reveal any information given to you in confidence by your client without their consent, even after a case has finished[16]. This leads to one of the most frequently asked questions in this area – what do you do if your client admits to you in confidence that he or she committed the crime they are on trial for, but insists on pleading not guilty?

On the one hand, to reveal what you have been told to the court or the prosecution would be a serious breach of confidentiality. On the other, you know that you cannot deceive or mislead the court. The answer, which predates the Code, is a compromise. You cannot reveal what you were told, as this not only breaches confidentiality but also contravenes your client's right to a fair trial – due to the principle of innocence until proven otherwise, the defendant is entitled to test the prosecution case, as the burden of proof is on the prosecution is demonstrate that he or she is guilty beyond reasonable doubt. Remember, an advocate must be objective and you should never think a client "deserves" to be found guilty.[17] However, while you can and should test the prosecution case, you cannot advance a positive case of your own. This is because if you

---

[11] Code of Conduct of the Bar of England and Wales, para. 708(b)
[12] Ibid, para. 708(d)
[13] Ibid, para. 704
[14] Ibid. para 708(f)
[15] The lay client is the person named in the litigation, i.e. the claimant or defendant. The term is used to distinguish from the professional client, who is the solicitor employing the barrister.
[16] Code of Conduct of the Bar of England and Wales, para. 702
[17] You should also note that just because a defendant says they are guilty, this may not be the case. People sometimes plead guilty even when innocent, for example to protect a family member or as a result of mental disturbance.

make any submissions which suggest your client is not guilty, you are knowingly misleading the court. For example, you cannot claim your client has an alibi and while you might suggest to a prosecution witness during cross examination that they were too far away to identify the defendant, you could not suggest that they had mistaken him or her for another person. This will severely hamper your case and makes it very difficult to run any successful defence. Furthermore, an experienced prosecutor may well realise what you are doing. As such, you advise your client in such a situation of these consequences and remind them that pleading guilty at this stage will be more advantageous in terms of sentencing than being found guilty after trial.

Duties to third parties and the profession

Advocates also owe a number of duties to third parties and the public as a whole. This is summarised in paragraph 301(a)(iii) of the code, which prevents a barrister from engaging in conduct "likely to diminish public confidence in the legal profession or . . . otherwise bring the legal profession into disrepute". Some of the key duties in this area include:

- Maintaining absolute independence from external pressures[18]
- Not to give money or presents to, or receive them from, clients or third parties[19]
- To treat witnesses with respect, avoid questions which are merely scandalous or calculated to insult a witness or other person and avoid naming third parties in open court if to do so would impugn their character.[20]

Reflection Questions

1. Do you agree that the above qualities are required by an effective advocate? Can you think of any other attributes which are required?
2. Think of three public figures past or present who you consider great orators. What made them such effective advocates?
3. Does being an ethical advocate necessarily mean you are a 'moral' advocate?

The Technique of Advocacy

Effective preparation

"Good advocacy depends on good preparation"[21]. This cannot be repeated enough, as it is almost invariably the case that a well-prepared advocate with limited advocacy skills will triumph over a badly-prepared advocate, however brilliant he or she is on their feet.

---

[18] Code of Conduct of the Bar of England and Wales, para. 307(a)
[19] Ibid, para. 307(c) and (d)
[20] Ibid, para 708(g) and (h)
[21] M. Hyam, *Advocacy Skills* 3rd Edition (Blackstone 1995) p.10

Undertaking research

Researching the issues raised by a case is always the starting point for any advocate. While legal research is an important skill of its own which requires far more detailed explanation elsewhere, there are some particular research techniques which directly relate to the art of advocacy.

As soon as you receive the papers for any form of advocacy, from a mooting competition to a Supreme Court case, you should ensure you read them carefully and in full. Many advocates will "skim read" the papers first, in order to get a general understanding of the facts and legal issues, but a good advocate will always then read everything they have been provided with in detail, as just one word in a statement of case or piece of written evidence may be enough to alter the likely outcome[22]. Once you have read the paper, the next step is to identify the legal issues that are being raised. This may be very straightforward, for example in a criminal case where your client is pleading guilty, you will merely have to look at the relevant mitigating and aggravating factors for sentencing. However, the legal issues may be extremely complex and could involve many different areas of law, thus a structured approach is preferable.

Once you have identified the legal issues, you should begin your research. It is advisable to start by looking at relatively general sources, particularly if the case involves an area of law you are not familiar with or have not studied recently – even the best advocates cannot remember all of the relevant law! While textbooks and similar resources can be of use, most advocates in practice would start by looking at practitioners' works, which are expressly designed to be used by lawyers. Unlike the textbooks we use in universities, practitioner textbooks contain much less historical and academic discussion of the law, focusing instead on stating what the current position is on each topic and considering in detail how the courts have dealt with such cases in recent years. They are also preferred as they can be cited in court with more authority than textbooks designed for students. Most of these books are named after their original author (often from many centuries ago) and some of the most well-known practitioner works include *Chitty on Contracts*, *Clerk & Lindsell on Torts* and *McGregor on Damages*. Another very useful source which you may well be familiar with is *Haslbury's Laws of England,* which provides authoritative coverage of all areas of law, although it is updated less regularly than the more specialist practitioner works. Today, many of these works can not only be found in law libraries but also through electronic legal databases.

By reading around the subject you will begin to gain a clear picture of the legal arguments in your particular case. While reading through practitioner works or textbooks, you should note down every case or piece of legislation which appears to be of relevance to the advocacy you will be performing. This will then provide a starting point for your detailed research into individual cases and other sources of law. It may be tempting to read the summary of a case in another work and immediately decide to rely upon it, but you must ensure that you read any law you wish to rely on in full, whether it is a judgment, a statute or an EU directive – you may well find that an important exception or definition can be found elsewhere which strengthens or weakens your argument considerably.

Finally, if you have been provided with any authorities by your opponent (for example in the form of a skeleton argument) you should ensure that you read and analyse such sources, as you may find points of weakness or at the very least gain a greater understanding of what your opponent might argue. You should

---

[22] For example *Owens v Dudley Metropolitan Borough Council* [2011] EWCA Civ 359; Times, April 21, 2011 where a special needs counsellor was entitled to be part of the Teacher's Pension Scheme due to being described as a "teacher" in a clause of her employment contract.

of course also ensure that you check all law relied on by yourself and your opponent is current and has not been over-ruled, repealed or altered.

Written preparation

Now that you have a detailed understanding of the legal issues in your case, you will need to prepare your arguments. Any persuasive argument will need to combine the relevant facts in a case with the appropriate law, in order to support a logical conclusion which favours your client. In some cases your submissions may be relatively obvious, while in others it may take much thought and hard work to construct an appropriate argument, but in either case you will want to make some record of what you plan to say, in order to rely on it while performing your advocacy.

The first and most important point to note is that each advocate may prepare differently. There is no "right" way to prepare and what may allow one person to perform fluently and authoritatively in court may cause another to struggle miserably. However, even if there is no "right" way to prepare, there are certainly some "wrong" ways which you should avoid. We will now look at some of the most common methods of written preparation and examine which are more effective.

Writing out a speech in full

Many people with little public speaking experience choose to write out a script for what they will say. This is not necessarily a bad idea for someone who rarely speaks in public and does not plan to improve in future, however it is to be avoided in legal advocacy. First and foremost, writing a speech is extremely time-consuming. If you get into the habit of relying on drafting your submissions in full, you will not only waste time that could be better spent improving the content of your arguments but also never practice speaking without careful preparation. Considering that it is extremely common for advocates in practice to only receive case papers the night before, or even on the morning of, a court hearing, this is an essential skill to learn. This leads on to another problem with the approach, which is that an effective advocate must always be flexible and ready to take a new approach. If you rely on a written speech and are then surprised by a question from the judge, or a point raised by your opponent, you will find it very hard to respond. Finally, while some experienced orators can make a written speech sound natural and persuasive, the usual result of a script is that an advocate looks down at his or her notes rather than making eye contact with the judge and the overall result is a dull and toneless presentation which does not project confidence or competence.

Speaking without notes

At the other end of the scale, some advocates attempt to speak entirely without written notes. While this may be appropriate in very brief submissions or for extremely experienced advocates, it is a dangerous route to take. By speaking without any written reminders, you are relying entirely on your memory and your ability to be spontaneous. If either of these fails you, the result will usually be one of two extremes: you either dry up as you can't think of anything to say, or you start to ramble and lose the thread of your argument. Neither will help persuade a judge.

Using outline notes

Probably the most common approach among advocates in practice is to write a relatively sparse outline of what they plan to say. You may do this by writing out a number of headings, or using bullet points or numbered lists. Some people combine this with using note cards, although in practice it is usual to use an advocate's notebook. This is a balanced approach which provides some structure and, in case of emergency, a reminder of the overall line of your argument, without creating the disadvantages of a full speech. However, until you gain more advocacy experience you should not feel that you need to confine yourself to bare headings – for example, you may wish to create sub-headings or fuller bullet points, note down in full how you will address the judge or how you will pronounce cases or legal Latin. It is also perfectly sensible to script just the first few sentences of your submissions, as this will give you the confidence to get started – most new advocates find that once they get started the words flow much more easily!

Practical preparation

Just as with your written preparation, you will develop you own methods to prepare for appearing as an advocate. What follows is a checklist of tips and suggestions which will help you to be as prepared as possible when that time comes.

- **Prepare clear notes:** The format of your notes is just as important as their content. It may sound obvious but make sure that your notes are in large enough text to be easily readable at a glance, as you will want to keep eye contact with the judge as much as possible. You should also try and organise notes so that you can avoid turning pages or dealing with large stacks of paper as much as possible.

- **Practice, practice, practice:** Even the most experienced advocates will run through submissions on their way to court and the more you practice, the more confident and fluent you will be on the day. There are many different ways to practice and you do not necessarily need another person with legal knowledge, or even another person at all. While practising in front of another advocate will give you the most specific feedback, a lay person such as a friend or family member can still advise you on your delivery, volume, body language and eye contact even if they don't understand the legal concepts you are discussing. However, make sure that you ask for honest and objective feedback! You can also practice alone and a common technique is to practice in front of a mirror. While you might feel very self-conscious at first, you can practice making eye contact and your volume and speed of delivery, which you cannot if you just go over your submissions in your head. For a more high-tech approach, you might want to record your submissions in audio or video format, although if you do so make sure you listen or watch your performance in full, however awkward it may feel! However you choose to practice, you should time your submissions if your advocacy is expected to last for a certain period. Bear in mind that you will usually speak faster on the day than when practising.

- **Pack carefully:** You should of course ensure that you remember any documents which you will rely on or present to the court and/or your opponent. Ensure that you bring spare copies for all parties who may need them. Of course you will need to bring any notes that you wish to rely on, but also make sure that you have extra paper and pens as you will want to make notes during your opponent's submissions. If you expect to be working with bundles of documents then post-it notes are also a useful item to bring, as they can help you mark pages or sections. Finally, never assume that water will be provided (although it usually will) and bring a bottle of your own.

- **Expect and accept being nervous:** Unless you are a part of the very small minority of fortunate advocates who never feel anxious before performing advocacy, it is inevitable that you will feel nervous at some point, whether it is the night before or the moment the judge enters the court. This is to be expected and you should not feel less of an advocate because of it, as many of the most experienced and respected advocates in Britain still suffer from nerves before every case. In the words of Andrew Hochhauser QC, who has been in practice for over 30 years yet still gets no more than three hours sleep before a big case, "The day you stop feeling nervous, is the day you are no longer at the top of your game."[23]

- **Ensure you arrive on time:** Nothing is less conducive to good advocacy than arriving at court late, flustered and out of breath. Always ensure that you leave plenty of time to travel to the court and build in sufficient time to compensate for traffic, delayed public transport etc. If you are visiting somewhere you have not been before, make sure you look up directions in advance and that you are clear on where you need to report to on arrival. It is much better to arrive too early than at the last minute, particularly because if you do arrive early you will get the chance to get accustomed to your surroundings.

Basic court etiquette

Despite recent reforms, the courts of England and Wales still retain considerable amounts of a long and sometimes obscure legal tradition. One of the areas in which this is most apparent is in the "rules" regarding court etiquette. Few of these rules are legal in nature, and many are essentially unwritten, however failing to adhere to them through discourtesy or ignorance is one of the fastest ways to lose favour with the court and while a judge will not decide a case based on the behaviour of an advocate, it may well mean he takes less note of your legal arguments and is less likely to grant any leeway on contentious points.[24]

If a judge feels that you have breached etiquette, the common method of informing the advocate is to say "I can't hear you". Ensure you remember this, as stories abound of junior advocates simply shouting louder and louder at the judge, rather than rectifying their error! However, (most) judges are willing to overlook minor errors and will take account of inexperience. If you do make a mistake of etiquette, a swift apology will usually rectify the situation. At the very least, you will avoid the fate which befell an American lawyer who repeatedly upset the judge during a criminal trial in a Federal District Court. In his final words to the jury, the judge said:

> "I also realize that you had a difficult and a disagreeable task in this case. You have been compelled to sit through a disgraceful and disreputable performance on the part of a lawyer who is unworthy of being a member of the profession; and I, as a member of the legal profession, blush that we should have such a specimen in our midst."[25]

Court dress

Unfortunately for traditionalists, there have been a number of reforms to court dress in recent years. While advocates are still expected to wear wigs and gowns in full trials and in the higher courts, many interim applications and lower court proceedings are now conducted in business suits. However, the apocryphal story still circulates at the Bar of the advocate who was ignored by judge because he was wearing coloured socks. This is an exaggeration but it is still important to dress correctly for any advocacy – the usual dress for a man will be a dark business suit, plan shirt and muted tie, while for women a dark suit or

---
[23] Priya Malhotra, 'The Nuts and Bolts of Trial Advocacy' *The Circuiteer* (London, Autumn 2010) p.17
[24] In practice, you should also note that there are disciplinary sanctions available, the most extreme being found in contempt of court, which can carry a prison sentence.
[25] As cited in the US Supreme Court, considering the attorney in question's appeal against his conviction for contempt of court. *Offlutt v United States*, 348 US 11 at p. 17n

dark skirt and white blouse is advised. A good rule of thumb is to dress the same way you would for an important job interview at a law firm or barristers chambers. Dress required for religious reasons will of course be acceptable but try to otherwise keep jewellery at a minimum. Even if you are taking part in advocacy where no dress code is imposed, you will find that dressing professionally improves your confidence and will make you feel more like an advocate.

Addressing the court

When addressing the court, it is vital to use the correct form of address for the judge or judges in question. While few judges will strenuously object to being addressed by a higher title than they merit, it is extremely offensive to refer to a senior judge by a more junior title. As part of your preparation for any piece of advocacy, you should confirm who you will be addressing and ensure you know the correct form of address.

Court	Judge	Mode of address
Supreme Court	Justice of the Supreme Court	My Lord/ My Lady or Your Lordship/ Your Ladyship[26]
Court of Appeal	Lord/ Lady Justice of Appeal	My Lord/ My Lady or Your Lordship/ Your Ladyship
High Court	High Court Judge	My Lord/ My Lady or Your Lordship/ Your Ladyship
	Master	Master
	District Judge	Sir/ Madam
Crown Court[27]	High Court Judge	My Lord/ My Lady or Your Lordship/ Your Ladyship
	Circuit Judge or Recorder	Your Honour
County Court	Circuit Judge or Recorder	Your Honour
	District Judge	Sir/ Madam
Magistrates Court	District Judge or Lay Chairman	Sir/ Madam
	Lay Chairman	Sir/ Madam if a barrister, Your Worship if a solicitor
	Other lay members	Your colleagues

[26] Note that the plural of judges referred to by these terms is My Lords/ Your Lordships when there is a mixture of male and female judges

[27] Note that judges in the Central Criminal Court and the Recorders of Manchester and Liverpool are referred to as "My Lord/ My Lady". See PD [1982] 1 All ER 320

When addressing higher judges, you need to know when it is appropriate to use "my Lord" and "your Lordship". The technical answer is that "my Lord" is used when addressing the judge in the vocative sense, while "your Lordship" is used for the accusative. In plainer terms, use "my Lord" when you would refer to someone by name, whereas "your Lordship" replaces "you".

> ## Example
> How to address a judge
>
> If you wanted to ask "Kate, have you had the opportunity to read the Appellant's skeleton argument?" where Kate is a judge in the Court of Appeal, you would say:
>
> "My Lady, has Your Ladyship had the opportunity to read the Appellant's skeleton argument?"

Citing cases

While cases are used less frequently in court than many students expect, particularly in courts of first instance, it is still very important to refer to legal authority correctly. An advocate who does not will at best appear very inexperienced and at worst may actually confuse the judge as to which case they are referring to.

When reading a case out loud, there are two conventions which you may not be familiar with. Firstly, you do not pronounce the "v" between the parties' names as the letter 'v', but rather use the word "and". Secondly, the citation must be read in full, not abbreviated as it is on the page. This can be summarised as:

> ## Example
> How to refer to cases in court
>
> "(Court) Party 1 AND Party 2 reported at (volume) of the (law reports) for (year) at (page number)"

Thus, if an advocate was referring to *Carlill v Carbolic Smoke Ball Company* [1893] 1 QB 256 in support of a point, they would actually say:

> "... which is supported by the Court of Appeal decision in Carlill and Carbolic Smoke Ball as reported in volume one of the Queen's Bench reports for 1893, at page two hundred and fifty-six."

Language and formalities

A common mistake many students make when first attempting advocacy is to try and speak "like a lawyer". This normally means trying to use as many long words as possible, dramatic body language and an affected 'posh' accent. The end result is usually more humorous than persuasive! Unlike what you may have seen in films, on television or on the stage, most advocates take a relatively simple approach to addressing the court. While obviously you should use the breadth of your vocabulary and avoid language which is overly casual or unprofessional, the most important thing is to make yourself understood. A judge is far happier to hear a straightforward argument which he or she can follow and understand than be the unwilling audience to an impenetrable monologue of legal jargon. In Sir Ernest Gowers' famous guide to plain English (which should be an invaluable aide to law students and indeed to some lawyers) he explains:

> *"Much official writing . . . needs merely to be clear, workmanlike and inoffensive. It had much better be flat and clear than eloquent and obscure . . . for the reader is looking only for plain, honest bread and butter and he does not want it spread with jam, or even caviar, any more than he wants it spread with glue or engine grease."*[28]

This equally applies to oral advocacy, although once you have mastered the basic advocacy flourishes of eloquence, as long as they remain relevant and comprehensible, can certainly be added to your repertoire.

Appropriate language

So what is appropriate language? It is perhaps easier to define what is *not* appropriate. In our everyday conversations, we include a lot of words and phrases which are merely 'filler'. Some of the most common examples include:

- **'Um' 'Er' 'Erm' etc.** – We use these filler words so frequently and so naturally that you may well not realise just how often they appear in conversation. Every student who first attempts advocacy will find themselves using these words, and indeed even the top advocates in professional practice are unlikely to be able to avoid them completely. However, you should try to minimise your 'umming and erring' as much as possible, as it breaks up your arguments and makes you sound as if you are either unsure of what you will say, or not confident in the truth of it. In actual fact, we usually use such filler words to fill in the gaps in our sentences, which means that a simple trick to cut down on using such words is to stop speaking as soon as you are about to say 'um' or 'erm', then resume with the next part of your sentence. This will give the impression of a dignified pause, and you will find such pauses becoming shorter and less frequent the more you practice.

- **'Like' 'you know' etc**. – Another common tic in modern speech is the use of these words and phrases, which we again use to fill in the gaps. In almost every case, they add nothing to the meaning of your words and you should try and avoid them altogether, as they sound unprofessional and repeated use will grate on the ear of the listener (try listening to interviews with famous footballers or pop stars and note how often these phrases are used, and how annoying they become when you start to notice them!).

- **Slang** – While the courts do not expect advocates to speak in perfect English, slang words and phrases should obviously be avoided unless necessary (for example you are repeating the words of a witness). In particular, never use 'OK' or 'yeah'. Where possible, also try and avoid contractions such as "can't", "don't" and "wouldn't" and use the full phrase instead.

- **Your opinion** – Remember that your opinion is actually completely irrelevant. The judge wants to hear your submissions, not your own personal view of the law or the facts. Therefore avoid phrases such as "I think", "I believe" or "in my opinion"; use "I submit" or "it is submitted" instead.

- **"Thank you"** – Traditionally, it is not considered polite to "thank" the judge – instead, you should say "I am grateful My Lord (or Your Honour etc.)".

---

[28] Sir Ernest Gowers, *The Complete Plain Words* (Sidney Greenbaum and Janet Whitcut Eds., first published 1986, Godine 2002) p.5

- **"OBJECTION!"** – Despite what you might see in courtroom dramas, or even in real courtrooms in North America, standing up and shouting "objection" is the height of bad manners in a British courtroom. If you do wish to object to something your opponent has said or wishes to do, the usual method is to try and catch the judge's eye, or if absolutely necessary to stand and wait for the judge to address you. In either case, you should explain in a reasonable tone why you object to what is occurring without casting aspersions on your opponent.

Essentially, you should stay as close as possible to your natural style of speech while avoiding the above pitfalls. In particular, do not worry about "sounding" like a lawyer – as long as you are clear and comprehensible and avoid slang, regional accents are common in the courts. To add one final note of warning, you should never, ever interrupt a judge, while you should always allow a judge to interrupt you.

Useful phrases

The following is a list of useful phrases which are frequently used by advocates in the courts. They are written to address a higher judge but you can of course substitute the correct form of address in each case.

- "May it please Your Lordship . . ." – This is a common way of beginning a speech or new submission. At the beginning of a case or advocacy exercise, you will usually continue on ". . . I am Mr/Mrs/Ms X and I shall be representing YZ Limited, the defendant in this case".
- "My learned friend, counsel for the claimant" – You should always refer to other advocates as your "learned friend", rather than by name. Note that traditionally barristers refer to a solicitor as their "friend", but this can be seen by some as slightly insulting (as it suggest they are not learned!) and in some areas this convention is slowly falling out of usage.
- "I am obliged to Your Lordship . . ." – Similar to "I am grateful", this is an elegant way to respond to a question or point made by a judge, even if inside you are furious that they have found the weakness in your argument! For example "I am obliged to Your Lordship for raising the point regarding contributory negligence. While Your Lordship is correct to state X, it is submitted that . . .".
- "May I draw Your Lordship's attention to . . ." – A common way to introduce a case or piece of evidence. An alternative is "If I may direct Your Lordship to . . .".
- "Is Your Lordship familiar with the facts of this case?" – When relying on a case, there is no guarantee that the judge will have come across the case before, or even if he or she has, whether they remember it fully. Rather than directly asking the judge if they know the case, you should use the above phrasing. This is because there is a legal fiction that judges do indeed know all of the law on every point, even though this is obviously unrealistic in practice.
- "May I assist Your Lordship any further?" – This is a useful phrase to end your submissions, as it allows the judge(s) to ask any questions they may have.

Body language

Non-verbal communication can be just as important as the words that you use. First and foremost, you must always stand when addressing the judge, or when being addressed by him or her. It is also common courtesy to rise when a judge enters or leaves the courtroom.[29] You should also ensure that you do not

---

[29] Note that in some hearings in the lower courts, such as hearings "in chambers", you may address the judge when seated. If unsure, err on the side of caution and stand unless or until told otherwise!

address the judge or anyone else in the court with your hands in your pockets, as this is seen as disrespectful. Another important rule of etiquette is that you will listen courteously to your opponent (or assiduously recording notes) rather than fiddling with your pen, cleaning your fingernails, whispering to fellow advocates etc. Be careful not to make any gestures which could be seen as disrespectful, such as raising your eyebrows during a contentious submission or rolling your eyes or yawning if your opponent is long-winded. You should also be aware of the importance of body language when making your own submissions. This is addressed in more detail below.

How to persuade the court

Persuading the court is the ultimate goal of legal advocacy. This is an inherently subjective process and the success of any particular style or method of advocacy might vary according to the personality of the advocate, the personality of the judge, the level of the court, the presence or absence of a jury, the strength or weakness of the case and many other factors. Realistically, there is simply no substitute for experience – the more advocacy you perform, the better you will become at judging how to persuade a particular court on a particular point. However, there are some basic guidelines which can help you develop your own persuasive style.

The delivery of your submissions

Verbal communication

We discussed the formalities of *what* you say above, but in order to persuade the court you also need to consider *how* you will say it. Perhaps the most obvious requirement is that your submissions are actually audible to the Court. Different advocates speak at different volumes and you do not need to shout at the judge, but you must ensure your voice carries. Advocacy takes place in widely differing settings, thus you will need to modulate your voice between, for example, speaking to a judge sat a few feet from you and speaking to a bench a considerable distance away with construction work being undertaken in the courtroom next door!

Another key element of communication is the pace at which you speak. The majority of advocacy students begin by speaking far too quickly, both because we generally speak quite fast in conversation and because nerves tend to make you speed up, to get your submissions over with as quickly as possible. As a rule of thumb, you will need to slow down your natural speaking pace for advocacy, although not to the extent that you will bore the judge. The classic advice given to all new advocates is to "speak at the speed of the judge's pen" which remains a sound philosophy – if the judge is clearly struggling to note down all the points you are making you are going too quickly, while if he is looking out the window then you have obviously slowed down too much!

Finally, do not forget the importance of tone and emphasis. It is easy to become so aware of volume and speed that your delivery, while well-paced and audible, becomes somewhat robotic. Try and modulate your voice so that key points or resonant phrases are emphasised and your tone is not monotonous, as this will cause a judge or jury member to lose interest in the content of your arguments.

Non-verbal communication

Most importantly, you should aim to establish eye contact with the judge (and members of the jury if relevant) as much as possible. It is almost impossible not to pay attention to someone who has made eye contact with you, while it is very easy to lose track of what is being said by someone staring out of the window or hunched over their notes. On a related point, you should try and avoid excess gesticulating or walking around the court. The vast majority of effective advocates will stand still and deliver their submissions without hand movements or other gestures. If you find that nerves cause you to move or fidget, or you 'talk with your hands', then a simple solution is to clasp your hands in front of you or behind your back. Similarly, you should never have anything in your hands when you stand up to make a submission (such as a pen or pair of spectacles) as it is inevitable that you will start to fiddle with it at some stage! While dramatic posturing might seem effective at first, it is actually of little use as judges and juries might miss the actual content of your argument and even turn against you if they think you are 'showing off'. The same goes for displays of emotion, although this was more common in the past and remains more acceptable in other jurisdictions, as the Supreme Court of Tennessee made clear:

> "[in the case at first instance] counsel for [the] plaintiff, in his closing argument, in the midst of a very eloquent and impassioned appeal to the jury, shed tears, and unduly excited the sympathies of the jury . . . while the question has never arisen out of any such behavior in this court, we know of no rule or jurisdiction in the court below to check them. It would appear to be one of the natural rights of counsel which no court or constitution could take away . . . if counsel has [tears at his] command, it may be seriously questioned whether it is not his professional duty to shed them whenever proper occasion arises."[30]

The content of your submissions

While the content of submissions depends greatly on the advocacy that you are undertaking, certain general principles can be identified which are present in almost all effective submissions. Many of the following are adapted from the work of Michael Hyam in analysing effective pieces of advocacy.[31]

Put yourself on good terms with the court

We have already discussed the importance of legal etiquette, but correct use of the formalities can also improve the persuasiveness of your submissions. By following the correct etiquette, you will appear professional, intelligent and respectful. This will naturally predispose the court to listen carefully to your arguments. To put it in everyday terms, think about how much more willing you would be to listen to someone who asks you if they may ask you a question, as opposed to someone who begins "oy you"!

It is also vital to set out the order in which you intend to make your submissions as soon as possible. It is far easier for the judge to follow a number of different points if you tell him or her in advance "Your Honour, I propose to make five submissions on this issue, namely . . .". Not only will this help give your case a clear structure but you will also find that it prevents the judge from interrupting you if he knows you will be addressing a certain point later.

---

[30] *Ferguson v Moore* 39 SW 341 (1891) at 343 *per* Wilkes J.
[31] See generally M. Hyam, *Advocacy Skills* 3rd Edition (Blackstone 1995) and in particular page 30

State the law as simply and accurately as you can

Many law students are amazed how little actual 'law' is discussed in court. Outside of the higher appellate courts, trials generally involve far more discussion of the evidence than of theoretical legal concepts and in a straightforward case, such as a road traffic accident or contract dispute, no 'legal' issues may be discussed at all. Unlike an academic essay or answering a problem question, you will not be telling the judge that there is such a concept as the duty of care and that this was formulated in the case of *Donoghue v Stevenson*[32]; instead you will be adducing evidence to prove that the duty was owed and that it had been breached.

However, occasionally you will be dealing with legal issues[33], and of course in any jury trial you will need to explain to the jury what the law states. The starting point when discussing points of law is to keep it as simple as possible – even when addressing a judge, imagine you are addressing an intelligent lay person. As much as possible, explain the issues rather than the law, particularly when dealing with a jury. For example, a member of the jury will more readily understand being told:

> *"You must decide if the defendant had any intention of returning the victim's bicycle"*

rather than hearing that:

> *"A person appropriating property belonging to another without meaning the other permanently to lose the thing itself is nevertheless to be regarded as having the intention of permanently depriving the other of it if his intention is to treat the thing as his own to dispose of regardless of the other's rights; and a borrowing or lending of it may amount to so treating it if, but only if, the borrowing or lending is for a period and in circumstances making it equivalent to an outright taking or disposal."*[34]

State the facts of the case clearly, but try and 'paint a picture'

Just as with the law, state the facts as clearly as possible. It is important that the judge and/or jury understand exactly what has transpired and which facts are agreed between the parties, as opposed to those in dispute. Only include relevant details and avoid overloading the listener with extraneous or irrelevant information.

However, this does not mean you should not use your rhetorical skills. While it is unethical to misrepresent any facts, it is perfectly acceptable to present them in the most favourable manner for your client. For example, if you are representing the prosecution in a criminal trial, you might emphasise the shocking and sudden nature of the violent assault, while the defence might focus instead on the provocative behaviour of the victim beforehand. One of the most effective advocates at painting a picture was Alfred (later Lord) Denning, who was a well-respected barrister prior to his (in)famous judicial career. Even on the bench, his rhetorical style remained apparent. Take, for example, the opening passage of his judgment in *Lloyds Bank v Bundy*[35]:

---

[32] [1932] AC 562
[33] Particularly if as a student you undertake advocacy exercises such as mooting
[34] Theft Act 1968 s.6
[35] [1975] QB 326

"Broadchalke is one of the most pleasing villages in England. Old Herbert Bundy, the defendant, was a farmer there. His home was at Yew Tree Farm. It went back for 300 years. His family had been there for generations. It was his only asset. But he did a very foolish thing. He mortgaged it to the bank. Up to the very hilt. Not to borrow money for himself, but for the sake of his son. Now the bank have come down on him. They have foreclosed. They want to get him out of Yew Tree Farm and to sell it. They have brought this action against him for possession. Going out means ruin for him. . . . At the trial his plight was plain. The judge was sorry for him. He said he was a "poor old gentleman." He was so obviously incapacitated that the judge admitted his proof in evidence. He had a heart attack in the witness-box. Yet the judge felt he could do nothing for him."

Even Mr Bundy's advocate could not have presented the facts in a more persuasive light!

Spell out your argument by combining facts and law

This is the heart of your submission. As you will know from answering problem questions, one of the hardest skills to master as a lawyer is combining the relevant law with the specific facts in a case to present a coherent argument as to why a party should or not should not succeed. It is best to start with basic, uncontroversial truth – that a fact is agreed or has been proven, or that the relevant law imposes a particular test. You should then proceed in small, logical steps, drawing on the relevant evidence, to construct your argument. Where possible, return to any overarching theory or theme which runs through your case, so that your audience knows where you plan to go with your argument.

Anticipate, as far as you can, your opponent's case

Just as important as advancing your case is undermining the arguments of your opponent. The common law legal system is unique in its adversarial approach, where cases are seen as a battle rather than an opportunity to compromise. Therefore, while adhering to professional courtesy, you should take every opportunity to pre-empt or respond to the case advanced by the other side. However, bear in mind that your opponent will be doing exactly the same!

Come to a logical and justified conclusion

All substantive submissions should end in a logical and definite conclusion. Just as an essay must answer the question posed, so should effective advocacy offer an answer to the legal dispute at issue. Remember, just as with an essay, you should not adduce new arguments in your conclusion, but instead summarise what you have already examined in detail. An oft-quoted maxim is that good advocacy will "show the judge the way home" – by the end of your argument, he or she should not only be convinced that you are correct but be willing to adopt your reasoning as the substance of his or her judgment. Never leave the judge in any doubt as to what you are asking for, and why you should be awarded it.

Practical Questions

Using one of the practice methods outlined above (preferably with another person) undertake the following exercises, while trying as far as possible to use appropriate language and comply with all the necessary formalities:

1. Explain to the judge how one would make a cup of tea.
2. Describe the facts and explain the decision in a case of your choice.
3. Taking a problem question from one of your academic subjects, practice putting the case for someone you were asked to advise.
4. Once you have done so, try arguing the case for the opposition.

Ask your audience to assess you, or record yourself, and provide feedback on the following areas:

- Volume, tone and speed of delivery
- Eye contact and body language
- Court etiquette and appropriate language
- Clarity of your submissions
- Persuasiveness of your submissions

Advocacy in Court

Introduction

In this section we will look at some of the different types of advocacy that a barrister or solicitor-advocate might be asked to perform in court. This is far from an exhaustive list of all the advocacy that even a typical case can entail, nor is it intended to provide a complete guide to the areas that are examined. The aim of this section is to introduce you to some of the more common types of advocacy which you will undertake both during your legal training and in a legal career. It will be assumed that you are familiar with the basic techniques of advocacy and the requirements of appropriate language and etiquette.

Opening and closing speeches

Opening speeches

An opening speech is designed to set out an advocate's case, giving the judge (and potentially the jury) an overview of what the advocate will be attempting to prove. It is worth noting immediately that most opening – and closing – speeches are far less dramatic or definitive than those you may have seen in films and on television. It is the evidence which is proffered over many hours, days or even weeks which will decide a case, rather than a particularly impressive piece of rhetoric at the very beginning or end of a trial. Nevertheless, a strong opening speech not only helps you structure your case, but also establishes an impression of competence and confidence which can only benefit your more substantive arguments.

The main content of your opening speech will be the facts of the case, both what is agreed between the parties and what you will set out to prove. If you are opening a case in a civil court the judge will usually have had an opportunity to read the papers prior to trial and will thus have a general idea of the facts of the case. In criminal trials, the tribunal of fact (i.e. magistrates or a jury) will have much less idea of what is to come, and thus a fuller summary is required. As one manual on advocacy describes it:

> *"The triers of fact [i.e. the jury if there is one, otherwise the judge] are about to board a bus, driven by you. It could turn out to be a mystery tour, where everyone finishes up at your intended destination (the end of the trial) but no one is quite sure how they got there or what they saw on the way. Indeed, some passengers may have seen different sights from the rest, some or all may have missed some very interesting sights along the way simply through ignorance. That's not what you want. Your opening speech must be like the very best guided tour – one where the travellers know from the off where they are going, how they are going to get here and what they are likely to experience along the way."*[36]

With this in mind, you must be careful not to overextend yourself when stating facts that are not agreed. All facts in dispute will need to be proved, and thus unless you are completely confident that your witnesses will say exactly what you are suggesting, try not to state your case too highly or too specifically.

Closing speeches

A closing speech should act as the natural bookend to the advocate's case. As mentioned above, dramatic posturing and emotive language is more suited to the stage and screen than to real-life courtrooms, yet you should still aim to be as persuasive as possible. By the time of your closing speech, the judge and/or jury have heard all of your evidence, and that of your opponent. Your job now is to summarise everything they have heard and all the arguments you have raised, creating a logical and coherent whole which should lead inexorably to the conclusion you wish to draw. This will mean not only emphasising the facts and law which have favoured your client, but also dealing with unfavourable evidence and the arguments of your opponent. In terms of the content of your speech, it is important to know who has the last word, as Munkman explains:

> *"If it is intended to say something (in advance) in refutation of arguments likely to be raised by the defence, the refutation should appear after the affirmative arguments have set the case on a firm foundation. In a defence reply the rule is the other way around: it is necessary to refute the arguments of the other side and get them out of the way before establishing a positive case."*[37]

The rules on who opens and closes a case and when they are permitted to speak are complex, but for our purposes can be summarised thus: in a criminal case, the prosecution will begin but the defence always gets the last word, while in civil trials a claimant both opens and ends the trial.

---

[36] The City Law School, *Advocacy* (OUP 2010) p.111
[37] J. Munkman, *The Technique of Advocacy* (first published 1951, Universal Law Publishing 2007) p.161

Dealing with witnesses

Working with witnesses

Witnesses are one of the most interesting, powerful and potentially damaging pieces of evidence which advocates must handle. Even when a witness has consistently given the same story at every opportunity and has no reason to depart from it, you cannot be sure what will be said on the stand.[38] An expert advocate knows not only what questions they want to ask of a witness (and what answers they hope to get in return!) but also how to handle that witness to minimise the chance of failing to prove a point. This means that while we shall focus on dealing with witnesses in a trial situation, careful preparation is required to ensure that you have the structure of your questioning planned out and you know what you hope to gain from their testimony. However, avoid writing a definitive list of questions, as the unpredictability of a witness's answers means that you must stay flexible.

Questioning skills

Because you are essentially putting your case through examining witnesses, it is very easy to forget that you need to be clear and comprehensible to the person answering your questions. Many inexperienced advocates fall into the trap of asking more than one question at a time, for example:

> *"When you say mathematics, what do you mean by mathematics? What are mathematics about? What did you learn? I will not ask you how far you went, but what sort of things did you learn in mathematics?"*[39]

This will either confuse your own witness, or if you are cross-examining may give the witness the opportunity to avoid your questions. Also bear in mind that you should try and keep questions short and simple, in order to maintain the 'flow' of the evidence and if dealing with an evasive or hostile witness, to avoid giving the witness too much time to think.

Open and closed questions

In the context of examining witnesses, questions are usually divided into two categories: open and closed. An open question is one which does not limit what the witness may answer, leaving them open to respond as they wish. Examples might include:

- Why were you in the street?
- Where did you go after that?
- What happened after you fell over?

These questions allow the witness to tell their story in their own words, and make it easier not to 'lead' the witness (see below). However, you can find that using too many open questions allows witnesses to move away from the point you are trying to make, forcing you to depart from your planned structure. Excessively open questions can actually harm your case, as Hyam explains:

---

[38] Bear in mind that in England and Wales it is not permitted to 'coach' witnesses, i.e. go through their testimony prior to trial
[39] From the cross-examination in the infamous Tichborne case which involved an imposter claiming to be the missing heir to a fortune. As reported in J. Munkman, *The Technique of Advocacy* (first published 1951, Universal Law Publishing 2007) p.42

> *"Don't, save in very exceptional circumstances, give the witness a free reign: 'Just tell us in your own words what happened'; this merely invites at best a rambling and extensive account or a crude alphabet of the topic, or at worst the admission of evidence which is irrelevant, inadmissible or damaging to your case."*[40]

Closed questions are those which only allow a limited range of answers. These questions are used to obtain a specific answer from a witness, although be careful not to lead a witness if using closed questions in an examination-in-chief. While closed questions allow you to control the witness closely, you do not want to give the impression that they are not being allowed to give their own account. Examples might include:

- What time was it?
- What street were you driving on?
- What was written on the notice?

Leading questions

You may have heard fictional advocates object to "leading the witness" but what you may not know is exactly what this means. A leading question is one which suggests the answer in the wording of the question. One example often given is "when did you stop beating your wife?" which clearly implies that the witness does indeed beat his wife. The importance of recognising a leading question is due to a very important rule: **it is not permissible to ask a leading question during examination-in-chief** (or re-examination). This is because witnesses should tell their story in their own words.

Avoiding leading questions is extremely difficult, particularly when you know what you want the witness to say. As a general rule, if you do not want to lead a witness avoid any question beginning with "did you . . ." or "didn't you" as this usually implies what the witness did. Instead, use interrogatories such as "what", "who", "where", "when" or start questions with words such as "describe" or "explain". Some examples can be found below:

- You want to find out where the witness was
    - Leading question: "Were you standing outside the door to the department store?"
    - Non-leading question: "Where were you at this point?"
- You want to find out what the witness saw
    - Leading question: "Did you see the defendant running out of the store?"
    - Non-leading question: "What did you see?"
- You want to find out where the defendant went
    - Leading question: "Where did the defendant run?"
    - Non-leading question: "Please describe what you saw happen next"

---

[40] M. Hyam, *Advocacy Skills* 3rd Edition (Blackstone 1995) p.170

Examination-in-chief

Examination-in-chief describes the process of prompting your own witness to tell their story to the court. Thus during the claimant or prosecution's case, they will call witnesses to prove certain facts and counsel for that party will examine them in-chief before the defence has the opportunity to ask questions. Similarly, during the presentation of the case for the defence, the defence advocate will examine his or her witnesses-in-chief. As mentioned above, the most important rule is not to lead the witness. You should try to let them give their evidence in their own words, using questioning to keep them from rambling or digressing. Try to avoid repeating "what happened next?" and "then what happened?" and instead use the techniques described above to keep the witness on point. Indeed, it can be said that "the essence of successful examination-in-chief is 'to lead, without appearing to lead'"[41].

Another tip to make your examination-in-chief as painless as possible is to try and establish a rapport with the witness. Be courteous, say "please" and "thank you" and remember to smile! A relaxed witness will give fuller and more persuasive testimony than one who feels on trial themselves. One exception to the rule on leading during examination-in-chief is on facts which are not in dispute. This is useful to bear in mind when beginning the examination as it is often hard to think of how you will begin. Thus you may ask "do you live at 98 Royal Drive?" or "are you employed by Jones & Smith Limited" if these facts are accepted by both sides.

Cross-examination

One of the best pieces of advice when considering cross-examination is that it should be a *cross*-examination – many budding advocates find themselves badgering the witness to admit a point, which is a counter-productive technique. Instead, you should use your freedom to ask leading questions to guide a witness into a position where you can elicit the answer you want. Unlike examination-in-chief, leading questions are not only permitted but expected and a good advocate will leave opposition witnesses as little room as possible to avoid questions. Therefore, at least at first, you should aim to lead with every question, essentially telling the witness what answer they must give. Combine this with closed questions so that the only answer can be yes or no. Remember that even if you do not advance your own case, it is equally important to undermine your opponent's case. Do not be afraid to ask questions you know the witness will deny, as their denial might be evidence in itself. However, avoid bare accusations where possible – effective advocates often establish certain facts with seemingly innocuous questions which can then make any denial far less impressive. For example, if you are trying to attack the testimony of a witness who claims to have seen your client escaping the scene of a crime:

- Did you see my client running away from the injured man?
    - Yes
- Are you sure?
    - Yes

At this stage, you are left with no option but to move on, or to carry on a pantomime "no you didn't" "yes I did" argument which will not reflect well on you or your case. A more patient advocate might approach this issue differently:

---

[41] J. Munkman, *The Technique of Advocacy* (first published 1951, Universal Law Publishing 2007) p.42

- It was around 11 o'clock at night at the time you claim this occurred?
  - Yeah I think it was around 11
- So it was dark was it not?
  - I suppose so
- There are no streetlights down that alley are there?
  - I can't remember any
- You were not wearing your spectacles were you?
  - No I forgot them
- So you can't be sure who you saw can you?
  - Well I think it was the defendant

While the witness has not agreed with you, the jury will now have the defence's account of events freshly implanted in their mind – that it was dark, that it might have been another person who committed the assault, that the witness may not be reliable. Note that at no point has the advocate suggested the witness is untruthful.

Re-examination

Re-examination is an optional right for the party calling the witness. It is only permitted to re-examine a witness on matters arising out of cross-examination, thus you should not use this opportunity to rehash what was said during examination-in-chief or ask questions you forgot to ask the first time around. If there is no need to re-examine, do not do so. Bear in mind that you are still not allowed to ask leading questions when re-examining a witness.

Bail applications and pleas in mitigation

What is a bail application?

After a person is charged with a crime, there will be a (sometimes considerable) period of time before they appear in court for trial. In the meantime, it is of vital importance as to whether that person will be allowed to remain in society on bail, or instead remanded in custody. For many people, being kept in custody may feel like a prison sentence, particularly for those who have not spent time in the criminal justice system in the past. Even though they are assumed to be innocent until proven guilty at trial, a person spending time in custody may lose their job and even their home, along with the inevitable impact on their relationships and mental well-being. Considering these grave consequences, and the fact that around 13,000 people are in prison on remand at any one time[42], with a further estimated 80,000 on bail[43], bail hearings are both extremely frequent and extremely important.

The Bail Act 1976, section 4, grants a general right to bail except in certain circumstances (for example if the defendant is charged with murder, manslaughter or rape and has a previous conviction for one of these

---

[42] Ministry of Justice, *Offender management caseload statistics 2010*
[43] As announced by the Prime Minister, David Cameron, in June 2011. HC Deb 30 June 2011, vol 530, col 1133

offences, he or she will only be granted bail if they can demonstrate 'exceptional circumstances which justify it'[44]). However, this does not mean that defendants are automatically granted bail. They must still apply to the court to be released on bail and while there is a presumption that bail will be granted, this is by no means certain as schedule 1 of the 1976 Act sets out the reasons for refusing bail. Thus the role of an advocate in a bail application is either to demonstrate that there are good reasons to oppose bail (if acting for the prosecution) or that these reasons are not sufficient to prevent the grant of bail (if acting for the defence). The following is written to focus on the role of the defence, as in practice the objections to bail by the Crown Prosecution Service are decided in advance.

Preparing a bail application

The starting point in any bail application is to examine the objections to bail. If the prosecution has no objections, it is usually very likely that bail will be granted without further argument. However, depending on the severity of the crime and the particular defendant, the prosecution may object, stating one or more of the reasons in schedule 1 of the 1976 Act. The relevant section states:

> ### Statute Extract: Bail Act 1976
>
> Schedule 1, Part I
>
> 2. The defendant need not be granted bail if the court is satisfied that there are substantial grounds for believing that the defendant, if released on bail (whether subject to conditions or not) would—
>
> (a) fail to surrender to custody, or
>
> (b) commit an offence while on bail, or
>
> (c) interfere with witnesses or otherwise obstruct the course of justice, whether in relation to himself or any other person.

There are other reasons set out in schedule 1 for bail to be refused, which will not be considered in detail here (examples include where the accused must be kept in custody for his or her own safety, or the accused is already serving a prison sentence for a previous offence).

Once you have established the objections to bail, your next step will be to consider how to argue against them. This can usually be done in two ways:

1. Arguing that the objections are unfounded or invalid – for example, that the prosecution has no grounds to suggest your client will fail to surrender to custody (i.e. fail to return to court for trial) because she has never failed to surrender in the past, she intends to plead not guilty (and thus will appear to clear her name) and she lives with her mother, who is a respected member of the community.

2. Accepting that the objections are valid, but can be addressed by conditions on the bail which your client is willing to abide by – for example, although it is true that in the past your client has committed a number of alcohol-related violent offences while on bail, this time he is willing to abide by a strict curfew and not to go within a mile of his local city centre.

---

[44] Criminal Justice and Public Order Act 1994, s.25, as amended

Bear in mind that you should discuss the potential conditions on bail with your client in advance, as they will not thank you for offering limitations on their freedom which they have not agreed to. You will also wish to check which conditions are feasible, particularly in regards to the surety and security. While there is technically no limit on what can constitute an acceptable condition on bail, some of the most common include:

- **A surety:** One of the most effective conditions, a surety is a person willing to ensure that the defendant will attend the next court hearing. In exchange, they are required to acknowledge that if the defendant does not attend, the surety will be liable for a specified sum of money, which has to be paid to court. Sureties are often family members, friends, employers or local community leaders. The amount of the surety is dependent on the person's financial circumstances and character.
- **Security:** Similar to a surety, a defendant may provide their own security for surrender. This may be in the form of money, or valuable possessions. While a surety only becomes due on the defendant failing to appear, a security must be deposited with the court immediately.
- **Reporting to a police station:** In order to ensure that a defendant remains in a certain area, he or she may be required to report to a police station at specified intervals, which will usually depend on the risk of flight. Common conditions can range from more than once a day to once a week, or more creative requirements such as the football hooligans required to sign in at their local police station during the first half of each of their teams' matches[45].
- **Curfews:** Increasingly common, particularly when dealing with younger defendants, a curfew requires the defendant to remain in a certain place during certain times of the day, for example to stay at home between 9pm and 6am.
- **Staying away from an area or person:** When there is a risk of further offences being committed or that a defendant will interfere with witnesses or evidence, they may be required to stay away from an area or person as a condition of their bail.
- **Staying in an area:** Alternatively, a defendant may be required to stay within a certain area or at a certain residence, such as the town where they live or at a bail hostel. Foreign nationals or defendants with strong links to other countries may be required not to travel abroad, or even hand in their passport to their local police while on bail.
- **Electronic monitoring:** Another condition which is being used more and more often, electronic monitoring or "tagging" is usually combined with another condition, to ensure a defendant keeps to a curfew or a certain geographical area.
- **Prevention of an activity:** Where a certain activity appears to encourage or assist a defendant to commit offences, they may be prohibited from doing this while on bail. Some recent examples include a teenage hacker forbidden to access the internet or possess any internet-capable devices[46] and an extremist politician banned from attending demonstrations[47].

---

[45] BBC News, 'Sheriff sets unusual bail conditions for Old Firm fans' (4 March 2011) http://www.bbc.co.uk/news/uk-scotland-glasgow-west-12648367
[46] The Telegraph, '"Hacker' Ryan Cleary released on bail' (27 June 2011) http://www.telegraph.co.uk/technology/news/8601344/Hacker-Ryan-Cleary-released-on-bail.html
[47] BBC News, 'EDL leader Stephen Lennon remanded for bail breach' (5 September 2011) http://www.bbc.co.uk/news/uk-england-london-14795553

Delivering a bail application

In practice, where a defendant is seeking bail and the prosecution let it be known that they will object, his representative will seek out the prosecutor before the bail hearing and try to agree conditions on bail which will persuade the prosecution to drop its objections. However, if this is not possible then both advocates will have to advance their arguments as to whether bail should be granted to the judge, who will make the final decision.

Bail applications do not normally last particularly long and thus you will want to make your points briefly and succinctly. A logical structure is to address each objection of the prosecution in turn. First attempt to cast doubt on its relevance by relying on favourable facts such as the defendant's past behaviour or positive changes such as a new relationship or treatment for an addiction. If the court does not appear convinced, or the objection is clearly well-founded, then you can progress to suggesting conditions on bail. Bear in mind that it will be the court which decides the conditions and thus you are not bargaining with the judge or judges, but rather placing potential solutions before them which you will need to persuade the court to adopt. While you are trying to secure the least restrictive bail possible for your clients, remain realistic about what is achievable – if the defendant has a long history of fleeing bail, his claim that he is a reformed man will have little weight. While you should not plan to rely on the court's sympathy, if the refusal of bail will have clear consequences such as your client becoming unable to care for an elderly relative or leaving young children with no means of support, these should certainly be brought to the court's attention.

What is a plea in mitigation?

In some respects similar to a bail application, as it involves using a defendant's history and circumstances to advocate their freedom, a plea in mitigation occurs much later in the criminal litigation process. As the name suggests, the plea is a final opportunity to ask the court for leniency when imposing a punishment on a defendant, and as such occurs in two situations:

1. When the defendant has pleaded guilty
2. When the defendant has pleaded not guilty, but has been convicted

Unsurprisingly, you will normally find the judge more receptive to your arguments if your client has pleaded guilty from the beginning, rather than being convicted after the time and expense of a criminal trial.

Preparing a plea in mitigation

In order to mitigate a sentence, you must first familiarise yourself with what punishment the judge may impose. The maximum sentence for a crime is usually found in the statute which governs the area, but more detailed guidance on sentencing is provided by judges and the Sentencing Guidelines Council[48]. Once you know the range of sentences available, it is worth consulting the SGC Case Compendium[49] which will point you to the specific cases where sentencing guidelines for each offence were discussed. By using a combination of these sources, and a practice book on criminal law, such as *Blackstone's Criminal Practice* or the CPS Sentencing Manual[50] you will also be able to identify the aggravating and mitigating

---

[48] Guidelines are available at http://sentencingcouncil.judiciary.gov.uk
[49] Available as a PDF at http://sentencingcouncil.judiciary.gov.uk/docs/web_case_compendium.pdf
[50] http://www.cps.gov.uk/legal/s_to_u/sentencing_manual/

factors for the relevant crime. As you would expect, the presence of aggravating factors will usually result in a sentence toward the higher end of the available range, while mitigating factors can indicate a more lenient punishment would be suitable.

The next step is to establish which of the aggravating factors are relevant to your client. While you do not want to highlight these too much, it is counter-productive to ignore them as the prosecution will certainly mention such factors and the judge will wish to hear your response. After you have done this, perform the same feature with the mitigating factors. This process will usually require a conference with your client as you will be looking for information on your client's background, previous criminal record, involvement in this crime (for example a common aggravating factor is acting as ringleader, while a minor role may support mitigation) and in particular your client's present situation. Just as with a bail application, evidence of reform such as steady employment, a stable home or willingness to be sentenced to addiction rehabilitation will be relevant to your plea. You also need to establish the defendant's financial means if a fine is a likely punishment and ask if there are any character witnesses you could call. Make sure that you see evidence of any personal claims your client makes, as claiming a non-existent job or family in your plea will have severe consequences for both you and your client. Finally, you should give your client objective and realistic advice as to the range of likely punishments.

Delivering a plea in mitigation

> *"In a plea of mitigation you always start with one advantage. No judge wants to send a man to prison if, consistent with his duty to the public, he can avoid it. He will therefore be eager to hear and act on any argument which will enable him to pass the appropriate sentence, mitigated but not unnerved by mercy. If you always bear this in mind when making a plea, you will avoid the irrelevant, the sentimental and the absurd."*[51]

The structure of a plea in mitigation is usually straightforward. You do not want to waste the court's time and it is highly likely that the judge has sentenced many similar offenders before, so will not be impressed with a long speech. Bear in mind that you will be speaking after the prosecution has summarised the case and revealed the defendant's prior criminal record.

Begin your plea by setting out the points you plan to make. It is a good idea to briefly review the sentencing policy in the area before discussing aggravating and mitigating factors. If no aggravating factors are present, ensure that you impress this upon the judge. If there are such factors in this case, avoid highlighting them where possible but do not expect to persuade the court to ignore them. You will then want to cover all the mitigating features which are present, although remember to keep your submissions short and to the point. Where possible you will want to back up these submissions with witnesses as to the defendant's character, although bear in mind the previous remarks made about ensuring the reliability of any witnesses you call. Finally, conclude by politely suggesting what you believe is a reasonable and realistic sentence to the court – but bear in mind that if the guidelines make it clear that this is a case of imprisonment, it is much better to admit that prison is inevitable and ask for a relatively short term, rather than trying to achieve an impossible outcome.

---

[51] M. Hyam, *Advocacy Skills* 3rd Edition (Blackstone 1995) p.10

Practical Questions

1. Imagine you are representing Ms Donoghue at first instance in the case which led to the House of Lords decision *Donoghue v Stevenson*[52]. Draft an opening speech, setting out what you plan to prove and which legal issues you will examine.

2. With a friend playing the part of a witness, practice examination-in-chief. Take them through a memorable day in their life, while adhering to the rules about leading questions.

3. Read the famous cross-examination of Hawley Crippen by R. D. Muir[53]. Note down the techniques Muir used to expose the implausibility and inaccuracies of Dr Crippen's testimony.

4. Choose a person, real or fictional, that was convicted of a crime. It could be an infamous criminal, a character from a book, film or television show, or a case study given to you by your tutor. Research the crime for which they were convicted, then plan and deliver a plea in mitigation on behalf of this defendant.

5. Attempt the Ministry of Justice interactive exercise 'You be the Judge', available at http://ybtj.cjsonline.gov.uk/

Further reading

Advocacy skills

R. Du Cann, *The Art of the Advocate* (Penguin 1993)
K. Evans, *The Golden Rules of Advocacy* (Blackstone 1993)
M. Hyam, *Advocacy Skills* 3rd Edition (Blackstone 1995)
I. Morley, *The Devil's Advocate* 2nd Edition (Sweet & Maxwell 2009)
J. Munkman, *The Technique of Advocacy* (first published 1951, Universal Law Publishing 2007)
D. Pope and D. Hill, *Mooting and Advocacy Skills* (Sweet & Maxwell 2007)
D. Ross QC, *Advocacy* 2nd Edition (Cambridge University Press 2007)
The City Law School, *Advocacy* (Bar Manuals) (Oxford University Press 2010)
F. Wellman, *The Art of Cross-Examination* (Standard Publications 2007)
J. Welsh, *Advocacy in the Magistrates' Courts* (Routledge-Cavendish 2003)

Wider reading

Aristotle, *The Art of Rhetoric* (Penguin Classics Reissue 2005)
R. Dowis, *The Lost Art of the Great Speech* (Amacom 1999)
A. McBride, *Defending the Guilty: Truth and Lies in the Criminal Courtroom* (Penguin 2011)
N. Neil Browne, *Asking the Right Questions: A Guide to Critical Thinking* 10th Edition (Allyn & Bacon 2011)
G. Robertson, *The Justice Game* (Vintage 1999)
P. Rodenburg, *The Right to Speak: Working with the Voice* (Methuen Drama 1992)

---

[52] [1932] AC 562
[53] Old Bailey Proceedings Online (www.oldbaileyonline.org, version 6.0, 16 September 2011), October 1910, trial of CRIPPEN, Hawley Harvey (48, dentist) (t19101011-74).

2
Answering Problem Questions

Andy Vi-Ming Kok

Aims and Objectives

After completing this chapter, you should be able to:

- Understand the need to answer problem questions
- Identify what a problem question is
- Analyse the differences between the skills required to answer problem questions from those required to answer essay questions
- Identify the issues raised in problem questions
- Using research, deploy relevant legal principles to answer problem questions
- Apply the law to the facts of a problem
- Clearly and methodically structure your answer to a problem question
- Provide concise and focussed conclusions to the issues raised in the problem question

The Purpose of Problem Questions

Assessments

You will be examined in various ways on a law degree. A common type of question you will encounter is the so-called "problem question".

Problem questions are popular with examiners as they test students' abilities to apply the law to factual scenarios. It is also generally believed that it is harder to plagiarise an answer for a problem question than an essay question, as problem questions tend to be bespoke i.e. specific to that assessment.

As such, you will find that problem questions feature in both in-semester assignments as well as end-of-semester examinations.

The advice here on how to answer problem questions will generally apply to both situations.

Real-life situations

In essence, problem questions reflect the real-life work of lawyers. A lawyer is typically presented with a real-life problem that requires a legal solution. In asking you to answer problem questions, your lecturers are merely preparing you for a professional working life in the future.

When clients approach a lawyer with their problems, they do not want to be given an extended account of some legal principle, however accurate that account may be; they would also have little interest in having a long line of judicial authority or statutory provision recited to them in depth. They certainly will have little interest in an academic debate on the merits of the law, or the respectable dissenting judgment of an eminent judge from an early 1900s case.

Instead they want to know how the law would deal with the situation they find themselves in, and what the most likely outcomes would be for them if their case was to progress.

What is a Problem Question?

Although a problem question attempts to replicate real-life scenarios faced by lawyers in practice, it is the case that the problem questions you will encounter are most likely to be fictitious i.e. made up by the lecturer who set the question.

At times, the fictitious scenario can appear quite absurd and unlikely to happen in real-life. Do not worry about that – the reason your lecturer would have constructed that scenario was to be able to assess your ability to analyse complex issues which do not have clear-cut answers.

Therefore, a problem question takes the form of a set of facts about a certain event or series of events. The facts are then followed by a question requiring you to discuss either the general legal position or certain specific legal issues flowing from those facts. For example, you may be asked to discuss the legal rights and remedies available to a particular party, or the legal position more generally.

Problem questions are sometimes also called scenario questions, or case studies.

It is not an essay question!

This might seem very obvious to you after everything we have said in this chapter; however, as lecturers we still see answers to essay questions masquerading as solutions to problem questions. And more often than we would like to!

The problem tends to stem from the fact that in your hurry to get started on the answer, students tend to speed read through the problem question and allow key words or events from the problem question to dominate your attention.

For example, in a criminal law problem question involving a complex set of facts revolving around a homicide, it is a common mistake of students to quickly pick up on the fact that there might be an issue of self-defence involved, and then proceed to write a four page essay on self-defence: its developments, relative merits, recent controversies, calls for reform, and so on. In the worst cases, the students even forget to firstly establish that a crime had indeed taken place before they embark on the long essay on self-defence!

Needless to say, an answer to a problem question that is simply a long essay on a selected aspect of law would not score very high marks. In order to answer a problem question properly, your solutions need to be concise, to the point and focussed on all the issues raised in the problem.

What you need to demonstrate

Problem questions test:

- Whether you can analyse a set of facts and identify the relevant legal issues, rules and principles that they relate to;
- Whether you can methodically research and come up with the laws that are relevant to the factual scenario presented in the problem question;
- Whether you can apply legal rules and principles to the given factual scenario and critically discuss the various legal possibilities; and
- Whether you can organise your knowledge and present a comprehensive, clear and logically coherent answer.

What is critical is that you appreciate that the skills required to answer a problem question well are different from those required for producing a good essay question answer. You certainly need to be able to do more than just outline the law and its development. Your answer needs to apply the law to the facts, and to reach a well-considered conclusion.

Being a successful lawyer involves more than just knowing the law. More often than not, it also requires you to be able to apply that knowledge of the law to factual scenarios. Application of the law is defined in its broadest sense, for example, you should be able to see the arguments from both sides, and be able to put together coherent and convincing arguments for the party you are representing.

In many ways, that is what a judge does too – they identify the issues raised by the case before them, they think about the different legal principles that might be of relevance and apply those principles to the facts, reaching a reasoned conclusion from that application.

Stepping away from the law for one brief moment, you will probably have realised that the skills required to answer problem questions are in fact skills that you employ on a daily basis. For example, if you regularly play games on your computer or mobile telephone, you are in fact applying sets of principles to find solutions to the problems or challenges posed.

How Should You Answer a Problem Question?

Always start by planning and structuring your answer.

Planning your answer

It is very important that you carefully plan your answer before you start writing it down. Proper planning will ensure that your answer remains focused on the question and does not include any irrelevant material.

You should:

- Read the question carefully and underline or highlight the facts you think may be relevant for the purposes of answering the question.
- Look at the points you have underlined or highlighted, and make notes on:
  - Why they are relevant, the legal issues they raise and how they impact on the legal position
  - Whether there is anything else that is legally relevant or necessary to know in order to reach a conclusion, even if it is not expressly mentioned in the given facts.

It is a good idea to read the question at least twice so as not to miss out on any key issues.

Be ruthless about excluding irrelevant points. Not all of the information you are given will necessarily be relevant and one of the things being tested is your ability to focus on the relevant issues without being misled by irrelevant information.

Be prepared to ask yourself the following questions:

- Who did what to whom?
- Where did it take place?
- When did it take place?

Quite often in problem questions, multiple parties will be involved – see the example on the next page. If so, make a clear note of their roles within the facts of the scenario.

Tips

- Your problem question tends to end with instructions as to whom you need to advise, and against whom. Follow those instructions.

- Every party listed in the problem question tends to be there for a reason – it is rare that you will be expected to simply ignore any particular party!

Example of a problem question

Note that although this example is from contract law, the skills involved in answering a problem question are applicable to other modules too.

Please also note that in order to be able to provide you with a working example of how to answer a problem question, it has to be presumed that you possess a certain degree of knowledge of contract law. To aid those of you who may be new to contract law, simple explanations of key legal terms will be inserted in square brackets after the terms. Please note that as this is not a book on contract law, those explanations will be brief.

Example: problem question

Terracotta Tiles Ltd manufactures and sells roof tiles, from its warehouse outlet in Stroud, Gloucestershire and online via its website.

Due to the economic downturn, Terracotta Tiles Ltd decided to reduce the number of styles of roof tiles it manufactures. On Wednesday 1 September 2011, the discontinued lines were advertised for sale in the local newspaper and on the front page of Terracotta Tiles Ltd's website:

"SALE: Quality roof tiles from Terracotta Tiles Ltd. Massive reductions on the following discontinued ranges: Square, Round and Diamond. Order now! The first five customers who order more than £1000 worth of roof tiles will receive a free golf umbrella each. We promise you will not be disappointed."

Roger was a local builder who required roof tiles for the extension he was completing in Charlton Kings. After seeing Terracotta Tiles Ltd's advertisement in the local newspaper on 1 September, he telephoned and spoke to Adam Terracotta, enquiring about the price for 1000 Square roof tiles. Adam Terracotta told him the Square tiles were offered for sale at £2 each. Roger said he would think about it, and get back to Adam Terracotta if he was interested in purchasing the roof tiles.

On Friday 3 September, Roger wrote to Terracotta Tiles Ltd, stating that he would like to purchase 1000 Square roof tiles. He posted the letter at 6 p.m. that evening.

At 9 a.m. on Monday 6 September, Steve, the owner of a large DIY shop in Cheltenham, visited Terracotta Tiles Ltd's warehouse outlet. He entered into face-to-face negotiations with Adam Terracotta on the price for buying the entire stock of all three discontinued lines of roof tiles from Terracotta Tiles Ltd.

Whilst Steve was negotiating with Adam Terracotta, Rafael ordered 300 Round roof tiles from Terracotta Tiles Ltd's website. He paid for his order by entering his credit card details online and received a confirmation message stating that his order had been processed and the tiles would be dispatched as soon as possible. The automatic payment collection system set up on Terracotta Tiles Ltd's website immediately debited the full payment from Rafael's credit card account. According to

> the terms of Terracotta Tiles Ltd's website, which Rafael had clicked 'I agree' to but had not read, acceptance of an offer takes place when Terracotta Tiles Ltd dispatches the goods to the customer.
>
> At 10.30 a.m. that same day, Adam Terracotta and Steve entered into a contract for Steve to buy the entire stock of all three discontinued lines of roof tiles from Terracotta Tiles Ltd.
>
> Having sold all those tiles, Adam Terracotta then opened his post which had arrived over the weekend and at 9.30 a.m. that Monday morning. Amongst the post was the letter from Roger.
>
> He then looked at the online orders, which included Rafael's order.
>
> As Adam had sold his entire consignment of Square, Round and Diamond roof tiles to Steve, he was concerned that he would be unable to supply Roger and Rafael with any of the roof tiles that they had ordered.
>
> Advise Adam Terracotta of his legal position.

Tips

Do not:

- Start your answer by repeating verbatim large chunks of the question – the examiner is not interested in your ability to simply copy text.
- State in your answer that "I am going to advise Adam"; Instead of stating that, you should just get on and do it.
- Make general sweeping statements like, "This case involves contract law". The assessment or examination is in contract law, so it must involve contract law!
- Miss out facts from the question, simply through oversight.
- Invent facts which are not there. Quite often the examiner deliberately leaves out key facts so that you can look at the alternatives.
- Waste your time challenging settled facts in the question e.g. in the example above, there is no need to debate the time that Adam and Steve entered into an agreement – you can take the 10.30 a.m. as read.
- Spend time deliberating on whether an issue can be proved in a court of law. Evidential matters are not usually the subject of assessment in a law problem question unless it is in the Law of Evidence module.

Structuring Your Answer

There are four steps to follow in structuring an answer to a problem question:

I – Identify the issue(s) raised by the given facts and place them in context by indicating the area of law they are governed by.

L – Outline the relevant **Law** i.e. legal rules and principles.

A – Apply the law to the facts you were given.

W – What is the outcome? I.e. you must always reach a conclusion on the legal position.

These steps are explained more fully below.

Note that different authors use different mnemonics or terminology, but essentially they share a common approach to answering legal problem questions. Some other mnemonics you might come across include:

IRAC = Issue, Rule, Application, Conclusion

IDEA = Identify, Define, Explain, Apply

CLEO = Claim, Law, Evaluation, Outcome

PLAN = Problem, Legal rule, Application, Note outcome

IPAC = Issue, Principle, Application, Conclusion

KKAR = Key facts, Key law, Applying the law to the facts, Reaching conclusions

Step 1 – I: Identifying and Contextualising the Relevant Issues

Step 1 (the first thing you should do in your answer) is to identify the relevant issue(s) or problem(s) raised by the facts you have been given. In other words, you should indicate exactly what you have been asked to do. For example, the question might ask you to "discuss whether A has any legal claim against B and, if so, the nature of any such claim".

An issue is a question raised by the facts that needs to be answered by reference to the relevant legal principles.

The general issue will usually be clear from the wording of the question, but its resolution may depend on an analysis of more specific issues. Where this is the case, you should also refer to those more specific issues. For example, you may be asked to discuss whether a binding contract exists between two parties. It may be clear from the facts that the answer to that general question depends on the more specific issue of whether there was a valid offer by one party and a valid acceptance by the other. For example, in such a case you might say: "The issue for determination is whether a binding contract[1] exists between A and B. This in turn depends on whether A made a valid offer to B and whether B validly accepted that offer".

---

[1] Legal terms for this example are: a legally binding agreement, bargain, promise or set of promises that the law will enforce; an undertaking made by one person (called the "offeror") to another person (called the "offeree") offering to be bound by certain contractual terms if the offeree agrees to accept those terms; consented or indicated approval. Acceptance of an offer is necessary for the formation of a contract.

For an assignment or examination, it will likely be the case that the problem scenario will be a complex one, involving multiple issues. Therefore, you should methodically identify all the issues, and relevant sub-issues.

It is vital that you deal with each of the issues and sub-issues carefully and separately. Remember that this stage is crucial as each of the following stages builds on the work you do here – if you miss out on key issues at this stage then it is unlikely that those issues will get considered later on, resulting in a loss of marks. Keep in mind that in an assessment situation, it is unlikely that your lecturer will set you a very straightforward problem question; therefore you need to keep all options open.

You should then place the legal issues in context by identifying the area of law they will be governed by (e.g. by stating that the position is governed by the Law of Contract's rules relating to the conclusion of contracts and, more specifically, offer and acceptance.).

Remember to keep to the relevant legal principles only. A problem question is not an invitation to discuss everything you know on X. Remember that no lecturer will ever set you a brief that amounts to "Write all you know about offer and acceptance".

Taking the position just between Roger and Adam Terracotta in the example, the main issue would be whether a contract exists between them. However, there are a number of sub-issues to be considered:

- The legal status of Roger's telephone call to enquire about the price of the tiles.
- Roger's statement that he would "think about it, and get back to Adam if he was interested . . ."
- The position of the letter posted to Adam on Friday 3 September.
- The fact that the letter was only opened and read by Adam on Monday 6 September.

Note that Step 1 should not take up much of your answer. At most it should be a couple of paragraphs long.

Step 2 – L: Outlining the Relevant Law i.e. Legal Rules and Principles

Step 2 (the second thing you should do in your answer) involves outlining or summarising the specific legal rules and principles that govern the solution to the problem. You should assume that the person reading your answer has no legal knowledge, and you should explain all the relevant legal rules and principles they will need to know in order to understand the legal position. Do not, however, write down everything you know about that area of law – only mention those aspects that are directly relevant to and necessary for answering the specific question posed.

Wherever possible you should mention any relevant statutes, cases and other legal authorities as support for your statements of what the law is. In written assignments you will need to include full references for all the authorities you cite. That will not be the case in a closed-book examination.

It may be difficult to know where to begin, especially if you are new to studying law and the problem question happens to be one of your first assignments.

Start by looking at your module guide and lecture notes from the relevant module and establish if any of the topics you have studied to date might be applicable to the issues you had previously identified (under Step 1). It is unlikely that you will be set an assignment question on topics you have not yet covered in class.

Make a list of all those topics.

Further examine each of the topics on your list to see if they are relevant. At this stage, you might want to also quickly read the cases listed on the reading lists for those topics, and any related statutory provisions, to see if they might shed more light on the relevance of those topics to your problem question.

Tips

- Quite often, the facts in problem questions set by lecturers are inspired by the facts of real cases;
- However, be aware that your assessment problem questions are unlikely to be based on one case alone, or that a single case could provide the answer to your problem question. Therefore be careful that you do not base your entire answer just on one case that has factual similarity to your problem question.

There is no harm in seeking guidance from others – discussions with your fellow students can often be helpful, especially if you are all doing the same problem question. Be careful though not to fall foul of any university regulations on unauthorised collusion or plagiarism if you speak to other students. As a last resort, you may also choose to approach your lecturer. As it is an assessment they will be limited with what they can tell you; they will certainly not be able to tell you what areas of law to concentrate on, but if you approach them with your own list of legal issues that you think are applicable to the problem, they might be prepared to give you an assuring "You are on the right track" nod.

<u>Remember that if this is an assessment (mid-term assignment or end-of-term examination), you will certainly be expected to demonstrate knowledge and understanding of a number of legal issues. Unlike essay questions, problem questions are highly unlikely to focus on a single legal issue only.</u>

You are also expected to weave those relevant laws into the facts of the problem question, but we will come back to that issue at the next step.

Having established which topics are potentially relevant, you will need to do further research to establish good knowledge and understanding of the pertinent laws.

Your module guide, lecture notes and recommended textbooks are good starting points for this research. These should provide you with a sound basic understanding of the law in the areas relevant to the problem question.

Once you have mastered the basics, you should go on to fuller reading of the relevant cases and other legal authority. These should take your knowledge and understanding up another level, such that you should be able to further dissect the subtleties of the problem question. Make notes of the full citations of your further reading as you will need to reference them in your assignment.

Having established a sound understanding of the relevant legal principles, you will need to clearly lay them out in your answer.

Remember that this is a problem question, so your answer should not be a long rambling essay on the law in this area. What your lecturer would be looking for in your answer would be clear and concise statements of the law closely related to the issues raised by the facts of the problem question.

Give yourself checklists to make sure you are on the right track:

- Are you writing large chunks of law with no reference to the facts of the problem question at all?
- Are you including far too much irrelevant detail e.g. facts of cases you have read?
- Are you discussing matters not raised by the problem question?
- Are you engaging in detailed 'academic debates' on matters such as law reform?

If you had answered yes to any of those questions above, then your answer would certainly be lacking in focus for a problem question. Get back to the facts of the problem and make sure that the law you discuss is closely related to those facts.

Revisiting the position just between Roger and Adam Terracotta in the problem question example, we had identified the main issue as that of whether a contract exists between them. We also established that within that relationship, there were a number of sub-issues to be considered.

Firstly, on the issue of Roger's telephone call to enquire about the price of the tiles, it would appear that the relevant legal issue would be whether such an enquiry would amount to an offer, or merely an enquiry for further information, with no binding contractual effect. The law on this matter should be fully explored. Cases such as *Harvey v Facey*[2] & *Clifton v Palumbo*[3] should be analysed in detail.

Another sub-issue concerned the letter posted by Roger to Adam Terracotta on Friday 3 September, which was only read by Terracotta on 6 September.

Legal issues arising there would include offer and acceptance, linked to whether Terracotta's original advertisement amounted to an invitation to treat [An invitation made by one person inviting another person to make an offer to contract] or an offer. These legal issues should again be explored in detail.

As Roger had posted the letter and it was possible that the letter could have constituted an acceptance, then you should go on to evaluate in detail the postal rule of acceptance [A letter purporting to accept an offer is binding from the moment it is posted]. Authorities such as *Adams v Lindsell*[4] & *Henthorn v Fraser*[5] should have been applied in the relevant parts of the discussion.

Your answer should also have noted that an acceptance could still be valid and binding even if the postal rule did NOT apply – it would just be that the time of acceptance would have been different.

---

[2] [1893] AC 552
[3] [1944] 2 All ER 497
[4] (1818) 106 ER 250
[5] [1892] 2 Ch 27

Remember at all times that you are answering a problem question, and not writing a long essay. Therefore always check that the law you are stating in your answer is closely related to the facts of the problem.

Tip

If you make sure that you refer to at least one of the parties in the problem question by name within every couple of paragraphs that you write, then the likelihood of your answer going off on an 'essay-style' tangent would be considerably reduced.

Note that Step 2 should take up a good portion of your answer – at least a third to half of your answer should be focussed on Step 2.

Step 3 – A: Applying the Law to the Given Facts

Step 3 (the next thing you should do in your answer) is to apply the legal rules and principles you have outlined in Step 2 to the facts you were given.

In many ways, this is the most important of the four steps, as it goes to the heart of answering problem questions. You will be surprised how many weak answers to problem questions skip this step altogether i.e. the student simply writes long essays on what the law is (step 2), and then jumps to the conclusion (step 4) by merely stating "Therefore, based on everything I have stated above, X must be liable for breach of contract to Y"!

Answers of that nature will not score high marks.

For this step, you will be expected to analyse and critically apply the relevant legal rules and principles to the facts of the problem. To put it another way, you now need to create links between the law and the facts of the problem question at this stage.

To do this you will need to:

Firstly, indicate which of the facts are legally significant and why they are significant.

Then indicate whether there are any additional facts that you have not been given but would need to know in order to reach a clear conclusion, and why it is necessary to know them.

Where there are ambiguous or "missing" facts, consider all the possible alternatives and how the legal position would differ for each of them. (For example, the answer to the question of whether or not a contract exists between two parties might depend on whether party A became aware of party B's acceptance before 1 January 2011. If there is no clear given information, you could then say that if A did become aware of the acceptance by that date there would be a contract, but that if he didn't there wouldn't be one.)

However, you should **not** "go beyond" the given facts by discussing possibilities that clearly didn't occur. (For example, if the question expressly says that party A did not become aware of B's attempted acceptance, do not discuss what the position would have been had he been aware of it.)

Where possible, you should also compare or distinguish the facts that you have been given from those of other similar Court cases covered in the syllabus. For example, you should point out any similarities between the facts you were given and the facts of any decided case; indicate what the Court's decision was in that other case, and highlight any differences that might lead a Court to reach a different conclusion.

Remember to methodically take each issue and sub-issue one at a time, and apply the relevant law to them. It would be a mistake to attempt to apply the law globally to all the issues raised in the problem question. If you do so, your answer will appear muddled and you will miss certain key points in the application process.

You should reach conclusions on each issue and sub-issue as you progress through this application stage. All of these conclusions will then feed into your main conclusion in step 4, but do not leave it until then to reach conclusions on the individual issues.

As previously mentioned, it is unlikely that the problem question you have been presented with has a straightforward 'yes or no only' answer. Instead, the facts of the problem will inevitably require you to consider alternative outcomes, depending on how certain facts are interpreted, or what the additional but yet unknown facts are.

Be prepared therefore to consider alternative conclusions and do take a balanced approach to your answer. Although the rubric may have asked you to 'Advise Adam Terracotta', that does not mean that you bend the legal rules to find in Adam Terracotta's favour. Think carefully about whether viable counter-arguments exist for each point that you make.

Also, just because there is no clear-cut answer to the problem does not mean that you can simply abdicate your responsibility to analyse methodically or reach reasoned conclusions. Commonly, weak answers to problem questions will simply ignore challenging alternatives with sweeping statements like "it has already been proven that . . .", or "that has been established by the facts" without any real analysis.

Another common trait in weaker answers is that of leaving any application and conclusion to the hypothetical 'court', 'judge' or 'jury' i.e. the student will skip any discussion of an arguable either way point by using a sentence like "As the facts are unclear, it will be up to the judge to decide what the outcome will be", or "it is up to the jury to determine guilt in criminal cases". Even if it is challenging because there appears to be no clear-cut answers, you must methodically consider all possible angles of how the law will apply to the facts of the problem question; you should then at least attempt to reach reasoned conclusions. Be prepared to accept that a number of alternative outcomes might all be viable, and say why.

At this stage more so than any of the others, it is vital that you:

- Link the law closely to the facts of the problem question. Remember that the brief is not to write an all you know essay on . . . ; and
- Support your application and analysis with relevant cases or other legal authority. When you do so at this stage, the supporting authorities should be closely applied to the facts of the problem question, rather than simply 'tagged-on' at the end of sentences (usually in brackets) – see below for examples.

Taking the first issue between Roger and Adam Terracotta in the example above:

> Roger was a local builder who required roof tiles for the extension he was completing in Charlton Kings. After seeing Terracotta Ltd's advertisement in the local newspaper on 1 September, he telephoned and spoke to Adam Terracotta, enquiring about the price for 1000 Square roof tiles. Adam Terracotta told him the Square tiles were offered for sale at £2 each. Roger said he would think about it, and get back to Adam Terracotta if he was interested in purchasing the roof tiles.

The key point was whether a telephone call to enquire about the price of the tiles would have been an offer, or an enquiry only, with no binding contractual effect. Good answers should state that, "In *Harvey v Facey*[6], the Court held that a telegram sent enquiring about whether a property was for sale and if so the lowest price for it, was merely an enquiry seeking further information rather than an offer. Applying this to the facts of Roger's telephone call to Adam Terracotta, it is unlikely that a court will find that Roger had intended any more than make a price enquiry. This was especially as Roger said he would 'think about it, and get back to Terracotta if he was interested . . .' As such, the telephone call from Roger to Adam Terracotta on 1 September did not bear any contractual consequences."

A weaker answer however, might simply state, "The telephone call to enquire about the price of the tiles was an enquiry only, with no binding contractual effect. *(Harvey v Facey)*"

Tips

Ask someone who has not read the problem question to read your draft answer.

Ask them to guess from your answer what the facts of the problem question are.

If in the process of this 'reverse-engineering' they come up with a full and accurate account of the facts in your problem question, then you have successfully achieved 2 things:

- You have covered all the points raised by the problem question; and
- You have not strayed too far into writing a law 'essay', rather than an answer to the problem question.

Obviously the reverse position is also true i.e. if they fail to reconstruct the factual scenario of your problem question from your answer, then you may have missed out key facts, or merely written a rambling 'essay'.

Note that like Step 2, Step 3 should take up a good portion of your answer – at least a third to half of your answer should be focussed on Step 3.

---

[6] [1893] AC 552

Step 4 – W: What is the Outcome? i.e. Reaching a Conclusion

Finally, your answer should state your conclusion on the issue(s) you were asked to discuss. This should be a global conclusion that ties in all your conclusions to the issues and sub-issues earlier.

Although only brief, this step is nonetheless important – if you imagine that each of the parties in the problem question are in fact real people, affected by the issues raised in the problem question, they would want to end their consultation with you with clear conclusions of what the most likely outcomes are.

There will be occasions when you may have to give a 'it depends' conclusion – that is fine so long as you have carefully analysed the law and methodically applied it to the facts of the problem.

You must also make sure that your conclusion is consistent with your analysis and application.

Note: Your actual final conclusion is not as important as ensuring that it follows logically from your discussion of the law and the application to the facts. It should not be more than one paragraph in length.

An Example of Applying ILAW to Answering a Problem Question

Let us revisit the problem question example, and attempt to apply all four steps of ILAW to it:

> ### Example: problem question
>
> Terracotta Tiles Ltd manufactures and sells roof tiles, from its warehouse outlet in Stroud, Gloucestershire and online via its website.
>
> Due to the economic downturn, Terracotta Tiles Ltd decided to reduce the number of styles of roof tiles it manufactures. On Wednesday 1 September 2011, the discontinued lines were advertised for sale in the local newspaper and on the front page of Terracotta Tiles Ltd's website:
>
> "SALE: Quality roof tiles from Terracotta Tiles Ltd. Massive reductions on the following discontinued ranges: Square, Round and Diamond. Order now! The first five customers who order more than £1000 worth of roof tiles will receive a free golf umbrella each. We promise you will not be disappointed."
>
> Roger was a local builder who required roof tiles for the extension he was completing in Charlton Kings. After seeing Terracotta Tiles Ltd's advertisement in the local newspaper on 1 September, he

telephoned and spoke to Adam Terracotta, enquiring about the price for 1000 Square roof tiles. Adam Terracotta told him the Square tiles were offered for sale at £2 each. Roger said he would think about it, and get back to Adam Terracotta if he was interested in purchasing the roof tiles.

On Friday 3 September, Roger wrote to Terracotta Tiles Ltd, stating that he would like to purchase 1000 Square roof tiles. He posted the letter at 6 p.m. that evening.

At 9 a.m. on Monday 6 September, Steve, the owner of a large DIY shop in Cheltenham, visited Terracotta Tiles Ltd's warehouse outlet. He entered into face-to-face negotiations with Adam Terracotta on the price for buying the entire stock of all three discontinued lines of roof tiles from Terracotta Tiles Ltd.

Whilst Steve was negotiating with Adam Terracotta, Rafael ordered 300 Round roof tiles from Terracotta Tiles Ltd's website. He paid for his order by entering his credit card details online and received a confirmation message stating that his order had been processed and the tiles would be dispatched as soon as possible. The automatic payment collection system set up on Terracotta Tiles Ltd's website immediately debited the full payment from Rafael's credit card account. According to the terms of Terracotta Tiles Ltd's website, which Rafael had clicked 'I agree' to but had not read, acceptance of an offer takes place when Terracotta Tiles Ltd dispatches the goods to the customer.

At 10.30 a.m. that same day, Adam Terracotta and Steve entered into a contract for Steve to buy the entire stock of all three discontinued lines of roof tiles from Terracotta Tiles Ltd.

Having sold all those tiles, Adam Terracotta then opened his post which had arrived over the weekend and at 9.30 a.m. that Monday morning. Amongst the post was the letter from Roger.

He then looked at the online orders, which included Rafael's order.

As Adam had sold his entire consignment of Square, Round and Diamond roof tiles to Steve, he was concerned that he would be unable to supply Roger and Rafael with any of the roof tiles that they had ordered.

Advise Adam Terracotta of his legal position.

First issue:

Due to the economic downturn, Terracotta Ltd decided to reduce the number of styles of roof tiles it manufactures. On Wednesday 1 September 2011, the discontinued lines were advertised for sale in the local newspaper and on the front page of Terracotta Ltd's website:

"SALE: Quality roof tiles from Terracotta Ltd. Massive reductions on the following discontinued ranges: Square, Round and Diamond. Order now! The first five customers who order more than £1000 worth of roof tiles will receive a free golf umbrella each. We promise you will not be disappointed."

Identify
- Was the advertisement (both in the newspaper and on the website) an offer or an invitation to treat?

Law

Advertisements and items on display are usually invitations to treat only – you should refer to cases like *Fisher v Bell*[7] and *Partridge v Crittenden*[8].

That is because they tend to be invitations to others to 'come and make offers'.

This position extends to online advertisements: as an example, you could refer to the Singapore case of *Chwee Kin Keong v Digilandmalcom Pte Ltd*[9] [the law in Singapore on such matters is based on the common law principles here].

The Courts also consider it unlikely that the person placing the advertisement will intend to be bound by all who come forward in response to the advertisement – it may be physically impossible to satisfy all demand otherwise.

The fact that these were discontinued lines of tiles suggests that Terracotta only has a limited supply, therefore his intention was surely NOT to be bound to everyone who orders tiles from him.

The counter argument: some advertisements could exceptionally be unilateral offers e.g. *Carlill v The Carbolic Smoke Ball Co Ltd*[10].

Apply

Adam Terracotta's advertisement in the local newspaper was very similar to the advertisement placed in *Partridge v Crittenden*[11], so it is more likely to be an invitation to treat.

The advertisement on Terracotta's website is likely to be treated in the same manner, following the case of *Chwee Kin Keong v Digilandmalcom Pte Ltd*[12].

Also, the fact that Roger had to telephone Terracotta to enquire about the price suggests that the terms of the advert were not sufficiently precise to constitute an offer.

The counter argument: Does Terracotta's advert fall into this exceptional category of unilateral offers? For it to do so, the advertisement must be sufficiently specific such that the actions of any buyer would constitute acceptance, as was the case in *Carlill v The Carbolic Smoke Ball Co Ltd*[13]. Another common law case that strongly supports this proposition is the American one of *Lefkowitz v Great Minneapolis Surplus Store Inc*[14], where it was held that if the advertisement is clear, definite and explicit, and leaves nothing open for negotiation, it constitutes an offer, acceptance of which will complete the contract.

---

[7] [1961] 1 QB 394
[8] [1968] 1 WLR 1204
[9] [2004] SGHC 71
[10] [1893] 1 QB 256
[11] [1968] 1 WLR 1204
[12] [2004] SGHC 71
[13] [1893] 1 QB 256
[14] 86 N.W.2d 689 (Minn.1957)

Does the offer of the golf umbrellas to the first 5 customers support this conclusion? I.e. do the umbrellas act in the same way as the £1000 deposited with the Alliance Bank in the case of *Carlill*[15], or the 'first come, first served' at $1 each for the 3 coats in *Lefkowitz*[16]?

Unilateral offers usually take the form of "if you do this, I will do that" – is it obvious that Terracotta had put himself in that position here?

The free umbrellas could themselves be subject to contractually binding agreements, as per *Esso Petroleum v Commissioners of Customs and Excise*[17].

The promise "not to be disappointed" is mere advertising puff, with no contractual significance.

What is the Outcome?

In essence, having looked at both sides of the argument, you should come to a conclusion whether the advert was an offer or an invitation to treat. The arguments tend to favour a finding of an invitation to treat due to the lack of clarity as to the terms (e.g. price) in the advertisements, but both conclusions are acceptable if correctly argued and supported with authorities.

Practical Question

When you have covered the relevant section of the Law of Contract in your studies, apply the four steps of ILAW to the section below:

Second issue

> Roger was a local builder who required roof tiles for the extension he was completing in Charlton Kings. After seeing Terracotta Ltd's advertisement in the local newspaper on 1 September, he telephoned and spoke to Adam Terracotta, enquiring about the price for 1000 Square roof tiles. Adam Terracotta told him the Square tiles were offered for sale at £2 each. Roger said he would think about it, and get back to Adam Terracotta if he was interested in purchasing the roof tiles.
>
> On Friday 3 September, Roger wrote to Terracotta Ltd, stating that he would like to purchase 1000 Square roof tiles. He posted the letter at 6 p.m. that evening.

Practical Question

Following on from the practical question above, identify at least another two issues raised by this problem question, and apply the four steps of ILAW to each of those issues.

---

[15] (n9)
[16] (n13)
[17] [1976] 1 All ER 117

Referencing

An ability to refer to legal authorities in support of your statements will improve your mark (in a closed book examination, it will be useful even if you can only remember the name of the statute or one of the parties involved in the case). Full and accurate referencing is however required in all assignments and other written work handed in for assessment. As Law students, you will be expected to use the OSCOLA system of referencing – please refer to: http://www.law.ox.ac.uk/publications/oscola.php.

In Summary

- Always read the problem question carefully
- Follow any instruction you are given in the rubric
- Be methodical
- Always link the law to the facts of the problem question
- Application of the law to the facts is the top priority
- Do not waffle on unnecessarily – keep it concise and to the point
- Reach reasoned conclusions

Practical Questions

Find an old problem question assignment you have completed. Analyse your answer to ascertain whether you have adhered to the points in this chapter.

If you have not, try rewriting that to reflect what you have learnt here.

Get an independent third party to read both versions of your answer and provide you with feedback on the differences.

2a

Career Planning

Fred Motson

Working in the legal profession

Many of you will at least be considering a career as a lawyer. In this chapter, we will look at the different types of roles that lawyers play in the English legal system, along with other employment in the legal sector. We will also discuss the variety of organisations and practice areas which make law such a unique and diverse field in which to work. We shall begin with the traditional roles of solicitor and barrister. It should be noted that at the time of writing (July 2012), the Legal Education and Training Review is on-going. When this joint project of the Solicitors Regulation Authority, Bar Standards Board and ILEX Professional Standards is completed late in 2012, recommendations may be made and adopted which dramatically change how students are taught about law and the legal profession, and how they qualify to become a lawyer. Because no final recommendations have been made, we will in this chapter consider the current position rather than try to predict the future.

Life as a solicitor

How do I become a solicitor?

Step 1: Obtain a qualifying law degree

As you are reading this book, you are probably already on your way to the first stage in becoming a solicitor, which is to obtain a qualifying law degree (QLD). What constitutes a qualifying degree is decided jointly by the Law Society and the Bar Standards Board. You may well already know that in order to obtain a QLD, you need to study (and pass!) modules on Public Law, Law of the European Union, Criminal Law, Contract Law, Tort Law, Property Law and Equity and the Law of Trusts. Bear in mind that because these subjects only need to make up half of your degree, you will have the opportunity to study a number of optional subjects. While these optional subjects offer a chance to expand your knowledge, it is not mandatory for you to study any specific options to work in that practice area. Note that students who do not study Law as an undergraduate subject can, after completing a degree in another area, take the one-year Graduate Diploma in Law (GDL) course in order to become eligible. It is also possible to qualify as a solicitor through the ILEX Diploma route (see below).

Step 2: The Legal Practice Course

Once you have completed your law degree, you are assumed to have the academic legal knowledge required for practice. However, there is one more stage of training you must complete. This is the Legal

Practice Course (LPC), which is designed to provide would-be solicitors with the knowledge of practice and procedure required to work as a solicitor. There is currently no academic requirement for eligibility for the LPC beyond a QLD, and thus even a third class degree classification will not bar a student from this study. However, it should be noted that a number of LPC providers do set higher academic requirements, and obviously a lower classification may affect your ability to obtain a training contract. There are currently around 50 LPC providers, based in major towns and cities across England and Wales[1]. Between these institutions, just over 15,000 places were available on the course in 2010–2011 (the last year for which statistics are currently available)[2]. Some LPC providers are private companies, most notably BPP and the College of Law, who have licensed LPC (and BPTC) centres across the country. Other courses are run by University Law Schools. Because the content of the course is regulated by the SRA and the Law Society, there is little practical difference between these types of institution.

Perhaps the most important issue to consider when deciding where to apply for your LPC is the cost of studying the course. The fees for the full time course (which is the option chosen by around 80% of applicants) range from around £7,000 to £13,000[3], depending on the provider. In general, London-based providers are the most expensive. The general principle by which the LPC is expected to be funded is by firms paying for the course for those whom they wish to take up training contracts the following year. This is why applying for a training contract should be done while still at university and we will discuss this in more detail below. For those who do not apply for or obtain a training contract which includes LPC funding, there are a number of other options which can make the LPC more affordable. Firstly, different providers offer different grants and scholarships so it is important to research potential institutions thoroughly. In particular, university-based providers may offer large discounts to students who have studied their LLB or GDL qualification with them, and some universities offer a combined LLB/LPC course known as the "exempting degree – although this is currently only offered in the south of the country by the University of Westminster, and in the north by the Universities of Huddersfield, Nottingham Trent, Northumbria and Central Lancashire. Another way of helping manage the cost is to apply for scholarships from third parties, such as the Law Society's Diversity Access Scheme or Local Authority Grants. Finally, it is possible to borrow the money from a financial institution but this will of course require you pay it back, plus interest, in future and you should only proceed after seeking advice from an independent financial advisor.

If your LPC is being funded by a training contract provider, then they will almost certainly specify which institution or institutions they wish you to attend. For almost all applicants, the procedure is to apply through the Central Applications Board (www.lawcabs.ac.uk) which is a not dissimilar experience to the UCAS applications you will already be familiar with. You can apply to up to three providers, ranked in order of preference, although you should bear in mind that some institutions would expect to be ranked first in order to offer you a place. Applications should be made early in your final year of undergraduate study. Prior to commencing your LPC, you also need to register with the Solicitors Regulation Authority as a student member. Student enrolment is generally very straightforward but you must pass the "suitability test". In short, this means that you must declare: any criminal convictions, cautions or warnings; any assessment offences committed during your academic studies; any evidence that you cannot manage your finances (such as being declared bankrupt); and any disciplinary action taken against you by

---

[1] For an up to date list, including contact details, please visit http://www.sra.org.uk/students/courses/lpc-course-providers.page
[2] Strategic Research Unit, *Trends in the Solicitors' Profession: Annual statistical report 2010 – executive summary* (The Law Society, 2011)
[3] Figures taken from Chambers Student Guide, accessible at http://www.chambersstudent.co.uk

another regulatory body. If any of this applies to you, it is important to disclose it with full evidence in your application. It does not necessarily prohibit you becoming a solicitor, but you may need to provide further information (for example, a police warning for anti-social behaviour when you were a teenager is considerably less serious than a conviction for fraud).

You will commence your LPC in September and it will last for either one (full-time) or two (part-time) academic years. Since 2008, the LPC has been split into two stages. Stage 1 is designed to cover the core areas in which all solicitors are expected to be trained: Business Law and Practice, Property Law and Practice and Litigation (both civil and criminal). Stage 1 also includes learning about Taxation, Wills and the Administration of Estates. During your study of these areas, you will also develop knowledge of Professional Conduct and Regulation, along with key skills such as legal writing, drafting, interviewing and advising, legal research and advocacy. In Stage 2 of the course, you are given the opportunity to study optional Vocational Electives – each student must choose three of these and the options available vary by institution. Most electives involve detailed study of particular practice areas, thus common examples include Family law, Employment law, Commercial dispute resolution etc.[4]

Again, the methods of teaching and of assessment vary depending on the institution and the number of students studying the LPC that year. However, the key difference between the LPC (and indeed the BPTC) and undergraduate study is that you spend far more time in the classroom each week. This can involve a two or three day timetable involving very long days (often nine or more hours), or a four or five day timetable where you are expected to attend morning or afternoon sessions. Much of your time will be spent in relatively small groups, more akin to a tutorial than a lecture, where you will be focusing on learning and applying practical skills. However, an increasing number of providers do use lectures to communicate general concepts, backed up by interactive small group sessions. Because you are also expected to do extensive background reading and online learning in your spare time, you should bear in mind that it is much harder to balance a full-time LPC programme with other commitments, such as part-time employment or childcare, than undergraduate study. Assessment will usually take place through a mixture of exams (to test your knowledge of practice and procedure) and more practical assessments, designed to test specific skills such as drafting legal documents or performing advocacy. As this is postgraduate study, the pass mark in all assessments is 50% (rather than the 40% you may be more familiar with currently). Resits and referrals are possible but all assessments must be passed within five years of attempting your first LPC assessment. Higher marks can earn a Commendation or Distinction. It should be noted that the award you receive is generally seen as less important than a degree classification, as most employers are only concerned with their trainees passing the LPC rather than their actual grade. However, if you have not secured a training contract prior to commencing LPC studies, then you will find that a higher mark will help in applications.

Step 3: Undertake a training contract

This brings us on to the most difficult, but most important, part of becoming a fully qualified solicitor. After completing your LPC, you are not yet a solicitor, merely a more highly qualified student! In order to be admitted to the roll of solicitors, which will allow you to practice, you must complete a two-year training contract (although as we shall discuss below, you must apply for your training contract much earlier). A training contract is full-time employment with a firm of solicitors, where you learn "on the job". Each firm is different, and the experience of a trainee in the commercial litigation department of a Magic

---

[4] SRA Education and Training Unit, *Information for providers of Legal Practice Courses* (SRA, 2012)

Circle firm will be worlds away from someone undertaking a training contract in a small high street firm, however the most common method of training is to rotate you through different "seats" – which essentially means being placed in different departments for a fixed set of time. Most commonly, a trainee might spend six months in four different seats. The aim is to not only provide specific training in the most relevant areas, but also to allow new recruits to see different aspects of the firm and develop a wider skillset. Most of your training contract will be extremely practice-based, but you do need to keep a record of what you have learnt and this may be requested for review by the SRA. You are also expected to complete the Professional Skills Course, which your employer will pay for along with your travel expenses. At regular intervals your supervisor(s) will informally review your performance and at least three times in the two years you will have formal appraisals of your development and progress[5]. Assuming everything goes to plan and your firm wishes to take you on permanently, you will be informed at a set point during your second year of their decision. If you are not fortunate enough to be offered a full position, you will still complete your training contract and can then apply to work as a solicitor for another firm.

In practical terms, obtaining a training contract is far from guaranteed. On the face of it, the statistics look very positive when one considers that the number of students passing the LPC examinations is usually roughly equal to the number of training contracts available. In recent years the number of places has dropped[6] however even accounting for this the odds still look very good. However, these figures are misleading. The vast majority of training contracts are offered two years before they are due to start, thus if you wish to pursue a career as solicitor you should be making applications in the second year of a standard three year law degree. Because of this, most students who commence the LPC do so because they already have a training contract (and usually their firm is also paying at least some of the course fees). It is thus difficult to get an accurate picture of the real chances, however one can say that obtaining a training contract is statistically still much more likely than obtaining pupillage, but far more difficult than finding graduate employment in most other sectors. It is also worth noting that while most good students who enter the area find *a* training contract, this may not be in the type of firm or practice area in which they would have wished to work. Certainly, applications to the "Magic Circle" firms are as competitive as those to the top barristers' Chambers. One positive point for would-be solicitors is that unlike those looking for work at the Bar, applicants for training contracts have no limit on the number of firms they can apply to. Pay varies dramatically depending on the size of the firm and the sector in which they work however the minimum annual salary is £16,650 (£18,590 in Central London)[7], although this is to be abolished in 2014[8]. Top commercial firms in London will at least double these figures, and some American law firms operating in England have offered £50,000+ for first year trainees.

What does a solicitor do?

The traditional view of solicitors and barristers is that a barrister appears in court, while a solicitor spends their time preparing cases and meeting with clients. There is certainly an element of truth in that generalisation, however the work of a solicitor can be extremely varied, particularly across different types of firms and different areas of law. Key differences might include: the type of work carried out; the number of different cases handled; the type of clients you work for; the amount of time spent with clients/in the office/

---

[5] SRA Education and Training Unit, *You and your training contract* (SRA, 2012)
[6] Rothwell, R. *Report shows drop in training contract places*, The Law Society Gazette 1/4/2011
[7] http://www.sra.org.uk/sra/news/minimum-salary-2011-2012.page
[8] http://www.sra.org.uk/minimum-salary/

in court; and perhaps most importantly the overall objective of your work. In the words of one local government solicitor:

> *"six months into Articles [what is now called a training contract], I had made a small contribution to protecting numerous women from violent husbands, prevented tenants being evicted and harassed, and obtained compensation for employees injured at work. My university friend in the City firm for which I was, apparently, destined had spent six months in Sheffield compiling a list of documents for one major piece of litigation which she knew very little about. She had, of course, earned four times as much as me during that period and was already being charged out to clients at more than I am now as county borough solicitor."* [9]

However, there are a number of key elements to the work of most solicitors, although they may be present to a greater or lesser extent for each individual.

Contact with clients

As mentioned above, traditionally solicitors are seen as the "public facing" branch of the legal profession. While this distinction has become increasingly blurred (as discussed later in this chapter) it is still true to say that most solicitors spend a lot more time communicating with clients than most barristers do. This contact is obviously varied – you might spend more time on the telephone or conducting email correspondence, but for important matters such as a first meeting with a client or taking a witness statement then face to face contact is essential. Furthermore, it is important as a solicitor to not only speak to clients when you need information from them or are providing legal advice, but also to act more generally as a point of contact and source of information for your clients, who are of course your customers. This might involve developing productive relationships with senior employees of a large corporation, or at the other end of the scale giving someone facing criminal or immigration proceedings a sympathetic hearing.

Providing advice

Of course, one of the most important parts of your client contact is in providing clear and accurate advice. It should be noted that giving advice in practice is somewhat different to the impression you may have from your academic studies – each case involves real people with real problems and thus you need to consider the context in which you give your advice, rather than simply trying to find the "right" answer as you might when discussing a problem question. For example, in an employment dispute where your client believes they were unfairly dismissed from their job, your legal knowledge might suggest that any eventual litigation would almost certainly be decided in favour of your client. However, they might be currently unemployed, supporting a large family and emotionally ill-prepared for a court hearing. Thus the correct advice to give would involve exploring options with your client to settle the matter out of court. Equally, a solicitor practising in criminal defence work does not try and decide if their client is guilty, but rather gives advice as to the consequences of, for example, refusing to comment if interviewed by the police. Thus the role of a solicitor is not to pre-empt the judge, but rather to ensure a client is aware of all of his or her options and the likely chances of success, and likely consequences, of these alternatives.

---

[9] Forbes, D. *The (first) year in the life of a borough solicitor*, J.L.G.L. 2003, 6(3), 41–43

Case management

Away from communicating with your clients, as a solicitor you are also responsible for taking their case forward. In a high street practice, this might mean you are responsible for every step from their first meeting with a member of your firm up to enforcing any eventual judgment in their favour. In other disputes, and particularly in larger firms, solicitors would usually specialise in one area – for example, there might be a pre-litigation department, an alternative dispute resolution department and then a litigation department with specialists in each step of the process.

Case management is a wide term, but it generally entails making sure that the practical steps needed are taken within deadlines, while keeping in mind the overall direction of the dispute. Some common examples of important steps in managing a case would include corresponding with the legal representatives of other parties, obtaining evidence such as witness statements or the reports of expert witnesses, preparing for court hearings, keeping track of costs and ensuring the client is kept up to date on the progress of the case.

Different types of firms

We have already mentioned that the work of a solicitor can depend largely on the type of firm they are employed by, and because most solicitors are unlikely to work for more than a handful of firms at most in their career, it is important to make the right decision as to where you will work early in your legal career. On the whole, it is advisable to obtain a training contract at the level of firm in which you plan to remain.

Magic Circle and Silver Circle firms

At the very top of the list of solicitors firms in England and Wales are the so-called "magic circle". This term is used by lawyers to refer to the largest commercial law firms in the UK, namely Allen & Overy, Clifford Chance, Freshfields Bruckhaus Deringer, Linklaters and (although some feel that they are not a magic circle firm) Slaughter & May. While the outlook and international reach of these firms varies, they are generally seen as the most profitable and globally-recognised law firms headquartered in the UK. A number of major city firms which have made great strides in catching the magic circle were branded the "silver circle" by *The Lawyer* magazine in 2005[10] – the exact membership is again disputed but generally involves domestic-focused commercial firms with particular strength in corporate and real estate practice. Notable members include Berwin Leighton Paisner, Herbert Smith and Macfarlanes. At all of these firms, trainees and associates are expected to work extremely long hours, often spending more than one night a week staying at their desk, and can also expect to work over most weekends. However, the rewards are commensurate – starting salaries are extremely high and within a few years most recruits will be on a six-figure wage. Work in these firms varies, but is heavily focused on corporate, commercial and financial matters.

Other City firms

Behind the firms which top the various rankings for turnover and profit, there are a large number of well-respected, large firms which offer legal services to UK-based companies. These firms will still mainly appeal to those who wish to work in commercial law and while salaries and working hours are not quite at magic circle levels, still require serious commitment in exchange for considerable financial rewards. At some smaller commercial firms, the pay may be lower and the facilities less impressive but there is often more scope to take on larger cases early in your career, and you may deal with more private clients alongside large businesses.

---

[10] Griffiths, C. *Top of equity: Firms break into millionaires' club as partner earnings rise* (The Lawyer, 15 August 2011)

International firms

As an international centre of business, London has always been a very attractive destination for a number of international firms. Apart from UK-based firms with an international presence, there are a large number of foreign-headquartered firms with London offices. Traditionally, most are American firms such as White & Case, Baker & McKenzie and Latham & Watkins. However, there are also firms from across the globe, based in countries varying from Belgium to Brazil, and Nigeria to Kazakhstan. For most firms, there is again a focus on corporate and real estate practice areas. Some of the highest salaries in the entire legal sector are offered by the US firms in particular, but long and often unsociable hours are the result of working for a firm which may be based in a very different time zone. Members are also likely to be expected to work on secondment abroad at least occasionally, which you should bear in mind if interested in this area.

National firms

This level of firm covers those which are more UK-focused than the above categories, but which are spread across the country. The size of these firms usually allows for a level of specialisation among their solicitors, but the overall portfolio of work is usually wider and can often include a much wider range of practice areas that the firms we have looked at above, including crucial areas such as criminal, family and employment law. Some national firms, such as DLA Piper and Eversheds are similar to City firms in their areas of work and you should research firms in this area carefully to ensure that their practice, and their location, will be suitable for you. As they may have offices in a number of cities and areas, you should also be prepared to travel frequently and possibly relocate.

Regional firms

A regional firm may simply sound like a smaller version of a national firm and this is true in some cases, but often so-called regional firms are specialised, high-end providers of legal services which simply happen to based outside of London. Such firms are particularly found in other major cities such as Birmingham and Manchester, and can be as prestigious and selective as top City firms. You should bear in mind however that salaries are generally lower, and these firms are wary of applicants from other areas who may see them as an "easier" alternative to seeking a training contract in a City firm.

Specialist and boutique firms

Because the law is such a large and varied area, there is plenty of scope for a law firm which specialises in just one niche. There are many such firms in the UK, although most will be based in London or local to a particular industry. Examples range across practice areas such as sports law, media law, telecommunications, equestrian law, art law and intellectual property. Because the work is focused in one area, applicants must show at the least a real interest in this field and previous industry experience can be very highly valued, making such firms a particularly attractive option for mature students.

High Street firms

It has been estimated that more than half of all training contracts are offered by high street firms[11]. As the name suggests, this category refers to outfits with a single set of premises which conduct the majority of their work within the local area. Such firms can still vary widely, from long-established firms with a literal "high street" presence, to sole practitioners. Practice areas tend to be much less specialised, as the potential

---

[11] Chambers Student Guide, *Different types of law firm*, http://www.chambersstudent.co.uk/Articles/316

client pool is smaller, although generally there will be less of a commercial emphasis. As such, high street solicitors would often practice in areas such as wills and estates, property and conveyancing, crime and family law and personal injury areas. Because high street firms tend to be much smaller, their salaries are often lower than their larger rivals and they will have much less of a national presence. As such, it is important to research your local firms if you are interested in this route, and in particular you need to note that not all high street firms can afford to offer training contracts every year. While, as mentioned, you may not get the huge pay packet of the commercial firms, high street work provides great variety and a chance to run your own cases far earlier than in a large organisation. You are also likely to spend more time with clients, and to work far more sociable hours.

Other organisations

We will look at other legal careers later, but it is worth noting that large numbers of qualified solicitors do not work for a law firm at all, but for businesses in other sectors which need qualified legal staff. As such, training contracts are available from organisations as diverse as television channels, supermarkets and oil firms, along with more predictable businesses such as banks and insurers. Alternatively, you may choose to undertake a training contract and then transfer "in-house" by applying for a job as a solicitor for a company. Such roles tend to be less well paid than their equivalent in private practice, but compensate for this by offering a shorter working week and benefits such as more paid holiday allowance. The biggest in-house employer is of course the UK government, which requires huge numbers of lawyers both in "legal" areas such as the Crown Prosecution Service[12], and across all departments of the civil service. Most central government jobs can be found through the Government Legal Service[13] and you should also bear in mind that with 4,000 solicitors and trainees working in local government[14], this is an area worth exploring if you have an interest in public law in particular.

Other organisations which require trained lawyers include charities and pressure groups, and in particular those which provide legal advice. This is prevalent in areas such as family law and immigration law and some of these organisations have been accredited to offer training contracts. Again, the salary is unlikely to match private practice but the opportunities to become engaged in important litigation at an early stage of your career are considerable, and if you have passionate beliefs in such an area, it is one way of ensuring that you can make a clear contribution.

A career as a solicitor

Whichever type of firm you choose, if you obtain a training contract and complete it successfully then you have become a qualified solicitor, and will be added to the roll of solicitors by the Law Society. At this point, assuming you remain in private practice, you will become an Associate Solicitor (usually shortened to associate), where you are a fully-qualified solicitor but work under the direction of more senior members of the firm. Promotion from this role leads to becoming a Senior Associate. However, the ultimate goal for most solicitors in private practice is to become a partner in the firm (as you will probably already know, law firms are run as partnerships). A salaried partner is one who remains on a set wage, but will usually receive a (often large) bonus annually to reflect the firm's performance, whereas a "full" or equity partner is one who is entitled directly to a proportion of the distributable profits of the partnership.

---

[12] http://www.cps.gov.uk
[13] http://www.gls.gov.uk
[14] For more information see the Solicitors in Local Government website at http://www.slgov.org.uk/

At top magic circle firms, this means partners can expect millions of pounds every year. In smaller and high street practices, the figure is understandably far lower, however the status and influence of being a partner is still a desirable goal.

It should also be noted that in recent decades there has been a distinct move to increase the number of solicitors in the judiciary, which had traditionally been seen as the preserve of former barristers. A solicitor of the requisite number of years standing has, under the Courts and Legal Services Act 1990, the same rights to apply to any judicial post as a barrister.

> ### Reflection Questions
> 1. Think about specific reasons why you would or would not pursue a career as a solicitor
> 2. Does a career in private practice appeal to you more or less than in-house work?
> 3. What type of law firm do you think would best suit your skills and personality?

Life as a barrister

How do I become a barrister?

Step 1: Obtain a qualifying law degree

Just as for a solicitor, a barrister must hold a qualifying law degree. As above, there is no need to study any particular subject, although it should be noted that a number of chambers actually prefer to recruit GDL students, believing them to have a wider knowledge base than those who committed to a first degree in law.

Step 2: Join an Inn of Court

Unlike solicitors, who are regulated solely by the Law Society (and accompanying regulatory body the Solicitors' Regulation Authority), barristers are not only controlled by the Bar Council (and Bar Standards Board) but also by their "Inn of Court". This ancient tradition remains a crucial element in qualifying as a barrister. The Inns of Court were a number of organisations which sprang up in London in the 14th Century to provide lodgings for legal advocates[15]. Four of these Inns survive to this day: Gray's Inn, Lincoln's Inn, Inner Temple and Middle Temple. All four Inns are based in the Temple area of London; however they are open to all students in England and Wales intending to practice at the Bar. Traditionally the Inns were a place to live, to work and to socialise and also provided much of the legal training needed for would-be barristers. Today, the educative role has been taken over by universities and the Bar Professional Training Course (discussed below) but membership of an Inn remains mandatory for any student wishing to study the BPTC.

However, membership extends beyond a merely technical requirement. The Inns remain a social hub for barristers at all stages of their career, and in order to promote networking between members each Inn requires student members (i.e. those studying the BPTC) to attend 12 "qualifying sessions" during their

---

[15] Rider, C. *The Inns Of Court And Inns Of Chancery And Their Records* http://www.innertemple.org.uk/index.php?option=com_content&view=article&id=36&Itemid=30

studies. Usually held in the evenings, these sessions may be purely social, such as "guest nights" where students can show off the Harry Potter-esque surroundings to family and friends, and dinners where students sit with barristers and judges. They may also include a cultural element, such as concerts, plays or religious celebrations. Other qualifying sessions focus on improving important skills, such as mooting or debating competitions. Finally, residential weekends are offered, which count as multiple qualifying sessions and combine the above activities, also allowing easier access for students based further away from London.

The qualifying sessions thus provide networking opportunities, an opportunity for students to find out more about the profession, and an element of training. However, the Inns also fulfil another crucial function, without which many students may not ever reach the Bar. Because pupillages are usually only offered one year in advance, fewer applicants obtain pupillage prior to commencing the BPTC than on the LPC. Furthermore, even then few pupillage providers offer to cover the cost of the course, or at best will deduct this from the amount paid during pupillage. As such, the Inns of Court are very much relied on by the profession to provide funding for promising students who would otherwise be unable to afford the course. Many students interested in a career at the Bar spend a lot of time worrying about which Inn they should join, but in most areas the Inns are essentially identical – it is no longer true to say that any particular Inn focuses on a particular practice area, and the level of diversity at each Inn is broadly similar. Where the Inns do differ is in the precise terms of the large amounts of funding they provide students (estimated at around £4.5 million every year[16]). As such, applying to an Inn with the most relevant scholarships is often a good idea, unless you have specific reasons for choosing a different institution.

Step 3: The Bar Professional Training Course

As the emphasis on scholarships in the last paragraph might have suggested, the cost of the Bar Professional Training Course (BPTC) is one of its defining features. Because lower numbers of students study the course compared to the LPC and the teaching style demands frequent small group sessions, the cost of the course is extremely high. Currently the lowest fees are just under £11,000, while the highest reach £16,000[17]. Until the 1990s all students on what was then known as the Bar Vocational Course (BVC) had to attend the Inns of Court School of Law in London. This has been widened with new providers entering the market but the course is still only available in London, Birmingham, Bristol, Cardiff, Leeds, Manchester, Nottingham and Northumbria. As such, many students need to consider the cost of living in a major city for the year of study. If you do not obtain funding from your Inn of Court, the other funding options discussed for the LPC above, such as grants from external bodies and career development loans remain viable, but again you should think very carefully about any arrangement where you will have to make regular repayments.

In order to apply to the BPTC, you must apply in your final year of undergraduate study. The current deadlines are for the system to open in November and close in January (with the aim of commencing the course in September). Students can apply to a number of providers, but only to three in the first round. If unsuccessful (note that unlike the LPC, the BPTC is oversubscribed and so only around 60% of applicants receive places[18]) then a second round takes place where applications are sent to other nominated providers. Because of a concern that too many students were being admitted to the BPTC who had little chance of obtaining pupillage (a problem we will discuss in the next section) an Aptitude Test was proposed (known

---

[16] Bar Council statistics, accessible at http://www.barcouncil.org.uk/becoming-a-barrister/finance-and-funding/funding-and-scholarships/
[17] Figures taken from Chambers Student Guide, accessible at http://www.chambersstudent.co.uk
[18] Bar Standards Board data, accessible at http://www.barstandardsboard.org.uk/qualifying-as-a-barrister/bar-professional-training-course/how-to-apply-for-the-bptc/

as the BCAT) and at the time of writing, has just been approved by the Legal Services Board despite some controversy over how effective the test will be[19]. More information about the test, along with sample questions, can be found on the Bar Standards Board website[20]. As mentioned above, you will also need to join an Inn, and this involves a similar disclosure of any criminal record as mentioned above regarding the SRA.

The content of the BPTC is not entirely dissimilar to the LPC, although there is more emphasis on advocacy and appearing in court, at the expense of areas such as conveyancing and taxation. The content of the course is theoretically divided into knowledge areas (Civil Litigation & remedies, Criminal Litigation & sentencing, Evidence, Professional Ethics and two optional subjects) and skills, which along with more general abilities include Opinion-writing, Conference skills, Resolution of Disputes Out of Court and Advocacy. The course is taught similarly to the LPC, but with an even greater emphasis on small group sessions and much of the course is taken up with practical exercises. Some BPTC providers do use larger lectures rather than full small group teaching and this may be something to consider when choosing your institution. Assessment is similarly split between knowledge-based assessments (which since April 2012 have been standardised across all providers by a Central Examinations Board) and practical assessments, such as assessing advocacy through the cross-examination of an actor playing the part of a witness. The optional subjects are similar to the LPC electives, allowing students to gain a greater knowledge of specific practice areas. The level of classroom time is also similar to the LPC, as is the option of studying the course part-time over two academic years.

Step 4: Obtain a pupillage

On completion of the BPTC, and assuming you have completed your twelve qualifying sessions at your Inn of Court, you will be "called to the Bar" at a ceremony at your Inn. At this point, you are officially a Barrister – but you are not qualified to practice. In order to do so, you must complete a pupillage. In many respects a pupillage is comparable to a training contract – it involves shadowing senior lawyers to understand more about legal practice and procedure, while being paid to do so. However, pupillage lasts one rather than two years and is split into two equal periods of six months. There is also a strict limit (twelve sets) on the number of chambers to which you can apply each year.

In the "first six", pupils are not allowed to undertake any work of their own. Instead, they will shadow one or a number of barristers in the set, known as "pupil masters" – often carrying out research and discussing cases, as well as watching these practitioners in court. Once this is satisfactorily completed, the pupil can begin their "practising six" or "second six", in which they *may* take on legal work – both providing legal advice and appearing in court, as long as they have permission from their supervisor. In some sets, particularly those which are smaller or focus on court-based work, this might mean a pupil appearing in court within days of beginning this period (although the work is likely to be low-value civil claims in County Courts, or minor criminal offences in the Magistrates' Court). In larger sets, particularly commercial sets where barristers may appear in court infrequently, the second six may be very similar to the first six with little opportunity to take on individual work. During the twelve months of pupillage, trainees must also complete the Advocacy Training and Practice Management Courses (provided by the Inns of Court or local circuits elsewhere in the country) along with a Forensic Accountancy Course within the first three years of practice. If all of these conditions are met, the pupil will obtain a practice certificate at the end of the twelve months, allowing him or her to accept instructions (i.e. take on cases from solicitors).

---

[19] See for example Manning L. *LSB approves introduction of Bar Course Aptitude Test* (The Lawyer, 25 July 2012)
[20] http://www.barstandardsboard.org.uk

The idea of paid pupillage is relatively new – until 2003, there was no obligation to pay pupils (and perhaps understandably, few sets did!). This was mainly because a set of barristers' chambers is actually just a group of self-employed professionals who happen to share a building and the services of one or more clerks, rather than a company or a partnership. Therefore, the cost of employing a pupil reduces the other members' earnings. Since 2003, a compulsory wage has been set (which currently stands at £12,000 plus expenses[21]), which was intended to increase diversity at the Bar (as it was felt that only those independently wealthy enough to work for free for a year could afford unpaid pupillage). The response has been, to say the least, mixed – some believe the minimum salary is an excellent idea which has had the intended effect, while others believe that it has actually made access far harder. This is because the number of pupillages has declined dramatically since unfunded pupillages were abolished, meaning that only the top candidates (who in the eyes of most sets remain Oxbridge-educated students who are likely to come from privileged backgrounds) can obtain a much sought after pupillage. Indeed, one law student went as far as to sue the Bar Council, claiming that this caused racial prejudice – although his claim was swiftly dismissed by the Employment Appeal Tribunal[22]. However, two facts are not in dispute: firstly, most pupillage providers pay well above the minimum award (up to £50,000+ for commercial sets); secondly, there are not enough pupillages for everyone.

The level of competition for pupillages can be frightening. We saw above that it is by no means guaranteed that a would-be solicitor can obtain a training contract, and the picture at the bar is even more unforgiving. In the words of the "Health Warning" which the Inns of Court, BPTC Providers, BSB and Bar Council agreed to publish to all prospective students:

> "... you should also consider some of the 'facts and figures' concerning a career at the Bar before you commit yourself. In brief, approximately 1700 students take the Bar Course every year and, typically, the number of pupillages offered is about 480 each year. Some students who complete the Bar Course return overseas or turn to other professions. However, students are allowed to seek pupillage for up to 5 years after completing the Bar Course, so the competition for pupillages is extremely intense. Over 3,000 individuals may be applying for pupillage in any particular year, and some Chambers have over a hundred applicants for each pupillage placement, and at present there are only a limited number of pupillages at the Employed Bar."[23]

If anything, this health warning could be said to be overly optimistic, as the number of pupillages has fallen steadily since 2007[24]. The warning mentions the effect of the large number of students who are studying or have completed the BPTC making applications, however what should also be noted is that these applicants are likely to have far more impressive CVs than students in their final year at university, making it extremely difficult to obtain pupillage prior to the professional course. When one considers the cost of the BPTC, it is clear that for many students it is no more than a gamble to attempt to reach the Bar. One final point to bear in mind is that unlike in the solicitors' profession, where would-be trainees can apply to as many firms as they wish, the limit of twelve applications per year makes your selection of chambers crucial.

---

[21] Bar Standards Board Code of Conduct, Annexe R
[22] *Iteshi v The General Council of The Bar*, Unreported (EAT, 30 March 2012 – available at http://www.bailii.org/uk/cases/UKEAT/2012/0161_11_3003.html)
[23] Health Warning for prospective Bar Professional Training Course students, available at: http://www.barstandardsboard.org.uk/media/1363162/final_health_warning_for_bsb_website_24_jan_2012.pdf
[24] Bar Council statistics, http://www.barcouncil.org.uk/about-the-bar/facts-and-figures/statistics/#EntryStats

What does a barrister do?

Depending on the area in which they work, and their particular professional clients (i.e. the solicitors who employ them), the majority of barristers spend most of their time engaged in one of three activities: researching the law, advising on the law, and presenting a case.

Advocacy

Barristers have always been seen traditionally as "hired guns", who come into a case at the last minute in order to present a party's arguments in court. While the work of many barristers is far wider than this (and as we shall discuss below, solicitors are increasingly moving into the field of advocacy), it remains the defining feature of the profession. Barristers are trained specialists, expected to have the knowledge, ability and ethics to argue any case for any client. Indeed, the so-called "cab rank rule" holds that a barrister must take on a case if he does not have a full workload and it is in his area of expertise[25]. The rule is so-called as it is the same as a taxi driver at the front of the rank – he or she must take the next fare, whether or not they particularly want to! As we shall see, the amount of advocacy you would perform depends on the area in which you choose to work, but this also might change the type – while criminal defence lawyers do (to an extent!) get to present eloquent speeches to a jury, the majority of advocacy actually involves a more nuanced approach of patiently building a case than the dramatic speeches you might see in films or on television. You may also be carrying out a lot of advocacy during settlement negotiations or interim court hearings, rather than necessarily always appearing in full trials. However, a flair for public speaking remains a crucial skill for any would-be barrister.

Researching the law

Even the most persuasive advocate in the world would struggle to win a case if he or she did not prepare fully. As such, a lot of a barrister's time is spent in law libraries or on a computer, finding the cases and judgments they need to support their case. You may well already feel that it is hardly possible for any one person to know that much law when revising for your exams, so you might be relieved to know that barristers are certainly not expected to be able to recite all relevant authorities on command.

Advising on the law

As well as using legal research to prepare for a hearing, barristers are often asked by solicitors to research a point of law simply to provide advice. It is common for a solicitor to seek a barrister's Opinion (a formal document which they are paid to provide) on any complex legal points in a dispute, or on more pragmatic issues such as what evidence should be collected or what level of damages the client should expect. Some barristers also deal directly with lay clients, which they are allowed to do on completing a public access course.

Different types of chambers

Unlike among solicitors firms, chambers are not easily classified into different categories. On the whole, chambers are divided by their areas of work, thus one might talk about a "criminal chambers", a "commercial chambers" or a "common law chambers". However, it is worth noting that the size of chambers can vary dramatically – some sets have less than ten tenants, while others are well into the hundreds. The size of a chambers is not an indication of quality, although smaller chambers are likely to

---

[25] Bar Standards Board, *Code of Conduct of the Bar of England & Wales – Part VI Paragraph 602* (As updated 31 March 2010)

be more specialised while the largest sets often take a very wide approach with different practice groups for each area. As you might imagine, personal relationships can, for better or worse, play a much larger part in smaller sets.

One of the biggest differences between chambers is how much time their members spend in court – practice areas such as crime and common law generally mean most members are in court at least weekly and often almost every day. At the opposite extreme, commercial sets often deal with long-running litigation that has lasted for months or even years and so their members may spend most of their time advising on the dispute and carrying out conferences and negotiations. It is also worth noting that different sets may take on work at different levels – some specialise in lower-level courts such as the Magistrates Court or Immigration Tribunal, while others take on lots of cases in the Court of Appeal and Supreme Court, which offers the opportunity for more junior members to assist Senior Counsel. Finally, you should note that just as with solicitors, there is an Employed Bar who work in-house at major companies and for public sector organisations. There are just under 3,000 employed barristers, representing around 20% of the Bar[26].

A career as a barrister

Assuming you are lucky enough to obtain pupillage, you are well on your way to becoming a barrister. However, just as with a training contract, you need to ensure that you impress during your time in training. Towards the end of your pupillage year, you will learn whether the set of chambers have decided to offer you a place to work with them once you are qualified – this is known as a 'tenancy'. The chances of being offered a tenancy are generally good, assuming you have done well during your pupillage, but it is by no means guaranteed. Pupils who are not offered tenancy will need to apply to another set (although this can often be done relatively informally, whereby their pupil supervisor tries to find other opportunities at similar chambers) or undertake a "third six", which is the choice to remain a pupil for another six months while looking for tenancy elsewhere.

As we discussed above, tenants at a chambers are self-employed and so once you have established tenancy, the amount you work and the amount you earn is dependent on the number of cases you obtain. As such, it is very important to have a good relationship with the clerks (whose role we consider further at the end of this chapter) who allocate work. Because chambers are not businesses, there is not really an opportunity to obtain "promotion" and so for the most successful and talented barristers, the highest mark of competence is to be made a QC, which stands for Queen's Counsel. This was traditionally seen as a very secretive process, where popularity was perhaps more important than ability[27]. As such, in 2004 a new independent Selection Panel was appointed to ensure a more transparent process. Becoming a QC, sometimes called "taking silk" (because a QC is entitled to wear a silk gown in court) usually allows a barrister to charge higher fees for his or her services, and will attract the most prestigious clients. Similarly to partners at the largest law firms, top QCs can earn hundreds of thousands, or even millions, of pounds each year[28]. Of course, the other very prestigious appointment for senior barristers is to become a member of the judiciary. To give one example of how the Bar still dominates this profession (although as we will discuss this is changing), all twelve of the current Supreme Court Justices[29] originally practised at the Bar.

---

[26] Bar Council statistics, http://www.barcouncil.org.uk/about-the-bar/facts-and-figures/statistics
[27] Elliot, C. and Quinn, F. *The English Legal System* 12th Edition (Longman, 2011)
[28] Aldridge, A. *Barrister fees spiral ever up as the economy trundles ever down* (The Guardian, 8 December 2011)
[29] At the time of writing in mid-2012

> **Reflection Questions**
>
> 1. Think about specific reasons why you would or would not pursue a career as a barrister
> 2. Does a career in private practice appeal to you more or less than in-house work?
> 3. What obstacles can you identify for a law student wishing to become a barrister?

Solicitor or barrister?

Perhaps the most common question students grapple with after they decide on a career in the legal profession is which route to choose, although it should be noted that it is possible to cross-qualify, allowing solicitors to become barristers and vice versa. Below are two tables, which demonstrate both the differences and similarities between the professions.

Differences between the professions

Barristers	Solicitors
Training: The BPTC focuses on practical skills, particularly advocacy. At least some experience or ability to speak publicly will be extremely helpful. Most guides to success at the Bar would suggest that a 2:1 or 1st class degree is required, barring any mitigating circumstances.	**Training:** The LPC includes practical skills but covers a wider range of practice areas, such as taxation and trusts. Most larger firms would expect at least a 2:1 classification in your law degree but high street firms may be less concerned with academic performance.
Qualifying: Pupillages are extremely competitive, with only a small portion of applicants obtaining success. It is rare for pupillage to be awarded prior to deciding to study the BPTC (and paying the fees!)	**Qualifying:** Training contracts are relatively competitive but the proportion available per applicant is considerably higher. It is common to secure a training contract before committing to the LPC.
Entering the profession: While not all pupils obtain tenancy, the conversion rate is relatively high and almost all those who successfully complete pupillage do end up obtaining work as a barrister. Pupillage also allows access to the employed Bar.	**Entering the profession:** Particularly in larger firms, it is very common for a much larger number of trainees to be taken on than there are places for associates. Furthermore, over two years conditions can change dramatically.
Daily work: Most barristers spend a considerable amount of time in court. As a result, they also travel frequently (although as they are self-employed, not luxuriously!). Lengthy client contact is rare. Barristers are mainly responsible for timetabling their work outside of court and most of this work is carried out alone.	**Daily work:** Most solicitors only attend court to monitor proceedings and assist their client, rather than to appear in front of the judge. Far more time is spent with clients. Solicitors usually need to keep to a tight schedule and there is less freedom as to when and where to work. It is also common to work as part of a team.
Career opportunities: As a freelance professional, a barrister can earn huge sums if successful and sought after, but has no guaranteed income and only earns as much as he or she works.	**Career opportunities:** As an employee, solicitors have employment rights such as paid holiday and many firms offer benefits such as private healthcare. Salaries are very dependent on the area of practice.

Similarities between the professions

Barristers	Solicitors
Training: Both the BPTC and the LPC are expensive courses which demand a considerable commitment from applicants. Both courses teach the main rules of procedure and the process of litigation. While the level of skills training differs, the LPC can provide excellent advocacy training, as the BPTC can develop skills such as client conferencing. Evidence of both academic achievement and practical ability is required to succeed in either profession, and so an impressive CV is vital.	
Qualifying: Obtaining a placement as a pupil or a trainee is a difficult task which requires commitment and patience alongside the ability to stand out. Areas which are particularly popular or highly paid are particularly competitive and only the top applicants will obtain a place. However, there is no reason why a truly committed student cannot achieve a place at even the most impressive firms or chambers.	
Entering the profession: Again, obtaining tenancy or a role as an associate solicitor are far from guaranteed, but for all but the most unlucky trainees, it is generally true that excellent performance during your training period will demonstrate why you are worthy of a permanent role. For both professions, completion of this period also means qualification as a practising lawyer, allowing you to move into "in house" work. As mentioned above, it is also possible to cross-qualify.	
Daily work: All lawyers need the same crucial qualities – intelligence, the ability to communicate, professionalism, strict ethics and meticulous time management. The increasing number of solicitor-advocates means that following this route still allows the opportunity to be appearing in court regularly, while public access means that barristers can deal with lay clients directly. Indeed, the type of work carried out can often be more dependent on the practice area you choose, rather than your particular profession. For both professions, a successful career will also demand long hours and a lot of hard work. Solicitors and barristers both need to be able to cope with difficult, often last-minute issues and exercise their own judgement to assist a client.	
Career opportunities: Both solicitors and barristers can become judges, at all levels of the judiciary. Cross-qualification and in house work remain options at any stage in a lawyer's career. More widely, the skills taught and experienced gained in qualifying to become a lawyer are highly valued across all sectors and many companies are keen to recruit trained lawyers, even into non-legal roles. It has also been suggested by some academics and lawyers that in light of changes to the legal profession (which we will discuss later in this chapter) solicitors and barristers will increasingly be seen as a single group, to be compared to those without a professional legal qualification.	

Practice areas

This section is intended to highlight some of the main areas in which solicitors and barristers work. However, the list is far from exhaustive.

Chancery and Tax

You may have already studied parts of this area, and you certainly will before the end of your degree when you undertake your Equity and Trusts module. Chancery is so-called because it was the Lord Chancellor's decisions which built up the area of law we now know as equity. This practice area covers issues such as trusts and probate, which involves the way people dispose of their money and possessions, both during their life and after death. In a commercial context, chancery can relate to some of the most complex legal mechanisms, such as off-shore banking, international finance and insolvency proceedings. A related area, sometimes included under "chancery" is tax law – it is a priority for many businesses and wealthy individuals to legally avoid paying tax wherever possible, while of course the government and HMRC would take the opposite view. This leads to a lot of work for lawyers who are able to understand and utilise Britain's labyrinthine taxation laws.

Civil Liberties and Human Rights

British citizens have been able to take their cases to the European Court of Human Rights since the 1960s but since the introduction of the European Convention on Human Rights into domestic law via the Human Rights Act 1998 there has been an explosion in cases involving the rights enshrined in the Convention. Closer to home, many of our fundamental rights are actually protected in our historical common law and so civil liberties lawyers may also deal with issues such as the actions of the police, the legality of demonstrations and protests and the treatment of prisoners. There are overlaps with areas such as the criminal law, welfare and social security, immigration law and more recently the legislation passed relating to terrorism. As such, lawyers practising in this field need a broad knowledge of the law and can expect to advise and represent clients at all levels of the legal system.

Commercial

One of the largest, and most prosperous, areas of law, "commercial law" includes almost any legal issues involving business or trade. This can range from the routine legal work all companies need, for example insurance disputes or issues relating to the sale of goods, up to huge disputes worth hundreds of millions of pounds. Commercial clients come in all shapes and sizes and as well as a good grasp of the relevant law, it is crucial for anyone practising in this area to have a real understanding of, and interest in, business itself. Commercial law tends to involve less court-based work and so other key skills include attention to detail and the ability to explain complex legal issues in simple economic terms. Other related areas include shipping law, construction law and competition law.

Criminal

Criminal law can be neatly divided into prosecution and defence work. The vast majority of prosecutions in England & Wales are brought by the Crown Prosecution Service (CPS) on behalf of the state. Thus if you are interested in this area, you are likely to apply for the CPS Legal Trainee Scheme[30] which was re-launched in 2012 to provide a number of pupillages and training contracts. Criminal defence work remains in the hands of private practice, and there are of course large numbers of law firms and barristers chambers which undertake criminal defence work (and occasionally work for the prosecution). Some practices specialise in high profile clients, but most rely for at least part of their work on legal aid, representing people from all walks of life who are accused of a crime. Because of this, it is not, except at the highest levels, a particularly highly-paid area but it is one that can be exceptionally rewarding, offering the opportunity to help provide justice for both the innocent and the guilty. However, this can also be a mentally demanding role, as your duty is to your client and thus you may be required to prosecute someone you feel is innocent, or defend someone you believe is guilty – and do so to the best of your ability.

---

[30] http://www.cps.gov.uk/careers/legal_professional_careers/legal_trainees/

Employment

There are almost 30 million people in employment in the United Kingdom[31], which is a very large pool of potential clients! Employment lawyers handle all aspects of disputes in the workplace – most obviously, claims for unfair dismissal, but also issues such as redundancy, industrial action, discrimination at work and whistleblowing. Because employment cases are usually heard by the Employment Tribunal and parties must pay their own costs, there is often scope for relatively junior lawyers to handle their own cases, and for advocates to appear regularly in front of the tribunal early in their careers.

Family

Another very large area of law, family law is self-descriptive. Work in this area generally revolves around two key area, which can be described as "money and children"[32]. As such, family lawyers will handle cases involving marriages, separations and divorces, along with issues relating to children such as custody, child support and adoption. Because of the issues involved, family litigation can often be extremely emotive and an effective family lawyer has to learn to be able to sympathise, but not empathise (in other words, to acknowledge that your client may be very upset and provide comfort, but to retain an objective view of the case). Depending on your specialisation, family law can involve a lot of alternative dispute resolution (for example conciliation and mediation to try to resolve a dispute over contact with a child, or negotiations over a pre-nuptial or divorce settlement); or it can involve large amounts of disputed cases being decided in court (to give one example, it is rare that cases involving custody of a child are settled amicably).

Immigration

Immigration is, as you will know, a hot political topic and because of the competing pressures of large numbers of people wishing to start a life in Britain, and legislation to limit the number of immigrants who can enter or remain in the country, legal disputes are common. At its most dramatic, immigration law involves everything from asylum seekers claiming that they will be tortured or killed if they are not permitted to remain to issues of unlawful detention and breach of human rights. Other immigration issues are less divisive, such as obtaining visas for students and employees or advising a wealthy businessman on how to obtain dual nationality. Similarly to criminal practice, immigration law involves a lot of client contact and time in court hearings. Another similarity with criminal law is that an immigration lawyer needs to be able to partake in cases which might involve very serious issues and very upsetting evidence, while still remaining objective.

Intellectual Property and Patents

Patent law has always been a crucial issue, as it is of course vital for companies and private individuals to protect their intellectual property (i.e. their right to be recognised as the author or inventor of something, and to be compensated if others use it). Traditional "hard" intellectual property involves patents, which are the legal rights to the sole usage of an invention. However, to an increasing extent this has been overtaken by "soft" intellectual property, which involves issues such as copyright (which covers literary,

---

[31] Data from Office of National Statistics http://www.statistics.gov.uk/hub/labour-market/people-in-work/employment/index.html
[32] LawCareers.net, *Family* http://www.lawcareers.net/Barristers/PracticeAreas/Family.aspx

dramatic, musical and artistic works, as well as sound recordings, films and broadcasts[33]), trademarks and "passing off" (where one person tries to sell something by pretending that they are from a particular source). You only need to read a newspaper to see the amount of work this includes, with major issues such as digital piracy and counterfeit goods costing companies huge sums of money.

International/European Law

As you will know, as a member of the European Union the UK is obliged to follow European law, which takes precedence over domestic legislation[34]. Disputes regarding EU law can be heard in the British courts, and also by the European Court of Justice. Furthermore, as we discussed above the UK can also be taken to the European Court of Human Rights. Lawyers who practice in this area will usually specialise in a particular field, so for example a solicitor may be an expert in European competition law, or a barrister may spend much of his or her time taking on immigration cases involving a human rights issue. Furthermore, the UK also participates in other international bodies such as the World Trade Organisation and the International Criminal Court. British lawyers might also be asked by foreign nationals to advise on European or International disputes. Obviously, a willingness to travel is an advantage if you wish to work in this area, as is speaking more than one language.

Property/Landlord and Tenant

The English common law was originally developed out of the law of property, and today it remains a crucial area, as evidenced by land law remaining one of the core modules for a qualifying law degree. For many high street practitioners, the work involved in buying and selling properties such as houses and small business premises was traditionally a mainstay in their practice. Today, with alternative providers of conveyancing and the rise of "do it yourself" legal services, there has been a reduction in this level of work. High street firms also take on smaller-scale landlord and tenant disputes.

Property law is also crucial at a commercial level and lawyers in this area are often undertaking similar work, but on a larger scale. Commercial property can also include public law issues such as obtaining planning permission for a new supermarket, environmental law issues such as disputes over emissions from a factory, and high value contract disputes between landlords and tenant companies.

Media and Sport

Two relatively new areas of law, media law and sports law are similar to areas such as construction, in that they tend to involve a mixture of other practice areas but applied in one industry. Thus a media lawyer working for a television station might been asked to advise on potential libel (tort law), crack down on illegal file-sharing (intellectual property law), resolve a dispute between a journalist and management (employment law) and negotiate the rights to broadcast a new series (contract law). Equally, sports lawyers advise on everything from civil liability for injuring another competitor, to the complex regulations governing sponsorship, advertising and broadcasting rights, to the appeals available to an athlete who has failed to pass a drugs test.

---

[33] Copyright, Designs and Patents Act 1988 s1(1)
[34] European Communities Act 1972

Personal Injury

Even if you are yet to study tort law, which is the foundation for most personal injury claims, you are probably aware of its importance as a practice area from the plethora of advertisements for legal services available to victims of road traffic accidents or so-called "trip and fall" cases. While there are now moves to try and limit the amount of costs recoverable in these actions, due to a rise in so-called "ambulance chasing"[35], the introduction of Conditional Fee Agreements (popularly known as "no win no fee") in 1999 led to an explosion in personal injury claims. As such, there is plenty of scope to practice in this area, either in a dedicated firm or in a more general organisation. For both solicitors and barristers, personal injury work involves a lot of time with clients and in court, with junior lawyers handling lower value claims which are usually dealt with relatively swiftly, while more established practitioners take on claims worth hundreds of thousands and even millions of pounds.

Public Law

Public law is another core academic subject which plays a major role in legal practice. Most obviously, if you are interested in public law then work for the central or local government offers the opportunity to focus on these areas, such as judicial review. However, there is also room to specialise, as public law covers areas as diverse as state-assisted housing, education, healthcare, welfare and benefits and social services. Public lawyers also work in fields such as property law (from the planning perspective) and European law (as public bodies are often affected by European and human rights law). Generally much of public law operates "behind the scenes" and so the opportunities to take on major court cases can be limited, although cases that do make it to court are often appealed all the way to the Supreme Court, because of the importance of establishing a principle.

Reflection Questions

1. Thinking about the practice areas above, are there any that particularly appeal to you? And/or are there any which you would not work want to work in? Why is this?
2. Can you think of any other practice areas which are not outlined above?
3. Would you prefer to work in a firm or set which specialised in one area, or in a variety?

Legal executives

How do I become a legal executive?

Many people outside the law assume that all lawyers are either solicitors or barristers. However, this is not the case and legal executives play an increasingly large role in law firms in England and Wales. Below we shall look at the role of a legal executive, and highlight the similarities with the role of a solicitor, but one of the key differences is the route to qualification.

---

[35] See particularly the 'Jackson report', Jackson, R. *Review of Civil Litigation Costs: Final Report* (TSO, 2010)

Unlike solicitors and barristers, a legal executive does not necessarily need to complete a qualifying law degree but can instead study the academic law through the ILEX Level 3 Professional Diploma and Level 6 Professional Higher Diploma. However, assuming you have indeed already completed a qualifying law degree, the regulatory body CILEx (standing for the Chartered Institute of Legal Executives) offer a special "Graduate Fast-track Diploma" which takes approximately one year to complete (although time off can be awarded if you already work in the legal field, for example as a paralegal). The Diploma is taught by distance-learning, or face to face at around 70 accredited institutions across the UK[36]. Students must choose two practice units (from a choice of Civil Litigation, Criminal Litigation, Company & Partnership Law, Conveyancing, Employment Law, Family Law and Probate) along with studying Client Care skills. As such, the course is relatively short, allowing it to be taught by part-time study (usually in the evenings, allowing students to "learn as they earn" by working full time). However, the course remains rigorous (it is assessed at final year undergraduate level) and considerable amounts of independent study are required. The downside is that there is far less skills training outside of client care than on the LPC and BPTC – but the cost of the course is far lower (£2,187 as of 2012[37]). Legal Executives do not need to complete a training period equivalent to pupillage or a training contract. Instead, they become a graduate member of the Chartered Institute. After five years of qualifying employment in legal work, you may apply for admission as a Fellow of CILEx, which makes you a fully qualified legal executive.

What does a legal executive do?

Legal executives have long played an important role in law firms, and the forerunner of CILEx was first founded in 1892. Today, there are around 20,000 members of CILEx, with 7,500 of those having become fully qualified lawyers[38]. In terms of day to day work, legal executives meet clients, manage cases and attend court. In fact, they can carry out exactly the same work as a solicitor, with the only difference being that they must do so under the supervision of a solicitor. As such, legal executives can establish themselves as key members of a law firm, and recent changes in the legal profession (mainly under the Legal Services Act 2007) have allowed legal executives to become partners in law firms. The 2007 Act also allows CILEx members to undertake further training to obtain rights of audience, allowing to appear as an advocate in the lower courts. Finally, the Act also allows Legal Executives to apply for positions in the judiciary.

A career as a legal executive

Due to the part-time nature of CILEx qualifications, many of those who study to become a legal executive are already in employment, for example as a paralegal or working in local government. During your course and once you have obtained the graduate certificate, CILEx suggest that your average salary would be in the region of £20,000–£35,000. On reaching Chartered status, this can rise considerably and top legal executives in major firms can command six-figure salaries. It is also possible to dual qualify, taking the LPC after becoming a legal executive, and doing so can lead to exemptions from some LPC subjects and possibly from obtaining a training contract, allowing you to become an associate immediately after completing the LPC.

---

[36] http://www.cilex.org.uk/study/lawyer_qualifications/cilex_lawyer_study_centres.aspx
[37] http://www.cilex.org.uk/careers/careers_home/graduates/law_graduates/chartered_legal_executives/cilex_costs__fees.aspx
[38] http://www.cilex.org.uk/media/facts__figures_for_the_media.aspx

Other legal careers

Paralegals

"Paralegal" is a very wide term which is often used to cover almost any working in the legal sector who is not a member of the professions discussed above. To give a more precise definition, the Institute of Paralegals (which is a professional body for paralegals, but, unlike the Law Society, Bar Council and CILEx, not a regulator) provide the following guidance:

> *A paralegal is someone who does legal work even though they have not qualified as a solicitor or barrister. By "legal work" we mean advising and assisting with the law in the same way that a solicitor advises and assists clients. Doing clerical or administrative work in a legal environment does not count as legal work . . . Many paralegals have different job titles: caseworker, contracts manager, legal assistant, compliance officer, housing assistant, company secretary, volunteer adviser, counsellor, trade mark clerk etc. Many senior legal secretaries also do paralegal work despite still being called legal secretaries. You are potentially a paralegal if you do paid or unpaid legal work for your employer or for clients or someone else. Your job title is irrelevant. What counts is that you do legal work sufficiently often to legitimately be considered as a (non-lawyer) legal practitioner. Only one in three paralegals works for a solicitors' firm. The rest work for the government, the not-for-profit sector, companies, charities, industry etc.*[39]

As this definition suggests, there is far less formal regulation of the work of paralegals and thus there are no formal qualifications required in order to work in this sector. However, most employers would expect prior legal knowledge, and thus it is common to find paralegals with a law degree or GDL. It is also quite common to find BPTC and LPC graduates who have not been able to obtain a training placement working in the paralegal sector. As you saw in the definition of a paralegal, only a minority work in law firms, where depending on experience and ability, paralegals carry out work from basic photocopying to dealing with their own cases under the supervision of a solicitor. In businesses paralegals might provide legal advice, assist in departments such as human resources or finance, or review contracts and other legal documents. Because the sector is so diverse, it is difficult to expand further on the role of a paralegal, and for the same reason salary statistics are unreliable. However, figures from career websites[40] would suggest that the average salary is around £20,000–£25,000, although individuals may earn far more or less than this median.

Of particular interest to law students, and indeed to lawyers, is the introduction of Alternative Business Structures (ABSs) under the Legal Services Act 2007. These organisations will be allowed to provide legal services, while employing both lawyers and non-lawyers. You will find huge amounts of information and comment on the potential impact of this reform, both in textbooks and online, and this is really an area in which you need to conduct your own research as the position is changing constantly. However, it is safe to say that if ABSs become popular, there will be a large increase in the number of potential employers of legally-minded, but not necessarily professionally-trained, young graduates. On the other hand, it may further diminish employment opportunities for solicitors and at the Bar.

---

[39] Institute of Paralegals, *Am I a Paralegal?* (http://www.theiop.org/membership/what-is-a-paralegal-2.html)
[40] Sources: http://www.reed.co.uk, http://www.totaljobs.com, http://www.monster.co.uk

Law Centres and advice workers

Sometimes grouped in the same category as paralegals, advice workers and those employed by one of the 55 Law Centres in England & Wales have a more specific, client-facing role. Law Centres are not-for-profit organisations which provide free legal advice and representation, relying on public funding to cover their costs. Other organisations, both charitable and for-profit, also provide low-cost or free legal advice. Working in this area will, similarly to being a paralegal, involve having some legal knowledge (preferably a law degree) but will usually allow for much greater client contact, as you will be dealing with people and their disputes on a day to day basis. While some issues can be crucial, for example involving criminal, family or immigration law, this career path does obviously lack the opportunity to work in high value commercial litigation.

Barristers clerks

As we discussed earlier, while barristers are self-employed, each chambers will share the services of one or more clerks. Junior clerks generally act in an administrative role, with responsibilities such as preparing "bundles" of documents, supervising the sending and receiving of case papers and assisting barristers in making arrangements for travel etc. More senior clerks are perhaps the most important figure in a set of chambers, as they will handle the booking of barristers by solicitors. As such, it is their role to not only facilitate communication, but when needed to recommend the appropriate member of chambers and to ensure that all members have an appropriate workload.

Clerks are not necessarily expected to have a law degree and many junior clerks will begin work after completing GCSEs or A-levels. However, legal knowledge is obviously an advantage and will assist in obtaining more senior positions. As with pupillages, the pay varies widely depending on the size of the chambers, the geographical location and the type of work undertaken by that set. Junior clerk's salaries tend to range from £10,000 to £25,000, but senior clerks earn considerably more than this and may even reach six figure salaries at larger sets.

Licensed conveyancers

A conveyancer is a legal professional who specialises in the purchase, sale or remortgage of a property. They are regulated by the Council for Licensed Conveyancers, who offer training directly via distance learning, and accredit qualifications offered by Colleges of Further and Higher Education. Conveyancers can be found working in legal practices (and may well be in considerable demand from specialist property ABSs) but can also set up their own business or work as a sole practitioner.

Costs draftsmen

Costs draftsmen are another highly specialised legal profession. They are used to assess and prepare detailed bills of costs, both when an unsuccessful party is challenging the amount of their opponent's costs, and also when a client complains about their own solicitors costs. Costs draftsmen are usually self-employed, working on a freelance basis, but larger solicitors' firms may employ some costs lawyers on a permanent basis. Again, training and accreditation is needed, in this case through the Association of Costs Lawyers.

Court workers

There are a whole plethora of roles available in Her Majesty's Courts and Tribunals Service. Some roles offer an entire career, while others may be valuable as work experience while applying for work in one of the legal professions.

- **Legal Advisers**, who are qualified barristers or solicitors used in magistrates courts to explain legal issues to lay (non-legally trained) magistrates and advise on court procedure.
- **Court Clerks**, who act as the judge(s) assistant. The Clerk of the court controls proceedings, for example ensuring evidence is placed before the judge, that all case papers are correctly filed and keeps the judge updated of any developments outside the courtroom.
- **Ushers**, who keep order in the court. Their role includes calling the parties and witnesses into court, administering the oaths (that witnesses promise to tell the truth) and escorting the jury in and out of court.
- **Court reporters**, who are trained to record court proceedings word-by-word. This requires excellent shorthand and legally trained applicants are welcomed, as they will find it easier to understand the proceedings which they are reporting.

Practical Questions

1. Now that you have studied this chapter, draw up a sketch plan of your ideal legal career. Consider what qualifications you would obtain and where you would study them, what area of law you would enter in what capacity, and your ideal employer.
2. Using online research, identify five organisations offering pupillages or training contracts in your geographical area in the field in which you wish to work.
3. Talk to a lawyer about their life in the legal profession. This could be a friend, a family member or one of your tutors, who may well have practised law prior to entering academia.

Building blocks for your career

In this chapter we are going to examine how you can start laying building blocks in place to maximise your chances of a successful career, whether in law or in another field. We will begin by discussing planning and development activities which you can carry out now to help decide on your goals and plot your route to achieving them. We will then go on to talk about how you might do this, looking at some of the most important activities which you should carry out prior to making job applications. Finally, we will consider some crucial points to note if you plan to pursue a career at the Bar or as a solicitor.

Planning your career

Assessing your abilities

You may already have decided on the exact role you wish to obtain, have decided on the area in which you wish to work but not the position, or still be extremely open-minded about what career you might pursue. However, as you progress through your degree it is important to start thinking about your future, and in particular about how to evaluate your current skills and abilities. The purpose of this can be twofold: it may help you decide what careers would particularly suit you, or indeed what might not; and even more importantly it will highlight the areas in which you need to develop your skills, experience and knowledge in order to stand out as a candidate when it is time to apply for full-time employment.

There are many types of skills evaluation and you may well have already completed similar exercises at school or college. A suggested format is given in the practical questions at the end of this section, but you should feel free to adapt this to your own particular needs. However you choose to assess your abilities, the most important aspects are to be honest in evaluating your current performance and to prescribe practical steps which you can take to improve. You should also ensure you regularly return to your personal development plan, noting which areas show improvement and considering alterations if you are struggling to improve a particular skill.

Choosing the right path

Once you have an honest assessment of your abilities, it should be clear where your strengths and weaknesses lie. While you should not assume any skill is irretrievable, if you really do not like doing something it is usually better to focus on a path in which this skill is not required (for example, if you hate public speaking, even after attempting to work on this skill, a role requiring lots of advocacy is probably not the best aim). Therefore, you should carry out careful research into the area in which you plan to work. In legal terms, this would mainly involve deciding on which profession to join (solicitor, barrister or legal executive) and perhaps even more importantly which area of law in which to practice, as this will have a large impact on the type of skills required in applicants.

Focussing on your goals

Once you have identified a role or roles which you would like to work towards, it is important to set targets and try your best to meet them. It might seem very early in your life to be dedicating so much time and energy towards planning a career, but you should bear in mind that the effort you put in now can be the difference between achieving your goals or falling short. That being said, you should not place yourself under undue pressure or set unattainable targets for yourself. A good way to avoid this is to use so-called S.M.A.R.T. targets, which since their invention thirty years ago[41] have been adopted in both the private and public sector for career planning and more general development. Such targets are:

---

[41] By George Duran, see Duran, G. 'There's a S.M.A.R.T. way to write management's goals and objectives' *Management Review* (1981) Volume 70 Issue 11 pp. 35–36

> ### S.M.A.R.T. targets
>
> **S**pecific – You should ensure that you set targets, rather than merely identify aims[42]. For example, rather than simply saying "I will communicate better", you might set the target of joining your University Debating Society.
>
> **M**easurable – You want to be able to track your progress, so for example if you decided to improve your attendance record, you could start keeping track of how many lectures and tutorials you attended and setting specific goals.
>
> **A**chievable – There is no point setting a target that you can't achieve and indeed it can actually have a demoralising effect. For example, if you have already completed most of the assessments for a module and your average marks are in the 40–49 bracket, setting a goal of obtaining a first class mark overall is unattainable. A better goal might be to achieve a mark of at least 60 in this final assessment.
>
> **R**elevant – Equally there is no use setting irrelevant targets. Your targets should be directly beneficial to you and should also be relevant at this current time – for example, if you are in your first year of undergraduate study, researching pupillages is unlikely to be of great use and your time could be more profitably spent doing something else.
>
> **T**ime-bound – Always set (realistic) deadlines for your goals, and ensure you keep to them.

Practical Questions

1. Carry out a skills evaluation on yourself. Draw up a table listing key skills in a column (you might think of these yourself, look at job specifications for areas in which you are interested or take skills or find lists on careers and recruitment websites). In each row, include columns such as how you would rate your current ability in that area, what evidence you could provide to demonstrate this, and how you plan to improve on this skill.
2. Draw up a set of SMART targets that you can carry out in the next three to six months. Ensure that these targets are achievable, but will require some effort to attain.

Getting legal work experience

Whatever role you wish to pursue in the legal profession, work experience is essential to obtain employment. At the most general level, it is the best method of finding out what life is actually like as a legal professional in a particular practice area. More specifically, it is a chance to look inside a particular chambers, firm or company if you are considering applying for a permanent role. Finally, as the legal employment market is so competitive, increasing numbers of firms and chambers now expect applicants to have carried out work experience, making the process something akin to a pre-application job interview. Below, we shall look at the main types of legal work experience (although as we shall go on to discuss, valuable experience can also be gained outside the legal field). Bear in mind that legal employers will often ask why you want to be a barrister, solicitor, legal executive or other legal professional, thus it is well worth sampling work in other areas in order to be able to make an informed comparison.

---

[42] Drew, S. and Bingham, R. *The Student Skills Guide* 2nd Edition (Gower, 2001)

Work placement

What is it?

Work placement is the usual term for work experience within a firm of solicitors, although they can also be known as "vacation schemes". Just as solicitors' firms vary widely, from giant Magic Circle firms to small high street practices, so do work experience opportunities. However, most larger firms will have a relatively formalised scheme, usually taking place during the summer holidays (and sometimes during other academic breaks such as Christmas and Easter). The length of schemes can vary, with some lasting mere days, while others can be up to a month. It is also worth noting that at larger firms, particularly those practising commercial law, it is common to pay attendees of these schemes. This may be just travel expenses, but can in some cases amount to hundreds of pounds per week[43].

Unsurprisingly, at larger firms there are likely to be quite a large number of other would-be lawyers on each scheme, and thus group events such as seminars or workshops are likely to be organised. Firms are also interested in your communication and social skills, thus social events may well be part of the schedule. Outside of these events, you will spend most of time shadowing a relatively junior member of the firm (a trainee or junior associate) and assisting them with their work. As you might expect, it is rare for a person on a training scheme to be entrusted with anything particularly important or sensitive, so you should prepare to be photocopying and fetching coffee for at least some of the time you are there! However, you may well be asked to carry out some legal research, proof-read legal documents or even to take notes at meetings and your ability to carry out all of these tasks will be noted by your supervisor. At smaller firms, you may get the opportunity to shadow a more senior practitioner or to become more involved in the day-to-day work of the firm, although you are less likely to have the varied programme of arranged events that commercial firms offer. Smaller practices are also more likely to offer more informal work-shadowing opportunities, but as these may not be advertised it is often worth contacting local firms yourself to enquire.

How do I apply?

Most commercial firms have a specific application process, involving application forms or sending a CV and cover letter, and will set a deadline for applications each year. Some vacation schemes, particularly those which offer paid work experience, may even include other requirements such as competency testing and interviews. While the application process can be time-consuming, you should bear in mind that it is excellent practice for later applications for pupillage or a training contract, so if you experiment with different answers, make a careful note of which applications are most successful. There is no central application process, or approved list of vacation scheme providers, although you can find the details of most major firms' schemes on legal careers websites. Another excellent place to find information about work experiences schemes is at law fairs, either through your university or in your local area.

More localised firms or those specialising in other areas than commercial law may not have the recruitment resources to offer such a formalised application process. If you are interested in work experience outside commercial law (and even would-be commercial lawyers can often benefit from seeing legal practice form a different perspective) then you may need to carry out some research to find firms in your area. Most will have information on their website about work experience, but if this is not available, you should certainly take the initiative and contact them to enquire if they offer any work experience opportunities.

---

[43] Lawyer 2B, *How to survive: Vacation schemes* (The Lawyer, 20 June 2011)

What should I know?

- When applying for vacation schemes, there is no rule that you can only undertake one in a particular holiday. However, you should be aware that firms do not appreciate applicants failing to take up offered places, so ensure that you can attend every day of a placement and ensure none of the schemes you apply for overlap.

- Do not be tempted to write a "one size fits all" work experience application and send it to all the firms you are interested in. Just as with applying for a training contract, a targeted approach will pay dividends so ensure that you carefully research each firm you apply to, and write your application to reflect this.

- If you are applying to a legal practice which does not have an online application process, or enquiring about the availability of work placement, a little research can go a long way. For example, you should ensure you find out who is responsible for work experience, so that you can address your cover letter or email to the correct person.

- Try to be as flexible as possible. If you are willing to be accommodating as to the dates of your scheme, and which department you are placed in, you are more likely to obtain work experience and will make a good impression.

- When on your work experience, bear in mind that you are being assessed (either formally or informally). As such, make sure your performance reflects your abilities and in particular ensure that however dull the work you are assigned, you complete it efficiently and accurately. Other crucial qualities to demonstrate are punctuality (never arrive late), enthusiasm (ask questions where possible, stay late or attend extra events if asked), social skills (be friendly yet respectful to members of the firm) and professional (keep your mobile phone away and don't browse Facebook on the office computer!).

- This final tip seems rather obvious, but from the number of careers websites, blogs and guides to work experience which mention it, it is clearly a perceived problem. Do not, at all costs, drink too much at social events! On a related note, attempting to chat up junior members of the firm, recruiters running the scheme or your fellow attendees will not make a good impression . . .

Mini-pupillage

What is it?

Mini-pupillage is the Bar's equivalent of work placement schemes. A mini-pupillage is an opportunity to attend a set of barristers' chambers and gain an insight into the working life of a barrister. Mini-pupillages tend to be shorter than work placement schemes, with most lasting between 3 and 5 days. Because chambers are smaller organisations than law firms and do not possess recruitment departments, mini-pupillages tend to be less regimented that work placements. Depending on the size of the chambers, the area of practice and most pragmatically, the amount of work being undertaken that week, mini pupils experience can vary widely – even at the same chambers!

On the whole, mini-pupillage usually involves being assigned to one of the members of chambers, who you will shadow during your work experience. This will usually mean that you spend at least some of your time attending court and watching proceedings. While you can of course attend a court in your own time, going with counsel involved in a case can be very rewarding, as you may get the opportunity to discuss the case before and after the hearing and ask any questions you might have. Other common parts of mini-pupillage include reading and discussing case papers, carrying out legal research and potentially being invited to social events. Realistically, it can be a matter of luck as to whether you are shadowing a barrister who is busy and willing to get a mini-pupil involved, or someone who is less approachable or simply has a rather boring week of work in chambers!

How do I apply?

The crucial difference to note with mini-pupillages is whether they are assessed or unassessed. Assessed mini-pupillages are designed for those who plan to apply (or have already applied) for full pupillage and as such are difficult to obtain and may involve a rigorous selection process. As regards unassessed experience, the application process varies between chambers, with some sets organising specific dates throughout the year, with online applications and deadlines, while others take an ad hoc approach, expecting prospective mini-pupils to send a CV and covering letter requesting a mini-pupillage. As with law firms, the first place to look for more information is the website of the chambers you wish to apply to. Bear in mind that not all sets offer mini-pupillage, and most will expect you to have some knowledge of the area in which they practice, so you might for example find it difficult to obtain work experience at a criminal chambers before studying Criminal Law as part of your degree.

What should I know?

- Because mini-pupillages generally involve shadowing one particular barrister, the best way to obtain mini-pupillage can be to ask contacts at the Bar if they would be willing to give you work experience. You should not be afraid to ask, but obviously ensure you do so in a respectful manner and accept that many barristers simply do not have the time to allow this.

- Just as with work placement schemes, you are being assessed throughout your time at chambers. You should also remember that the Bar is a close-knit community, so particularly good or bad performance might well be related to other barristers or chambers. In order to make the best possible impression, ensure you arrive early, take a real interest in all the activities you undertake and attempt to develop a good relationship with the barrister(s) you shadow.

- Only the largest chambers are likely to arrange specific social events to coincide with mini-pupillages, so the onus may be on you to try and get involved with chambers' social life. If you are invited to go for lunch, or a drink after work, with members of chambers you should if it all possible accept, as it is an opportunity to show your social skills and to network with practitioners.

- After any work experience you should always thank those who have helped you, but this is perhaps particularly important after a mini-pupillage if you have spent most of your time with a particular person. An email or written thank-you letter is always appreciated and will ensure you leave a good impression.

- Another very general tip, but one of particular importance to mini-pupils, is to dress as smartly as possible. As you are likely to attend court, you should be dressed in appropriate attire, which will usually mean a suit and tie for men and a suit or smart blouse and skirt for women.

- If you do attend court, take notes of who you went with, what case you saw and what was interesting about it. If you end up applying for pupillage at that set, being able to recall a particular case which aroused your interest is an impressive demonstration of how much you gained from your experience.

- As mini-pupillages are quite short, you should certainly aim to undertake more than one. There is no upper limit, although for the purpose of pupillage applications around five is generally seen as a sensible amount. You should of course prioritise areas in which you wish to practice, but time spent in a different field or even in a solicitors firm can be impressive, as it demonstrates that you have taken time to evaluate other career options.

Pro Bono work

What is it and how do I apply?

Pro bono publico is a Latin phrase which roughly translates as "for the public good". In law, it refers to providing legal services for free. For legal professionals, this might involve taking on a full case without payment, for example for an individual who cannot afford legal representation or for a charity or interest group. While you could not take on such work prior to obtaining a practising certificate (on completion of your training contract for solicitors, or pupillage for barristers) there are many organisations which use law students to assist on pro bono under a supervising legal professional. Who is eligible to take part, how they should apply and what work they will be doing thus varies from organisation to organisation. The table below summarises some of the most common pro bono options.

Provider	Area of law	Description	Applicants sought
University/ Law School	All areas	Most universities and providers of legal training now have a dedicated pro bono unit, either providing direct support or working in conjunction with other schemes. A full list is available from http://www.studentprobono.net	You will need to be a student at the relevant institution in order to take part. There may be further restrictions, such as which course you are studying or your year of study.
LawWorks	All areas	Formerly the pro bono provider for solicitors, LawWorks is now a charity in its own right which works with law firms, mediators and students on various pro bono projects. Along with their own projects, they keep a large database of other pro bono opportunities for students. More information can be found at lawworks.org.uk	Dependent on the particular placement, but there are roles for students from secondary education through to qualified lawyers.
Bar Pro Bono Unit	Varied	The Bar Pro Bono do not recruit volunteers directly except for occasional administrative roles (which are still good experience but do not involve legal services). They do however use student volunteers to raise funds for the Unit.	Open to law students, but would most suit those considering a career as a barrister.
Free Representation Unit (FRU)	Employment and Social Security	FRU has been the starting point for many barristers, as it is one of the few pro bono organisations that allows students to present a client's case to a judge in a real hearing. FRU provide advice and representation in the employment tribunal and social security tribunal.	To be an Employment Representative you must be into the May of your final year or a graduate or GDL student. Social Security Representatives must be the above or LLB students who have reached May in their penultimate year.

Legal Charities	Varied, but emphasis on crime, discrimination and human rights law	There are huge numbers of charities which provide people with legal advice and support. Some of the most notable include Amicus, whose interns work on the cases of death row inmates in the United States; the Disability Law Service which provides legal advice to the disabled on areas such as welfare and discrimination law; the Immigration Advisory Service who offer representation and advice on immigration and asylum law; and many many more.	Dependent on the charity, but most have specific roles for those with legal knowledge, such as law students towards the end of their degrees. A good starting point for ideas is the student section of the LawWorks website which contains a list of major charities seeking law student volunteers.
McKenzie friends	Family law	A McKenzie friend is a person who is not legally qualified but who provides assistance to litigants in person in family law (i.e. those unrepresented by a lawyer). A number of organisations seek law students for this role, the most notable being the National Centre for Domestic Violence (NCDV) – who also provide other pro bono opportunities in this field.	No specific requirements but you will be required to pass an application process. Find out more at http://www.ncdv.org.uk/VolunteerForNCDV.html
Citizens Advice Bureaux	Varied, focus on debt, welfare, employment and housing	Citzens Advice Bureaux (CAB) can be found across the UK and they are always keen to recruit volunteers to help advise members of the public, particularly with a legal background.	Anyone can volunteer, although you will of course have to go through an application and training process. More information can be found at http://www.citizensadvice.org.uk/index/join-us.htm
Law Centres and local groups	Civil law	Law Centres perform a similar role to the CAB, but with a more directly legal focus and with the services of professional lawyers. Law Centres rely on volunteers to run and are large recruiters of law student volunteers.	Find your local Law Centre at http://www.lawcentres.org.uk/involved/ and contact them to find out information on vacancies and other opportunities.
i-Probono	Varied	i-Probono is a non-profit website designed to put students in touch with those seeking pro bono volunteers.	Visit the http://www.i-probono.com to register as a student member and browse the current opportunities available.

What should I know?

- Pro bono work can be incredibly rewarding as well as a boost to your CV. However, you must remember that by agreeing to carry out pro bono work you are assuming a duty both to the provider and to any clients who may use the service. As such, you must make sure that you have the relevant knowledge and the time to carry out the work you are given.

- It is not mandatory to volunteer in the area in which you wish to practice, and for some practice areas pro bono work is unlikely to be available (most notably commercial law). However, you should carefully consider what skills you will develop from a specific pro bono opportunity.

- The best starting place for pro bono work is definitely your educational institution. If your university does not offer a pro bono scheme, consider setting up your own – not only will it then allow you to carry out pro bono work, but creating such a scheme is an impressive achievement in itself. LawWorks offer help and advice in setting up a new clinic.

- Remember that large amounts of pro bono work involve dealing with members of the public. You will need to develop good communication skills to handle your clients, but always remember you are the legal adviser and so must be able to hold your ground even if they do not agree with your advice.

- Your supervisor is there to act as a safeguard and as a mentor. Do not be afraid to seek advice from your supervisor, whether it is because you are confused as to the law or unsure how to deal with a particular case or client.

- Because pro bono work involves 'real life' legal practice, you must comply with the ethical obligations placed on all lawyers. This includes avoiding conflicts of interest, acting honestly at all times and maintaining client confidentiality.

Marshalling

What is it?

Unlike in other countries, it is not possible to join the judiciary of England & Wales until you have practised as a legal professional. Despite this, it is possible to gain valuable experience by shadowing a judge. This procedure is called marshalling. Unlike the forms of work experience discussed above, marshalling is an essentially passive process – while you might be asked to assist the judge with basic tasks (most often helping carry papers!) your role is not to get involved, but rather to observe. During marshalling, you will spend your time sitting with the judge in court hearings, but also get the opportunity to see the judge in "chambers", which is the area at a court reserved for judges between appearances in court.

Marshalling is looked upon very favourable by employers, particularly at the Bar where Chambers appreciate candidates who have made this effort to see the role of the advocate from the other side of the Bench. It also allows you to witness court proceedings close-up and you may be lucky enough to shadow a judge who will happily talk at length about his or her views on the advocacy and case management of the legal representatives, giving you invaluable insight into what are (and are not!) effective methods of presenting a case.

How do I apply?

Many students are unaware of the opportunity to marshal and for practical reasons the judiciary do not want to encourage a flood of marshalling applications. This means that there is relatively little information available on marshalling compared to other forms of work shadowing. It should be noted that the official

Judicial Shadowing Scheme run by the judiciary is **not** available to students, being aimed instead at practitioners who wish to join the judiciary.

Therefore traditionally marshalling has been seen as being offered on an *ad hoc* basis, most commonly where a student happens to know a member of the judiciary through family or social ties. This is certainly a viable option and if you are lucky enough to know a judge then you should certainly enquire if they would be willing to let you shadow them. However, if you are part of the majority who are not this fortunate, there are still ways to get marshalling experience. All four Inns of Court offer marshalling schemes, so if you are a member of an Inn (remember any student intending to study the Bar Vocational Course may join) this should be your first port of call. It is also possible to arrange marshalling by contacting your local court, where you should contact the court manager or listing officer at the court to ask if marshalling is available, and if so how to apply.

What should I know?

- Most marshalling lasts between a day and a week. During this time you are likely to be in court every day so you should ensure you dress appropriately and are able to attend punctually.
- Ensure you address the judge you are shadowing correctly (the correct form of address depends on the seniority of the judge). They may ask you to address them by their first name but this is not guaranteed so err on the side of caution[44].
- Depending on the judge you shadow and the court in which he or she sits, you may spend your entire experience following one trial or at the other extreme see hundreds of brief applications. In either event, ensure that you read up on the relevant area of law in advance. Not only will this help in conversations with the judge, court proceedings are a lot more interesting when you understand what issues are being discussed!
- When sitting in court, remember you must always remain silent and attentive, and **never** forget to turn off your mobile phone!

Practical Questions

1. Using a resource such as Pupillages.com or the Law Society's "Find a Solicitor" (http://www.lawsociety.org.uk/choosingandusing/findasolicitor.law) research firms or chambers in your local area that specialise in work you would be interested in witnessing. Find two or three organisations which offer mini-pupillage or work experience and make a note in your diary of their application window.
2. Research pro bono opportunities at your institution and find out if there are any opportunities for you to get involved.
3. Ask family and friends if they have any contacts within the legal profession who might be able to offer you work experience, and follow up on any leads.
4. Make a careful note of the date of your university's Law Fair and ensure you attend!

---

[44] Vora, R. *Marshalling – what is that?* (AllAboutLaw, 2010) http://www.allaboutlaw.co.uk/index.php/careers/work-experience/marshalling-what-is-that/

Improving your CV

In this section we are going to look at a number of different ways, outside of legal work experience, that you can directly increase your chances of achieving a legal career. In the most basic sense, the activities and opportunities that we will discuss below will improve your CV, but more generally they will make you a stronger candidate and far more able to answer the dreaded competency questions[45] which make up large parts of applications for legal employment. The list below is by no means meant to be exhaustive, and you should bear in mind that almost anything you achieve can be a selling point if properly presented. A final note of caution – while we will discuss how you can present these activities in their best light, do not be tempted to exaggerate or invent experience in your applications.

Legal skills

Mooting

Mooting began in England at least five centuries ago, at the Inns of Court (which provided, and continue to provide, training for would-be barristers)[46]. It was invented to develop advocacy skills prior to the development of the modern system of legal education, although lost popularity over the centuries as books became more prevalent. More recently, mooting has enjoyed a resurgence and is now seen as a crucial part of educating lawyers who intend to work in litigation.

A moot is the argument of legal issues in a hypothetical case. It is not concerned with disputing the facts of the case, thus mooting does not involve examining witnesses and other evidence – it focuses **instead** on pairs of participants being able to construct a logical and well-presented argument as to why their interpretation of the law should be followed. There will be two parties, the appellant and the respondent, who are each represented by a Lead and a Junior counsel. There will be at least one judge (who will run the moot and intervene to ask questions of counsel), who decides both who has 'won on the law' (i.e. would win the case in real life) and also who has 'won the moot' (i.e. has performed best) – this may not be the same team!

Mooting is a very useful activity, and will give you a range of transferable skills:

- It gives you experience in public speaking;
- It develops your advocacy skills – i.e. the ability to persuade others as to the validity your opinion;
- It trains you in a specific form of logical reasoning, which will be of a benefit for you especially if you intend to pursue a career in litigation;
- Mooting lets you explore areas of law you would otherwise not deal with in detail during your course. Almost invariably, preparation for a moot gives you a broader picture of legal arguments in some areas than your course normally would;
- It teaches you other skills which you will need to develop in order to enter the profession – such as how to write a skeleton argument, preparing a trial bundle and appropriate court etiquette;
- Mooting is not only an exercise of presentation, but also one of research. You will learn valuable legal research skills, especially using practitioners' references as opposed to textbooks.

---

[45] These are questions such as "Describe in 500 words a time when you demonstrated leadership" or "Name two instances when you worked successfully as part of a team"
[46] Lynch, A. *Why do we Moot? Exploring the Role of Mooting in Legal Education* [1996] LegEdRev 3

If you do plan to practice as a barrister or a solicitor working in litigation, mooting also gives you the chance to meet top-ranking barristers and judges and get a feel of the workings of "real" courts. Needless to say, participation in mooting is looked on extremely favourably by Chambers as well as by Solicitors' firms. There are numerous opportunities to get involved with mooting and most universities which offer legal courses will have a mooting programme, which may be run by either faculty members or students. Some universities also offer a dedicated mooting module as an option for undergraduates. Even if your university is not currently actively promoting mooting or you are not able to participate this year, bear in mind that creating or joining a mooting society at your institution is also excellent experience. Alongside any internal mooting competitions at your institution, you should be aware that there are many national and international mooting competitions for law students, with some of the most notable including:

> **The English-Speaking Union Essex Court National Mooting Competition** – This is the longest running national competition and offers cash prizes for winners and finalists, as well as mini-pupillages at the prestigious Essex Court Chambers. http://www.esu.org/programmes/universities/competitions/national-mooting-competition
>
> **OUP National Mooting Competition** – Another national competition, this time offering prizes along with the opportunity to gain work experience at law school BPP's pro bono centre. http://www.oup.co.uk/academic/highereducation/law/mooting/
>
> **Philip C. Jessup International Law Moot Court Competition** – An international competition which has been running for more than half a century, the Jessup Cup is contested by participants from over 500 law schools in more than 80 countries. http://www.ilsa.org/jessuphome
>
> **ICLR Annual Mooting Competition** – Run by the Incorporated Council of Law Reporting, this competition is supported by the Law Society and usually offers free subscriptions to otherwise expensive case reports as a prize. http://www.iclr.co.uk/learning-zone/mooting
>
> **London Universities Mooting Shield (LUMS)** – Only available to students studying at institutions in the greater London area, LUMS is of particular note because it is organised by students. It is supported by a number of well-known law firms, chambers and education providers. http://www.lumshield.co.uk/
>
> **The Inner Temple Inter-Varsity Moot** – This competition takes place at the Inner Temple (one of the four Inns of Court) and offers undergraduate students the opportunity to experience a weekend at the Inner Temple along with high-quality competition. http://www.iclr.co.uk/news-and-events/sponsorship/inner-temple-inter-varsity-moot

Debating

Debating utilises very similar skills to mooting, as it encourages participants to research an issue thoroughly, construct a logical and persuasive argument and to present this argument orally in public. However, debating allows for wider scope than mooting and as such is used well beyond the boundaries of legal education. As such, it is accessible to almost anyone, from almost any age, and undergraduate law students are no different.

Debates can be run very differently according to the rules used, but in almost all debates there will be (at least) two sides, arguing for and against a particular proposition. This can be almost any statement, from political issues (such as "This House would allow unlimited freedom of speech" or "This House supports unilateral nuclear disarmament") to social concerns ("This House would legalise recreational drugs" or "This House would ban violent computer games") to moral and religious arguments ("This House believes religion does more harm than good" or "This House would kill one to save many"). In a specifically legal context, debating will usually involve issues of law, although these are likely to be more general than in a moot or a negotiation. Thus a legal debate might revolve around the reintroduction of the death penalty, or the abolition of trial by jury.

Most debates will take one of two forms – either there will be distinct "teams", who will argue back and forth in turn, or there will be a more general debate in a large group, with an organiser ensuring that each member has an opportunity to speak in turn. Most of the largest debating competitions use a set of rules known as 'British Parliamentary Style', which involves four teams of two people each. Perhaps the most prestigious tournament in the UK is the John Smith Memorial Mace, featuring over 200 teams from universities across Britain and Ireland[47]. Most universities will have a Debating Society or similar body, although you may find that this is organised outside of the Law School.

- Important skills developed by debating include.
- Giving you experience in public speaking, often in front of a large audience.
- Training you to argue a point which you might not yourself believe – just as in a courtroom when you must represent a client whatever your opinion, in a debate you may find yourself arguing for or against a proposition on which you hold strong views.
- Just as with mooting, debating also teaches you how to conduct very specific research in order to support your arguments.
- You often need to respond quickly in a debate, to point out a flaw in your opponent's argument or respond to a point of their own. As such, it develops your ability to think on your feet and to react to changing circumstances, which are crucial legal skills.

Negotiation

Almost all lawyers require good negotiation skills, whatever their role or area of practice. As such, legal employers are impressed by applicants who have already had the opportunity to develop their abilities in this area. As with skills such as mooting, some universities offer dedicated negotiation teaching (and it is a mandatory part of the curriculum for the LPC and BPTC) but as an undergraduate student your best opportunity to improve your formal negotiation skills may be to join one of the many negotiation competitions available.

Your university or college might offer internal competitions or modules, and there are also a number of national competitions between higher education institutions. Most negotiation competitions involve pairs or teams, although some do involve individual competition. You should also note that while most negotiations take place between two parties, competitions can involve negotiations between three or more parties, adding another level of complexity.

The most prestigious national competition is the CEDR Negotiation Competition[48], which is open to all law schools in England and Wales. As such, it includes universities, GDL providers and institutions

---

[47] http://www.esu.org/programmes/universities/competitions/john-smith-memorial-mace
[48] http://www.cedr.com/skills/competition/

offering the BPTC and LPC vocational courses. Each year regional finals are held, with qualifiers then spending a weekend at the National final. The winners of this final are then entered into the International Negotiating Competition, representing the UK against teams from law schools all around the world.

By taking part in negotiation:

- You can learn how to analyse a legal or commercial problem and identify potential compromise. In real legal practice, most clients would rather settle a dispute, even if they have to sacrifice some elements of their claim, than to face the cost, delay and uncertainty of lengthy litigation.
- You will improve your communication skills, which does not just include being able to advocate your own arguments but also more subtle skills such as non-verbal communication, active listening and perceptive questioning.
- You will learn a lot about the different styles and strategies people use when negotiating. This is invaluable knowledge for your legal career, as different styles require a different approach and a truly effective negotiator will be able to adopt the correct tactics in differing circumstances.
- Legal negotiation is also another opportunity to network with students, academics and lawyers from different institutions and as many negotiations are carried out in teams, to improve your teamwork skills.

Extra-curricular activities

Employment

While activities such as negotiation and mooting demonstrate that you have developed specific legal skills, your employment history remains one of the most important indications as to your overall suitability for a particular position. Obviously for many of you, full-time employment has not been and will not be an option prior to applying for legal employment. However, almost any previous employment is relevant to an application as it demonstrates crucial skills such as punctuality, reliability and independence. Work in the legal sector is obviously particularly impressive, whether this is a part-time position at, for example, your local Citizens' Advice Bureau or paralegal or secretarial work for a law firm. Because of the cost of courses such as the BPTC and LPC, some students choose to work for a period after graduation to hopefully save funds to support themselves on their chosen course and this can be a good opportunity to look for legal employment.

As stated above, non-legal employment is also valuable, but here you need to ensure that you emphasise the transferrable skills which are evidenced by your role. For example, working at weekends in a shop might demonstrate that you can communicate with members of the public, employment as a receptionist could show organisational ability and a job in a fast food restaurant is evidence of teamwork and potentially management skills. The other advantage of providing your employment history to recruiters is that it is a good source of more practical references, which will complement academic references from tutors.

If you are a mature student, or have taken time out between levels of education, then you may have a fuller employment history. If this is the case, again ensure that you use this as a positive, rather than concealing the length of time you have spent outside the legal sector. Many firms and chambers actually prefer to recruit mature applicants (i.e. those who have not applied directly after full-time education) and thus you can present your experience as a unique strength.

Positions of responsibility

As a lawyer, you will be placed in a position of considerable responsibility, where you will be partly or solely responsible for the conduct of numerous cases each year. Any errors on your part can be extremely costly, either financially (in the civil law) or with even more serious consequences (such as loss of contact rights with a child in family law, or imprisonment in criminal law). As such, one of the most crucial attributes you must demonstrate to any legal employer is that you are worthy of such responsibility. For some of you, this may be demonstrated at least partially by your previous employment.

However, in addition to employment, there are other ways in which to demonstrate responsibility and oversight, and it can be particularly impressive to show that you actively sought such a role, rather than it merely being part of your job. Therefore, you should ensure that your CV adequately demonstrates that you have held positions of responsibility. Some examples of such positions include:

> **At school** – You may have held a position such as head boy/head girl/prefect, or mentored younger students. Other positions of responsibility might be captaining a sports team or leading a club or society.
>
> **At university** – Similarly to above, if you held any official role in a university club, team or society this is well worth mentioning. Other responsibilities at university might include being involved in open days or helping out at freshers week, acting as a student representative for boards or committees, assisting a lecturer or PhD student with research and helping organise events.
>
> **Extra-curricular** – Outside of education, involvement in organisations such as youth clubs, local teams or charity events can all demonstrate your ability to take on responsibility.

Volunteering and charity work

Even if you have not been placed in a particular position of responsibility, any and all evidence that you are willing to get involved in activities in your own time demonstrates enthusiasm and commitment. Perhaps the most impressive evidence of volunteering is spending time in a legal setting, for example working at a Law Centre, Citizens' Advice Bureau or on a pro bono project. Charity work is also always a positive addition to your CV and gives plenty of scope to demonstrate a wide range of skills. If you are involved in organising events, you can show management and organisational skills, while if you raise money for charity you might use this as evidence of your communication skills and ability to persuade others. While it is important not to over-burden your time, if you have the opportunity to volunteer for any role at university it is usually a good idea to at least consider doing so.

Skills

If you have other skills that are not evidenced by any of the other sections on your CV, ensure that you do bring them to the recruiter's attention. One common error is to not mention any ability to speak another language – while you should not claim more fluency than is truthful, if you have even moderate proficiency this should be mentioned. As litigation and legal communication is increasingly carried out electronically, any IT skills should also be discussed and you should consider the possibility of obtaining a qualification to demonstrate this (which may well be freely available from your educational institution or employer).

Other interests

Often used as a "filler" section on a CV, you should bear in mind that setting out your interests can also be a positive part of your application. Think about what interests you, and in what ways that can demonstrate skills or otherwise impress an employer. Research can be crucial here – for example, if you find out that the law firm you are applying to has recently won a cricket tournament, your experience of playing in your local side might be of great interest. Similarly, if a Chambers is proud of their string quartet, ensure you mention your grade 6 violin qualification! It is also worth trying to match your interests to the work the firm or Chambers takes on – for example, helping out with a student radio station might be particularly relevant to a firm which specialise in media law, while a commercial Chambers might be particularly interested to note that you founded and ran a small business enterprise.

> **Practical Questions**
>
> 1. Update your CV, both in terms of design and content. You might want to research guidance on effective CVs online or better yet make an appointment with your careers service to look at your CV.
> 2. Once you have an updated CV, download a job specification or application form for a similar position to your ideal employment after education (for example, a training contract application to a similar-sized firm in your chosen practice area). Look at the skills the recruiter is asking for – does your CV evidence these?
> 3. Pick out the skills in which you have the least relevant experience and make a plan of practical steps you can take in the next six months to gain experience in these areas.

Training contracts and pupillages

When you get to the stage of applying for training contracts or pupillages, you should consult as wide a range of resources as possible. With that in mind, the following section is intended to provide.

Selection tips

- In order to most efficiently carry out the considerable work of selecting where to apply, it is best to split the process into three stages – firstly, narrow down your options; secondly, research these options in depth; and finally select where you will apply.
- As a starting point, decide on the geographical area(s) in which you would be willing to work. This will considerably narrow down the number of potential employers. Bear in mind that for most legal work outside of high street practice, you will need to be based in a relatively major city.
- Next, decide on which areas of law you would be willing to practice in. Bear in mind that unless you are planning to enter an organisation with a single speciality (such as criminal law) it is likely that, at least in the early years of your career, you will have to take on some cases in other fields than your main interests.
- When looking at which areas a firm or chambers practices in, make sure that you carry out more research than simply what categories they are listed under on online databases such as pupillages.com.

A law firm may have advised a handful of footballers on property transactions and thus claim expertise in Sports Law, but that is not an area in which they will be looking to recruit or to provide work. Similarly, smaller firms or Chambers may have one or two members who specialise in a particular area, but again this is likely to mean that they are not looking to employ more people with these interests.

- At this point you should have considerably shortened the overall list of pupillage or training contract providers. At this point, you need to start carrying out more detailed research about each possible recruiter. This is essential and helps in many different ways – not only will it save time when applying, but it can also give you a much better idea of your chances of success.

- A good place to start is to go through each of the possibilities remaining on your shortlist and look at the type of people they have recruited in recent years. This is easily done as members will be listed on the firm or chamber's website, with the most junior usually at the bottom. Look at the CV or pen-picture of those who have joined in recent years and consider:
  - What university did they attend? Does the firm seem to predominantly recruit Oxbridge or non-Oxbridge candidates?
  - What qualifications did they achieve? Would it seem that GDL or LLB students are more likely to be offered a role?
  - How old are new recruits? Does this firm or chambers seem to prefer students fresh from education or those who have worked in other sectors?
  - Are there any extra-curricular activities which seem to be particularly favoured? For example, is mooting experience a common theme, or are sporting achievements highlighted?

- Sadly, while not an issue in the majority of the legal sector, you may also wish to note the diversity of the organisation. If there is a dearth of women and/or ethnic minorities among recent recruits this may need to be borne in mind. Note however that a lack of diversity among more senior members is unlikely to be an issue, as this reflects the demography of the profession many years ago.

- This should help narrow your list further and give you a good idea as to where you are most likely to succeed in your application. At this stage, you should be close to beginning to apply, although bear in mind that for pupillage you are limited to selecting 12 chambers, so may need to narrow your list further.

Application tips

- The most important tip of all is that there are no shortcuts when it comes to applications. Admittedly, multiple applications can take huge amounts of time and deadlines often conflict with your studies, however you should remember that each application is a potentially career-determining opportunity and that the more time you spend (within reason) on the application, the higher your chances of reaching the next stage of recruitment.

- As such, avoid the temptation to copy and paste substantive answers (obviously copying and pasting basic information such as A-level qualifications is perfectly acceptable). Each firm or chambers will have its own individual character and requirements for applicants, thus each application should be treated on its individual merits. While you may well want to reuse a clever turn of phrase or a particularly impressive experience, ensure that you carefully plan your answer to each competency question from scratch each time.

- Make sure you stick to word limits given for a question. If a recruiter asks you to describe an example of leadership in 600 words, anything above 600 words suggests that you are either inattentive (did not read the question properly) or a poor communicator (unable to explain what is needed within a set number of words). However, anything below around 500 words is a missed opportunity, as you should be using these questions to sell yourself and your skills as much as possible.

- On this note, look at your application form as a type of written advocacy – you are trying to persuade the recruiter to interview you, so ensure you mount a persuasive argument. Also bear in mind that your application will form the basis of any interviews, so be prepared to discuss anything you mention on the form.

- Proof-read, proof-read and then proof-read again! Lawyers are expected to be meticulous and in some areas, even a comma in the wrong place in a legal document could cost your clients millions of pounds. Thus spelling mistakes, poor grammar or typos reflect very poorly on your application.

- Once you have (repeatedly) proof-read your application, pass it on to a friend or family member, as they may spot mistakes that you have missed.

- Don't leave applications to the last minute – online systems tend to crash as the deadline approaches, and an early application will in any event demonstrate that you are both enthusiastic and efficient.

- Finally, learn to deal with rejection. Every applicant will face rejection at some stage of the process in many of their applications, and this is perfectly normal. If you are rejected by your "dream" employer, focus on applications to other institutions rather than letting this damage your enthusiasm.

Interview tips

- Make sure you prepare thoroughly for an interview. This includes practical planning, such as working out where the interview takes place and how you will get there, but also rereading your application form and thinking about how you plan to answer questions.

- It is obviously not possible to predict exactly what you will be asked, but you can usually assume that the most impressive achievements stated in your application will be discussed – and equally, that you may be questioned about areas where you appear to have less experience.

- Equally, ensure you read a broadsheet newspaper in the days leading up to your interview, as employers will often ask questions about the legal aspects of major news stories.

- Expect and be prepared to answer the three standard questions every legal employer wants to know:
  - Why do you want to be a barrister/solicitor?
  - Why do you want to practice in this area?
  - Why do you want to work with us?

Non-legal careers

Just because you are studying a legal qualification, there is no obligation on you to become a lawyer. Indeed, many of you reading this book now will be at least considering alternative careers and even if you are set on entering the legal sector, it is always useful to have a "plan B". In this section, we will look at the key skills developed by a law degree and some of the destinations outside the law where such skills are highly prized.

Transferable Skills

Research skills

As you will know, to achieve a degree in Law you need to carry out large amounts of research, finding relevant cases, legislation and articles in order to support your arguments. This develops a number of inter-related research skills, such as:

- The ability to find relevant information amongst large amounts of material – for example, finding one case among the millions reported that supports your point.
- The ability to extract the crucial points from large amounts of material – for example, identifying the *ratio decidendi* from a case report that is hundreds of pages long.
- Using hard-copy sources (such as your institution's law library) alongside electronic databases such as Westlaw and LexisNexis.
- Check whether information is corroborated and up to date (for example, checking that a case has not been over-ruled or that a statute has not been amended).

These skills are highly valued by employers because they demonstrate that you will be able to handle large amounts of information and also synthesise large amounts of research into summaries of the most important points. This might be particularly useful in areas such as finance or government work, where there are often large amounts of technical data which needs to be read and summarised.

Analytical and evaluative skills

Legal education also teaches you how to analyse the information that you collect and to evaluate how it applies to real life scenarios. The obvious examples of this during your law degree are problem questions, where you have to identify the issues involved in the problem, summarise the relevant law and then analyse how it will apply in this particular situation. Such questions are obviously mainly designed to assist you in developing the skills needed for handling real-life disputes but these skills are eminently transferable – in any walk of life, the ability to evaluate a situation and analyse potential options and consequences is extremely useful.

The other very important skill developed in answering such questions, and generally in studying the law, is the ability to think and argue logically. Techniques such as the IRAC method of answering problem questions (Issue, Relevant law, Application to facts, Conclusion) may seem to be purely academic, but are in fact a way of showing you how to construct a well-supported argument. In many industries, particularly in businesses where you are seeking to persuade customers or investors, it is crucial to be able to not only present an argument but also support it with a series of logical steps, thus persuading your audience that they should agree with your proposition.

Problem solving and creative thinking

Of course, when you are asked to answer a problem question or to discuss legal issues, you are not only expected to analyse the dispute but also to offer your assessment of the chances of success. As you progress through legal education, this will develop from being able to give a basic 'yes they should sue'/'no they should not sue' answer, to a more nuanced approach where you can take into account other factors such as the cost of litigation compared to the amount potentially recoverable or the suitability of alternative dispute resolution. Again, such an approach may seem very legalistic but can be easily adapted for other circumstances – in any form of employment, you or your company will face problems which require not only the evaluation of different options but the selection of the correct choice.

On a related note, studying the law also teaches creative thinking. As you will know, much of your time studying common law and legislation is not spent dealing with the general rule in a particular area, but the exceptions and loopholes which have been developed to surmount it. This ability to always consider alternative routes or seek out opportunities to benefit from ambiguities or lacunas is highly prized in areas such as finance, commerce and insurance.

Communication skills

Of course, one of the most important skills taught as part of both undergraduate law degrees and the professional courses is how to communicate effectively. At university, this will usually mean an emphasis on written communication, assessed through coursework and exams where the standard of not only your written English but also your ability to script a logical and persuasive argument is crucial. However, tutorial-based teaching also develops your oral communication skills and legal extra-curricular activities such as mooting, debating and negotiating can further demonstrate this ability.

Of course, certain careers are particularly reliant on communication skills, such as journalism, politics and sales-based roles. However in any job in any sector, the ability to communicate clearly and precisely is a valuable asset, whether this is with clients, managers or subordinates. Law graduates are seen as not only persuasive communicators, but also capable of being able to "translate" complex information (such as an archaic judgment) into simple, easily-understood summaries.

Attention to detail and time-management

Of course, another commonly-held belief about lawyers is that they spend much of their time poring over the small-print in contracts and agreements. This is of course only true of a small minority, but it does mean that many employers do see law graduates as particularly precise and able to spot even the most insignificant detail. There is some justification for this, as the way in which you study the law, for example reading long case reports to find one crucial sentence, or picking up on the one word in a problem question that dramatically alters your advice, does develop these skills.

Time-management is another crucial skill and law degrees are known for requiring large amounts of work alongside intellectual ability. Explaining how you are expected to not only develop practical skills but also retain huge amounts of knowledge, such as the names and details of hundreds of relevant cases, can demonstrate to an employer that you are able to work efficiently and effectively.

Where can a Law degree take you?

The private sector

Business

Of course, "business" is an exceptionally wide area and there are roles within the commercial sector for talented people whatever their background. However, a law degree can be particularly valuable as it is seen as one of the most intellectually challenging subjects to study, thus demonstrating your intelligence and perseverance. Specific legal skills can be utilised in different roles – we already mentioned one example, of advocacy skills being very useful to those working in a sales capacity. Other examples might include using your written communication skills in a customer-service role, using your evaluative skills as a business analyst or demonstrating your problem-solving skills as a consultant.

Finance

Financial institutions usually deal with lots of complex data, must comply with huge amounts of regulatory law and have to attract and advise clients. As you might imagine, these requirements make law students particularly attractive employees, as they can exercise the skills we discussed above to assist in all of these areas. In particular, legal graduates are able to understand not only complex technical terminology but also ethical considerations such as confidentiality and conflicts of interest, which can be crucial in this sector. In particular, legal graduates are often found working in regulatory and compliance roles.

Human Resources

Human Resources is increasingly an umbrella term for a wide array of different positions, many of which are ideally suited to those with legal training. Most obviously, a knowledge of employment law and an ability to analyse and advise on disputes are crucial attributes for working in a department which provides the link between an employer and their employees. However, there are other HR concerns which can be particularly suited to someone with legal training, such as analysing contracts to ensure they are correct and comply with legislation, being entrusted with organising and maintaining a payroll system or assisting with the grievance procedures and the resolution of disputes.

Insurance

Another industry in which contracts and legal regulation are crucial, the insurance sector recruits legal graduates. As well as offering the opportunity to directly draw on your legal knowledge, a career in this area is likely to utilise your analytical and creative thinking skills as well as requiring excellent communication with clients and claimants.

Publishing and Media

We could subdivide this area further into legal publishing and media, and the wider non-legal sector. In terms of legal publishing, there are of course many large companies which specialise in producing legal textbooks, practitioners' works, legal reference books and law reports. Roles can range from the creative, providing the written content for such publications, through using your legal research skills to collate and update the masses of legal information required, to more managerial or editorial positions. There are also many opportunities in both dedicated legal media (publications and websites such as *The Lawyer* and *Counsel* magazine) and for legal journalists for mainstream news outlets. In the wider sector, law graduates' communication skills and attention to detail make them attractive candidates for any journalistic or editorial role. There are also opportunities to work in advisory capacity, providing advice to publishers and publications on issues such as copyright, broadcasting rights and defamation.

Politics

Many Members of Parliament are law graduates, and Prime Ministers from Margaret Thatcher to Benjamin Disraeli to Tony Blair all practised law prior to successful political careers. There are obvious overlaps between the two professions, such as the ability to communicate and to persuade, and for many law students the opportunity to actually change, rather than merely work within, the law is a tempting one. There are also many roles in policy development, research and compiling reports, both within the government (as we shall see below) and in pressure groups and non-governmental organisations (NGOs).

The public sector

The Civil Service

One of the largest employers of legal graduates, the Civil Service is the organisation which staffs government departments, agencies and non-departmental government bodies. Unlike politicians, civil servants are expected to be impartial and objective, able to implement whatever policies the elected government proposes. There are almost half a million Civil Servants in the UK[49], many of whom have a background in legal education. Various 'Graduate Fast Stream' programmes offered by the Civil Service offer graduates the opportunity to experience a multiplicity of placements and postings in their early career, with the intention of developing high-quality staff eligible for promotion to the highest levels of the Civil Service. Because Civil Servants staff such a wide range of departments and organisations, there is the opportunity to work in an area in which you have a particular interest, or to spend time in different and challenging environments. The Civil Service also offers good job security and clear career paths to work towards.

Supranational and International bodies

We have discussed work in UK politics or within the Civil Service, but there are also many opportunities in international bodies such as the European Union and United Nations. A qualification in law can attract employers in this area by demonstrating the same skills we have discussed above, and such careers offer the opportunity to travel and work abroad. Speaking another language is recommended if you wish to pursue a career in this area, but by no means mandatory.

Local government

At the other extreme, there are many interesting and well-remunerated positions available below central government level. Counties, districts, boroughs and urban authorities all require personnel and actively seek to recruit those with legal knowledge and training. There is a wide variety of roles, from working in specific areas (for example environmental protection or regulating local business) to more general positions utilising your transferrable skills.

Law enforcement

A knowledge of the law is a major advantage in enforcing it, and so law graduates can be found at all levels of the law enforcement – not only the police force, but also bodies such as the prison service, immigration

---

[49] On a headcount basis, there were 489,000 Civil Servants in July 2012. Figure taken from official website at http://www.civilservice.gov.uk

and customs, environmental agencies and the security services. As well as the legal knowledge they can provide, law graduates are seen as ideally suited for such work by having strong analytical skills, linked to the ability to remain objective and evaluate all information prior to making a decision.

Academia

As you will know, the study and teaching of law requires considerable resources, particularly considering that law is usually taught most effectively in relatively small groups. As such, there are opportunities for teaching law from schools to colleges to universities to the providers of professional courses such as the LPC.

Reflection Questions

1. Whether or not you are planning a career in the legal profession, what other options would you consider as alternative careers?
2. How do you think your own skills and abilities would suit such a role?
3. What do you think are the major advantages and disadvantages of choosing an alternative career after completing legal education?

Further reading

Written resources

Chambers Student 2012: The student's guide to becoming a lawyer (Chambers and Partners, 2012) – note much of this information is available on the website cited below

Harrison, C. *From Student to Solicitor: The Complete Guide to Securing a Training Contract* (Sweet & Maxwell, 2010)

Kramer, A. *Bewigged and Bewildered? A Guide to Becoming a Barrister in England and Wales* (Hart Publishing, 2011)

Robinson, C. *Ultimate Guide to Training Contract Success* (Ultimate Guides, 2010)

The Training Contract and Pupillage Handbook (Published yearly and available free from your university)

Weiner, S. *21st Century Solicitor: How to Make a Real Impact as a Junior Commercial Lawyer* (Hart Publishing, 2011)

Wolfe, G. *The Path to Pupillage: A Guide for the Aspiring Barrister* 2nd Edition (Sweet & Maxwell, 2010)

Online resources

AllAboutLaw http://www.allaboutlaw.co.uk/
LawCareers.Net http://www.lawcareers.net/
Lawyer 2B http://l2b.thelawyer.com/
Pupillage and How to Get It http://pupillageandhowtogetit.wordpress.com/
Roll On Friday http://www.rollonfriday.com/
The Chambers Student Guide http://www.chambersstudent.co.uk
The Junior Lawyers Division http://juniorlawyers.lawsociety.org.uk/
The Law Careers Advice Network http://www.lcan.org.uk/
The Pupillages Pages http://thepupillagepages.com/index.php

4
General Study Skills for Law

Dave Hodgkinson

Introduction to General Study Skills

In this piece we are going to develop some ideas about general study skills.

The first thing for us to consider however is that we are, thank goodness, all different. So the following chapter comes with a caveat – take it with a pinch of salt. There is no hard and fast rule here and it will be a case of finding what works – for you as a student and you alone.

The usual problem is that a student is worried about missing information from lectures and tutorials. Well, the advice is do not worry – the information will come to you, you will pick it up through reading and preparation, talking to others and immersing yourself in whichever topic is the focus of your concern. So relax. You will be a far better 'learner' if you are able to have the confidence to say 'this will come to me and I will succeed'. Free your mind from the panic and worry and you will learn it. You won't forget it in the exam and you will put forward an excellent piece of coursework and have a smile bigger than a Cheshire cat when your grades come back. You can do this so stop fretting.

So here is by far the biggest single tip which can be given with regard to general study skills – be confident in your own ability.

How best to learn these skills?

The first thing you should do is open your mind; it is clear that you can do this degree and succeed. That is a given. You would not have obtained a place on the award if you did not already have ability, sense, drive, tenacity, understanding, experience and desire. But that does not make you fully equipped for this next stage. It will be a step up and by reading on you might find some tips and ideas to assist you further in climbing up the ladder of success. However, you need to open your mind. Not just to the fact you can do it, but to the information you are about to receive. It is necessary to accommodate and assimilate the information and, in doing so, not only obtain a good degree but also learn.

That's what this is about, in case you didn't already know. It is to enable you to learn and utilise the information in obtaining a job, moving onto practice or other areas of academia, or just having the knowledge and enjoying the 'buzz' you get from it. We will look at different ideas as to how to succeed. Some other writers call them 'tools' however really they are innate skills which you already possess. Ideas as to how to do the job correctly which you already know and really only need a little bit of guidance as to how to put the ideas into practice.

So, 'law lives' and it is also something you already know about: you know the differences between rights and wrongs. You know what is and what is not the law for the most part already. If you don't believe this then take a moment and think what the law might be which governs the area when you buy an iPad and it is faulty. You will already know the most part of all the issues. All you have to do now is to learn how to support your knowledge with authority. All we have to do then is learn the authorities and the rest our academic mind will deal with. It is a little 'scary' but just be free and easy with yourself and the information will come to you.

However, it's not quite as simple as that! You have to work at it you know and in this section you will find some suggestions to enable you to study and improve your general skills in order that you can learn and recollect and present and do exams and get that degree. They are only 'ideas': there is no paradigm method so just try out the suggestions and see which works for you. Perhaps they all will? Think about this – information in lectures and tutorials and from reading and researching goes in your brain and so it's only a matter of being able to recall that information. This really is what general study skills are about – the ability to store and recall information when required to do so.

There are a few 'tricks' however, but ultimately it's all to do with thinking. You are going to think a great deal. You should think, query, mull over and question information. In doing so, you will learn and have the ability to recall.

Some lecturers will call it understanding. Indeed, this is what is required to be successful. It can be split into other areas such as analysis and application however at the end of the day it's all about understanding and to understand something we need to think about it.

'Chip away at the block' – you have probably heard that phrase before and that is what general study skills are – they are like the chisels a sculptor would use to chip away at the block of stone and create the masterpiece; where do you think Rodin's *The Thinker* came from? Initially, a block of marble we should imagine. Yet with hours of hard work and chipping away, eventually he produced a masterpiece.

To recall and understand you also need to store the information. This storage capacity can be increased and assisted by utilising your general study skills.

One way to think is to ask what it means? If you do this will make yourself consider the elements of the particular area and this will lead to that storage and the ability to recall.

Learning to learn

Of considerable importance is learning how to learn. Some of you will have just completed A-Levels, GNVQs or the like. Others may have been out of study for a period of time. In either case, University study requires a different approach and a different attitude to learning, with much more of the emphasis on students directing their own study and managing their own time, individually or as part of a team. We call this "independent learning" and by being able to take control of your studies and motivating yourself to go beyond doing the bare minimum you will come to gain a much deeper understanding of the subject and this will foster greater success for you as a student.

Time management as a skill

The volume of work can be deceptive – typically a student will have 10-12 hours per week of directed learning e.g. lectures and tutorials. The fact that the Student Union Bar may be open all day is not an indication that this is where you spend time out of lectures – the Learning Centre and Library are open for longer! The rest of the time is actually set aside for students to undertake the preparation, reading and research necessary to intelligently approach taught activities and to contribute in a meaningful way. This puts pressure on students to manage their time and discipline their learning activities. In addition it requires students to reflect on what they have learnt and take a critical approach relating to how they develop.

It will be very useful for you to come to understand when you are most productive in your learning. Some students find that treating their degree like a "9 to 5" job works, and their entire day is structured around study but they will "down tools" at 5pm and switch off until the next day. Other students perform at specific points of the day (some are morning people, others are "night owls"). The key is to get yourself into a routine with which you are comfortable and where you know you're doing your best study, and stick to it. A useful exercise would be to draw up a timetable with study periods identified. Even if you find you're less "structured" than our 9 to 5 example, having this written down will be a useful prompt to you to ensure you're putting in the extra work necessary to achieve the higher marks. If you need any direction on how much study you need to put in, consult the module guide. These will often identify how much directed teaching there will be, but will also indicate how many additional hours of independent study is roughly expected. If not, just ask your lecturer.

Finally, it is important that when you're working out your study times, you factor in breaks. Few people can realistically hold their concentration at the top of its performance for much more than 30 minutes at a time. So long as you can be disciplined enough not to let them take too long, regular breaks will help you keep mentally alert.

Practical Question

Once you've received your lecture/tutorial timetable for this term/semester, write it up into a spreadsheet and create your own study plan around it. It doesn't have to be the 9 – 5 model, and could go very late into the evening/over weekends if this is how you work best. Ensure that you're giving sufficient amount of independent study time to each of the modules you're taking under guidance from the module handout or lecturer. You might also want to think strategically about when you study for each module – you might find that you prefer to do your pre-lecture reading in a study block right before that particular lecture so it is fresh in your mind. Alternatively, you might elect to do it well in advance, so you've had time to consider and reflect upon it – it's all down to what works best for you . . .

Reflection

This is a key skill. You reflect and think. Review your notes and say to yourself "what did I learn today?" or "what does it all mean?". Rodin, our sculptor, would have stood back from his stone of marble thousands of times and reflected on where it was going, how it was shaping up, what he should do to make it better. You must do the same. It is more difficult to write something down here instructing you how to reflect than it is just to do it in itself. But this is what you do –

1. Read the notes you have taken and think about how they relate to the subject.
2. Find the substantive element – the essential element which you need to learn in order to progress. Ask yourself what the key area is.
3. Think about it and reflect upon its place in the overall scheme of law; what does it mean?, how does it affect the situation?, is it 'good law' or 'bad law'; this is absolutely key.

You might be shocked at that last reflective thought but here is another home truth for you – you do not have to accept everything that you are told. There are many different views as to the law. This is the beauty of it and perhaps one reason why you have chosen to study it – all views compete and there is never any single right way or a wrong way. Indeed, look at all the famous judgments where certain judges give dissenting judgments and hold views totally in contradiction of the majority verdict. Why does the Supreme Court overrule the Court of Appeal? *Because there are different views of competing ideas.* Do you find this proposition hard to believe? Well, law is adversarial in this system. This means there are always two or more sides. It's a competition. Claimant v Defendant, Crown v Defence – lawyers on both sides advocating that their point of view, their interpretation of the law, is the best one, or the one to be favoured by the court in the current circumstances.

The "trick"

All you need to do is learn the basic authorities and then put your own opinion forward by thinking about what they actually mean. Paint your own picture. The canvas is yours.

Original thinking

There is nothing wrong in reflecting on the lecture or the books and thinking to yourself – 'I accept that, and I realise I have to apply the authorities as they are, but I can hold another view as to how they relate with one another and the eventual outcome in this thing called litigation, or academia, or my coursework, or my exam, or I can take issue with the journal writers'.

Indeed, you will notice how academics who write journals tend to do nothing other than call into question another academic who is writing on the same area. They usually begin, 'whilst I recognise the valuable contribution that Smith puts forward in relation to this legal matter, he is, in actual fact, quite incorrect and has missed the point entirely'. So – be bold, be brave, and *have your own view*.

Think: it doesn't matter what you say as long as you have authority for it (and remember you can use authority in the reverse, in the negative, to show why a particular point is not as it first seems).

Read more widely than the lecture . . . and the law

A University education is more than reading books and articles about your specific subject. In an area like law, broader political, social and economic issues have a significant and direct effect on the subject matter. While your studies will reflect the real context of law as a social and political phenomenon you will need to be open to the developments in the world at large. Reading broad sheet newspapers, intelligent watching of the television and discussion and interaction with students studying other disciplines will not only help you to be a more informed person but will be of direct benefit to your understanding of your subject. If you don't know what the fuss is about something you have seen on the news for example, you might want to start finding out.

Do it

Law is a 'doing' subject, not simply a paper chase. Your abilities to communicate, to argue and to interact socially are all as vital to the learning process as they are to the legal process. To this end you will be required to engage in a variety of activities in your tutorials and assessments no matter which University you attend to study law and these will include oral presentation, working in teams, undertaking independent research and the general development of a variety of skills some of which you might not have known you even have. In order to get the best out of all of this you need to 'throw yourself' into these activities because it is your contribution and your work that will make things work for you. Doing these things might also give you the chance to discover whether you really have got what it makes to be a jet set deal-making solicitor or whether your fortunes will be better served at the Bar.

Be "picky"

Sometimes you will find that you are confused or that the subject is difficult or that there is too much reading. All students should feel this – it is after all a degree, rather than a GCSE, that you are studying for. Do not be afraid to ask questions, to make mistakes or to seek guidance in how to manage your workload. Remember that the lecturer is there to ensure that you make the best of your potential. He or she will specifically help you with these things. They are, after all is said and done, teachers.

Think about your aims

Whilst it would seem that the process of learning about law is the main aim of study, it is clear you will need to know how you are progressing and how your skills are developing. The onus is on you, for the most part, to set yourself goals for managing work and reflecting on how you are progressing. In most modules you will not be given homework/tutorial preparation per se. Those who have recently completed study in further education will be used to being set regular tasks that allow you to gauge how you are doing. Frequently this will have given you goals and tasks that may or may not have contributed to the overall mark you gained for your study. You do not generally have this particular form of feedback at University. This means that you are the creator of your own destiny. Try this cliché out and think about it – 'You're going to reap just what you sow'. Do you expect to be working and preparing for an extensive part of your University day? If the answer to this is "yes" then you are already on the way to becoming a better student. This all comes back to the theme of becoming an independent learner. The more you're willing to put in, the more you will get out.

Lectures

It is absolutely crucial to realise that the lecture will only cover the basics. This information might be quite shocking. You may have expected to go into the lecture and be presented with all the information necessary so that you can just go out and pass your exam or your coursework. Ah well it doesn't quite happen like that. The best way for you to know what you can get out of the lecture is to understand what the lecturer wants to do. He or she has an *objective*. This objective is to deliver a certain piece of information or describe a current situation in relation to the law, or deal with a particular case and how it affects others and so on. But the lecturer simply has an objective. There might be a number of objectives depending on the length of the lecture. Now, the lecturer will set this out for you either in a module guide or in the previous week's lecture, but you will know the (aims and) objectives of the lecture. It is possible that you have been asked to carry out some prior reading – well it is to be hoped you did it.

What are lectures then? They are an opportunity for introducing you to a new area. They might follow on from a previous subject and they have the ultimate aim of delivering a large amount of information to you. Because of this, you have perhaps been provided with a module or study guide – something which sets out the topic to be covered in the lecture. Now, you have to find out what kind of student you are here – are you the kind who wants to write down every word which comes out of the lecturers mouth and prepare some scrappy notes and not listen and miss important things and be unable to realise when something important is being stated as opposed to something supplementary to the topic? Or are you going to engage, think, listen and learn. Because the lecture is the first chip at the block, or the first opportunity for you to think about the subject.

Relax

A good skill is in fact to just relax, think, not panic and take your time. You can do all the reading after the lecture. You can speak to the lecturer afterwards if you wish for clarification. You will revisit the areas in your own time and in the tutorials. So – relax and enjoy the lecture. Think of it like going to see a live performance. You might not like the show and find it boring or you might think it is the most fantastic play you have ever seen. But the fact is you don't sit at shows writing out copious amounts of notes and worrying about whether you are getting the entire story correct do you? This is because – you watch it and you do get the story. It's like watching *Coronation Street* – you can watch an episode and then recall enough about it to tell somebody what happened.

This then is because you are relaxed and your mind is absorbing all the information. You see it and hear it and so it must be in your brain. You should of course get the notes which are important and so you need to be discerning and ensure that you get the core part of the information – the meaning of a case, how the statute affects the position, the comparison between the judgments, and so on. Everything else can be researched and pieced together afterwards – the more chipping you do the better. How much should you take in during a lecture then? The best thing is to use the *Coronation Street* illustration above – just get enough information that you have the basics and you could explain it to somebody afterwards. Imagine you are at a party and you don't know anybody and so the host introduces you to a stranger. What will you talk about? There must be things which you know all about, like sport or current affairs or something. But you wouldn't start to chew their ear off with in depth details and complex points would you? So, just get enough from the lecture so you could go up to a stranger afterwards and say "Hey, I'm going to tell you the basics of . . .". In other words, you want to get the information into your basic understanding so that you can recall a sound base in the fundamentals.

Basic method of information gathering

Take your notes and work through them. Go to lectures and listen. Ensure you do those tutorial questions. Motivate yourself to look at the online resources such as Westlaw or LexisNexis, or any academic journal/article databases your university may give you access to.

Pre-reading

Choose the relevant materials. If you think you are reading in the incorrect area then stop! Look at the directed reading in the module guide. Speak to your lecturer. Review the chapter in the textbook. Then read. Quickly. The skill is to get the basics. Think about a sound base in the fundamentals. This is all you need at this stage to start chipping away at the block. The skill is to read fast enough to understand but not so fast as to not take it in. Enjoy it. Consider it. Think about it.

Links within the subject matter

How does your knowledge so far link with the subject matter which is being presented to you? It might seem 'alien' at the moment, but you will have moments of enlightenment and you will benefit from your preparation. Think about how the authorities relate to the overall information about the subject matter. For example, a case might fit two areas and act as authority; however it will clearly be best suited to one. Be discerning and remember – it's a matter for you to work out which one and present your case compellingly. Be bold.

Before the lecture

Ensure that you know how long the lecture is. It might sound silly, but go to the toilet beforehand – the last thing you want is your attention distracted either in the sense that your body is telling you you need to go to the toilet, or that you are waiting for a suitable moment to leave the lecture. Leaving the lecture will disrupt your thinking and you could miss the one vital piece of information which forms the basis and objective of the lecture.

You will develop an understanding of the individual lecturer styles; then if you wish perhaps it would be a good idea to speak to the lecturer beforehand to ask them what they expect and whether there is any specific reading which could assist your learning for example.

Remember the crucial focus is the substantive issues or topic which is the objective of the lecturer. The area could be outlined at the beginning – don't take notes here; just listen and think. Always keep in mind that the lecture is going to give you a sound base in the fundamentals. This will be the foundation upon which you can build your understanding and knowledge.

How do you obtain and retain enough information from the lecture then? Well, in only three ways – listening, taking notes and thinking.

Listening

Listening is a very important skill. Listening and not letting your mind wander is the ultimate goal! This means that you listen. Not just hear what is happening – but listen. If you do not listen then you cannot think. You miss the meanings and you will be unable to inform others about the lecture afterwards.

Listening assistance

Have a look at the module guide and any study materials beforehand. Start chipping away by thinking what the lecture will be about. This is the one single thing which you can do to improve your learning and retention. Just have a good old shuffle through the notes and think what it is about. Do not be a rough canvas – smooth that canvas down, prime it for the information. So tip one – have a look what the lecture is about and think about it. Use a highlighter and mark out some of the areas you think are the most important. Then, in the lecture, you can use a different coloured highlighter and see if you were correct! If not, it doesn't matter – you have the main areas for thought anyway. Playing this game will make you listen as well. So here is something you can put on your shopping list: two different coloured highlighters.

Problems in listening

Biggest Problem? Noisy friends and other students around you who are not going to do as well as you. Ditch them and get into the serious business of why you are even at in the lecture theatre. Make sure your friends know that it is important to you. You will soon find they follow suit. Do not stand for others who are disruptive with mobile phones or talking under their breath when the lecturer talks or passing notes. All of this will prevent you from listening and getting the information you need. You should ensure you have minimal distractions to maximise your ability to listen and engage and get the most out of the lecture. Never mind what they think – you will be the one with the big smile on your face when you get a great mark back from your assessments.

Also, and you might not like this, but some lecturers can be a bit 'quiet'. Therefore, *sit near the front*. Don't worry about what others think – they will soon forget about your seating preference and you will not be self-conscious at all. What you will be doing is hearing everything and listening and learning. Be attentive. View the lecture as a crucial learning experience.

Taking notes

It is clear that as well as listening you will most likely need to make some notes. The best way is to pick and choose. If you are not sure about something then make a small note in the module guide and go back to it later. If you spend time trying to write down all the lecturer's thoughts you will actually lose your way and end up not listening or taking effective notes.

The main thing is to get the key issues and concepts. Try to think about what the lecturer is saying and how he or she expresses information; you will soon find that where emphasis is placed this will be the important stuff. A good lecturer will be able to get everyone to write things down just by the use of their voice. Now, let's be honest and say that some lecturers are better than others. This means it is YOU who has to tune in and think what is important and what is not so important. Think of it like a judgment – the *ratio decidendi* is the important stuff and the *obiter dicta* the not so important. Well, just do this with lectures. Listen all the time, take down a note of the *ratio* and follow up the *obiter dicta* later.

> ### Practical Question
> Try taking notes on a news bulletin, or factual television programme. Find out what works best for you in terms of striking the balance between taking down details without losing your focus on what is actually being presented.

Style of note-taking

You know this better than anyone because it's your style. But you need to learn what is best. Try some long hand, writing it out – but ensure this does not encroach on your listening or understanding. It does have advantages because you take from the lecture all the information possible however this is only beneficial if you then sit down and extract the correct information. This would be more chipping away and indeed, 'cleaning' your notes in this way aids learning if you think about what is being transferred from 'rough to neat' form. There is a problem with this style though – you might not have understood the focus of the issues being delivered in the lecture. Think about it like this – even a child could take down a verbatim note of the lecturer's dictation – but would that child understand it? The answer is most probably no. So if you adopt this style you should only do so if you can take down the notes and THINK at the same time. Some students can do this, simply switching off to everything around them and focussing solely on the lecturers words, writing down every word and also thinking about what is being said at the same time. Try it, if it works for you then great!

However, it would be prudent to see if you can develop your own style of shorthand. It is not meant here that you learn, the Pitman or Gregg methods of shorthand! There are no doubt ways of taking notes 'faster' that you can develop yourself. A good tip is to think about words which are commonly used in lectures and making a symbol for them. For example, the word 'judge' could be a symbol such as a curly wig, or the word 'case' could quite simply be a tiny straight line. You will know what these things mean because you develop them yourselves. You can also apply this for a group of words which the lecturer says. For example, instead of writing out 'Act of Parliament' each time the lecturer says it, why not just write 'AoP' or even some symbol of which you know the meaning.

> **Practical Question**
> Search online for some common short-hand symbols for words that often come up in lectures. You might want to start using these, or developing your own.

Electronic assistance

You could think about using technology to assist you. There are clearly many different 'tools' available to you as a student from laptops to voice recorders and even smart phones. However take care – utilising such a recorder should not mean that you simply press 'record' but then do not engage with the lecture. Only use a recording device if you feel you would be better just focussing. Use the device to aid your studies, not as a replacement for listening. This piece has been talking all through about you thinking; well using a form of electronic recorder is not a substitute for thinking in the lecture. Basically if you get one then do not abuse it – just use it as a 'back up'. It's also worth keeping in mind that, increasingly, lecturers will have their lectures video recorded, and then post it up on the school VLE. If this is the case at your university, it could also be a handy back-up, or useful around revision time.

A good plan for any notes you take

Date everything
It helps because you can put the notes in order and see how the subject matter 'fits' together.

Paginate your notes
For ease of reference and if you have loose-leaf notes you can be certain how the topic has been set out before you.

Create a system

Think about putting your notes into a folder or some other kind of system. Perhaps you will lift the information from your written notes and onto your computer (make sure you back up your files!). This is all good because it requires you to think about the subject matter.

Highlight important areas

It will assist you greatly if you can easily identify cases and statutes from your notes. Indeed, some people learn by memory and you could find that you are able to 'see' these highlighted pieces of information on the paper at a later date.

Review

Go back over your notes and ensure you know what to do for the tutorial which covers the particular area.

Finally, think!

What does it mean?

> **Practical Question**
>
> Take some notes and highlight certain areas. Then read them over very quickly a couple of times and put on a shelf. Then the next day have a quick skim of the highlighted points. Later that same day, sit back and think about what you can remember.

Post-lecture reading

It is clear you must read around the area with a more focussed view after the lecture. This will help you to achieve depth of analytical thought and hone your mind to the work necessary for the tutorial. Read wider if you can, gain breadth as well as a depth of information. You could also carry out a little research which will all assist the retention and understanding. Use whichever online resource – a facility by which you can locate legal sources, such as cases, enactments or journals – your University provides and locate some journals in the area. Read these and they will help you. In fact, you will find that you start to understand more and more and in doing so you will be training your mind to all sorts of abilities.

Research trails for thinking

A research trail for these purposes means that you keep a record of the path you followed in order to arrive at the answer or conclusion to the problem posed. It is a good method of learning because it will enable you to reflect on the information you found along the way; it might also reveal something at a later date which you initially thought was less important than it actually is. Lawyers create their own research trails for this very reason. Indeed, if you go on to practice you will find that quite often it is the points which you initially thought were minor or of no or little relevance to the task in hand which actually turn out to be the most important point upon which the case turns. It could also reveal other lines of research and in doing so will enable you to show your lecturer in courseworks that you have researched the area. This will inevitably lead to higher grades! You will find that your lecturer will welcome originality.

Using a research trail will help you to study and learn the issues. You must consider how you will utilise those skills in problem solving. Creating a research trail will enable you to think and help you to formulate your answer. Again, there is flexibility in approach however a suggested guide for your research trail would be:

Question
Outline here what issues you are researching.

Thread of argument
Outline the cases and/or legislation that lead you to those conclusions.

Research trail
Detail the books/search engines used along with the search terms you used. This is a description. It should trace exactly what you did to find your answer. Include the books/search engines/methods you used, along with the words you searched under and the results of those searches. You should also include any unsuccessful lines of research and state why they were unsuccessful.

Conclusion
What is the basic answer to those questions? You should include a summary of your findings. Explain the legal arguments and case law justifying your conclusion.

Tutorials

Of course, it will be difficult if you feel like you are pushing a stone uphill and you will need to gain some feedback. Indeed, learning law is a little like jumping hurdles in a horse race; you have to jump a hurdle – for example understanding a difficult legal concept – and then you will be on the straight for a while, then you will come to another hurdle. You need to focus on the job in hand and keep 'chipping away'.

At University your best opportunity to find out how you are getting on is through performance in tutorials. This is in fact where you will have the opportunity for feedback and to test your understanding. You should read around and consider all your tutorial questions in advance and go fully prepared. Make sure that if you have been asked to do prior reading that you do it. If you have been asked to prepare answers to questions then answer them. You will be able to find the majority of information you need in relation to tutorial preparation from textbooks, however, you might have been asked to read a case or a specific statute and so if that is true then make sure you read it! This comes with a caveat; if you truly cannot prepare the tutorial fully then you should still go. Do not avoid the tutorial; you will learn something from it and so long as you do not make a constant habit of not preparing, your lecturer will no doubt understand and prefer that you showed willing and attended.

Finally, never be frightened of putting your view across. You should contribute your views in tutorials because then the lecturer will be able to reflect and consider them, engage other students in discussion and your learning will be more rounded and deeper for you.

There is no such thing as a silly question!

If you've a question, do not be afraid to ask it. The chances are other people might be thinking the same thing and even if the question is of little relevance, some discussion will come out of it which will lead you down the correct path. If you do not understand what is going on or are unfamiliar with the subject being discussed you should view this as something that needs to be addressed. It is a bit like getting a poor mark in a piece of homework. This clearly indicates that there is a gap in your understanding (of either the material or the homework question you were asked) and help you find a way to improve. In some modules your performance/attendance in tutorials or similar sessions might actually be taken into account as the basis (or part of it) of your module grade. Regardless of whether this is the case in a particular subject, your opportunity to find out how you are doing comes from your interaction in tutorials. Tutors are not there to make you feel stupid, but they will probe you to find out how far you understand and can apply the subject at hand, allowing you to tell just what you do know or do not.

Assessments

The set assignments/coursework that you are presented with in each module are terminal assessments in most cases. They are terminal for two reasons – firstly they are aimed at finding out what you have learnt at the end of a section of study. They are also terminal because it is too late to discover that you should have done more work if you get a poor mark in your assignment – only in rare circumstances will you get an opportunity of getting it right a second time. Moreover, Universities set down stringent rules relating to late submissions or excuses for poor quality of work. If your computer crashes or you have a hang over the night before the deadline watch out! You may fail your work if it is not submitted on time. Managing your time and keeping on top of your work therefore becomes of critical importance. *Procrastination is the thief of time.* Here is the single biggest tip for the general study skill necessary in this area – get it done. Now!

Preparation

Preparation is the key to success in written assignments, examination and oral presentation. It is the foundation upon which you build the rest of your 'answer'. It is the key to communication and gives you a route to your objective. You must understand all the facts – be it a problem question, a case which you have to present to the lecturer or a mooting activity. Chip away at these facts and get them clear in your mind. If you are fully conversant with all the facts you can apply the law to them or, for example, if you are asked a question in a presentation you are far less likely to be taken by surprise if you are fully aware.

No matter what the type of work is which you are being asked to present, follow these rules to achieve awareness of the factual issues:

Chronology

A time line. What happened and when did it happen? You should be fully aware of when the issues arose.

Dramatis personae
A character list. Who are the parties involved in the moot scenario? Which person is the defendant in the problem question? You should know exactly who is who.

Link
You then think about the links. Who did what and when?

Discrepancy
Look for discrepancies or other problems which do not quite seem to 'ring true'. This will help you especially if you are being asked to consider possible defences or to advise someone as to their liability.

Application
Lawyers problem solve. That's it. In order to do so they apply the law to the facts and the facts to the law. Following this mantra is the key to success. It does not matter whether it is an exam question, a written piece of coursework or a presentation – simply apply the law to the facts and you have the basis for an excellent answer or response.

Content and structure of answers

You will have seen a pattern emerging that it does not matter what you are being asked to do – assignment problem question or essay question, examination, moot, presentation – because the content and structure are all extremely similar. Save for a little alteration here and there, a general study skill is to address everything in the following manner:

Coverage of legal issues
Ensure that you identify the issues – look for all relevant possibilities of law and decide which are the most fundamental. You can brainstorm the piece – simply take some paper and a pen and do a spider diagram about which areas you think the question is about. If you do this in an exam you can mark it as 'rough work' and put a line through it at the end, however think about the 'human element' of the lecturer – they will see it and it will have the effect of making them realise you are creating a foundation. It could even contain some information which was relevant however you did not deal with it in the question.

Relevance of law
Now take the notes from your lectures, files, text books, primary sources and everything else and take time to work through them and see which are really relevant areas. Keep an open mind and allow the issues to float freely. Bring your 'best' points to the front and 'rubbish the bad'. A pattern will emerge of the issues to be discussed.

Correct and appropriate use of authority
Remember – 'it doesn't matter what you say as long as you support it with authority'. *Apply the law to the facts and the facts to the law.*

Emphasis
Tell the 'marker' that some areas are more important than others however they all go together to make the whole. Do not spend time on irrelevant material however try to deliver a 'full' piece which is informative and understanding.

Structure: introduction, development of argument, conclusion

Set out the piece correctly. It is important for the 'marker' to be able to follow your points. If you 'jump' around the issues it will become disjointed and lack of clarity will obscure your answer. Stay focused.

Basic assignment techniques

You must use footnotes to cite your authorities – for example, this may be a case, Act of Parliament, judge's dicta. Also use footnotes to reference another text or journal, provide information not strictly relevant yet of academic interest and refer the reader to footnotes previously used in the assignment.

Focus on the question

Always ask yourself if you have identified what the question calls for and then, on completion of your assignment, again ask yourself if you have really answered it. Those in lower bracket will not "hit" the essential requirements of the answer.

Example

Consider the following question: What is a contract? Why do people enter into contracts?

The question is *not* asking you to explain the rules about the formation of a contract. Rather, it asks you to identify the central characteristics of a contract – that it is based on *agreement*, that it is a *bargain*, and that it may be made in writing or orally. You must start with a definition then identify those central characteristics. You can use the rules on formation once you've defined the central characteristics, but you should not launch into a mere description of the rules of formation and the relevant case law.

The second part of the question requires a basic understanding of modern commerce and some common-sense observations about why contracts are concluded. It does not require you to explain the rules of contract. Instead, it asks you to think about why people arrange their affairs via contracts and to appreciate what qualities a contract has and what purposes it achieves. Again, using your knowledge of the law can help your answer (e.g. contracts formalise agreements, provide evidence of agreement etc.) but simply stating the law does not answer *why* people enter into contracts.

Structure is important

Do not simply "throw" the piece on the paper. Try to begin with an introduction, then the main body of the piece and then a conclusion. You may wish to title them in the piece so the reader is aware of what you are saying. A good piece of advice is that once you've worked out your line of argument you say what you're going to say (introduction); say it (main body); then say what you've said (conclusion).

You must support any points you make with proper authority

Usually this means either case law, statute law or an academic journal. A textbook is not authority for the point you make unless it is citing from a source of authority. It is no good making a statement and then putting "Elliott and Quinn" in the footnotes. If you wish to use a piece of text in the assignment this is acceptable – but you must acknowledge the author and give the page number of the book in which the text appears. Try not to do this very much – it can mislead the reader into thinking you have merely lifted text from a book and that you personally do not understand what you are saying. Furthermore – use journals! Try to bring academic depth to the points you make. Offer comparisons; find writers who disagree. Look for competing authorities.

When using a case you must cite it fully

Do not simply put, for example: R v Clarke (1972). You must put: *R v Clarke* [1972] 1 All ER 219. This must appear in a footnote at the bottom of the page. The case name must appear in the text in italics. When using a statute you must put the year in which it was enacted!

It is important to include the following at the end of the piece: table of cases; table of statutes; and bibliography

The bibliography must contain the title of any books you use, the author, the edition, the year it was published, the place it was published and which company published it. This seems pedantic but it is typical of academic work.

Do not write in the first person

Never say, for example, "I think" or "It is my opinion" or "I propose this" and so on. You must write in the third person, for example "It is submitted that . . .", "The following proposition may be drawn". Get used to writing in this academic manner and find new ways of starting sentences and addressing the subject matter – but don't get too flowery!

Address each point you make fully and finally. Do not "jump about" within the piece

Some people deal with an area in one paragraph, leave it, and then finish it later. This is only acceptable if the way you are presenting the piece allows for it – otherwise the piece is not fluent and seems "disjointed".

Every word matters

Think: does what you are saying make sense? Be careful not to make bold, broad statements without also stating why it is that such a statement can be made. One word can alter the entire meaning of your piece.

The conclusion is paramount

You should have this more or less in your mind before you start the piece. This is the statement of your answer to the question at hand and it is often a good idea to make sure you have this firmly in your mind all the while that you're addressing the question, and that you build the piece to it. This will help provide structure and coherence to the main body of your argument/answer. Do not "fizzle" at the end. You should aim for a sustainable conclusion which is supported by everything that has gone before it.

Try not to simply present lists

It is academically unsound and again illustrates a lack of understanding. Far better to take two or three points from your list and address these fully, critically analyse, evaluate or discuss them – higher marks are obtained by showing an understanding of the issues involved.

You must not exceed the word limit

Brevity is the essence of wisdom.

Oral Assessment

Assessment comes in a variety of forms at different Universities, ranging from keeping a reflective diary, through writing papers, to oral presentations and simulated courtroom argument. Law is about a variety of forms of communication. Some of you may not wish to be a courtroom lawyer or even a lawyer at all. However, communication skills are essential in any walk of life so that at some level you will need to engage in verbal as well as written presentation. Do not be worried if you suffer from stage fright. The key is to talk and respond naturally and here is how:

- If you have some oral assessments – *do not worry!*
- Use your natural body reaction – we are designed to deal with fear.
- Take a few deep breaths – this will ensure you have oxygen in your brain ready for the off!
- "Meter" your first line.
- Just deliver it 'nice and steady' and you will soon find you are talking naturally.
- Do not worry about what people think. They will be concentrating on the issues, not whether you have fluffed something. You will soon forget all about them.
- Preparation is the key. Failing to prepare is preparing to fail.
- Never be afraid to take a moment to pause and compose yourself, if needs be.
- Know your case.
- Stick to a clear, logical structure – clarity is everything. Make sure you don't "jump about".
- Ensure you make regular eye contact – engage with your assessor. It is important to act naturally.
- Make sure you speak clearly and audibly.
- Listen!
- Respond naturally – script is almost useless because it hampers good advocacy by imposing restrictions and not permitting you to be flexible and responsive to the context of the assessment.
- Work through the problem you are posed.
- Think of it like a legal conversation. Do not be artificial.
- If you are fully aware of all issues you will be confident and far less likely to be taken by surprise. Prepare fully and know it like the back of your hand.

Reflections on Yourself as a Learner

A SWOT analysis stands for Strengths, Weaknesses, Opportunities and Threats.

Many businesses use the SWOT analysis as a means of finding out where they are and what they need to do. It is a good way of identifying positive and negative points about yourself and the situation you are in. As a law student you will need to think about what you, as a learner, and your University, as a learning environment, can do to build upon your existing strengths and what you need to do to get yourself acclimatised.

In filling out the sections of the table you will be able to identify yourself; then you should come back to it after a few weeks of study at your University and reflect upon your answers to see where you have improved; you will be very surprised as you will have no doubt come on leaps and bounds.

SWOT	What do you feel are your STRENGTHS that will help you in your law studies?	What do you feel are your WEAKNESSES that might hinder you?	What OPPORTUNITY is there for you in studying law?	What THREATS are posed by studying law? You could see these as 'difficulties'.
Your previous learning background				
Your existing skills and those that you wish to develop				
Your study techniques				
Your interest/ knowledge of law and legal issues				
Your time-management and time constraints				
Your expectations of study				
Your long term career aspirations				

5 Mooting

Per Laleng

Background to Mooting

What is it and why do it?

The non-lawyer is likely to come across the word 'moot' in the context of the expression "a moot point". A point is 'moot' if it is undecided, open to argument or debate. Sometimes, a point is moot if it is no longer practically applicable or relevant. Those pointers provide clues as to what mooting is all about. The activity of mooting involves arguing moot points of law in a simulated courtroom setting ('the Moot Court') using hypothetical facts often based on a factual scenario that is a variant on a leading case. The points of law are arguable and may not be of practical relevance even if the activity of mooting has a very strong practical dimension quite simply because it involves the practice of public speaking. More often than not, the Moot Court operates at appellate level (Court of Appeal or Supreme Court[1]). There are at least two reasons for this: first, it distinguishes a moot from a mock trial; and second, it allows for a sharper focus on the law, its interpretation and application to a set of facts.

Although there is often law involved in a mock trial, the objective of a mock trial is to establish contentious facts whereas a moot concentrates on contentious law. A mock trial seeks to test evidence in order to establish the facts. The procedure is conducted by way of examination, cross-examination and re-examination of witnesses on their own evidence cross-referred, where appropriate, to other evidence. In testing that evidence, the object of the exercise is in essence to be able to tell a story that is relevant to why someone is in court. There may well be legal arguments about what sort of evidence is admissible, or submissions about what sort of inferences can be drawn from facts that can be proved with the available evidence, but the primary focus remains on establishing the facts.

---

[1] Although the House of Lords only ceased to function as the court of last resort in the United Kingdom on 31 July 2009 and was replaced by the Supreme Court on 1 October 2009 (pursuant to the Constitutional Reform Act 2005), references to the Supreme Court should be read so as to include the House of Lords depending on the context. Note that it is the Supreme Court of the United Kingdom to include Northern Ireland and Scotland. The expression 'Law Lords' should also be read as references to Justices of the Supreme Court where the context so requires.

In a moot, the facts are given. Ordinarily, there will be little, if any, scope to challenge the facts in a moot scenario. This is consistent with the general rule against challenging facts in an appeal. The main focus is therefore on the law relevant to those facts. Because the context is usually an appeal, the Appellant is invariably arguing that the judge(s) below reached the wrong decision because they misunderstood the law or misapplied it to the facts. Conversely, the Respondent is arguing that the lower court was correct. The role of the mooter, just as it is for a practising advocate, is to explain persuasively why – as a matter of law – the lower court was wrong or right as the case may be. Unlike an argument down the pub or with your friends, a moot is a dialogue with the judges where mooters try to adopt the mannerisms and forms of speech used in a real courtroom. One aim of mooting, therefore, is to adopt the "conventions and traditions of courtroom speaking"[2] which should "reflect as closely as possible the form and substance of the legal arguments in a real court."[3] In turn, the Moot Court also attempts to reflect the set-up of a real courtroom subject to resource constraints as well as its own rules. There will be a 'Bench' where the judge or judges sit and a 'Bar' for the advocates or Counsel (hence 'barrister'). For obvious reasons, the Bench and Bar in a Moot Court are usually plain ordinary tables and chairs facing each other. From the perspective of the Bench, the Appellants sit to the left and the Respondents to the right with each 'Leader' sitting closest to each other. Commonly, there are two teams of two Counsel: on the one hand, the Lead and Junior Appellants and, on the other, the Lead and Junior Respondents. An adventurous Moot Court might also have a mooter acting as amicus curiae (a 'Friend of the Court') whose role is "to assist the court on specialist questions of law, or to alert the court as to the public policy implications of the possible outcomes in a case. The amicus curiae does not represent the adversarial interests of either party."[4] Unlike in a real court, there is no dedicated space for a jury or the press, and no-one acts as a solicitor. There is no court clerk, although there is usually a mooting officer or equivalent. That officer will act as timekeeper, may announce the case and bring the judges into the courtroom. Sometimes they may act as the video recorder operator as well.[5] A Director and/or Master/Mistress of Moots should ideally oversee all moots in order to maintain a degree of consistency between moots.

Historically, mooting was the preserve of the Inns of Court who used mooting as a way of educating aspiring barristers in the conventions, etiquette and stylised argumentation of the courtroom. The Inns continue to offer mooting, but increasing numbers of law schools now include mooting as an integral curricular or extra-curricular part of the law degree. There is also a burgeoning number of 'external' mooting competitions where institutions compete against each other.[6] Despite the occasional arguable claim that mooting contributes to the indoctrination of lawyers, there are intrinsic educational values to mooting. Like clinical work, mooting requires focused and dedicated research,[7] as well as entailing reliance on and development of a whole raft of skills from the interpersonal through to the more intellectual: an ability to communicate effectively, analytical and interpretative techniques, argument-construction, the capacity to distil information and to anticipate issues that may arise, time-management and self-organisation, teamwork and teambuilding. For an advocate, however, one of the most important qualities is the ability to 'think on your feet' in order to persuade, and mooting is an ideal means by which

---

[2] J. Hill, *A Practical Guide to Mooting* (Palgrave Macmillan, 2009) p.6
[3] J. Snape & G. Watt *The Cavendish Guide to Mooting* (Cavendish, 1997) p.2
[4] *ibid* p.21
[5] With the current exception of the Supreme Court, in a real courtroom, videos and cameras have to date not been permitted to record any of the proceedings. The reason for allowing it in a Moot Court is to provide feedback.
[6] A list of some available competitions can be found at http://learnmore.lawbore.net/index.php/Category:Mooting.
[7] See question 32 in *Cavendish guide to Mooting* on how to use a law library effectively for mooting purposes.

to practice this art.[8] Mooting is undoubtedly a confidence builder. Finally, and from an instrumentalist point of view, participating in mooting is good for the CV as it indicates a willingness to work hard and of being prepared to develop that habit.

Mooting: Elements of the Moot

The moot problem

On receipt of the moot problem, read it carefully. It is not a document to be skimmed. This tells you many things quite apart from the identity of the parties. It may seem obvious, but start with the facts. Be completely on top of the chronology of events and the role of any parties within that chronology (what they witnessed, did, said or omitted to do at a particular moment in time). Time lines are very useful in this regard and it is advisable to get into the habit of using them routinely. A time line is literally a line along the plane of time punctuated by events (including hypothetical events). To get an efficient overview of a case it is useful to use one time line per person, and if appropriate for any counter-factual[9] scenarios (for example, an expert suggesting an alternative outcome in a clinical negligence case). This way you get a number of lines, one above the other, which allows you to 'compare stories'. The level of sophistication is entirely up to you. This system will not only provide a useful overview of the whole case but is invariably helpful as an *aide-memoire* at any stage of the mooting process, including your research, as it may focus your attention on particular strengths or weaknesses of the case. It cannot be stressed enough how important it is not to lose sight of the facts as the outcome of many cases often turns on some fact unique to that case.

Then proceed to consider the procedural history of the fictitious case you are given. This is also important as it represents the start of the legal analysis. Which court is being appealed from? What is the status of the judge(s) whose judgment is being appealed? Is the judgment unanimous or in the majority if more than one judge? What is the route of appeal? What level is the Moot Court appealed to and so forth? If, for instance, the moot problem is in the field of criminal law, in particular an appeal against conviction, the underlying basis of the appeal will usually be that the conviction was 'unsafe'. If the moot problem relates to civil law, the bases of the appeal will be set out in the Grounds of Appeal. If any cases are referred to in the judgment or Grounds of Appeal, think about their status and relevance in general terms to the level of the Moot Court and so forth.

The Grounds of Appeal

The Grounds of Appeal set the limits to the legal discussion required by the Moot Court. It should be noted that the Grounds of Appeal are the only points of law that you are required to address. Even if you

---

[8] For a practising advocate, one of the most important qualities is the ability to represent another. In the context of a Moot, this quality is less significant as there is usually no real client.
[9] Something that did not happen, but could have done – it usually takes the shape of a "what if?"

would have drafted different Grounds of Appeal on the facts before you, you are stuck with the Grounds you have been given. There are at least two good reasons for this: first, and most significantly, although the legal system in this country is adversarial[10] in nature, it is also underpinned by a core value, namely that of Notice: in principle everyone is entitled to know the case against them in advance. The Grounds of Appeal give notice of that case in advance. Unlike in popular film or television dramas, in the real or moot courtroom worlds, advocates are not permitted to 'pull a rabbit out of a hat'. This would be unethical. So (on the assumption that you are properly prepared), if you find yourself surprised by an argument or a point made against you, it is quite possible that it falls outside the Grounds of Appeal and it would be legitimate to comment that you have not had adequate notice of that point. In the real world, this might lead to an adjournment of the hearing at the other side's expense whether it relates to a legal argument or more usually, late disclosure of evidence. The second reason is more practical. It is of course entirely possible for you to find yourself stuck with someone else's Grounds of Appeal in the real world too. For instance, you may one day pick up a 'return'[11] from a colleague who drafted the Grounds of Appeal but who cannot for a variety of reasons do the case herself. Thus, the Moot Court practice instils a practical discipline in this particular art of dealing with Grounds of Appeal drafted by someone else.

In short, the Grounds of Appeal delimit the area of legal doubt. It is worth bearing this important point in mind at all times: even if one side's case looks stronger than another's, the fact remains that there would ordinarily be no appeal in the first place if there was no area of doubt. It is the doubt that makes a point moot, or a matter for debate. And it is this area of doubt to which your submissions need to be directed.

A submission

A submission is an argument or a series of arguments explaining why your interpretation of the law is correct and why the appeal should be allowed or not as the case may be. Those arguments in turn usually have to be based on the law. The core submission(s) should be capable of being distilled into a relatively short proposition or statement that explains why the court below was either wrong or right. That short proposition will then have to be 'unpacked' by way of argument based on analysis of the relevant law. It is through research and analysis of the relevant law that you can build up the argument supporting your submission. Generally speaking and as a minimum, you need to use cases (or statutory material, if appropriate) as pegs on which to hang your argument – and to do that successfully, you will need to read the primary material, such as cases, to see whether they say what you (or the judges) think they say.

The reason why cases in particular are so important in English law is because of the doctrine of precedent or *stare decisis*. Loosely, this means 'to stand by things decided'. Thus if there is a case that decides the law in relation to a particular set of facts then that case would be binding. However, that basic proposition is subject to two significant qualifications: first, the level of the court deciding that case will determine *how* binding the decision is; second, even if the decision has been made by the same or a higher court, there may be an argument about *what* is binding bearing in mind that only the *ratio decidendi* of a decision can in principle bind. Let's take the two points in turn:

---

[10] As opposed to investigative or inquisitorial. An investigative system aims to discover the truth of a matter whereas an adversarial system is less concerned with the truth and more with winning. However, that goal can only be pursued within acceptable limits. A significant limitation is the requirement to act ethically at all times albeit with a sporting spirit.
[11] A case is 'returned' to another barrister if the original barrister cannot do it.

The level of the court

As noted above, the level of court in which a decision was reached usually determines how binding an earlier decision is. When faced with a decision which is apparently binding, the mooter has two realistic choices: either invite the court to overrule that decision or in the alternative, to distinguish it.

Overruling

Terminology is important here. 'Overruling' is to be differentiated from 'reversing'. A higher court will reverse a decision of the previous lower court in the *same* case if it decides that the lower court was wrong. Overruling happens when a higher court decides that a *different* case was wrongly decided. In this latter scenario, the first decision remains binding on the original parties, but not on the parties in the later or instant case. However, a lower court cannot overrule a higher court's decision and generally speaking the Court of Appeal cannot overrule itself whereas the Supreme Court can, if it chooses to do so, pursuant to the Practice Statement of 1966.[12]

The Supreme Court (formerly the Judicial Committee of the House of Lords) is the highest domestic court and the Practice Statement is often overlooked in the context of mooting. Whether this is due to lack of knowledge or confidence is unclear, but it should not be forgotten. The Practice Statement allows the Supreme Court to depart from an earlier Supreme Court decision "when it appears right to do so". That said, it should also be noted that the Practice Statement has generally been interpreted conservatively. In other words, the tendency has been for the Supreme Court not to depart from its previous decisions.[13] There is a two-stage test set out by Lord Scarman in *R v Secretary of State for the Home Department, ex parte Khawaja*.[14] The Supreme Court must be satisfied that "adherence to the precedent would involve the risk of injustice and[15] the proper development of the law" and secondly, that "judicial departure by the House from the precedent is the safe and appropriate way of remedying the injustice and developing the law." Thus, the concern is not only with the individual justice of the particular case as well as the development of the law in general but there is also the explicit suggestion that legislation should always be considered as an alternative means of remedying the apparent injustice caused by an earlier precedent. This links to the first part of the test, in particular its concern with maintaining certainty in law and will be a matter at the forefront of the Supreme Court's mind especially if a recent precedent is being challenged.

It is arguable that the Practice Statement may have become more significant with the advent of the human rights era heralded by the Human Rights Act 1998 and may become even more so with the arrival of the Supreme Court. All law, whether in the form of legislation or case law, has to be consistent with the European Convention on Human Rights. This opens up the possibility of arguing that earlier Supreme Court authority is inconsistent with the Convention and should be overruled. Similarly, there may be European Court of Justice ('ECJ') or European Court of Human Rights ('ECtHR') authority on a point in European Law which would bind the Supreme Court despite, perhaps ironically, the fact that neither the ECJ nor ECtHR are bound by their previous decisions. The newly constituted Supreme Court may be

---

[12] [1966] 3 All ER 77
[13] See for example, *Rees v Darlington Memorial Hospital NHS Trust* [2003] UKHL 52
[14] [1984] AC 74 at 106
[15] Arguably, the use of this word 'and' makes it a three stage test of sorts.

more 'independent' of the legislature than the House of Lords arguably was, and it may be more open to 'law-making' than its predecessor.

Other methods for arguing that the Supreme Court should depart from its previous decisions include finding inconsistent decisions from higher courts in the Commonwealth. Such decisions would only be persuasive, but that is the very art of advocacy. Or, an argument could be mounted to the effect that an older decision no longer befits modern conditions. A final alternative, to be noted in passing, is that it is also possible for the Supreme Court (or indeed the Court of Appeal) to depart from an earlier decision if the earlier decision was reached *per incuriam*. This means where the earlier decision was reached having overlooked an even earlier line of binding authority. The chances of this happening in the Supreme Court are pretty remote but much more likely in the Court of Appeal.

All of the foregoing methods involve asking the Supreme Court to depart from or overrule its previous decisions. This is to be differentiated from asking this or lower courts to *distinguish* its previous decisions. When distinguishing an earlier decision, the earlier decision remains binding on the original and indeed future parties on the same facts, but the argument is that the earlier decision is sufficiently different from the case before the court this time for the earlier decision not to be binding. We will return to distinguishing later.

You may have noted from the foregoing that there are a number of ways of persuading a Moot Court Supreme Court (as indeed the real Supreme Court) to depart from its previous decisions. The reasons proffered to justify such a departure are often grounded in policy arguments. For instance, the argument that an old authority does not suit modern conditions is at root a social policy argument. Arguments based on policy are always likely to figure at the forefront of any Moot Court problem set in the Supreme Court. Not only is this because the Supreme Court can 'ignore' its own decisions, but also because one of the criteria for permitting an appeal to the Supreme Court in the first place is that the case raises an issue of "public importance".[16]

It is worth considering briefly what is meant by 'policy' in this context. If one leaves aside the argument that all law is inherently political, policy is conventionally thought of as the self-consciously 'political' element of law. It has been suggested[17] that most policy-based arguments in the Supreme Court can be broken down into five types. One is ethical whereas the other four are non-ethical or goal-oriented.[18] The ethical policy argument is grounded in notions of fairness: broadly speaking, similar situations should be treated in a similar way. This is very much a Common Law (as opposed to Equitable) approach to fairness and is motivated by consistency. The alternative way of looking at fairness is to consider the fairness between the parties irrespective of prior law. This is a more Equitable approach to fairness, and is more likely to occur in the context of cases that have Equity-related features implicated in them. Non-ethical concerns may be constitutional ('the outcome should be for parliament rather than the Judiciary'), administrative ('the outcome may or may not be practical', "floodgates"), social ('what does society demand the outcome should be?') or based on economic analysis ('what is the efficient allocation

---

[16] Other grounds include the argument that the case is of great importance, due to its severity, complexity or level of money involved.
[17] J. Bell *Policy Arguments in Judicial Decisions* (Clarendon Press, 1983) and see J. Snape & G. Watt *The Cavendish Guide to Mooting* (London: Cavendish, 1997) p.119.
[18] J. Snape *ibid* pp.121–3.

of resources?'). Arguments raised by the Appellant or Respondent may therefore be a combination of these types of argument.

Thus, for instance, the Appellant may submit (irrespective of whether there is authority on the point in the Supreme Court) that law is not static but must adapt to changing social conditions, justice must be done to the parties in the case (an equitable approach), a change in the law will not automatically lead to uncertainty as the instant case is a 'qualification' and in any case, certainty in the law has differential requirements depending on the area of law concerned (for example, business requires commercial contractual law to be predictable whereas an individual risking loss of liberty due to an anachronistic rule of criminal law might legitimately expect the highest court of the land to be able to revisit the decisions in a particular area of criminal law); and finally, judges are in a position to judge social opinion given that they have as much access to the media, for example, as anyone else.[19]

As against these points, a Respondent might contend that it is for judges to declare and apply the law, not to create it; they can only pronounce on the arguments of the parties and if they should stray too far into the realms of 'law-making' then they risk parliament taking away the very limited powers they already have;[20] litigation is an unsuitable vehicle for making changes in the law and such changes will in any case militate against certainty (see the parallels with *Khawaja* here). Judges are there to do justice according to the law – not the parties – and can only use the evidence before the court. Clearly, these arguments are only illustrative and do not cover all the types of policy arguments mentioned earlier. Interestingly, in some ways the two positions seem to pit the 'liberal progressive' against the 'conservative'; and it is worth remembering in this context that just because the Supreme Court can overrule itself, it tends not to, preferring instead to maintain a degree (or illusion?) of consistency. It is therefore an inherently conservative institution.

Policy arguments may also have some relevance in the Court of Appeal, but some care must be taken because, as noted above, the Court of Appeal cannot in general overrule its earlier decisions. In the Court of Appeal, therefore, the starting point is to establish that the moot problem falls within either *Young v Bristol Aeroplane Co Ltd*[21] (civil) or *R v Taylor*[22] (crime). It is only if a case falls within the parameters of those two cases that the Court is at liberty to depart from an earlier binding authority. *Young* provides that the Court of Appeal can depart from a previous decision it has reached if:

1. there are two conflicting authorities on a point. If so, it can choose which one to follow; or if

2. one of its own earlier decisions conflicts with a later Supreme Court authority which does not expressly overrule the earlier Court of Appeal decision; or if

3. a Court of Appeal decision was reached *per incuriam* (i.e. without having taken into account the authority or law it should have done). If a decision was reached *per incuriam*, it is said that the chain of authority is 'broken'.[23]

---

[19] A common technique here, particularly where there is no evidence before the court one way or the other, is to ask the judges to "take *judicial notice*" of something that is implied to be 'common knowledge'. Granted, this is more likely to happen at first instance rather than in the Supreme Court, but there is nothing precluding this course of action if you feel sufficiently confident that something is common knowledge.
[20] There is a strong argument to the effect that the risk of this has now dissipated somewhat with the creation of a much more independent Supreme Court.
[21] [1944] 1 KB 718
[22] [1950] 2 KB 368
[23] J. Hill, *A Practical Guide to Mooting* (Palgrave Macmillan, 2009) p.40

If a Moot Court problem cannot get around an apparently binding authority on any of these bases in a civil law context, then the earlier authority is binding unless it can be distinguished.[24]

In the criminal context, the same exceptions apply but there is a little further latitude open to the Court of Appeal hearing a criminal appeal because it "may decline to follow one of it's previous decisions where to do so [i.e. to follow such a decision] would result in an injustice to an appellant" (*R v Taylor*). The reason why there is this relaxation in the criminal context is because criminal law can deprive Appellants of their liberty; and liberty is seen as a fundamental value in English law. In both the civil and criminal contexts, the reason why there are restrictions on the ability of the Court of Appeal to overrule itself is to prevent the fragmentation of law (i.e., again, to promote certainty). Thus, it is not enough to show that an earlier decision is demonstrably wrong even if this would help a submission where the *Young* and/or *Taylor* exceptions might apply.

The High Court is free to ignore decisions made by a differently constituted High Court. It follows that it is important to consider both the level of the Moot Court and the level of the court in the apparently binding decision. If a Moot Court is set in the Court of Appeal, therefore, it would be a poor strategy to argue that the lower court should have considered itself bound by another High Court decision. Such a decision would be, at best, persuasive. It is also worth noting in passing that decisions of the Privy Council are only persuasive, albeit 'much more' persuasive than any other court in the domestic hierarchy because the personnel who sit in the Privy Council are generally the same as those of the Supreme Court.

Distinguishing

If it is not possible to persuade a court that it should overrule an earlier decision then the alternative is to attempt to persuade the court that an earlier decision is not binding on the case currently before it. An earlier case can be distinguished from the instant case either on the facts ('the facts of the other case are materially different from the instant case') or as a matter of law ('the point of law in the precedent is not applicable in the instant case'). Both are ways of arguing that the *ratio decidendi* of the earlier case is not binding on the instant case. In either case, don't be afraid of being audacious! But in order to distinguish any case, you need to have an understanding of what the earlier cases says, in particular in its *ratio decidendi*.

The *ratio decidendi* of a decision

There is no universally accepted definition of a *ratio decidendi*. Broadly speaking, it can be thought of as "the rule of law contained in [a] decision that can survive from a case long after the original parties are dead and buried."[25] The *ratio* encompasses the reasons given for a particular decision or for coming to the conclusion of law in a case. It is therefore a matrix of the material facts, the law relevant to those facts and most significantly, the reasons given for the application of that law to those facts. But bear in mind that a true *ratio* cannot really be known until it is confirmed as such in a subsequent case. The *ratio* is, therefore, in a very real sense, open to argument.

---

[24] It is also worth noting in passing the case of *R (Khadim) v Brent LBC House Benefit Review Board* [2001] QB 955 where Buxton LJ held that a court is not bound by a proposition of law which an earlier court assumed to be correct without argument.

[25] J. Hill, *A Practical Guide to Mooting* (Palgrave Macmillan, 2009) p.44.

A. *'Material'* facts ('distinguishing on the facts')

The italicised word 'material' needs a little care. In law, that word is a term of art meaning 'legally relevant'. It may be a fact in a case that someone is 18 or lives in Leytonstone, but such facts are very rarely material to the decision. Of greater relevance might be what that person was doing in Leytonstone on the eve of their 18th birthday. Extracting the material facts of an earlier legal authority as well as of your case is therefore an important analytical function because it may well become a fruitful way of distinguishing (or differentiating) your case from an apparently binding legal authority. If it is remembered that the combinations and permutations of life are infinitely variable, then the value of the process of distinguishing becomes concrete. On the other hand, as noted above, an oft-expressed policy aim of the law is certainty: that like cases should be treated alike and people should be able to expect the law today to govern disputes that arise today. That word material becomes relevant in this context too because a court may take the view that the alleged differences between two cases are not as material as claimed and that an apparently binding authority should not therefore be distinguished. If the process of distinguishing could be deployed on the basis of the slightest factual difference, there would be no system of law at all. In other words, it is not always enough to simply state that one case involved doctors, for example, whereas the other involved lawyers because on the next level of abstraction, both are professions, and that could be enough to dissuade a court from distinguishing between two cases. The key, therefore, is to identify factual differences that matter, and the job of the advocate is to persuade the court *why* those factual differences matter. So to use the doctor/lawyer example, yes they may both be professionals but one usually gives advice and the other (depending on the facts) offers treatment. It is this process of identifying material differences in the facts that may permit distinguishing cases on the facts.

B. The *ratio* ('distinguishing on the law')

Just as there is no definitive definition of what a *ratio* (in a general sense) is, there may even be doubt over what the *ratio* of a specific case might be. After all, a *ratio* is only one (or more) person's interpretation of what a particular *ratio* of a case is. Contrary to popular perception, rather than being black & white, law is more often than not monochrome: it has different shades of grey and only in some cases is a rule hardened into the darkest black or pure brilliant white. This observation should not lead to despair, painting as it does a picture that is at the mercy of relativistic interpretation; rather it ought to lead to the realisation that through analysis and creativity, the law is subject to argument and change.

When distinguishing a case on the law, the task is to attempt to 'cut down' the ambit of the *ratio* by arguing that judges in the original (or a later case that applied it) formulated the *ratio* too widely, for example, by failing to take into account of a factor that should have been taken into account or by placing undue weight on other factors. In this way, the advocate does not ask the court to overrule an earlier decision; rather she asks the court to refine it. It almost goes without saying that this is more difficult than distinguishing a case on the facts and it requires courage and creativity to go down this route.

The *ratio* is conventionally compared with the *obiter dicta*, those comments which are made 'by the way' or not in response to the material facts in a particular case. For example, comments made in response to hypothetical facts raised by a judge in a case[26] or comments made on issues that are not

---

[26] See for example Lord Rodger in *Corr v IBC Vehicles* [2008] UKHL 13 who gives the example of someone jumping off a car park and killing someone at the bottom by landing on them when discussing a case where the deceased jumped off a car park but did not kill anyone apart from himself.

directly relevant in a case. Alternatively, *obiter* comments can be those that are made in response to material facts, but where the comments are made by a dissenting judge or a judge who reaches the same conclusion as the majority, but who gives different reasons from the majority (see for example, the various judgments in *Smith v Littlewoods*.[27] For another example consider the comments of Lord Atkin in *Donoghue v Stevenson*[28] which have latterly become the basis for a duty of care in the law of negligence. The narrow *ratio* in that case is that a manufacturer owes a duty of care to the ultimate consumer whereas his question "who, then, in law is my neighbour?" is strictly speaking *obiter*, albeit *obiter* comments which have become fundamental in later cases). But just because comments are *obiter* and therefore not binding does not mean that they should be discarded or ignored because they may remain persuasive. The case of *Donoghue* itself is ample authority for this proposition. Provided that such *obiter* comments do not run contrary to a clear and binding *ratio* which otherwise cannot be avoided, then there is no reason they cannot be used in the advocate's quest to persuade the Bench that her submission should be accepted.

Challenging the facts . . .

A final word of warning: just as a mooter is stuck with the Grounds of Appeal, it must also be emphasised that you are usually stuck with the facts. It will also be extremely rare in a mooting context (as indeed it is in the real world) that a mooter will be permitted to put forward new evidence that was not used at the original trial and it follows that it is usually a waste of time to research matters that go to the facts rather than the law (unless it is done simply to enrich your personal knowledge). Questions of fact are therefore rarely subject to appeal whether in a Moot Court or in real life. That said, there might occasionally be questions of mixed fact and law that may allow for limited challenges. For example, some facts may be a "question of degree". If so, this is a question of fact but may be open to challenge if no reasonable judge could have reached the conclusion in fact reached. Similarly, the issue of whether someone has attained a particular standard (for example, whether a party has been negligent) is also strictly speaking a question of fact; but again, this becomes appealable if no reasonable judge could have reached the conclusion reached by the judge who is being appealed or because the judge has adopted the wrong standard against which the facts are judged. If a judge makes a finding of primary fact when there is simply no evidence available to support that finding (although this is unlikely to be the case in a moot because you won't have all the original trial material in order to form a judgement about this), that then becomes a question of law ("was there evidence available to the judge to make that finding?"). Furthermore, inferences can be drawn from primary facts. Again, such inferences are still factual findings, but a judge can be challenged if, for example, he misdirected himself or if the inference was one which could not legally/reasonably be drawn. Finally, the meaning of words is also a question of fact.

---

[27] [1987] 2 WLR 480
[28] [1932] AC 562

Mooting: Preparation

Preparing for the moot

On receipt of the moot problem, there are a number of things that can be done before starting your research. What follows is by no means an exhaustive check list:

1. Read the problem slowly and don't panic!

2. Identify whether you are acting for the Appellant or the Respondent and then read the problem again from both perspectives;

3. Note the jurisdiction and route of appeal that the case has taken – different considerations will apply depending on whether you are in the Court of Appeal or the Supreme Court; or whether it is a civil or criminal case;

4. Draw time lines of the chronology of events (giving particular thought to apparent 'gaps' in that chronology. The gaps may not be true gaps or they may provide clues as to where the battle lines will eventually be drawn);

5. Start thinking about which facts are material (i.e. legally relevant);

6. Formulate the lower court's decision on those facts *in your own words* – you need to be able to discuss the moot problem fluently, and it is often a good idea to 'translate' the problem and the decision into language with which you are more familiar before reverting to the more stylised language of law;

7. Consider the Grounds of Appeal (what is it that the Appellant is asking the Moot Court to do and on what grounds). Mooters often lose sight of what it is that they are asking the Moot Court *to do* (allow or dismiss the appeal) or the central reasons why (usually, it is a variant of 'the lower court got the law wrong because . . .');

8. Decide who is to act as Leader and Junior. In the context of a moot, there are no real advantages or disadvantages in being one or the other;

9. Make a note of any cases referred to as you will later need to consider whether they say what the court (or one of the parties) thinks they say;

10. Before starting any research, it is worth spending a bit of time thinking about possible arguments for or against any of the propositions made in the Grounds of Appeal – even if those arguments do not seem very 'legalistic' at this stage. Your research may reveal cases that support your 'gut reaction' in due course;

11. Once you start getting a sense of what the moot is about then you start your research.

12. Very occasionally, you may feel that there is something about the facts or indeed the moot problem that just 'doesn't work'. This could be a function of bad drafting although it could also be a function of the way you are thinking about the problem. Don't be afraid to discuss this with the moot organiser or the drafter of the problem, although you should discuss this with your fellow mooters first.

Skeleton arguments

There is no reason why you cannot add to or modify this checklist – but it is also generally a good idea at some stage in this process to remind yourself of the rules of the particular mooting competition which you have entered. Different competitions have different rules. For instance, some competitions require skeleton arguments whereas others do not. As a rule of thumb, even if a particular competition does not require skeleton arguments, it is a good idea to produce one. Not only are skeleton arguments increasingly required in practice, but even where they are not (provided it is a good one), skeleton arguments help structure your submission and therefore help not only you, but also the judges. Although advocates represent their client, they are also present in court *to assist judges* – who contrary to popular belief, may not in fact know the area of law in which they have been asked to judge especially well![29] A good skeleton argument can therefore act as an *aide-memoire* not only for the moot advocate, but also for the judge. Many advocates consider their most successful cases to be those where the judgment of the court mirrors the skeleton argument that has been handed to the judge.

If skeleton arguments are required, then it is also usually the case that they should be exchanged before the moot. This means that you will need to disclose it to your opponent, usually simultaneously. Best practice is to place this in an indexed, paginated bundle along with your authorities.[30] The rationale for this is the same as that for being required to stick to the Grounds of Appeal: namely, so that the other side receives adequate notice of the case they will be facing. English law frowns on the idea of a party being 'ambushed' in court. That said, there is no rule of ethics or otherwise that states that you have to provide all your arguments to the nth degree in advance. That would be practically impossible and would do away with the need for any sort of oral hearing whatsoever. The clue as to the extent of detail required is indicated by the word 'skeleton': it is the bare bones of the points you intend to make whilst setting out all your main points. It follows from the metaphor that a skeleton argument should be 'fleshed out' during your oral submissions. The golden rule is to keep the skeleton as simple as possible – it can almost take the form of notes, provided that they make sense to another reader. Conversely, full sentences can also be used (sometimes this may be necessary if it is not immediately obvious how your points are linked or relevant) but long paragraphs are definitely discouraged. In any case, the skeleton should be the document that you will later use to guide the court through your case: it sets out a series of signposts designed to point the court in the direction of accepting your submission as to why the appeal should be allowed or dismissed as the case may be. In practice, when skeleton arguments are exchanged a day or two before an appeal, an appeal court may have reached a provisional conclusion on the outcome of the appeal on the basis of the skeleton arguments alone before the hearing has even started. Skeleton arguments are therefore a significant method of written advocacy and need careful preparation. Although they function as means of persuasion, they should never descend into fully justified monologues: logical simplicity should guide the exercise.

---

[29] It does not necessarily follow that this makes them bad judges.
[30] Because of the time constraints, it is important to think carefully about which cases you will consider to be "key" to your submissions.

Mooting: During the Moot

The moot

There may be slight variations in the format of a moot, but the following procedure covers most of them. The mooters will be in the courtroom in the absence of the judges. The judges will be brought into the room by a Master/Mistress of Moots or Mooting Officer who will announce the entry of the judges into the courtroom with "All rise!" Sometimes, the name of the case will be announced along with the names of the judges (if more than one, there will be a "presiding" judge). Once the mooters are face to face with the judges, whilst still standing, they will bow before the judges sit (you are bowing to the crest behind the judges). Everyone else then sits apart from the Lead Appellant who remains standing (one advocate and only one advocate should *always* be upstanding throughout the moot except when a judgment is being given). Once the judges are ready, the Presiding judge will call upon the Lead Appellant – whose name they will already have – to start. Different judges may start in different ways, but many will simply say "Yes, Mr/Ms X . . . ?" The Lead Appellant will then introduce herself along with all the other advocates along these lines: "May it please Your Lordships, I represent the Appellant along with my learned Junior Mr Y; My learned friends Ms A and Mr B are Lead and Junior Respondents respectively." It then helps to give a very brief introduction to the procedural history of the case before the court.[31] For instance: "This is an appeal against the judgment of Her Honour Judge C in which she found that the Appellant/Respondent was . . ." Thereafter, setting out the 'division of labour' on the Grounds of Appeal between the advocates may help signpost the way forward for the Bench. So, for example, "there are two Grounds of Appeal. They are that . . . [try to avoid reading the Grounds of Appeal out verbatim if you can. It will sound much more effective if you can repackage the Grounds of Appeal into some pithy and memorable phrases]. I will be dealing with the first point; my learned junior with the second. My Learned Friend Mr A will respond to the first ground . . ." and so forth. Quite often, the Bench may indicate that they are already aware of the procedural history as well as the facts and wish you simply to get on with it. If so, proceed gracefully along these lines: "I am obliged for the indication, My Lord, in which case I will proceed with my submissions. Your Lordships should have a copy of my skeleton argument in the bundle. It can be found behind the first divider at page 1. Your Lordships will see from that document that I intend to make [x number] submissions". If the bench permits you to introduce the case in more detail, keep the introductions brief and to the point. The time you spend on this may well come out of your allocated time. No other mooter needs to introduce the facts or procedural history after the Lead Appellant has done so (unless another advocate wishes to draw the Bench's attention to a particular point that the Lead Appellant omitted to mention, whether deliberately or not).

Once the introductions have been made, as suggested above, you should state how many submissions you will be making on the point(s) of your appeal, what they are in brief, what you are asking the court to do and then tell the court that you are about to start your first submission. Each submission may, of course, have a number of interlinked points, in which case you should signpost these at the outset of the first

---

[31] Some mooters ask permission to do this. There is no strict rule about this, but it is useful to start this way just to 'get going'. But again, the watchword is to keep this concise. Bearing in mind that the factual scenarios in a moot are pretty short anyway, displaying an ability to distil that factual scenario further may well gain you points.

submission and explain briefly how they are linked. After completing each submission, you should indicate to the court that you have completed that submission and that you are moving onto your next one. Once all your submissions are complete, you should ask the court for permission to conclude. Your conclusion should recap your submission briefly, emphasising your best points and yet again set out what you want the court to do (allow or dismiss the appeal). You ought to be able to do this in 60-90 seconds. It cannot be emphasised enough that finishing on a strong note is extremely important because your parting words are likely to leave a lasting impression. If you conclude on a whimper, then the court is unlikely to be persuaded. Once you have made your final point in your conclusion, you finish along the lines of "unless I can be of any further assistance, that concludes my submissions". *Remain standing* until the judges have finished asking you any questions and indicate that you can sit down. Different courts will then proceed either with the Junior Appellant following or with the Lead Respondent responding to the Lead Appellant. Those following can simply start with "My Lords, it is my submission . . ." or "My Lords, the appeal should be dismissed because . . ." or variants thereof. Finally, one of the Appellants usually has a few minutes to reply to the entirety of the Respondents' case. This Reply should only refer to points that have not already been raised by the Appellants the first time round and should only respond to points that the Respondent has actually made. In other words, it is not an opportunity for the Appellant to make points that they overlooked the first time round. It makes sense to find out the running order from the Mooting Officers beforehand in order to be prepared.

Addressing the Bench and referring to judges

On the assumption that you are reasonably well-prepared, the few minutes that you are on your feet will pass by very quickly indeed. Although the most important aspect of the submissions is the content of the arguments advanced, there are a whole host of other issues to consider when making those submissions. One thing which generations of mooters always seem worried about is how to address the Bench. Although it is true that the modes of address are steadily becoming less formalised with the passing of time, some stylised codes remain. Magistrates are "Your Worship", (Deputy) District Judges "Sir or Madam", Circuit Judges (and Recorders) "Your Honour", (Deputy) High Court judges, Appeal Court Judges and Justices of the Supreme Court are all "Your Lordships or My Lord/Lady". The different uses of 'Your' and 'My' when addressing the Bench are not always immediately obvious (for example, "My Lord will find the case on page 75 of Your Lordship's (or his) bundle"); but as a rule of thumb use "My" when addressing the judge directly, and "Your" in all other situations. A female judge would be addressed as My Lady/Your Ladyship unless she is part of a group of male judges in which case she is part of a group of "Your Lordships" and "My Lady" if addressed directly or "Your Ladyship" if addressed indirectly. It is still considered inappropriate by most judges for advocates to simply address them as "you". Despite this apparent excessive formality, don't lose sight of the fact that the judges are human, that it is possible they may not know the law as well as you do, that they also understand the phenomenon of nerves and that silence is ok. There is no rule of advocacy that says that you have to talk constantly. In fact a well-placed pause can be just as effective as a clever bit of phraseology.

A related point here is how you refer to judges in cases which you are using in the course of your submission. The pointers here are the initials after their name in the law reports. Broadly speaking, a judge of the High Court is a J and should be referred to as "Mr or Mrs Justice [Name]" (sometimes you see the expression JJ and that refers to two or more High Court judges and now, confusingly, Justices of the Supreme Court); LJ is "Lord or Lady Justice [Name]" who sit in the Court of Appeal; Lord before a name is a Law Lord sitting in the House of Lords and should be referred to by their full title if you are actually referring to their speech in your submission; if not, just Lord or (probably) Baroness (as in Baroness Hale); LC is "Lord [Name], The Lord Chancellor" (but note the office of the Lord Chancellor is no longer a judicial position); LCJ would be "Lord [Name], The Lord Chief Justice" (who is also, incidentally, President of the Criminal Division of the Court of Appeal and head of the Queen's Bench Division); MR is nowadays often a "Sir [Name], the Master of the Rolls" (also President of the Civil Division of the Court of Appeal) and if he is not a life peer you should also refer to his first name; P is "[Name], President of the Family Division"; C is "[Name] The Chancellor" (of the Chancery Division) who has supplanted VC "the Vice Chancellor" (confusingly, formerly the head of the Chancery Division because he was the Vice to the Lord Chancellor). Finally, if the judges are no longer in the office which they were in when they gave the judgment you refer to (this is likely to be the case quite often!), you should add "as s/he then was" after referring to them. You can check the current Law Reports for the identity of the current personnel in each court. This is a good habit to get into anyway. As a side note, remember that R (as in R v Smith) is "The Crown" unless the case is in the Privy Council, in which case it is the Queen or King depending on the date of the decision.

Referring to yourself and other mooters

When referring to yourself, it is nowadays considered acceptable to refer to personal pronouns such as "I" or "We", but you should avoid verbs such as "think" or "feel". What the advocate thinks or feels is irrelevant – the mooter is there to make submissions, contentions and so forth. So it is acceptable to say "in my submission" but not "I believe the judge was wrong when . . .." When referring to other mooters in the moot (as in real life), barristers are referred to as "My Learned Friend" (add their name if there is more than one in the room) or "Learned Counsel for the Appellant/Respondent". If your opponent is a solicitor, they would be addressed as "My Friend".

Nerves

Whether or not it is your first moot, it is pretty likely that you will feel nerves whether in the build-up or during the moot. Nerves are fine as long as they don't overwhelm you. It is quite common for much of the nerves to dissipate once you start talking, so whilst waiting to speak take some slow, deep and silent breaths. Nerves go hand in hand with adrenalin and adrenalin makes you alert. In this sense, some nervous energy is a good thing, and it has been said that the good advocate displays a "quiet confidence with a nervous edge."[32] If you are well-prepared, you will be fine, and you need to tell yourself that. Preparing your opening couple of sentences well should set you off on the right track.

Practising styles of advocacy

With time, you will no doubt develop your own style of advocacy. A few will adopt an abrasive style (often because that is what some clients demand), but the vast majority of successful advocates are those who are polite, calm, easy to follow, charming, respectful, quietly well-organised and efficient.[33] These are skills which can be developed with practice. And practice is not only what you do every time you

---
[32] J. Hill, *A Practical Guide to Mooting* (Palgrave Macmillan, 2009) p.82
[33] *ibid* p.63

moot, it is also what you do in front of the mirror, friends, a video camera or even with your fellow mooters. Unlike a real case where the adversarial nature of the process is such that co-operation is probably far down the list of priorities, many moots work much better if the mooters have practised together beforehand, as this helps to refine and define the real points in dispute – something which may otherwise only happen in the course of the moot itself for the first time, which in turn may require much more thinking on your feet than first anticipated. If you practice beforehand, you can spend more time thinking about the intonation of your voice, the volume at which you project it, the pace of delivery, eye contact, structure – including the use of pauses – and timing. By practising with another human, he or she can point out where you may need to develop in these areas. Because ultimately you have to make yourself understood, you need to avoid slang and you should aim to speak slowly and clearly. And because judges are also human beings, they need to be shown a degree of respect. Few judges would admit it, but it is quite possible for a judge to find against a party because the advocate has 'rubbed them up the wrong way'; so never interrupt a judge, don't raise your voice in an aggressive manner and don't ask a judge any questions (unless with a view to asking them to clarify a question you have not understood). As Hill notes, "judges want to hear calm, coherent and eloquent submissions, not the ramblings of somebody who appears to be on the verge of a nervous breakdown."[34] So, be prepared for judges to interrupt you. More importantly, try to anticipate what the questions might be so that you have a working answer to that question. Deal with questions without being side tracked too much. In other words, it is usually a good policy to answer the question straightaway and not by saying to the judge that you intend to deal with that particular point later in your submission. If you happen not to understand a question put to you, it is fine to ask the judge to rephrase the question ("Would your Ladyship be so kind as to rephrase the question?"; "I do not grasp your Lordship's meaning"); and if you still can't answer the question it is probably best just to say so ("I am very sorry, my Lord, but I cannot be of assistance on that particular matter").[35]

Practising advocacy either before a specific moot or by doing as many moots as possible is really the only way of improving your advocacy skills. Much can also be learned by watching others, whether or not they are qualified advocates. You can attend local courts or watch proceedings in the Supreme Court via the Web.[36] There are things to be learned by seeing what not do as much as by seeing what works. In any case, you should seek to watch at least one moot before you yourself moot for the first time lest the whole experience takes you by complete surprise.

Eye contact and notes

It is very important to maintain eye contact with the judges. There is some basic psychology behind this observation. People who avoid eye contact are often seen as "shifty, untrustworthy, incompetent or just plain boring."[37] By maintaining eye contact with the judges, you are also in a better position to 'read' the judges (even if subconsciously). You may pick up signals from them whether they are with you or against you, and if there is more than one judge, you may work out who needs more persuasion. In order to maintain eye contact effectively, you cannot be looking down too much.

---

[34] *ibid* p.81
[35] *ibid* p.140
[36] http://news.sky.com/home/supreme-court
[37] Hill *op. cit* p.68

One way that mooters end up looking down too much is as a result of having too many notes or other distracting pieces of paper in front of them. This observation should lead you to think about what sort of notes you should be using. It is almost universally accepted that it is very bad practice to have a 'speech' written out in full in advance. One reason for this relates to the fact that reading from a script will cause you to look down and thereby lose eye contact. A further and more important reason is that the likelihood that you will be able to deliver such a speech word for word within the time constraints is very remote indeed. Why? Because the Bench will be asking you questions throughout your submissions and that will inevitably throw you off course. It is also possible that the judges will accept one of your submissions without requiring any elaboration whatsoever, whereas they require considerably more persuasion when it comes to another one. If, for instance, you had prepared three minutes worth of 'speech' for each submission and the judges are only interested in one of them, that leaves you with six minutes to fill on one submission. Or, it is possible that you are asked about a point you had not given much consideration to at all – if you then spend two or three minutes responding to that, it means you have two or three minutes left on the 'speech' you had already prepared and left with the unenviable task of deciding what to cull on your feet. Because of this, it is far better to use short notes in the form of bullet points – a skeletal version of your skeleton argument that also includes points related to the 'flesh' missing from the skeleton argument itself. This will remind you of your main points, the order in which you intend to deal with them, and if you are deflected by questions from the Bench, it will be easier to put yourself back on track afterwards.

Using cards

Some mooters like to use cards on which they write their submissions. Cards are marginally more preferable to a fully-fledged speech, but they can still be distracting – and a number of mooters end up writing out a full speech on cards instead of on paper, which then leads to the same problems identified above. Cards can be a useful aid in some situations. For example, a card can contain a brief summary of the facts and decisions of an individual case, or salient points related to a piece of legislation, or a summary of the main points of a distinguished article. But if you use cards in this way, they need to be organised – perhaps alphabetically or in some other logical fashion – so that you can find them with ease if asked a question to which your cards may be relevant.

Citing authority

It is pertinent to consider the whole issue of presentation of case law at this point. Any well-presented case is predicated on being well-organised and prepared. Judges will be impressed by someone who is well-organised, and less so with someone who is not. Not only should you be on top of cases on which you seek to rely, but you also need to be conversant with those cases on which your opponents intend to rely. You might use cards for brief summaries of the facts, decisions and individual judgments (including, at the very least, names of dissenting judges) as well as containing brief notes or summaries of relevant passages with page references. When citing the cases, you should say something along the lines of:

> *"In support of this submission, I refer your Lordships to the case of Cobbe and (not "v" or "versus") Yeoman's Row Management Limited, reported in the first volume of the Weekly Law Reports for 2008, at page 1752 [being the case of Cobbe v Yeoman's Row Management Ltd [2008] UKHL 55, [2008] 1 W.L.R. 1752] and in particular the speech of Lord Scott of Foscote at paragraph 14. Your Lordships will find that paragraph on page x of the bundle."*

At this point, you need to *stop and wait* for the judges to find the relevant passage before, if necessary, directing them further to the start of the sentence where you intend to quote from. After quoting from the judgment (and try not to quote too much – break any long quotations up with commentary as you go along), you need to comment on the passage explaining and justifying your interpretation of it and why you say it supports your submission. Many mooters highlight the passages they intend to use in the judges' bundle with a highlighter in order to ensure that the judges find the start of the passage quickly, but it is worth checking the competition rules to see whether this is permissible because in the real world, highlighted passages are discouraged (as judges prefer to make their own marks on any judgments used). Another word of warning: *never* cite from headnotes unless they are word for word replications of the content of a judgment. Remember that although headnotes are attempts by court reporters to distil the *ratio* of cases, they are summaries and interpretations made by the individual reporting the case and they do *not* form a part of the judgment. They may act as a useful memory aid in the course of your research, but you should avoid references to them in the moot. It is also useful to refer to a mixture of old and new authority on a particular point in order to show a consistent line of authority.

Awareness and body language

When delivering your submissions, think about your body language if for no other reason that *the judges will see everything you do from the moment they enter the court room*. If there is a lectern, use it. It is useful as a prop not only because you can to an extent 'hide' behind it but also because you can hold onto to it in order to avoid too many hand gestures. Try to stand as still as possible and face the Bench head on: people who turn sideways will look as if they are trying to deflect questions put to them by the Bench. Otherwise, stand up straight with your hands or hand by your side or behind you; avoid stooping and place your weight equally on both legs without locking your knees. Be aware at all times of your surroundings, but at the same time avoid taking any notice of how your opponents might be reacting to your submissions (just as you ought to try to avoid making any movements or sounds when your opponent is speaking – such as shaking your head or speaking to your colleague louder than in a whisper. In practice you will discover times when it is permissible to interrupt your opponent, but in the context of mooting, you should avoid this at all costs unless specifically asked by the Bench[38]). Advocacy is adversarial, but it should never become personal and ought to be carried out in a sportsmanlike fashion.

By being aware of your surroundings, you can take cues from when the judges are reading, writing or are about to ask you a question. In all such cases, it is worth slowing down or even stopping as only the best multi taskers can take notes, read, listen and think all at the same time. Even when you are not speaking, it is worth paying attention not only to what is being said by your opponent, but in particular to what questions are being asked by the Bench. Those questions will give a fairly clear idea about what the judges are interested in. A good mooter will pick up on points made by the Bench in the course of questioning and incorporate these points into their submission. For example, if a judge has responded with a degree of incredulity to a point made by your opponent, when it comes to your submission, you might say "As My Lady X pointed out in response to my Learned Friend's submission on this issue, the conclusion is unsustainable (amend as appropriate)." When responding to any point made by your opponents, whether as a Respondent properly speaking or in the course of the Appellant's Reply (following the Respondent),

---

[38] There is one situation where it might be legitimate to stand up when your opponent is on her feet: if your opponent has been asked for a reference to the bundle of authorities, for example, and finds herself in an embarrassing silence and it is clear that she will not find it, you might stand up and offer to assist the court if you know what that reference is: "If I may assist the court . . ."

it is helpful to remind the Bench what your opponent's point was before stating your rebuttal. If you haven't already dealt with the point in your pre-prepared submission, this shows that you have been listening to your opponent's submission. You need to weave such bullet points into your pre-prepared submission as the moot progresses, which once again illustrates the advantage of having bullet points and notes rather than a word-for-word speech with its inherent space-constraints.

The submission (in more detail)

Although there have been references to the nature and structure of a submission in what has gone before, a few more general and generic points will be noted at this stage. These points can only really be generic because moot problems are many and varied. By way of overview, there ought to be a brief introduction followed by one or more submissions followed by a conclusion. All your submissions should as far as possible be supported by some form of legal authority even if you need to 'stretch' that authority somewhat at times. In the Supreme Court, as we have seen, you may be able to raise some purely moral or ethical arguments or other policy-based arguments, but it always helpful if this can be backed up by some form of legal authority (which may, of course, be simply a Law Lord appearing to back your point *obiter*). As you make your submission, you need to be building it up as you progress. If a point you make does not develop or build on what has gone before, it may be worth considering leaving it out altogether. Your ultimate objective is to persuade the Bench that your interpretation of the law is correct and therefore you should pepper your submission with phrases such as "I submit", "it is my submission that" or "I contend that". Think about what it is that you are asserting – whether you are the Appellant or the Respondent, you are always making a positive case i.e. setting out your case. Don't forget this, and don't forget that you are also asking the Moot Court *to do* something in response to your positive case. As a Respondent, you are more often than not defending the lower court's decision. But this is still to assert a positive case. In both situations, you also need to respond to the other side's positive case, which means you need to understand and engage with it in order to try to knock it down. You must do both tasks as best you can in the short time available to you. It is usually not enough to simply put forward your own positive case – if you only do that, it is more likely than not that the judge will ask you to deal with particular points made by your opponents if you have not done that in the course of your submission. And this may count against you in terms of marks.

It is always important to keep in your own mind a distinction between the general overview of your case and its detailed analysis. You should be able to give a short and generalised response to what your case is, if asked, and the remainder of your submission is the analysis which backs that basic case up. If you can summarise your basic case in a catchy phrase that you refer to at times throughout your submission (e.g. "a car is a dangerous weapon, and lethal in the hands of a drunk") then so much the better. If you can reduce a complex rule into something simple or metaphorically memorable, this is likely to curry favour with the Bench. But not only do you need to be able to put your case forward simply and succinctly you also need to pre-empt your opponent's case. As Hill says, "in order to know your case well, you need to know it from the other side's point of view."[39] This means that you need to think about what the other side will say about your case (the skeleton argument will give a strong indication of this) as well as what they will say about theirs. By thinking about your case from your opponent's point of view you can identify the weaknesses in your case and you will need to take protective measures against those weaknesses. The good

---
[39] J. Hill *op.cit* p.111

advocate turns their weaknesses into strengths by means of creative thinking. At the very least, you need to think about responses to the weaknesses before the moot and deal with them either in the submission itself or await the inevitable question on that issue. You should also identify weaknesses in your opponent's case and focus some of your submission on those. Even better is to identify the apparent strengths in your opponent's case and to create some doubts about those apparent strengths in the course of your submission.

In terms of structure to overlay the modes of address referred to earlier, your submission might proceed along these lines: after the general introduction set out earlier including what you are asking the court to do:

1. Introduction to your (basic) submission preferably by reference to a catchy phrase;

2. Set out your 'running order' by briefly explaining the logic and thinking behind your submission;

3. Detail of the reasoning behind your basic submission backed up by legal authority within the general structure of your positive case followed by responses to the Respondent's likely submission (but not in too much detail as it is possible that the Respondent's case might change in the course of the moot).

4. Brief summary of submission(s).

5. Conclusion which includes asking the court to do something.

As you progress through your submission, indicate or signpost along the way where you are up to in your submission. For instance, "my first submission is that the learned judge was wrong in his interpretation of X because of Y. In support of my submission I will be referring to the case of A and in particular the speech of Z. I will also rely on the well-known principle of AB and draw an analogy with CD" and so forth. After referring to the first case, it is then good practice to remind the judge where you are going next by saying "that is my submission in relation to the case of A. I will now consider the well-known principle of AB". It would be sensible to approach your submission with half an eye on your skeleton argument at all times as you can then signpost by reference to the skeleton rather than expect the judges to take constant notes. This approach may seem a little repetitive, but if you bear in mind that your task is to assist the Bench, then continually telling the judge where you are up to may in fact give the impression that you are in control of your submission and that it is important that the judges need to follow you and follow you completely in order for them to grasp the full force of your submission.

When preparing your running order you might want to pay particular attention to what your key submission is and where in the course of your submission you ought to make it. Invariably, you will have a key point and you should try to make sure it is as watertight as possible by considering what the likely questions are going to be related to it (judges will want to test your submission by playing with the facts of your case to see how far the point stretches) and thinking about where it will be most effective in your submission. Having a clear view about what your key submission is will also act as a reminder to yourself that you will need to slow down and emphasise that particular part. The corollary to this is that it is also very likely that you will make a bad point at some point. A bad point is not the same as an obvious point. A bad point is either a weak point, or even worse an unrealistic one. Because it is also important to avoid overloading your submission, it is worth thinking about what your bad point(s) might be and simply removing them from your submission altogether. It is far more common for mooters to have too much rather than too little to say, so it will do you little harm in spending a bit of time working out which points can usefully be excluded. If you are completely wedded to a weak point and don't want to discard it, at least put it on a 'reserve' list of points just in case you should find yourself well ahead of time – although this is very unlikely.

Concluding the submission and concluding thoughts

When concluding your submission, finish strongly. Reiterate your main points, ask the court to allow or dismiss the appeal as the case may be and finish with "Unless I can assist the court further, that concludes my submissions on this ground of appeal" or "I rest my case". Wait until the Bench gives permission to sit but recall that this is by no means the end of your job as you still need to listen to what your opponents have to say either because you have a formal right to reply or because you might unexpectedly be called upon to deal with a point that has arisen. If your teammate has yet to speak, it is also worth listening with a view to helping your teammate out should the occasion arise.

Different Moot Courts have different practices about whether they give a judgment or not. There is a whole host of different reasons for a variance in the practice. In many ways a judgment on the law is less important than feedback on your overall performance. It is the latter that is likely to stay with you for longer than a debatable judgment on a set of hypothetical facts (even if it may be very interesting to you to hear the opinion on the law from your judges). Try to take on board the advice given to you about your performance, but at the same time bear in mind that the particular judges in your particular moot represent but a small sample of the type of judge 'out there' even if they may share some common traits. In other words, listen to the advice, but don't get too hung up on what they may have to say. With practice you will develop your own inimitable style and in time, hopefully, you will look back on your first moot as a first and important but ultimately small step along the way. Similarly, different Moot Courts may have different marking criteria. So, if your concern is to obtain the best mark possible, you will need to consider those criteria carefully. Usually, they are a mixture of advocacy skills (the art of persuasion), knowledge of the law, preparation and presentation as well as time keeping. The latter is usually given a low weighting, but that does not mean it is unimportant. The key is to try to get the balance right by not placing over-reliance on one aspect to the detriment of another.

Mooting at University can help develop your advocacy skills, but more importantly it can deepen your knowledge and understanding of law. Amidst the theatre and the fun of oral advocacy it is important not to lose sight of that. In the first place, a moot gives students the opportunity to master the case and statute law and also the procedure that applies in a particular case that must be mastered if you are to argue the case properly. It also strengthens your ability to apply the law to situations of fact, or rather, to analyse situations of fact in legal terms. Perhaps most importantly of all, through the process of working through in very close detail the resolution in legal terms (although not perhaps in others) of one specific conflict it may also provide an insight into how the law operates in society. At least, it may provide such an insight if you don't forget to think about it.

Further reading

P. Clinch, *Using a Law Library: A Student's Guide to Legal Research Skills* (Blackstone Press 1992)
R. Du Cann, *The Art of the Advocate* (Penguin 1993)
K. Evans, *The Language of Advocacy: What to Say and How to Say it in the English-Speaking Courts* (Oxford University Press 1998)
J. Hill, *A Practical Guide to Mooting* (Palgrave Macmillan 2009)
C. Kee, *The Art of Argument* (Cambridge University Press 2007)
I. Morley, The Devil's Advocate: *A Short Polemic on how to be Seriously Good in Court* (Sweet & Maxwell 2005)

D. Pope & J. Hill, *Mooting and Advocacy Skills* (Sweet & Maxwell 2007)
K. Rawlins, *Presentation and Communication Skills: A Handbook for Practitioners* (Macmillan 1993)
D. Ross QC, *Advocacy* (Cambridge University Press 2007)
N. Shaw, *Effective Advocacy* (Sweet & Maxwell 2010)
A.T.H. Smith, *Glanville Williams' Learning the Law* (Sweet & Maxwell 2006)
J. Snape & G. Watt, *How to Moot: A Student Guide to Mooting* (Oxford University Press 2004)
J. Snape & G. Watt, *The Cavendish Guide to Mooting* (Cavendish 1997)
http://learnmore.lawbore.net/index.php/Category:Mooting
http://www.mootingnet.org.uk/

6
Negotiation

Fred Motson

Background

What is negotiation?

The *Oxford English Dictionary* defines to negotiate as:

"To communicate or confer (with another or others) for the purpose of arranging some matter by mutual agreement; to discuss a matter with a view to some compromise or settlement."[1]

This is a perfectly logical definition which includes the key features of a negotiation: communication between two or more parties and the aim to achieve agreement or compromise. However, negotiation is a far wider subject than this suggests and is not merely a concept but a practical skill of increasing importance in the legal profession. As you might expect, there are copious books, journals, websites and other materials provided by academics, businessmen, lawyers and others which all claim to explain exactly how to achieve success in a negotiation. The aim of this section is more modest – we will consider the styles and strategies most commonly used in a negotiation and how this relates to the legal context. We will also look at the ethical aspects of negotiating as a lawyer, and it is worth noting at this early stage that negotiating as a lawyer is often a more formalised, regulated process than negotiations in a business or social context.

Negotiation in the legal system is usually, although not exclusively, to be found in civil and family litigation, rather than criminal cases. Following the Woolf Reforms and the introduction of the Civil Procedure Rules, there is a greater emphasis on settling claims outside of court and as such negotiation is only increasing in importance as a practice area. As a lawyer you will almost inevitably be involved in negotiations at some stage, whether it is as a solicitor helping two parties enter into a commercial contract, or at the other extreme a barrister settling a case literally outside the courtroom door. To put the

---

[1] "negotiation, n.". OED Online. September 2011. Oxford University Press. 19 September 2011 <http://www.oed.com/view/Entry/125879?redirectedFrom=negotiation>

importance of negotiation (and other forms of alternative dispute resolution) in context, over 1.6 million civil cases were begun in the county court in 2010. However, just 63,000 trials took place in the same period[2]. This suggests that at least 96% of claims are settled prior to a final hearing and this of course only includes disputes which are not resolved prior to court proceedings being commenced. In many of these claims, negotiations will take place between lawyers to find a mutually acceptable settlement.

Strategies of negotiation

While negotiation is no different to other practical legal skills, in that there is no "correct" strategy which suits everyone, most commentators identify five typical strategies of negotiation. These emerged from the work of Kenneth Thomas and Ralph Kilmann, who developed a series of questions known as the Thomas-Kilmann Conflict Mode Instrument (TKI). This posits that people naturally choose one of five conflict resolution strategies, which are characterised by differing levels of assertiveness and 'cooperativeness'. While you may find one strategy suits you better than others, an effective negotiator can switch between strategies during a negotiation, in order to achieve the best possible result. It is also important to be able to recognise your opponent's strategy.

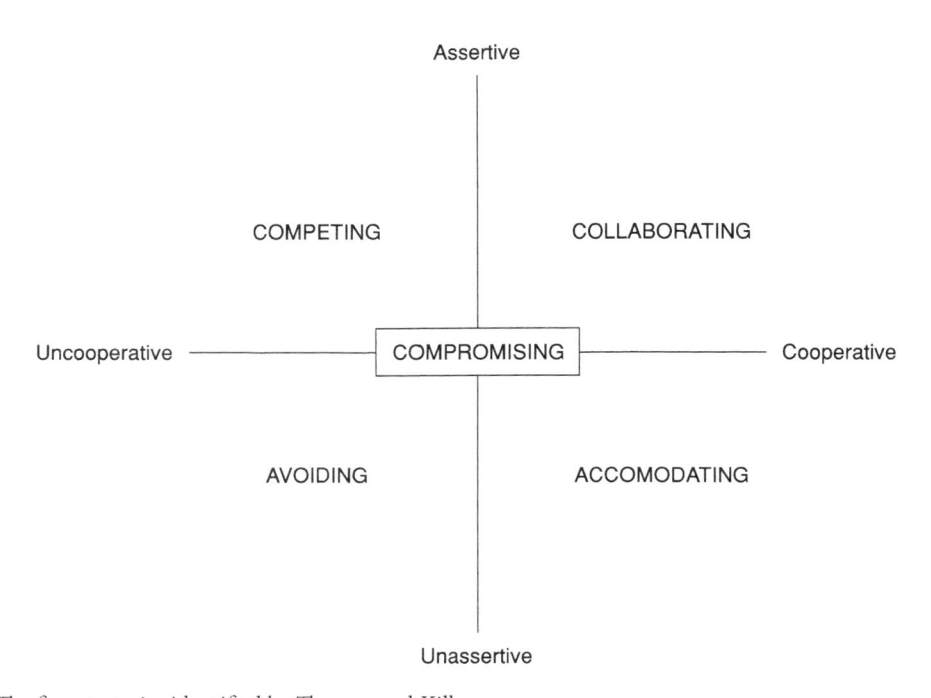

Figure 1: The five strategies identified by Thomas and Killman

Accommodating

One of the least common negotiating strategies, accommodation involves deferring to the other side and agreeing to all reasonable proposals they may suggest. As an overall approach to negotiation, this has

---

[2] Ministry of Justice, *Judicial and Court Statistics 2010*

been described as "at its extreme ... useless as a strategy"[3] and as you can imagine, most clients would not be happy for their representative to simply capitulate to their opponent. However, there can be a time in certain negotiations when accommodation becomes unavoidable and it is better to concede gracefully, or even allow the other side to believe you have chosen to be generous, rather than souring your relationship by refusing to accept the inevitable. This may be the case when your client is clearly in the wrong, or where the disruption caused by the dispute potentially continuing is far worse than the concession being requested.

If you are faced with an accommodating negotiator, then little advice would appear to be needed, as you will achieve success on every issue! However, you should bear in mind that you should remain reasonable and justify every argument, as too many concessions may make your opponent feel you have taken advantage of them and this might hamper any final agreement.

Avoiding

A negotiator who uses the avoiding strategy is one who not only avoids coming to an agreement but may also avoid discussing any issues or even their own demands. As you can see from the diagram above, a negotiator using this strategy is both uncooperative and unassertive, thus they do not wish to aid you or themselves. The most extreme form of avoidance is to refuse to negotiate at all, or to cancel or walk out during negotiations. Avoiding strategies are not normally recommended for use by legal professionals, as you are under a duty to your client to attempt to resolve matters. Even if you are given instructions to avoid negotiations, you should bear in mind your professional obligations to the court and the duties imposed by the Civil Procedure Rules. Any party who refuses to attempt alternate dispute resolution can – and often will – suffer the consequences when costs are assessed at the end of the litigation.

The one time you may decide to use avoiding tactics, or see them in your opponent, is when time is a factor. For example, if you are expecting an expert's report the following day which you feel will dramatically strengthen your arguments, you may attempt to avoid negotiating until this arrives. It may even be that both sides are willing to cooperate in their lack of cooperation, such as delaying any talks if a higher court decision is due on an important legal issue in the negotiations. If you do wish to negotiate and your opponent is using this strategy, you are left with two options: to persist, or to reschedule negotiations for a better time or with a more cooperative person.

Competing

The competing strategy is characterised by combining an aggressive approach with a 'win-lose' style (discussed in more detail below). A competitive or combative negotiator is one who does not believe both sides can benefit from the negotiation, and is determined to be the 'winner'. As one writer has described it, the "most extreme result will be that one side does get the whole cake and the other side doesn't even get a crumb"[4]. Indicators that your opponent is using a competitive strategy might include unreasonably high demands, a refusal to compromise or even listen to counter-offers, assertive behaviour and body language, and attempting to control the pace and agenda of the negotiation.

---

[3] F. Boyle, *A Practical Guide to Lawyering Skills* 2nd Edition (Routledge-Cavendish 2003) p.286
[4] Ibid. p.265

Maintaining a competing strategy throughout the negotiation can be counter-productive, as agreement is usually unlikely unless your opponent is extremely accommodating. However, if you are certain that you are 'in the right' on a particular point and/or your instructions allow no compromise, it may be worth using such an approach. If you are the other side of the table from a competitive negotiator, it is important not to be bullied into making concessions. Try to be as assertive as possible, while remaining polite – you do not want talks to descend into an argument. Ask your opponent why they feel they should not compromise and patiently outline your own case, to explain why you will not accede to their demands.

Compromising

This strategy is sometimes referred to as a 'problem-solving' approach. Both names are slightly misleading, as they suggest the negotiator might compromise at any cost. Instead, this strategy describes a negotiator who is looking to reach a final agreement which partially satisfies both sides. It is something of a cliché to say that a good compromise is one which leaves both parties dissatisfied, but this is often the maxim of the compromising negotiator. He or she may be willing to accept concessions on a point-by-point basis, 'trading' each gain for a loss elsewhere in the settlement. This strategy is particularly common when a negotiator feels under pressure to produce an agreement but does not have the confidence for the competitive strategy or the willingness to be overly accommodating. Such negotiators may be quite aggressive, actively seeking a comprehensive agreement at the expense of exploring points in detail, or they may take a conciliatory approach, for example pointing out the advantages of a quick settlement.

As already mentioned, you may resort to this strategy when the agreement itself is more important that its terms. This may be because the dispute has interrupted a continuing commercial relationship, or a deadline is approaching. It can also be a response to a negotiator using avoiding tactics, in order to 'force' a compromise. However, you should be careful not to give the impression that you are willing to accept *any* compromise, as this may make your opponent more assertive and less willing to compromise in turn. When facing a compromising negotiator, you should ensure that you keep a close eye on what is being discussed and agreed, to ensure that important issues are given sufficient consideration. Do not get carried away with the prospect of a quick solution and concede too much.

Collaborating

Finally, the collaborating strategy strikes a balance between assertiveness and cooperation, in order to create what could be seen as a new paradigm. Unlike the other strategies we have examined, collaboration does not necessarily involve either party making a 'loss'. For example, two neighbours may be in a furious dispute over who can use the single parking space on the street in front of their properties. Using the other strategies discussed above, the best solution imaginable would be a compromise where they take it in turns, or one pays the other for exclusive use. Neither of these solutions fully satisfies both parties, as one or both parties lose access to parking and are financially worse off respectively. A creative negotiator might instead ask the two neighbours *why* they want to use the parking space. It turns out that neighbour A is very proud of his vintage car and wants it parked somewhere he knows it is safe, although he very rarely drives the vehicle. Meanwhile, neighbour B runs a taxi service and needs quick and frequent access to his car, rather than storing it in his garage. Suddenly, a creative solution can be seen – neighbour A can leave his car in neighbour B's garage, giving him the street parking in exchange. Now both parties are in a better position than they were originally, due to taking a collaborative approach.

This concept of identifying interests, rather than focusing on stated bargaining positions, is one of a number suggested by Fisher and Ury in their influential work on this strategy, which they call "principled negotiation".[5] In their words:

> *"People find themselves in a dilemma. They see two ways to negotiate: soft or hard [i.e. accommodating/compromising or avoiding/competing] . . . There is a third way to negotiate, a way neither hard nor soft, but rather both hard and soft. The method of principled negotiation . . . is to decide issues on their merits rather than through a haggling process focused on what each side says it will and won't do. It suggests that you look for mutual gains wherever possible, and that where your interests conflict, you should insist that the result be based on some fair standards independent of the will of either side. The method of principled negotiation is hard on the merits, soft on the people. It employs no tricks and no posturing. Principled negotiation shows you how to obtain what you are entitled to and still be decent."*[6]

By looking at what both sides actually need, rather than what they are demanding, you can find creative solutions. When it works, collaborative negotiation can reach settlements which are simply not conceivable by other strategies. Such agreements, by benefitting both parties, are also more likely to be upheld and form the basis of more beneficial partnerships in future. If you wish to use this strategy, you need to learn to look beyond what an opponent is saying and think creatively to find a solution which will satisfy both parties' interests. A good starting point suggested by Fisher and Ury is to ask yourself two questions: "why do they want what they are asking for?" and "why are they saying no to what I am asking for?".[7]

However, there are some disadvantages to relying on the collaborative approach. Firstly, it requires both parties to be committed to this strategy of negotiating. If you attempt to collaborate when your opponent is pursuing a competitive strategy, you will either achieve nothing or end up conceding ground for no benefit. Even if all parties are willing to collaborate, it is usually a relatively complex and time-consuming process, thus is not suitable when settlement needs to be reached as soon as possible. Furthermore, while collaborative approaches can open up new solutions, they are not suitable for every case – for example, when one party is completely at fault for a financial loss caused to the other party, there is little point in collaboration as opposed to merely agreeing a level of compensation.

No strategy

It has been argued by some authors that there are "distinct advantages"[8] to adopting no strategy at all and instead waiting for your opponent to set the tone of the negotiation. By doing so, you force the other side into revealing their main concerns and you may pick up clues about their strategy and bargaining power by taking this approach. However, it is not generally recommended as not only do you lose the opportunity to set your own agenda, you may give the impression that you are weak, lazy or do not take the negotiation, or the wider relationship between the parties, seriously.

---

[5] R. Fisher and W. Ury, *Getting to Yes* 2nd Edition (Random House 2003)
[6] Ibid. p.6
[7] Ibid. p.25
[8] R. Lewicki, B. Barry and D. Saunders, *Negotiation: Readings, Exercises and Cases* 5th Edition (McGraw-Hill 2007) p.28

Styles of negotiation

It may seem somewhat artificial to distinguish between style and strategy in the context of negotiation, but there is a considerable difference between the two concepts. Strategy, as we have already discussed, comprises the specific tactics used by a negotiator and can alter during the course of negotiations – for example, someone may begin aggressively with a competing strategy, soften toward a more compromising approach, and as time runs out end up accommodating their opponent in order to get an agreement. Style meanwhile is a more general concept which describes the overall approach taken by a negotiator throughout the entire process. It is unlikely that someone using a win/lose style will shift to a win/win approach, or vice versa.

Many inexperienced negotiators will always use a win/lose style – where in their view the two sides begin at opposite extremes and the aim is to achieve a result as close to your own starting position as possible. This is perhaps particularly true of legal negotiators, who may be more used to the adversarial approach of the courtroom than collaborative strategies. This style is usually combined with a competing or avoiding strategy, but could be used with a compromising strategy where the aim is to 'win' more compromises from the other side than you allow them in turn, or with an accommodating approach where you are happy to 'lose' in the short term, due to external factors. Just as with the win/lose style, win/win can allow for the use of almost any of the five strategies (although avoiding strategies are unlikely to be pursued by such a negotiator). Even a competing strategy might be predicated on winning more/winning less rather than either side losing out. However, the win/win style is usually more cooperative than win/lose and suits less aggressive negotiations, such as non-contentious work.

Most books on negotiation will tell you that the win/win approach is always preferable to this style, however in the context of legal negotiations this is not necessarily the case. If you are negotiating to settle a case, where your client is clearly in the right and there is no future relationship between the parties to preserve, your duty to obtain the best possible outcome is more important than finding a 'fair' or 'balanced' agreement – "do not assume that lawyers and clients will necessarily agree on what is fair"[9]. However, the win/lose approach is more likely to lead to stalemate and it should only be used when the context justifies it. Realistically, the very concepts of 'winning' and 'losing' are extremely relative and thus it is better to focus on strategy rather than style – settling a claim worth millions for a nominal sum costs money but would be seen by most clients as a very successful result!

Ethics and rules

Duties to your client

As a lawyer, many general ethical principles apply to all the work you perform for your client. However, certain duties are particularly important to bear in mind when negotiating.

To remain within instructions

When acting as the legal representative of a party, you must always take care to remain within the instructions they have given you. These may be very clear, such as "do not make any agreement below £10,000", or more general, such as "only settle if you think we have to". You should try and get as specific

---

[9] C. Maughan & J. Webb, *Lawyering Skills and the Legal Process* 2nd Edition (Cambridge University Press 2005)

instructions as possible before negotiating, because you cannot exceed these limits. If you do, you may well have breached professional codes of conduct and will also be potentially liable in negligence to your client. If ever you are unsure whether you have authority, ask your client, or if this is not possible, make it clear to your opponent that you will have to relay the offer before any acceptance is possible. Remember, remaining within instructions is not just staying under or over specific limits, but also not proposing any solutions your client has not expressly authorised – this is particularly important when using a collaborative strategy.

To obtain the best possible settlement

It can be tempting in complex or slow-moving negotiations to grasp at any chance of an agreement. You must remember that even if the prospect of yet more argument is unappetising, you should always seek to do the best for your client, regardless of personal feelings. Obviously this is a matter of degree – rejecting a settlement that has taken weeks to achieve on the basis that your client could achieve a few pounds more is unreasonable. Experience will give you a better idea of when to settle, but as a general rule if any further gains are so unlikely or will extend the negotiations for so long that the client will actually be worse-off as a result, it is time to conclude.

Duties to your opponent

Not to conceal, misrepresent or invent facts

This is a difficult matter to address, as while you must not intentionally mislead your opponent or lie to them, your duty of confidentiality to your own client means that you should not volunteer damaging information. If you are aware of facts which will weaken your negotiating position, but that your opponent does not know, you are under no obligation to tell the other side. However, if you are asked directly about this issue, you must answer truthfully. For example, you are representing a client who is suing their travel agent after a flight was cancelled. You are claiming £1,000 for the replacement ticket bought by your client, although they have told you that they could have mitigated this loss by taking a slightly later flight for just £200. There is no need to reveal this fact, but if your opponent asks "was there any other way for your client to travel to their destination?" you must now admit what you were told.

To behave appropriately and reasonably

As a member of the legal profession, you must uphold professional standards. Obviously, this includes treating your opponent with respect and even if using an aggressive style, remaining inside reasonable boundaries. For example, you should not disparage your opponent or their client, use offensive language or make unfounded allegations. You should also keep to your word – if you made a concession which you later regret, you cannot simply deny that this was ever agreed!

Remember that you may have an extra duty as a lawyer, to use the law responsibly. Obviously you should not misrepresent the law but when dealing with a lay person this may also include drawing their attention to relevant legal sources, such as cases or legislation, and clearly and objectively explaining how this affects the current dispute. One common error made by legal negotiators is to refer to the law too frequently – just as when you are performing advocacy, the majority of your arguments should involve the facts of the case, with the law providing a wider framework.

To negotiate "without prejudice"

The majority of legal negotiations take place "without prejudice". This means that what is discussed during negotiations cannot be relied on in any later litigation, or revealed to third parties. This is a rule based on public policy, that parties should be encouraged to be as open as possible during negotiations in order to encourage settlement.[10] Thus if a party makes an offer to settle during negotiations without prejudice discussions, this is rejected and the matter goes to trial, it cannot be argued that the offer was an admission of fault. Even after a settlement is reached, anything discussed under this rule remains confidential indefinitely.[11] You should note that while this allows you to be more open in negotiations and explore potential solutions, you should not reveal information to the other side which your client has made clear is confidential.

Reflection Questions

1. Think about the five strategies outlined in this section. Which do you think would suit you best? Why?
2. When you have negotiated in the past, have you favoured a win/win or a win/lose style?
3. Due to their ethics, are lawyers more restricted in negotiations than other people?
4. Which of the ethical duties discussed above is most important?

Negotiation Skills

Preparing to negotiate

"In all negotiations of difficulty, a man may not look to sow and reap at once; but must prepare business, and so ripen it by degrees."[12]

Preparation for a negotiation is absolutely crucial in order to stand any chance of a successful outcome. Unlike other work lawyers undertake such as advocacy, litigation or drafting legal opinions, you will often have very little time to deal with new information when negotiating. Therefore the more preparation you undertake beforehand, the easier it is to cope with the speed of a negotiation.

Analysing the problem

As with all legal work, your first priority must be to thoroughly read over all the documentation you are given prior to negotiating. Even if you do not expect to deal with certain issues, it is advisable to read all of the available papers as you need to have an overview of the entire dispute in order to judge the level at which you may potentially settle. While reading through the facts and your instructions, you should note down all of the issues which will be raised at the negotiation and what objectives your client has. Once you

---

[10] *Unilever Plc v Procter & Gamble Co* [2000] 1 W.L.R. 2436
[11] *Rush & Tompkins Ltd v Greater London Council* [1989] A.C. 1280
[12] F. Bacon, *The Essays* (first published 1627, Penguin 2003) p.204

have analysed the facts of the case, you should also analyse the relevant law. Negotiation involves less 'black letter' law than many legal skills, as you are very focused on the practical aspects of the case, however you need to know the relevant law in order to properly assess your chances of success. You may even want to refer to the law during the negotiation, to support your arguments or justify an offer.

Remember that it is also important to analyse the case for the other side in similar detail. Not only might you identify weaknesses which can be brought up during negotiations, you will also find that you can predict what your opponent might ask for. This then allows you to consider your response on those points, and possibly even begin to plan what level of offer you would accept or possible concessions you would make. However, bear in mind that this is merely a thought exercise and you should never assume that your predictions will be correct! Finally, reread your instructions both at the beginning and the end of your preparation in order to ensure you do not exceed your authority.

Assessing your chances

No contested litigation can be assessed scientifically. A case which appears watertight on paper might collapse due to the presentation of, or lack of, a single piece of evidence, while what appears a hopeless position may be stronger than you realise. As such, you should not try to assess your chances exactly – some inexperienced negotiators will, for example, assume that "as my chances are around 50/50, I will aim to settle for half the value of the claim". This makes far too many assumptions about the case, about the course of negotiations and particularly about your opponent – remember that they may have some damaging weaknesses which you are yet to discover. Instead, you should take a holistic view. Firstly, are you expecting to make more concessions (for example negotiating the amount of compensation your client must pay), receive more concessions (such as where your client has been injured by the other party) or take a collaborative approach (for instance negotiating a commercial contract)? Secondly, how strong is your case? As explained above, this does not mean calculating a 68.31% chance of success, but rather considering whether you are very likely, moderately likely, not very likely or very unlikely to win – just as you would when answering a problem question. Once you have assessed your chances in this manner, it is easier to start thinking about what strategy or tactics you might choose in order to conduct the negotiation as effectively as possible.

Identify your BATNA

"Always know your BATNA before entering into any negotiation. Otherwise, you won't know whether a deal makes sense or when to walk away . . . People who enter negotiations without defining their BATNA ahead of time put themselves in a weak position."[13]

When considering how you will approach a negotiation, you also need to have in mind your 'BATNA', or Best Alternative To a Negotiated Agreement. This is the next best option if negotiations fail. This should be distinguished from a "bottom line" or "walk away point". For example, you have decided to travel to Australia and to fund your trip you are selling your car. You know from research that similar models have sold for around £3,000 in the past. An inexperienced negotiator might then think that they must not agree to sell the car for any less than £3,000. However, this is not necessarily the BATNA in this scenario. Your alternatives to any agreement today are to try and sell to someone else, or to not sell the car at all. As you

---

[13] Harvard Business School, *The Essentials of Negotiation* (Harvard Business School Press 2005) p.77

want to leave soon and you need the money before you go, these alternatives are not very attractive. Therefore, it may actually be more to your benefit to sell the car for say £2,500 than to walk away and then be forced to cancel your trip altogether. In other negotiations, your BATNA may help you to refuse an offer which you would otherwise accept. Imagine that you are looking for travel insurance for your trip and are conducting a telephone negotiation with an agent of an insurer. They begin by quoting you £200, but after some discussion offer £145, telling you it is their final offer. If you had not considered a BATNA, you might well think that you should now accept – after all, your negotiating skills have won you a discount of more than 25%. However, the prepared negotiator would have obtained a number of other quotes from alternative agencies, and knows that one insurer will go as low as £120. Knowing this, you can ask for a further reduction, safe in the knowledge that a refusal will mean that you can simply call the rival company.

Preparing a written plan

At this point you should have a good idea of what the case involves, and which party appears to have the upper hand. You are now ready to start specific preparation for the negotiation. It is extremely important to write out your plan for the negotiation, as this will help you remember everything you have identified and can also assist you in structuring the negotiation, particularly if your opponent has a tendency to digress or you reach stalemate on a particular issue. Your written plan would normally be no more than three sides of A4, with wide margins or line spacing to allow for notes during the negotiation, and should contain the following:

1. **The details of the negotiation.** Write out in full which parties will be represented at the negotiation, and if you know this detail, who will be representing them. This helps keep clear in your mind who is involved, and helps you remember their names!

2. **The aims of your client.** It is crucial to make a brief list of all your client's objectives. These may be financial (not to lose more than £14,000, to gain at least £100,000 etc.), practical (to avoid court, to keep negotiations confidential, to maintain a business relationship etc.), or personal (to obtain a written apology, to further a persona agenda etc.). Often they will be a combination of the three. Once you have identified all of the aims of your client, you should prioritise them as much as possible. For example, in a defective products dispute your client may be far more concerned with keeping their business reputation than avoiding paying compensation, thus maintaining confidentiality is more important than keeping the amount paid below a certain sum.

3. **Your opening position.** It is useful to write out a brief paragraph or set of bullet points outlining the overall position you will take. This can then form the basis of your opening statement. For instance, in the example given above you may write:

   "Made-up Company Limited is a well-respected and ethical company which deeply regrets what has occurred. However, we are not willing to be held to ransom over what is no more than an isolated mistake and wish to resolve this dispute quickly and efficiently. We certainly believe a reasonable settlement is possible and all parties should keep in mind our long and profitable prior relationship."

4. **Questions to ask.** Having read over the papers, you will have identified areas where more information is needed. Make a note of the questions you will ask concerning these issues as you will want to ensure that you explore them fully and extract as much information as possible.

5. **Issues.** This will be the largest section of your plan. You should, for each issue which requires discussion, set out your opening position, what you hope to achieve, argument in favour of your goals and potentially any concessions you might be willing to make. Bullet points are recommended, as this makes your plan easy to refer to during the negotiation.

6. **Best outcome/Worst outcome.** Finally you should write out what you would achieve in an ideal negotiation (which is usually success on each of the objectives already identified, perhaps tempered by some minor concessions if they seem unavoidable or will not negatively affect your client), and what you would accept as an absolute minimum. This should be relatively straightforward if you have already worked out your BATNA.

Communication skills

Verbal communication

It might appear somewhat redundant to discuss verbal communication – of course you will talk during a negotiation! However, what you say and, just as importantly, how you say it can have a huge impact on your opponent's opinion of you and as such their willingness to compromise with you. Effective negotiators in all walks of life know that establishing rapport with their opposite number can be the key to a successful outcome. If you are negotiating with someone who has trust and confidence in you, whether you are selling them goods and services or settling a multi-million pound claim, they are far more likely to listen to your arguments and accept a reasonable compromise. Even if rapport alone cannot produce a settlement, you will find that building a relationship in a negotiation will almost certainly improve the level of information you receive, such as about your opponent's true position or instructions.

Looking at purely verbal communication, the first and most obvious point to make is that your language should be appropriate to the negotiation. You should ensure you remain professional and avoid becoming too informal, as this may lead to imprecise agreements or give your opponent the impression that you are inexperienced; however you should also avoid the other extreme of negotiating as if you were addressing a higher court – a good negotiation is collaborative rather than adversarial. On a related note, avoid 'legalese' as much as possible – it usually adds nothing to a discussion and can actually make any agreement harder to interpret and enforce. Finally, even in the most heated negotiations, remember common courtesies and never air your personal opinions of either the parties or other negotiators.

As well as the content of your speech, you should consider your delivery. On the whole, negotiation does not require large amounts of oration or spectacle. As such, keep your tone moderate and speak at an appropriate volume for the room. One aspect of your delivery to watch out for is the pace at which you talk – ensure that you speak slowly enough for your opponent to follow your argument, particularly if they are making notes at the same time. Also remember that your voice can provide important clues, such as the inflection that you put on a word. Noting the grammar, read out the following two statements:

> *"Ten thousand pounds is a reasonable sum to settle on. My client would be prepared to repair your client's vehicle and drop his legal action."*

> *"Ten thousand pounds is a reasonable sum to settle on? MY client would be prepared to repair your client's vehicle AND drop his legal action!"*

The first sentence sounds like a ready acceptance of the deal on the table, while the second, despite using the same words, is a clear indicator that the negotiator expects a better offer. Remember that you might involuntarily provide your opponent with clues about your position by any sudden variance in the tone, pitch and pace of your speech.

Non-verbal communication

In face to face negotiations, body language and other non-verbal communication can be equally important in revealing a negotiator's true feelings and intentions. Some obvious examples include raising your eyebrows when surprised, frowning when unhappy or confused, leaning forward when angry or intrigued and many others. Just as poker players will watch for 'tells' from their opponents, an effective negotiator knows that body language can convey many signals about their own and their opponent's position. It is not generally advisable to become too fixated on watching for signals, as you may miss the content of your opponent's arguments, but if you see any signs that might indicate their feelings on a point then it can be an indication that you may want to probe further on that issue or alter your own strategy.

Equally, you should ensure that your own body language does not give away information you would rather keep from your opponent, such as having a weaker position than your strategy suggests. However, this does not mean that you need to sit stock still or maintain a permanent 'poker face'. Instead, you can use body language to actually improve your rapport with your opponent. Many negotiators use a technique called 'matching' or 'mirroring', where they try and mirror another's behaviour – not mimicking every movement but generally keeping posture, gestures and voice similar to that of their opponent. However, this can have its own pitfalls:

> *"There are dangers in escalating friendly behaviour [by mirroring] as well as the obvious problems of escalating aggressive behaviour. You may find yourself being more co-operative and giving more concessions than you had planned if your opponent is very friendly, or in a deadlock or walk out situation if you mirror your opponent's aggressive behaviour."*[14]

Even if you do not use this technique, you should be aware that open and relaxed body language is more conducive to rapport than stiff or aggressive tactics. This might include adopting a confident yet comfortable posture, leaning slightly forward when listening and most importantly maintaining eye contact as much as possible. Finally, remember that spatial relationships are extremely important to most people – while being closer to someone may suggest sociability and a willingness to collaborate, entering someone's 'personal space' can provoke a negative reaction, such as an aggressive response or feelings of intimidation. Also note that appropriate distances can vary between cultures and this may have a bearing on the space at which you negotiate.

Active listening

It is absolutely essential when negotiating that not only do you listen carefully to your opponent's arguments, but also that he or she *realises* that you are listening to the points they are trying to get across. There is a considerable difference between hearing someone talk, and listening to their words and we often unconsciously give the impression that we are not interested in what someone has to say. To avoid this, you need to ensure that you develop skills in active listening.

As the name suggests, active listening involves more than passively waiting for your own turn to speak. Firstly, it requires that your body language and behaviour indicates that you are giving the speaker your full attention. As mentioned above, this includes considerable eye contact, but also

---

[14] F. Boyle, *A Practical Guide to Lawyering Skills* 2nd Edition (Routledge-Cavendish 2003) p.265

techniques such as leaning gently towards your opponent with your shoulders square, giving the impression that you are concentrating on what they have to say. Keep your body language relaxed, rather than appearing coiled and ready to raise a counter-argument as soon as they finish speaking. It is also important when listening to longer or more complex arguments that you are following your opponent's train of thought. Simple gestures such as nods, smiles and brief interludes such as "yes", "I see", "of course" are easy to forget when you are concentrating on a negotiation but will put your opponent at their ease and reassure them that you do understand their concerns, even if you do not agree with them.

Effective questioning

Another crucial communication skill is the ability to ask the right questions at the right time. In almost all negotiations, the questioning face is extremely important as you are attempting to obtain as much information as possible, and this information may change the entire context of the negotiation.

Open and closed questions

There is a general distinction, not just within negotiation, that can be made between 'open' and 'closed' questions. An open question is one which allows a wide range of answers, such as "what are your client's concerns?" or "what are your views on this offer?" or even simply "why?". Open questions are useful to obtain a broad range of information and will encourage the other person to discuss their own opinions, views and ideas. However, bear in mind that too many open questions can allow a negotiation to digress from the main issues. Furthermore, an experienced negotiator might be able to avoid disclosing harmful information if a question is too open.

By contrast, a closed question is one which only allows very limited answers, often either "yes" or "no". For instance, you might ask your opponent "do you have video evidence of this event?" or "exactly how much money was lost on this contract?". Closed questions are used to elicit specific information, when you want a particular fact or answer without any extraneous additions, or you wish to pin your opponent down on a certain point. However, this means that excessive use of this technique might make your opponent feel they are being interrogated and thus less willing to compromise, or it may mean you miss wider information which could help your case. Therefore you should use a mixture of closed and open questions.

Questioning skills

You should not only combine open and closed questions, but also think about the *types* of question that you ask. In order to extract the most information, you will need to take a varied approach. For example, you may begin by asking very open, general questions which are really a prompt for your opponent to talk as much as possible, or probing questions to explore an issue you have little information on. If the answers to these questions hint at further information, you will then want to proceed to using clarifying and follow-up questions, such as "what exactly do you mean by 'some losses'?" or "so how else has this affected your client's career?".

Remember that even once you progress into the bargaining stage of a negotiation, there is still scope for further questioning. In particular, you can make use of hypothetical questions to gauge reaction to offers, for instance "if we were to make some concessions on the Brighton property, how would this affect your position in regards to the London office?". This allows you to explore options without committing yourself, and may prompt your opponent to think of alternative solutions.

Silence

Remember that "in interpersonal communications, most of us are uncomfortable with silence"[15]. You will know this from personal experience – if you are with someone you do not know well and both of you stop talking, there is a temptation to say something (or anything) to break the silence! Indeed, recent research suggests that just four seconds of silence in a conversation can "make one feel distressed, afraid, hurt, and rejected."[16] While you will not be aiming to have this effect on your opponent, you can certainly harness this human compulsion to speak by purposefully allowing conversation to lapse and letting your opponent break the silence. This will often result in your opponent offering information unprompted that can be of great use to your case.

Mistakes to avoid

Most questioning errors are relatively easy to spot, but they are also easy to make. One of the most common is the multiple question, where you ask a number of different questions at the same time. For example, you might ask a negotiator representing a company you suspect intentionally supplied your client with defective products, "so what exactly was delivered? Which products did you supply? Did you check any of them before they left your warehouse?". If your opponent is given this chance, he or she could answer one of these questions, such as what was delivered, and avoid mentioning what checks were carried out. Ensure that when you ask a question, you wait for an answer, rephrasing that same question if necessary.

Another common error is to suggest the answer within the question. If you listen to journalists and interviewers, you can see this technique in action. However, while it might be useful for them to ask "what did you think of that performance? It was not good enough, was it?" you should be very careful of doing the same. If you prompt an answer, such as in the example above asking "did you check the goods before they left the warehouse? I assume you must have opened some of the crates", you will normally get a yes or no response. This may be helpful if you need such a specific reply, but often the answer is of little help, as it may mean that had you asked a more open question, your opponent would have elaborated. It can also be an irritating habit generally and your opponent may feel patronised, or that you are attempting to misrepresent his or her arguments.

Structuring a negotiation

We have already looked at how you might prepare for a negotiation, but even the best preparation possible is of little use if you do not cover all the issues you have planned to discuss. This is why a clear structure is extremely useful in a negotiation. Not only will you ensure that all topics are covered, but as most negotiations take place under some element of time pressure you will also be able to track how quickly you are progressing down the agenda.

Unsurprisingly, a negotiation will begin with the introductory stage. At this point all parties should set out who they are and who they represent. This may sound obvious, but it is important to establish this exactly at this stage to avoid any misunderstandings – for example, a party may have separate representation to their insurers. Any major limits on your authority to negotiate should also be mentioned, for example if you cannot make a final agreement or will only be able to negotiate on certain issues. You will also want

---

[15] T. Gosselin, *Practical Negotiating* (John Wiley & Sons 2007)
[16] N. Koudenburg, T. Postmesa, & E. Gordijna, 'Disrupting the flow: How brief silences in group conversations affect social needs' (2011) 47(2) *Journal of Experimental Social Psychology* 512

to establish an agenda at this stage, namely the order in which you plan to discuss the issues on the table. You may find that this schedule is adapted as the negotiation progresses but it is useful to at least attempt to agree a basic structure. As discussed later in this section, you may not be able to decide this agenda but at the very least you might pick up some clues as to what your opponent considers the most important issues. It is usually more advantageous to agree a less than perfect agenda than to proceed with no agenda at all. If you cannot agree as to the order of issues, some simple compromises include negotiating the highest value items first, or following the order of issues in the statements of case or list of facts which you have been given beforehand. This is also a good opportunity to establish empathy with other negotiators and while you should not waste your client's time with long discussions about last night's television or the football results, some brief pleasantries can go a long way to establishing your image as a polite and professional representative.

After the introductory stage, some negotiators will give their overall position. This can be helpful to establish the basic aims of each party at the beginning and may lead to a more collaborative approach, particularly as both parties may have similar interests (agreeing as quickly as possible for example). However, some less cooperative strategies might mean you or your opponent choose not to reveal any information at this point. Once the negotiation begins in earnest, the structure will be very much dependent on the subject matter of the negotiations. In very straightforward cases, there may only be one issue to decide, while at the other end of the scale there may be a large number of complex issues and sub-issues to consider. In either case, the discussion of each issue should be a two-stage process. Firstly, there will be a period of questioning and exploring, where both sides are seeking further information about the issue and raising any specific concerns from their instructions. This is also the point to ask for or produce any written evidence which is relevant. Secondly, once both sides are satisfied that they know as much as necessary, you can proceed to the bargaining stage, where proposals and offers are made and responded to. This is considered in more detail below, but bear in mind that this stage should not be viewed as merely exchanging figures, as you need to support any offer or rejection with a logical argument for your choice. Make sure that any agreement made is recorded by both parties as soon as it occurs, as this will save time at the final stage.

This final stage is of course to conclude the negotiation. Again, we will look at this in more detail a little later but from a structural point of view, any conclusion should involve three elements: what has been agreed; what has not been agreed; and what further steps must now be taken (and when they will be taken). Bear in mind that in a real legal negotiation, you will also need to consider the issue of costs at this point (which party will pay you and your opponent's fees) and the form of any agreement you might make as it is usual to record such settlements in a formal legal order.

Making and responding to offers

One of the most complex skills in negotiation is making and responding to offers. Unless you have been given very strict instructions on what or how much can be offered or accepted, it can be difficult to decide exactly how low or high to pitch your offer. This is particularly the case when making an opening offer, as you have no previous figure to work from.

As a result, many inexperienced negotiators will allow the other party to make the first offer. While this might take the pressure off you momentarily, it can also be a disadvantage. To illustrate why this is, we will engage in a brief exercise:

> **Exercise: The "anchoring effect"**
>
> Answer the following questions as quickly as possible. Please do not look up the answers beforehand, as this defeats the purpose of the exercise.
>
> 1. Do you think the population of Australia is more or less than 30 million people?
> 2. Estimate the population of Australia to the nearest million.
> 3. Do you think the population of North Korea is more or less than 10 million people?
> 4. Estimate the population of North Korea to the nearest million.

In actual fact, the population of both countries is similar – Australia has a population of just under 22 million people, while North Korea has around 24 million inhabitants.[17] However, the majority of you reading this chapter will have given a higher estimate for Australia than North Korea. This reflects a principle known as the "anchoring effect" – because you were given implied reference points (30 million and 10 million) you are likely to have kept your estimates relatively close to these figures.[18] It should now be clear why the majority of experienced negotiators actually prefer to make the first offer – if they can set the reference point relatively low or high, the final figure agreed is likely to be in this range.

We now know why you should try to make the first offer, but that does not answer the question of what offer you should make. For the following discussion, we will assume you are representing a hospital attempting to settle a dispute with a patient who was negligently treated. You know that the patient originally asked for £100,000, while you are of course trying to keep costs as low as possible. To take the anchoring effect to its logical extreme, surely you should open with an offer of one pence? Of course, this would not be a sensible first offer, as it will merely insult your opponent and give the impression that you will not be open to reason. Instead, you want to make an offer which is as low as possible yet still credible. This leads us on to the concept of the ZOPA, or the Zone Of Possible Agreement.

Best for defendant				Best for claimant
Insult zone	Credible zone	Reasonable settlement zone	Credible zone	Insult zone
	Z	O P	A	
Lowest offer				Highest offer

Figure 2: The Zone Of Possible Agreement

---

[17] Source: CIA World Factbook population estimates, https://www.cia.gov/library/publications/the-world-factbook/rankorder/2119rank.html
[18] For further study of this phenomenon, a good starting point is the work of Amos Tversky and Daniel Kahneman.

As you can see from the diagram above, we can plot all the possible offers you or your opponent might make on a spectrum. At either extreme, the offer is so low or so high that it cannot be considered credible and may offend the other party. In the centre is the most likely zone of settlement where, assuming both negotiators are similarly skilled and willing to be reasonable, we would expect the final settlement to lie. Your aim in any such negotiation is to agree a figure as close to your end of the spectrum as possible. Remember that once you make an offer, you can only move closer to the centre, thus just as you should avoid the "insult zone" you should also leave enough room to negotiate!

If you find that agreement is not possible on a point, do not panic or automatically assume you cannot reach a settlement. Consider whether you can combine any other issues into your next offer, for instance agreeing to raise your offer or lower your demand if the other side will allow some leeway on another point. However, you should not try and renegotiate on any areas on which you have already reached agreement. If this does not break the deadlock, do not be afraid to move on to another issue. Often, giving both sides time to consider their position can lead to a softening of approach and this can be bolstered by agreement on other areas – once you have resolved so many other points, it may be more tempting to make a small concession to break the deadlock rather than lose the chance for a full settlement.

The end of a negotiation

Full agreement

If you have achieved an agreement on every point in issue, concluding the negotiation will mainly concern recording your settlement. Ensure that everything you have agreed is clearly recorded in a written document, which both sides accept and sign. This prevents any dispute later about exactly what was agreed. Make sure that you record enough details for each point – if party A will pay party B a sum of money, you should not only record the amount of the payment but also when it will be paid and how. You may also wish to record some brief notes as to why you agreed a certain point, such as "prepared to pay this due to concession on costs" or "admitted this figure was excessive, thus accepted lower amount". This is particularly important on any points where you have come to an even split, as while you will of course have only done so after reasoned argument as to why this was appropriate, you client may look at the agreement and assume you said "well let's just split this down the middle"!

Partial agreement

When you have only come to a partial agreement, you should still record everything which was agreed. If you have finally settled certain points, this should be in the form discussed above. If you have come to a partial agreement in the sense that you have provisionally settled certain issues, but reserved acceptance until you consult your client, this should be recorded as such. Make sure that you set a timeframe for this to occur, for example "will confirm or reject within 14 days". You may also want to discuss arrangements for a future session to again try to resolve any unsettled points.

No agreement

Occasionally a negotiation will result in no agreement whatsoever. You might think that this means there is nothing to do at the end of the negotiation, but this is not the case. It is important to consider why no agreement was reached – if for example you were progressing well but ran out of time, then it would be appropriate to schedule another session. If you have failed to agree because of a lack of authority or cooperation by one party, you may want to ask if another negotiation can be arranged with different personnel. Remember that you will have to explain to your client why you have not achieved any agreement, thus you should ensure you can justify ending the negotiation at this point.

> ### Self-Test Questions
> 1. What should you include in a written negotiation plan?
> 2. Name six ways to improve rapport through verbal and non-verbal communication.
> 3. What is the difference between a BATNA and a ZOPA? How are the two related?
> 4. What is the "anchoring effect"?

Improving as a Negotiator

Negotiating as a team

Much of the previous section is written as if you alone will be representing your client in negotiations. However, many negotiations take place between teams of people and it is important to note the specific skills which you will need to develop to be effective in such situations. The following points assume that you are negotiating with others of equal authority and may not be applicable where you are working with a person in a more senior or junior capacity.

- **Prepare together**
  - You are probably much more familiar with preparing for and conducting legal work alone, such as tutorial preparation, legal research and writing assignments. This means that it can be very easy to start preparing to negotiate alone and not compare notes until you are finished, if at all. This is a counterproductive approach which will waste your time and that of your partner. Before conducting any substantive preparation you should meet to discuss the issues and objectives in the negotiation. You may then decide to research separate areas alone and perhaps draft a negotiation plan yourself, but ensure that you meet to compare your findings and work out a joint negotiation plan. Even if you do work alone for some of the time, it is important that all members of the team have a good understanding of every issue, in case someone is not present at the negotiation itself.

- **Assign issues and roles**
  - Make sure that you and your teammates are clear on which issues you will take the lead on. It is more effective for one person to conduct the majority of negotiation on each point – this is so that your opponent knows who they should address their arguments to and to avoid two or more team members making different offers or adopting different tactics. When assigning issues, you would

normally aim to give each negotiator a similar workload. Take account of team members' experience and skills when assigning issues, for instance allowing a more combative negotiator to begin the negotiation or assigning a weak point to someone particularly good at accommodation.

- You will also need to discuss the roles and responsibilities you will each undertake. This might be strategic, such as the 'good cop/bad cop' approach where one negotiator uses an aggressive strategy while the other adopts a conciliatory approach, or more practical, for instance deciding who will open the negotiation or who will record the proceedings. Ensure that you discuss how you will deal with any offer of final agreement – will one team member take final responsibility or will you confer with each other before acceptance?

- **Speak one at a time**
  - One of the easiest, and therefore the most common, mistakes to make in team negotiation is to interrupt or talk over your teammate. It is almost inevitable that this will happen at some stage in a negotiation but you should work hard to keep this to a minimum. Not only can it negatively affect your relationship with others on your team, this behaviour will give your opponents the impression that you are unprofessional and may mean important arguments are not properly communicated.
  - This can be partly avoided by separating the issues as advised above. Another useful technique is to develop a signal for when you want to interject, such as nudging your teammate under the table or raising your pen. When your teammate is speaking, wait until they have finished and avoid the urge to interrupt unless absolutely necessary (for example if they exceed instructions). You can always write a brief note on the negotiation plan in front of you if you want them to ask a particular question or develop a specific point.

- **Analyse your performance**
  - It can be a great advantage to negotiate with someone else, as you have an excellent opportunity to receive constructive feedback from a fellow negotiator. Ensure that after every negotiation involving a team, you take part in a post-mortem review. At this meeting, you should talk about how you felt the negotiation went, whether you noticed any particular issues with a fellow negotiator and if you have any concerns about your own performance. Obviously you should be polite and not attack a teammate's performance but constructive criticism should be encouraged – if a colleague is continually interrupting you, they will not stop unless you point out what they are doing wrong.

Negotiation competitions

As a student your best opportunity to improve your formal negotiation skills is to join one of the many negotiation competitions. Your university or college might offer internal competitions or modules, and there are also a number of national competitions between higher education institutions. Most negotiation competitions involve pairs or teams, although some do involve individual competition.

If you do enter a negotiation competition, there are some specific issues you should be aware of. Firstly, you should familiarise yourself with the scope of the competition. If it is restricted to legal negotiation, you will need to conform to legal ethics and expect to research and discuss the law, while if there are entrants from a non-legal background you should focus on the practical issues rather than specific law. You should also be aware of the rules of the competition, most notably how long each negotiation will last and how it will be assessed. In particular, find out whether the balance of marks is awarded for reaching agreement, or for how you actually negotiate – often competitions are slightly artificial in that the questioning and positioning stage is more important than the actual settlement (or lack of one).

You should also bear in mind that many negotiating competitions will try to assess wider skills than plain negotiation. This might involve multi-party negotiations, having to work with another team, being given extra facts just prior to or during the negotiation, or intentional errors or ambiguities in your instructions. It is quite common for competitions to involve feedback sessions after each negotiation, where participants are expected to be able to analyse their own performance and discuss it with the judges. You will need to both critically discuss your own strengths and weaknesses, and justify why you took certain steps during the negotiation. Finally, do not forget to make a good impression – arrive early, dress smartly and network as much as possible.

Common problems

Bad habits

Even the best negotiators make mistakes and it is all too easy to develop bad habits. You should beware in particular the temptation to assume that just because a tactic worked once, it will always be effective. Listed below are some of the most common bad habits negotiators develop – when reflecting on your performance after a negotiation, try to consider if you are developing any of the following:

- **Expecting agenda control**
    - If you have prepared carefully and exhaustively, you will have created a structured plan for the negotiation. As this will usually involve prioritising issues, you will often have fixed in your mind the order in which you intend to deal with these issues at the negotiation. This is not a problem per se, however it can be difficult to adapt if your opponent does not wish to negotiate according to your schedule. In the worst case, you can then make serious errors, such as beginning by offering up a concession which you planned to give away at the end if a deal was close.
    - In order to avoid this habit, make sure that you bear in mind that your plan is just that, and in the words of Rabbie Burns, "apt to go awry". In more complex negotiations, it may be worth considering alternative agendas prior to the negotiation. If you face an opponent determined to set the agenda, you should not immediately accept but instead try to negotiate a compromise.

- **Advocating rather than negotiating**
    - This is a problem many negotiators face, but one which is particularly common among lawyers and law students, who might be more used to advocacy than negotiation. This habit is characterised by continuing to put your arguments and only disagreeing with your opponent, rather than seeking compromise or any common ground. While you should back up your offers and responses with logical, reasoned argument and put your clients' point of view, remember that there is no judge to decide the result of your negotiation and that it is very unusual to achieve the exact result your client wants.

- **Sticking to a single style**
    - You should make use of different styles when negotiating, rather than picking one approach and using it relentlessly. For example, if your opponent is extremely aggressive, using your own aggressive strategy is likely to be fruitless and could cause discussions to degenerate into an argument. Instead, you should be willing to change styles and strategies as required, always aiming to adopt the tactics which will make a favourable agreement more likely.

- **Overconfidence/Expecting to "come out ahead"**
    - This might not be a problem during your first experiences of negotiation but it is easy, especially after a number of positive results, to begin to expect to "win" every time. This can manifest itself in a number of different ways. Firstly, you might be overconfident in your own ability, which makes it more likely that you will fail to prepare fully or take unnecessary risks when negotiating (such as pitching offers too high or exceeding your instructions). Alternatively, you might be overconfident in your client's case, expecting that you will "come out ahead" despite the weaknesses in your arguments. Remember that for every negotiation where one party is stronger, the other is in a weaker position and some negotiations are essentially exercises in damage control, where you will have to accept an unfavourable compromise and your job is to keep these concessions as minimal as reasonably possible.

- **Monopolising team negotiations or over-reliance on your partner**
    - As mentioned above, team negotiations pose their own set of challenges. One of the most common issues which can arise in a team is that one partner or team member begins to dominate the pairing or group. This is of no benefit to anyone, as the dominant member may not be able to address all these issues in the requisite depth, while the skills and knowledge of his or her colleagues are not being utilised effectively.
    - If you feel that you are falling into one of these roles, it is important to discuss matters with the rest of your team as soon as possible. Ensure that you raise the matter tactfully, as no one wants to be accused of either dictating to the group or of not pulling their weight. Often, you will find that this problem arises due to poor preparation, where one party is taking on a larger share of the work, so a good starting point is to discuss how you can allocate issues more evenly.

Dealing with opponents

Unfortunately, however good a negotiator you become, the success of a negotiation always relies on *both* parties being willing to compromise. While an effective negotiator can usually surmount most difficulties, certain types of opponent can prove frustratingly difficult to deal with. Below are some common problems, with suggested solutions:

- **My opponent is not prepared**
    - As you know, preparation is crucial for a negotiation to be successful. However, you will find on occasion that your opponent has not prepared and this can create a number of problems.: it may cause delays as your opponent has to read or reread documents; it may mean your opponent is too optimistic as they have not understood all the facts; and it may well prevent agreement if your opponent is not clear on what they can or should agree.
    - If your opponent is clearly underprepared, you should try to assist them as much as legal ethics and common sense allows. While it might seem unfair to have to help the other side, it is far better for you and your client that the negotiation has a chance of success, rather than facing the delay and disruption a failed negotiation can cause. However, when assisting your opponent you must remember to give an objective view of the case, neither giving away information they would not have, nor misleading them as to their position. You should also bear in mind that an underprepared opponent will probably already feel embarrassed and if you appear patronising or overbearing in your assistance, you may make agreement less likely.

- **My opponent uses intimidation, personal attacks or inappropriate language**
    - Sadly some negotiators still believe that using a highly aggressive style is an effective method of negotiating. This can range from relatively mild intimidation, such as using a loud voice and adopting commanding body language, to extremes such as insults, abuse and sexual or racial discrimination.
    - If you are facing a negotiator who is aggressive, but behaving within reasonable boundaries, you should attempt to ignore their bluster. Aggressive negotiation is often an indicator of a weak bargaining position and you will often find that if you keep calm and persist with a rational, problem-solving approach your opponent will abandon the aggressive approach and become more willing to compromise. However, if your opponent behaves in an unacceptable manner and continues to do so even after you tell them that you are not comfortable with their behaviour, you are well within your rights to ask to deal with another negotiator or in extreme cases simply leave the negotiation.
- **My opponent is highly emotional**
    - Your opponent may not be adopting an aggressive style but actually negotiating on the basis of their emotions. While uncommon when negotiating with other lawyers, you may well face this problem with inexperienced negotiators or when dealing with lay people representing themselves.
    - When dealing with an emotional negotiator, remember to empathise, rather than sympathise. This means that you should try and understand their position and recognise why they might be feeling such emotions, without losing sight of your duty to your client. Thus if someone has suffered a traumatic injury for which they believe your side is to blame, you should show that you understand why they are upset, but you should not agree that your client is at fault or must compensate them! Often the best strategy is to suggest a short break in the negotiation to allow your opponent to compose themselves.
- **My opponent claims not to have authority**
    - Some negotiators, while claiming to represent their client, deny that they have full authority. You may find your opponent using phrases such as "I cannot make any commitments on that point" or "I can only give provisional agreement" or "let me talk to my client about our possible agreement".
    - If your opponent has no authority at all, there is no point in continuing the negotiation – you will gain nothing and may give away information without anything in exchange. If your opponent appears to only have authority on certain points, you will need to make a judgement call – if you think that you can create a self-contained agreement on those points you should attempt to do so, however if these issues overlap with areas where there is no authority, you should be careful not to give away too much. For example, imagine you are negotiating for one of the drivers in a road traffic accident. You may well be able to make an agreement that all future negotiations will remain confidential without considering any other issues, but you should not for example agree to accept liability when your opponent claims no authority to negotiate compensation – the next negotiation might well begin with your opponent demanding an extremely high figure in the knowledge that your client has accepted they must pay up!

- **I think my opponent has exceeded their authority**
    - Unless your opponent makes it clear in advance what the limits of their authority are, you would not normally know if they have exceeded them. However, it might occasionally be obvious that they are offering or demanding compromises which are far outside any authority they could conceivably possess. This is particularly true of negotiation competitions, where for example students are told in the rules that they cannot offer monetary compensation, only practical solutions.
    - If you are certain your opponent is acting beyond their authority, you should ask them to reassure you that they are entitled to make such an offer or even to check with their client. It may be that they have got carried away with the moment and will realise on reflection that they have exceeded their authority. It may seem counter-intuitive to do so, as you might be being offered a very advantageous settlement, however any agreement made outside of a negotiator's authority may well not be honoured by their client, making the negotiations a waste of time and money.
- **My opponent is making unrealistic offers or demands**
    - Occasionally you will come across a negotiator who makes demands far outside any zone of possible agreement and refuses to compromise, even in the face of rational argument.
    - Firstly consider whether your opponent is truly determined not to change their offer, or whether they are trying to use an aggressive style to force you to change your position. If you are satisfied that they will not compromise, and that this is unreasonable in the light of the facts put forward by both sides, do not be afraid to walk away, unless expressly instructed to settle at any price. A client would rather negotiations failed than that they were bullied into an unfair agreement.
- **My opponent has made a last-minute demand**
    - Some negotiators have a habit of all but agreeing on a deal, then making a last-minute demand. This is a common tactic in business negotiations, particularly in the sales sector – after all, if you have both worked so hard and agreed on so many points, what can it hurt to make one last concession?
    - Be very wary of anything proposed at the last minute. There can be a strong temptation to agree to anything at this point to gain an agreement, particularly if the negotiations have been difficult or a deadline is approaching. The correct attitude is to respond to this issue as you have responded to all other issues in the negotiation – listen to your opponent's point of view, then put your own and try to come to a compromise which both parties can accept.

Practical Questions

1. Research a negotiation competition on the internet. What rules does the competition have which you did not expect? How is the competition assessed?
2. Make a list of the most common mistakes you make when negotiating. For each entry, think of two practical steps you could take to avoid this error in future.
3. Think back to the last time you negotiated, whether in an academic, professional or personal capacity. Did your opponent do or say anything which you were unsure how to respond to? If so, how could you respond in future?

Further reading

F. Boyle, *A Practical Guide to Lawyering Skills* 2nd Edition (Routledge-Cavendish 2003)
R. Cialdini, *Influence: The Psychology of Persuasion* (Harper Business 2007)
H. Cornelius & S. Faire, *Everyone Can Win* 2nd Edition (Simon & Schuster 2007)
R. Fells, *Effective Negotiation: From Research to Results* (Cambridge University Press 2006)
R. Fisher, *Getting Past No* (Random House 1992)
R. Fisher and W. Ury, *Getting to Yes* 2nd Edition (Random House 2003)
S. Gates, *The Negotiation Book* (John Wiley & Sons 2010)
T. Gosselin, *Practical Negotiating* (John Wiley & Sons 2007)
C. S. Graham, *The Way of the Lawyer: Strategies and Tactics for Negotiations, Presentations, and Litigation* (American Bar Association 2011)
Harvard Business School, *The Essentials of Negotiation* (Harvard Business School Press 2005)
G. Kennedy, *Everything is Negotiable* 4th Edition (Random House Business 2008)
R. Lewicki, B. Barry & D. Saunders, *Negotiation: Readings, Exercises and Cases* 5th Edition (McGraw-Hill 2007)
D. Malhotra & M. Bazerman, *Negotiation Genius* (Bantam 2008)
R. Mnookin, S. Peppet & A. Tulumello, *Beyond Winning: Negotiating to Create Value in Deals and Disputes* (Harvard University Press 2004)
K. Paterson *et al.*, *Crucial Conversations: Tools for Talking When Stakes are High* (McGraw-Hill 2002)
A. Pease & B. Pease, *The Definitive Book of Body Language* (Orion 2005)
Dr N. Peeling, *Brilliant Negotiations: What the Best Negotiators Know, Do and Say* 2nd Edition (Prentice Hall 2010)
G. R. Shell, *Bargaining for Advantage: Negotiation Strategies for Reasonable People* 2nd Edition (Penguin Books 2006)

8
Writing Law Essays

Janette Porteous

Introduction

Assessment is an essential component of your learning process and, while being assessed may be a daunting prospect, there are good reasons behind it. Being assessed during your law degree gives you the opportunity to demonstrate not only your understanding and knowledge of a topic, but also to exhibit other skills you will have developed, such as your ability to analyse a legal problem or to evaluate competing arguments in relation to a particular legal issue. It also allows you to show good research and communication skills and to discover strengths and weaknesses in your own learning. Assessment will provide you with the opportunity to demonstrate the extent that you have progressed in your learning from one level (year) to another. Through the feedback and grade you receive for an assignment, you will be able to undertake any remedial action before your submit your next assignment, which will hopefully result in a better mark.

Prior to starting university, you will most probably have had experience in writing essays, for example, as part of your A-level assignments. As such, there is perhaps an assumption that you know how to write essays, and yet some of you may feel disappointed when you receive the mark for the first assessment you submit. This is because, at undergraduate level, there is a greater expectation that you will write to a higher standard and employ a number of key skills. No longer will it be acceptable for you to, for example, write a purely 'descriptive' essay or one that contains 'everything you know' on the subject in question. You will be expected to express yourself clearly, to be concise and precise in what you are saying, to be critical and analytical, to employ good presentation skills and to demonstrate the use of appropriately selected and diverse sources of law (both primary and secondary).

> "Written skills are not things that you learn once and for all and then continue to put into practice in the same way, year after year."[1]

---

[1] Webley, L. *Legal Writing* 2nd Edition (Routledge-Cavendish 2010)

Even if you feel confident in writing an essay, it is essential to continue to improve and to develop your writing skills to a higher standard. The purpose of this chapter is to offer you some advice and tips on writing law essays at undergraduate level.

Why Write Law Essays?

"An essay question is a way of examining your understanding and your considered and evidenced views on an area of law, practice or policy. Your answer displays your considered response to a question, which weighs up competing viewpoints. It shows how you reached your conclusions with the evidence that you have drawn upon to come to your final view."[2]

Some of you might question why essay writing should be part of a law course. After all, many of you will hope to become lawyers in the near future and your expectation will be that you will be solving your clients' legal problems and so will have no need to write essays. Nevertheless, there is a good rationale for including essay writing as part of your assessment diet. The assessor (who will often be your tutor) will want to use essay questions to evoke an in-depth answer to a complex question and will want to encourage you to demonstrate not only your knowledge of the subject-matter, but also other key skills, such as your ability to critique legal rules and to consider policy, social, ethical and other issues relevant to the question set. Including essays in your coursework allows you to demonstrate that you can select appropriate and diverse materials not only to demonstrate knowledge, but also that you have the ability to evaluate the selected sources in terms of reliability, validity and relevance. Research should be used strategically as a tool in analysis, critical thinking and evaluation and the assessor will be able to measure these skills in your essay.

There are, of course, other important skills that the assessor will take into account when marking your essay – they will want to see that you can organise your thoughts by writing them down in a structured and logical way. They will want to gauge that you are capable of stating and developing your *own* point of view on issues and not simply the point of view of others. The assessor will also evaluate how well you express yourself in the written form; your use of language and how well you present your ideas. Hopefully, you will have, by now, begun to see how useful the art of writing essays is. You will have the opportunity throughout your course to develop a range of writing skills that are often referred to as transferrable skills. The ability to write well and to express yourself clearly in the written form is important, as these transferable skills will assist you not only whilst you are at university but also in your professional life. In short, writing essays will help you to hone your writing skills and to be an effective communicator during university and in your chosen career, whether or not you become a lawyer.

The assessor may use essay questions in examinations along with problem questions. You may find this intimidating as you do not have the luxury of time to think about the question and to plan your answer, or the opportunity to undertake research. Nevertheless, the skills employed when writing an essay say for

---

[2] Ibid

coursework, are essentially the same. Perhaps the main difference is your inability to undertake detailed research and to use academic articles and other sources in the examination. You are essentially writing from memory but regardless of this perceived disadvantage, you should always refer to appropriate authorities and you may find it helpful to try to memorise a couple of brief quotes to enhance your answer.

What the Assessor is Looking for in Essay Writing

You now know that being assessed is a fundamental part of being a student. As such, you will feel more confident if you are aware of the kind of things the assessor will be looking for and, giving marks to, when assessing your essay. Knowing what the marker is looking for and *how* your written work is assessed is often seen as a mystery to students. Most of you will want to know the 'secrets' involved in marking your work so that you can achieve a good grade for your essay. In reality, there are no secrets.

> ### Example
> 'The assessment process, as far as it practicable – particularly with regard to the different types of assessment – should be clear and apparent from the students' point of view so that they:
>
> - understand the means by which a module is assessed;
> - know the criteria that are to be used in any type of assessment;
> - easily comprehend the grounds on which a mark or classification has been awarded.'

The assessment process begins with the module leader designing the assessment method for their module and they will want to ensure that this is valid, reliable and transparent. The assessor will have in mind what they want to measure. For example, when drafting an essay question they will want the question, in broad terms, to allow you to demonstrate your individuality and expression, to enable her to measure your writing style and to determine your depth of knowledge of the subject-matter in question. The assessor will want the essay question to motivate you to learn and to promote deeper understanding of a subject. They will also want the question to be fair and equitable and yet demanding; demanding in the sense that it should allow the 'better' student to be challenged and yet allow all students to have the opportunity to achieve a high grade.

> *"Assessment tasks and the feedback students receive on their work can show them what the intended learning outcomes mean in practice. Often it is only when students undertake tasks in which their evidence of achievement of the learning outcomes is being measured that they fully appreciate the nature and level of the competences they need to attain."*[3]

The assessment design will also focus on the **learning outcomes** of the module being assessed. All law programmes will contain learning outcomes for the programme as a whole and for each individual

---
[3] Race, P. *et al. 500 Tips on Assessment* 2nd Edition (Routledge-Farmer 2005)

module. What are learning outcomes and why do you need to know about them? Simply, learning outcomes may be said to be *what* is intended to be learned. Modern practice in higher education is to produce learning outcomes rather than simply list the topics to be studied. Topics will be listed but this list should not be confused with learning outcomes. The list of learning outcomes provides transparency in that you will be able to engage in your own learning by being aware of what the aims are for each module studied. Learning outcomes are often written is terms of what you should be 'able to do' by the end of the module. The following is from an undergraduate third year Family Law module:

> ### Example
> Upon successful completion of this module, the student will be able to:
>
> - **demonstrate** sound knowledge and understanding of the principal features of family law;
> - **critically assess** the legal and financial implications of relationships on relationship breakdown;
> - **analyse** the rights and duties of parents and others towards children;
> - **critically evaluate and synthesise** doctrinal, policy and ethical considerations involved in family law legislation and judicial activity;
> - **exhibit the ability to identify and retrieve** up-to-date and relevant legal information, to use primary and secondary sources and to read, discuss and critique the materials found;
> - **communicate well** and present knowledge or argument in a way that others may grasp; and
> - **work independently,** reflect on their own learning and to make use of feedback.

Learning outcomes play an important role in assessment strategy. The assessor will have in mind the learning outcomes for the module when drafting the essay question. It is therefore important that you familiarise yourself with the learning outcomes for each module you study – these are usually contained in the module handbook but if not, just ask your lecturer.

Once the assessor has written the essay question with reference to the learning outcomes – what do they take into account when assessing your essay? Not surprisingly the assessor will allocate marks for **content; structure** and **overall presentation**. However, at university level, the assessor will have certain other criteria in mind. For those of you who have studied for A-levels you will probably be aware of marking schemes. Marking schemes are not model answers; they are more to do with identifying the mark-bearing parts of a good answer and they are drafted in such a way to allow allocation of marks. At university the assessor will not use marking schemes as such – what they will use is assessment criteria. **Assessment criteria** will indicate the basis upon which your assessor will make judgments about your work in terms of **knowledge, communication skills** and **'legal skills'** – the criteria will be communicated to you.

Content

In simple terms, an essay consists of three main components: the introduction, the main body and the conclusion. You will gain most marks from the main body of the essay. The assessor will be looking for a structured approach and overall presentation of the essay, but, in addition, they will be measuring certain skills in your *content* and these might include your ability to:

- address the question set and cover all the important and relevant points;
- avoid irrelevant material;
- demonstrate knowledge and understanding of the relevant law;
- demonstrate knowledge of relevant policy, social, political, economic issues;
- apply analytical and evaluative skills;
- enter into a full debate and critique of the issues in question;
- present your arguments in a logical and structured way;
- produce well reasoned conclusions;
- undertake thorough and accurate research;
- analyse the material used;
- offer insights that are well considered and convincing; and
- use appropriate terminology.

The assessor may prefer to draft specific criteria in relation to content and convention will vary from institution to institution. The assessment criteria for content might, for instance, be expressed in the following terms:

Mark in the 40s (Weak to fair)	Mark in the 50s (fair to good)	Mark in the 60s (good to very good)	70s and above (excellent)
Content: based mainly on lecture material with only limited analysis/evaluation/problem-solving	competent use of source material with fair attempt at analysis/evaluation/problem-solving	good use of source material and thoughtful analysis/evaluation/problem-solving	source material used to maximum effect with sophisticated analysis/evaluation/problem-solving
insufficient evidence of clear understanding of the subject and ability to formulate own thoughts and ideas on the question	evidence of satisfactory understanding of the subject and ability to formulate own thoughts and ideas on the question	evidence of good understanding of the subject and ability to formulate and manipulate own ideas effectively	ample evidence of excellent understanding and ability to produce and manipulate original ideas effectively

Structure

"The basic structure follows the convention of moving from the general (the introduction) through to the specific (the main body) and back to the general (the conclusion)." [4]

---

[4] McMillan, K. & Weyers, J *How to Write Essays and Assignments* (Pearson 2007)

The assessor will be looking for a structured approach to the essay. She will want to see evidence that you have set out the content in a logical and coherent way and will award specific marks for this skill. The assessor will be specifically looking for your ability to:

- produce a clear introduction and conclusion;
- carefully organise your arguments in a logical and methodical way;
- link ideas and arguments coherently;
- demonstrate good use of subheadings, paragraphs and footnotes; and
- ensure that points made flow on from one another.

The assessor may prefer to draft specific criteria in relation to structure. Such an assessment criteria might, for example, be presented in the following format:

Mark in the 40s (Weak to fair)	Mark in the 50s (fair to good)	Mark in the 60s (good to very good)	70s and above (excellent)
Structure: little development of themes with no obvious logical progression from beginning, through middle to end	perceptible development of themes and logical progression to conclusions	clear and well thought-out organisation of points within a coherent framework of thought leading to logical conclusions	tight argument progressing through inter-connected stages with strong development of themes generated by perceptive interpretation of the question

Presentation

> *". . . directly or indirectly, presentation will make a statement about the overall care you have taken in conducting your analysis and preparing the content."*[5]

The presentation of your work may well be assessed formally i.e. as part of the assessment criteria. You could gain a few valuable marks for submitting your work in a professional way and by complying with your Law School's coursework requirements in terms of presenting your work. Even if the essay is not 'formally' assessed in terms of presentation, there is little doubt that good presentation will be something the assessor will consider when awarding your final mark. Good presentation not only helps the assessor to understand what you have written, but it also shows that you can present work to a professional standard. The skill of presenting work to a good standard will not only benefit you during your time at university, but will also feed into your professional life post-university.

Presentation is not just about 'superficial' appearance. That said, overall appearance will be one of the first things the assessor will notice when they come to mark your essay and before they consider the contents. First impressions can count.

---

[5] Ibid

The layout of assessed work will vary according to what you have been asked to submit and so a report, for example, will look quite different from an essay. If your assignment is in the form of essay then it is perhaps best to adopt a simple layout. You will need to produce a cover page – what you state on the cover sheet will be a matter of convention and your Law School may require certain key information. It is important to check with your Law School because, for example, they may not want you to put your name anywhere on the assignment so as to comply with their regulations on anonymous marking.

With regards to the contents of the essay, again it is worth checking what conventions your Law School follows. For example, you might be required to comply with formalities such as the following:

- you should word-process your work
- you should print on one side of A4 paper only
- you must ensure that your work is presented with one and a half line spacing or double spacing
- you must use 12 point font size for the main body of the text
- you must use either Times New Roman or Arial as your font
- you should ensure that page numbers are inserted and that they appear in the bottom centre or top/bottom right hand corner
- you should ensure that footnotes appear at the foot of each page, ruled of from the main text (you are encouraged to use footnotes)
- you can alter how your font is printed: *this is italics*; this is **bold** (try not to get too carried away – keep the layout simple and clear)
- you must attach at the end of the essay the following:
  - a full bibliography (in alphabetical order)
  - a table of cases, statutes and statutory instruments referred to
  - a table of any other sources you have used, for example: journal articles, newspaper articles, internet sources etc
- you must state the exact word count either on your cover page or after your concluding paragraph – do not include the footnotes, your bibliography or table of cases etc.

Presentation is not just about layout; what font you use or whether you have provided a full bibliography or table of cases. Presentation is also about:

- the way you express yourself in writing;
- whether you have let grammatical or spelling mistakes spoil your essay;
- whether your essay is structured (good use of paragraphs);
- whether you have given full and correct references and citations;
- whether you have 'abused' the use of footnotes (as a way of getting around the word count);
- whether there is evidence you have thoroughly proof-read your work (there is nothing more annoying to an assessor than sloppy mistakes and obvious errors that could be rectified at the proof-reading stage – always keep the assessor on your side!).

Assessment Criteria

"Once [lecturers] have decided on the learning objectives [outcomes] and the assessment tasks which will test whether students have achieved the desired outcomes, the next stage is to specify and communicate to students the criteria of assessment."[6]

Assessment criteria will indicate the basis upon which the assessor (and others, for example, the external examiner) will make judgments about your work. The assessor will articulate what they expect you to do in the assessment task and indicate the factors they will take into account when judging your work. This way, you will know what they had in mind when setting the task and what they are looking for when marking your work. Assessment criteria not only allow you to focus on what the assessor will want you to achieve but also go a long way to demonstrate uniformity, objectivity and consistency in marking and to ensure fairness to all students. Perhaps as important is that making the assessment criteria available to all students can help achieve predictability in marking. Knowing what the assessor is looking for in advance allows you to, in effect, assess your own work before you finally submit it. If the mark you give yourself, based on the assessment criteria, is not as high as you would like, then you will have the opportunity to evaluate and improve your work before final submission. How the assessment criteria are framed will vary from institution to institution and from programme to programme. Equally, assessment criteria will vary depending on the nature of the assessment task and the level (year) of study. As you know, a variety of ways will be used to assess you whether by essay writing, examinations, presentations and so on. Whichever method is employed, the assessor will provide detailed criteria. Criteria for coursework might, for example, look something like the following:

> ## Example
> In this essay the student should:
> - demonstrate relevant knowledge and understanding of the topic in question;
> - demonstrate the use of key skills such as the ability to analyse or argue a point;
> - think critically about the subject;
> - show the ability to select, interpret and summarise legal sources;
> - show evidence of the use of cases and other materials not only to inform but strategically as a tool in analysis, evaluation and problem solving;
> - produce sound arguments based on coherence and logic;
> - present structured arguments;
> - exhibit good communication skills; and
> - keep within the word limit.

---

[6] Johnstone, R. *et al. Improving Criteria and Feedback in Student Assessment in Law* (Routledge-Cavendish, 1998)

Knowledge criteria

Some institutions might provide criteria specifically for assessing knowledge outcomes and communication skills which will be 'standard' to all levels of the programme and apply to all types of assessment. Equally, the assessment criteria for knowledge might be written in terms of *what is required of you* in order to achieve a first class answer (and so on) for the knowledge element of the essay, for example:

1st (70%+) Within the constraints of the assessment activity, demonstrates complete, accurate and detailed knowledge of legal rules, principles, procedures, values, theory and critical debates (as appropriate). Where an assessment requires a selective treatment of a topic, there are no material omissions in the student's demonstrated knowledge.

If upon receipt of the return of your essay you were given a mark between 40-49% (a third class answer) for the knowledge element of your essay this is probably because you provided:

3rd (40%–49%) A basic knowledge of the principle areas provided by the question. The answer demonstrates substantial descriptive competence. There may be some relevant details, but key areas of knowledge are omitted. Likely to be absence of knowledge of theory, values, critical debate (etc.).

Communication criteria

The assessment criteria for **communication** might be written in terms of a 'general statement' that would be applicable to all levels of your programme and apply to all types of written assessment, for example:

> *"A good grade in Law is not achievable without good use of English. Clarity of expression is crucial in any attempt to describe or analyse the law accurately. Good grammar and properly constructed sentences are key factors in putting across a logical and convincing argument. Vocabulary, spelling, punctuation and appropriate paragraphing are also important. Simple, but clear statements, are normally preferable to long, convoluted and/or jargon-ridden ones."*

Thus far, you are beginning to see the kind of things the assessor will be taking into account when marking your essay. They will be allocating marks for:

- overall presentation;
- content;
- structure;
- knowledge; and
- communication skills.

You might be forgiven for thinking that you are already well versed in knowing what an assessor is looking for when marking essays. After all, none of the above will represent anything 'new' or 'different' to what you would expect an assessor (whether at school or university) to be looking for when allocating marks. Perhaps what will be less familiar are the *legal skills* to be assessed. Even if your Law School does not draft specific assessment criteria for say 'knowledge' or 'communication' – they will draft specific assessment criteria in relation to legal skills. The assessor will want to measure your ability to, for example:

- undertake *legal analysis and reasoning*;
- *evaluate* legal rules and the policy of the law;
- *solve legal problems*; and
- undertake *legal research*.

Legal skills criteria

Common to all universities will be specific assessment criteria relevant to the subject you will be studying whether it is 'say' Politics, English or Law. In the case of Law, the assessor will produce criteria to measure certain *legal* skills. It must be pointed out that there may be conventions peculiar to your Law School in relation to the legal skills they will want to assess, but as a general rule, for the subject of law, most assessors will want to gauge your ability to: undertake *legal analysis and reasoning*; *evaluate* legal rules and the policy of the law; *solve legal problems* and undertake *legal research*.

Quite often the assessor will draft statements in relation to the above skills which will be different at each level (year) of your programme. This is because these skills become progressively more demanding at the different stages of your programme. Here for example, is the assessment criterion for **legal research by level** and indicates what is required to gain marks either in the 1st, 2.1 or 2.2 category:

Level one: undertake legal research

1st (70%+) Identifies accurately primary and secondary sources and locates these sources consistently and appropriately. Demonstrates a full understanding of the relationship between sources. Presents evidence of the use of these sources in the body of work (not just in a bibliography). Essential, where appropriate, that a range of primary sources have been researched and used. Demonstrates own initiative in undertaking research.

2.1 (60%–69%) Has worked effectively to reading guidance provided by tutors. Demonstrates the use of sources beyond textbooks and lecture notes. Textbooks, where used, are scholarly works. Primary sources used in the preparation of work and evidence of understanding of the relationship between sources.

2.2 (50%–59%) Must produce evidence of the ability to locate both primary and secondary sources, but likely to be much reliant on texts and lecture notes.

Level two: undertake legal research

1st (70%+) Presents clear evidence of comprehensive and independent use of primary and secondary sources. Clear evidence of understanding of the relationship between different sources. Use of texts, where appropriate, or kind which offer critique as well as description of law. Use of sources not evidence simply by bibliography, but by deployment as the basis for analysis, problem solving and evaluation. Evidence that the value of sources has been weighed. Clearly gone beyond guidance reading offered by tutors.

2.1 (60%–69%)   Independent research beyond lecture note and textbook approach. Use of primary and secondary sources incorporated into work. Evidence that research being used, if not always effectively, as an analytical/evaluative tool. Less likely to have evaluated sources. Followed guidance offered by tutors systematically.

2.2 (50%–59%)   Evidence of use of primary and secondary sources, but likely to be heavily reliant on texts and/or lecture notes.

Level three: undertake legal research

1st (70%+)   Demonstrates use of appropriately selected but diverse sources to inform knowledge, analysis and evaluation. Clearly evaluates the selected sources in terms of reliability, validity and relevance. Has used research strategically as a tool in analysis, evaluation and problem solving. Highly likely to demonstrate reading beyond that offered as guidance by tutors.

2.1 (60%–69%)   Uses a variety of appropriate sources and has attempted to evaluate these sources with some degree of rigour. Clear and systematic use of primary sources. Strong 2.1 will have used sources beyond those offered as guidance by tutors.

2.2 (50%–59%)   Evidence of reading around the subject, but tends to rely on established texts and materials (including notes taken in lectures and classes). Some use of primary sources, but this may be limited. Opportunities to evaluate sources may be missed.

Marking your work is not an exact science or a mathematical exercise. You have seen that the assessor will take a number of factors into account when marking your work. The assessment of work is a matter for professional judgment for academic staff. Assessment is not, however, a matter of *exclusive individual judgment*. Rather, the professional judgment takes place within the framework of your university's regulations governing such matters; the judgment of academic peers both *internal and external* to the Law School and the collective judgment of the Subject Board of Examiners and the Award Board of Examiners. Both the internal and external examiners will have access to the assessment criteria and they will moderate your work with the criteria in mind.

It may appear that a great length of time has been spent on what the assessor is looking for when marking your work; however, there is good reason for this. At university level you will not usually have access to 'model' answers. The assessor will want you to work out the 'answer' for yourselves; they will want you to be independent learners and independent thinkers. By understanding the assessment criteria, you will know in advance what the assessor is looking for when marking your work and how to achieve a good mark. Moreover, the hope is that having awareness of the assessment criteria will help you to improve the standard of your work in the future. You will gain confidence in essay writing and you will have good knowledge of what is required of you. There should be no reason why, in principle, you should not be able to predict your own grade, within a few marks.

Knowledge of what the assessor is looking for ensures consistency and fairness in marking. Your university will follow its own conventions in relation to the assessment criteria and, as such, if you are unsure about any aspects of the assessment process, do ask your course or programme leader. To be informed ensures that you not only have awareness and understanding of the assessment processes but also that the assessment processes are transparent.

Where to Begin to Write a Law Essay

One of the first questions you may ask your university tutor is: What makes a good essay? Let me answer this question with reference to the following quotation:

> *"A good essay will be written well, well presented and contain only relevant material. And, above all, it will answer the question."*[7]

The second question you may ask your tutor is: where do I begin to write a law essay? This is probably the common concern of most students after their first question. The answer to this question cannot be given in just two sentences. Even if you are familiar with writing essays, some of you might not be used to writing law essays or extended essays of up to say 4,000 words. At undergraduate level, the expectation of the marker will be higher than that of an A-level assessor. In addition to testing knowledge, content, presentation and communication skills the assessor will be looking for more 'advanced' skills in these areas and, in addition, your ability to:

- adopt a more 'academic' (professional) style to your writing;
- not be merely descriptive but to employ analytical and critical skills;
- undertake wider reading and research and not to rely on your lecture notes or basic textbooks;
- use legal materials and to be able to evaluate those materials;
- engage in good essay writing skills – taking great care with your spelling, grammar, punctuation, syntax and so on;
- structure your essay; and
- make good use of paragraphs or sub-headings;
- present your work in a professional manner;
- reference your work fully and correctly; and
- keep to the word limit.

These are just some of the demands in terms of skills, required of you when writing a law essay and, at first glance, may seem intimidating. Perhaps this is why some students can struggle, particularly in the first year of their law course, to know where to begin to write a law essay and certainly one that will attract a good mark.

First and foremost, allow yourself plenty of time to complete the task.

---

[7] Askey, S. & McLeod, I. *Studying Law* 3rd Edition (Palgrave Macmillan, 2011)

Allow yourself plenty of time

A good starting point is to allow yourself plenty of time to research, plan and write your essay. You should also give yourself time to reflect on your essay before the date of submission so that you can edit, proof-read and make any necessary improvements. You will need to find out the hand-in date for the essay. Once known, you might want to work backwards from that date and begin preparation as early as you can by undertaking some preliminary thinking, research and reading.

> *"Managing our time is something like dieting. We know what we should eat, we know why we should eat that way and we know the benefits it will bring. However, how often do we start with good intentions and then let things slip? Time management can be similar. We know why we should manage our time, we often know what to do, but we just can't keep to it.*[8]

Time management becomes quite fundamental at undergraduate level. You will have to balance your time between curricular (such as attending lectures and seminars) and extra-curricular activities (for example, being a member of a mooting team) as well as finding time for yourself. All of these activities will need to be programmed into your day or week. There are sound reasons why, as a student, you need to be organised and manage your time well. Failing to manage your time effectively may lead to you becoming anxious or suffering from stress. You may start to feel 'out of control' particularly when a number of assessments are due to be submitted around the same time. As a result, you may start to suffer from physical symptoms such as headaches or emotional symptoms such as losing confidence in your abilities. Being a student is never going to be stress free and at certain times of the year, especially when you are being assessed, you may well feel particularly stressed. This is where, in part, managing your time well and being organised may help alleviate some of the pressures you may feel you are under.

There are other reasons why you need to start early and allow yourself plenty of time to do the task in hand. For example, it is never a good idea to leave research to the last minute. You should always leave time to acquire the relevant materials you will need in order to answer the essay question. You might have to acquire a relevant article through inter-library loan or some other student may have taken out on loan the materials you want. You will also need time to digest the materials found and to evaluate the selected sources in terms of reliability, validity and relevance.

Time management is about forward planning and to assist you in the task of planning (and being organised) you might wish to draft a timetable or schedule of work to help you manage your time effectively.

Draft a timetable

When you know you have an assessed essay due by a certain date you might find it useful to draft a schedule of work to do. This activity can help you to organise and manage your time better. Through planning the various stages in the process of writing an essay and listing the various tasks you need to do, and by when, you will begin to feel in 'control' of what is being asked of you. The schedule of work could be on the lines of listing the tasks you need to do and by when, for example:

---

[8] Price, G. and Maier, P. *Effective Study Skills* (Pearson, 2007)

Tasks	To be completed by . . . (enter date)	✓
Understanding the question set, recognition of the key (instruction) words; awareness of the word count and whether the question is divided into more than one part. Note the deadline for the assessment		
Undertaking preliminary reading and understanding of the subject-matter		
Researching – record the sources referred to		
Planning the answer to the essay		
Writing the essay		
Producing a full and complete bibliography, table of cases/statutes and referencing all materials used		
Improving your work before submission – proof read, check spelling/grammar and typing errors		
Final reflection – refer to assessment criteria; overall presentation. Adhering to any formal requirements or course conventions		

By producing a schedule or timetable and giving yourself plenty of time to complete the various stages (or tasks) in writing a law essay you should feel less stressed and more confident in your ability to produce and submit a good essay on time. Once you have drafted a schedule of work, the next stage is to read the question carefully.

Read and Understand the Question

This might seem obvious. However, it is much easier than you think to misunderstand or misinterpret a question. Quite often students will answer the question that they wished had been set rather than the actual question set. To avoid this, look closely at the wording of the question and note the instruction word or phrase at the end of the question. The assessor may formulate the essay in the form of a question, but they are more likely to be framed as instructions by an instructing word or phrase. The instruction tells you what you need to do. At undergraduate degree level it would be unusual for the assessor to use such words as 'describe' or 'list' or state the 'advantages and disadvantages' of something. The assessor is more likely to use, for instance, the following words or phrases:

- Analyse . . .
- Argue . . .
- Contrast and compare . . .
- Critically evaluate . . .
- Criticise . . .
- Discuss with reference to . . .
- Distinguish . . .
- Evaluate . . .
- Identify . . .
- Justify . . .
- Review . . .
- What is the significance of . . .

> **Example**
>
> "From a clinical perspective, mediation begins with the assumption that the parties are competent to define the issues facing them, discuss them rationally and ultimately agree them" (Roberts, 1997).
>
> **With the above statement in mind, *critically evaluate* the role of mediation in settling family law disputes.**

It is important to know what these instruction words/phrases mean and thereby determine what is being asked of you. In the example above, what does to *'critically evaluate'* something mean? It might be useful to breakdown the instruction words into two component parts and briefly define what each word means.

> **Example**
>
> **to *critically evaluate*,** a definition of each word could be:
>
> To be *critical* is to point out strengths and weaknesses i.e. give a balanced answer.
>
> To *evaluate* is to provide an objective assessment of the subject matter. Legal evaluation would include offering detailed critique of legal rules, policy considerations etc. and using appropriate theoretical models as part of the critique – whether political, social, philosophical, economic, ethical etc. It would include the evaluation of competing arguments and the ability to propose conclusions with persuasive justifications. If views of others are presented then they should be presented with comment and used as an evaluative tool rather than a descriptive tool. Here the assessor would expect to see the student's own insights – but these must be considered and convincing. Argument and/or evidence should support any conclusions. Objectivity should flow through the answer.

Practical Questions

Give a *brief* definition as to what you are expected to do:

Instruction words	Definition
Analyse	
Argue	
Comment on	
Compare and contrast	
Criticise	
Distinguish	
Justify	
Review	
Summarise	

Try not to make too many assumptions about the question. Rather, try to determine the main issues in the question and ask whether there are any sub-issues. It will be unlikely that the question will be straightforward and so be aware that the question may be open to more than one interpretation.

For example, you might encounter a question along the lines of "Should human rights operate within times of high terrorist activity?" This question is not asking you to put down everything you know about human rights law in terms of terrorism, police stop and search powers, powers of detention etc. Instead, it is asking for your considered opinion. Of course, you will need to use the relevant law to add weight to your argument, but simply describing the law around this area will not secure you a good mark. The question is asking you to engage with a debate. Whether you come down on the side that human rights should prevail under any climate, or that degradations in times of high terrorist activity are necessary to secure the safety of the majority doesn't matter. If you're able to present a balanced account using authority and reason to back your opinion (whilst recognising and refuting potential counter-points along the way) you will be rewarded with a much better mark.

> **Practical Questions**
>
> Source some past essay questions from your course tutor. Sit down and try to unpick exactly what you're being asked in each one? What is the question asking you to do? What are the sub-issues? How do you think you need to answer the questions? Once you've done this – email your lecturer to ask whether you're on the right track.

Once familiar with the question and the instruction words or phrases, you will also need to be aware of whether the essay is subject to a word limit, for example, 3,500 words. You should also note whether the question is split into parts. If so, you will need to know what weight you should give to each part of the question. If you are unsure about any aspect of the question you should ask your tutor for clarification.

Once you feel confident or, reasonably confident at this stage of what is being asked of you, next you will need to undertake some preliminary research and reading.

Undertake preliminary research and reading

You may have to refresh your memory on the subject-matter or topic referred to in the essay and re-familiarise yourself with the law on the area in question.

Start by referring to your lecture notes and any supplementary notes you may have written. You should also refer to your seminar or tutorial notes as the essay question you have been set may have been discussed, at least, in part, in a past seminar or tutorial. Next you should refer to the appropriate chapter(s) in the textbook(s) you use for the subject area of the essay question. This will help ensure that you have good knowledge and a basic understanding of the subject-matter. Remember you are only undertaking *preliminary* reading to aid knowledge and understanding, and so try not to overload yourself with too much information as this stage.

After completing some preliminary reading, you should be acquainted with the subject-matter of the essay. Next, refer back to the question. Start to pose questions that you think you will need to answer. Determine what the main issues in the question are. Ascertain whether there any sub-issues. By formulating a set of questions and answers, you will begin to have a better understanding of which resources you might need in order to answer the question. Now you are ready to begin to undertake further research.

Research

When grading essays, the assessor will award marks for research skills. Indeed, there will probably be specific assessment criteria in relation to legal research. You are advised to refer to the assessment criteria before you begin your research. This will give you an idea of what is expected of you in terms of research and, what you will need to do to achieve a high mark for this skill.

The assessor will envisage that your research will go beyond the information that can be found in a few textbooks. You will also be expected to source materials beyond that contained in a reading list. Researching for an assessment can be disheartening. This is because you can feel overwhelmed by the volume of information available, especially on the Internet. Knowing where to begin to research can often be seen as alarming as knowing where to start to write a law essay. This is why it is useful to think of the task of researching in terms of stages, for example:

- **Stage one:** find the relevant resources
- **Stage two:** read or scan the materials found
- **Stage three:** make your own notes on the materials found
- **Stage four:** reference your notes

Stage one: find the relevant resources

Much of a student's time will be spent in the library preparing for seminars, assessments etc. As such, it is fundamental to all students that they quickly become familiar with the range of facilities and resources to be found in the university library. It is only when you are confident in the knowledge of not only what materials are available in the library but also how to locate them, will you become an independent researcher.

You might begin your research by using the library catalogue to find textbooks relevant to the essay question. Whilst textbooks should not be the main source of knowledge, they can be useful for citing quotes from learned authors. Most textbooks will contain a reading list or list of references either at the end of a chapter or at the end of the textbook. The reference to further academic articles, textbooks, key cases and so on can help widen your research.

In order to answer the essay question, you may need to use cases as authority. It is advisable to research for cases beyond those that can be found in a textbook. Further search may come up with more relevant cases to your arguments. Try to read the case directly from source i.e. the law report. This way, you are more likely to have better understanding of the issues in the case and the reasoning of the judge(s). You may also find that useful quotes and other dicta from the case can be used in your arguments. If you are relying on case law, you will need to check the case in question has not been overruled. If you intend to refer to legislation then you should confirm the statute is still in force or ascertain whether any amendments have been made to the legislation.

Your research strategy should include academic opinion. An author of a journal article may comment on, for example, new legislation or a recent case and you may be able to use their opinion to support your own views. If relevant, refer to official reports and consultation papers produced by the government to enhance or evidence a point you want to make in your essay.

Depending on the essay question, you might need to refer beyond *legal* sources and refer to other disciplines to inform your answer. This is especially so if the question requires discussion of, for instance, policy, political, social, philosophical, economic, or ethical considerations. If this is the case, then you should be prepared to cross-fertilise between legal and non-legal disciplines. The university's library catalogue will help you find relevant textbooks.

An important part of researching is that the materials found should come from reliable sources. This means that you should have some awareness of the reputation of the author, and their expertise in a particular field. You should rely only on authoritative sources. Be discerning when referring to a newspaper article as your supporting evidence. This is because such articles are unlikely to be *legal* authority and comments made in the articles may not be based on facts but merely opinion or made by someone who has a political agenda or axe to grind. The same principle applies to sources found on the Internet. If you do decide to use materials found on the Internet or a newspaper article, you are advised to scrutinise the contents to determine validity and reliability. It is perfectly acceptable for you to criticise an author's work, but you should always review the work in an objective and considered way.

Try not to get too obsessed with gathering information (especially from the Internet) as you could become overwhelmed and lose sight of the task you originally set yourself. Once you have undertaken a trawl of the relevant materials available, the next stage is to read and make notes on the materials found.

Stage two: read or scan the materials found

> *"Learning new approaches to reading can save you time, and can increase your grades. Reading is also vital for stimulating your thinking, which is a key component for success."*[9]

As a university student you will have to do a lot of reading. It is not possible, however, to read all the materials you have found in the *same* way as you would read a novel. It would be a physical impossibility to read in full every case, statute, textbook, article and so on from 'start to finish' for every assessment you have been set. This is not always the case, and sometimes you will have to read a law report or article in full to gain insight or understanding. Nevertheless, as a general rule you should start to look at *how* you read in a different way, a way that fits in with the demands on your time. There are a number of textbooks and Websites available that give advice and tips on learning new approaches to reading which can save you time and effort. For example, *Effective Study Skills* by Price and Maier contains an excellent chapter on 'how to optimise your reading'. The authors offer guidance on how to improve your reading efficiently and how to learn to skim texts and increase your speed of reading. They advocate that it is possible to develop and improve your reading skills by:

---

[9] Ibid

- **increasing** your basic reading speed – the more you practice reading quickly, the more proficient you will become;
- **increasing** the amount of information your reading brain can absorb in one sitting – start to look out for 'key' words in the text that will direct your attention to specific parts of the text;
- **skimming** the text – this is a way of collating information from the text in the shortest possible time. You are not reading the whole page of the text, instead you are getting the gist of the text by looking for key words or phrases which will help you decide whether you need to read the whole of the text or move on to other material;
- **selecting** only the information from the text which will assist you with your essay;
- **annotating,** underlining or highlighting (with a fluorescent pen) key sections of the texts – but only if the text belongs to you;
- **reading** the text critically and trying to analyse or evaluate the content – in other words, be a critical reader; reflect upon what the author has said; evaluate what you have read and examine the strengths and weaknesses in what the author is putting forward. Remember it is okay to challenge the author's ideas and to make your own judgements on what has been written.

Another important 'reading skill' is for you to be an 'interactive' reader. This means preparing yourself before reading by asking yourself some questions. For example: "by reading this article, what do I hope to find out?" It also means that you 'engage' with the article by marking key passages of the text. You could highlight a passage in the article containing the author's opinion or pick out key references (cases etc) or underline the main ideas in the text (only annotate the article if the copy belongs to you). The overall function of being an interactive reader is to read purposefully and to keep concentration levels high. A useful aid to becoming an interactive reader is what is commonly known as the SQ3R technique. This stands for:

Survey – skim the text to get a feeling for the contents and determine whether the content of the text could be helpful to you;

Question – ask yourself what you hope to get out of the text – refer to the questions you posed in your preliminary reading – can the text help you answer some of the questions you posed;

Read – break up your reading into small sections; look for key information such as data or a quote you could use;

Recall – mentally go through the text and try to recall the main points/ideas;

Review – ask yourself whether the text has answered your questions or do you need to read further.

Only by practice will you become an efficient reader; increase your reading speed; learn to be selective in your reading and to become an interactive reader. Once you have found your way around the text and found other materials that will assist you with your essay assignment – you should then make notes on what you have found.

Stage three: make your own notes on the materials found

"It is often more effective to read a section in the book or case report and then write notes about the main points at the end of the section rather than writing at the same time as reading (and therefore simply copying out the whole book. . . .)"[10]

I remember in my first year of university I thought I had to makes notes on everything I read. I was not always sure what was relevant or irrelevant in a chapter of a book (or an article or case) and so I ended up virtually rewriting the chapter in my own notebook – using the words of the author and not my own. After many hours of hand writing my notes I soon realised that this was not only an impossible task but a fruitless one. I was drowning in reams of papers. I quickly learnt the importance of summarising the text into my own words and only making relevant notes. While it is essential to take notes (not least as a memory jogger) there is little point in simply rewriting the whole book or article or case that you have just read. As with other skills, note-making skills can be developed and honed as you progress in your studies. In much the same way as learning new approaches to reading, it is possible to learn new approaches to note-taking.

When beginning the task of note-taking, in might be useful to first scan the materials you have found. With practice, you should be able to recognise the parts of the material that are relevant to your task. Start with underlining key words or sentences or highlight with a fluorescent pen a particular paragraph as you read (work from a photocopy if the material does not belong to you). This way, when it comes to writing your own notes, you can direct your attention to only those relevant parts and not the whole material. If the material is your personal copy, you may not need to take notes at all – merely refer to the highlighted parts of the material when you come to write your essay, this will you save valuable time.

Next, you need to consider what format your notes should take. This is personal to the individual and some methods of note-taking may work well for you and others may not. When contemplating which method to adopt, a strategy to consider is choosing a method that works well for the subject-matter of the essay. If, for example, you have been asked to evaluate a recent piece of legislation, perhaps your notes could take the form of 'time lines' i.e. listing the reasons and sequence of events that led to the new legislation being enacted. Some students may adopt the 'linear' approach to note-taking. This approach consists of writing notes in bullet points (rather than full sentences). Others may be more experimental and use for example, flow-charts; matrix notes; mind-maps or grid notes. There are a number of textbooks available that will explain the different methods of note-making; the advantages and disadvantages of each method together with examples. See for example: Price, G. and P. Maier (2007) *Effective Study Skills*, Pearson.

Once you have worked-out a method of note-taking that suits you best, try to develop your own 'shorthand' and use your own abbreviations, for example, Cl. (claimant) or standard abbreviations such as TU (trade union). You might like to experiment with colour (colour coding) and for instance, write cases in red and statutes in green and quotes in blue. There is evidence to suggest that colour-coding may assist with memory and help trigger recall. Some students respond better to 'visual style' of note-taking rather than block texts and so you might want to use arrows to link information or put salient points in boxes.

---

[10] Webley, L. *Legal Writing* 2nd Edition (Routledge-Cavendish 2010)

Make sure your notes make sense and are organised. This way, should you need to refer to your notes in the future, you can easily read them and they are meaningful. Take time to reflect upon the notes you have made. Ask yourself: Have I picked-out all the important points in the material? Could I have paraphrased a section of the material better? Also, try to demonstrate how the notes you have taken will feed into your essay.

Stage four: reference your notes

"Referencing is attributing the work that belongs to someone else and which you are using in your essay. . . ."[11]

It is essential and indeed good practice to reference in full all work you have referred to as part of your research and reading. There are many reasons for this. The most obvious is that by noting the full reference, it will make it must quicker for you to locate the materials should you need to refer back to them. In addition, by noting the reference in full as you read and make-notes, it will make the task of drafting the bibliography, table of cases etc. much simpler.

If you decide to use a direct quote or paraphrase someone else's findings in your essay, it is imperative that you acknowledge whom the work belongs to. Failure to acknowledge that the work belongs to someone else and using their work in your essay may look (and indeed is) claiming that the work emanates from you. At the very least you could be accused of poor scholarship – which will affect your overall mark and, at worse, you could be charged with plagiarism. Plagiarism is taking others' words or ideas without stating whose words or ideas they are and where they came from. Plagiarism is a very serious academic offence and your university will have a range of penalties they can invoke if you are found guilty of such an offence – including expelling you from the university. To avoid any potential allegation of plagiarism, always put any direct quote in quotation marks together with the full reference. If you are paraphrasing an author's work make sure you credit the author and give the full reference of their work – you should cite the reference in your footnotes and bibliography.

It is worth mentioning at this stage that some students will have concerns that they are 'over relying' on others' work and that they may be penalised for this. Demonstrating that you have undertaken research and referred to a wide range of sources in your essay is always a good thing and will attract marks. By using research materials effectively in your essay will also attract marks. Materials found can evidence a point you want to make in your essay or using a quote can enhance the quality of your argument. You will have exhibited to the assessor a fundamental skill, that of a scholarly researcher with your ability to provide evidence to support any points you are making. You may feel frustrated that you have not come up with an 'original thought' – but in reality, as an undergraduate student, it might be difficult to come up with an original or new idea. Nevertheless, you can use evidence to support (or otherwise) your own views. Using other people's work should not stop you from commentating on, or criticising it, through reasoned argument or persuasion.

Once you have undertaken your research and made notes on the materials found, you are now ready to plan your answer.

---

[11] Ibid

Plan your Answer

'Fail to plan is to plan to fail. . . .'

Planning an outline of the essay gives a basic structure to work from. The planning stage will also assist in identifying the main ideas and help formulate the points you want to make in the essay in a logical sequence.

The actual writing of the essay will be much easier if you have a plan to work from. It will also ensure that you do not miss important points and will help to organise your thoughts. It should be noted here that whether you are required to write an essay for coursework or in an examination, you should always write a plan before you begin to write the essay in full.

A starting point when planning the essay is to revisit the essay question – make sure you are clear as to what is being asked of you. Make a preliminary list (headings) of the issues in the essay you will need to address and think about the order you will need to address them. Once you have done this, make further notes under each of the headings as to how you plan to explain or to develop ideas or illustrate the points you intend to make in the essay. You might want to go so far as to make a note of what you intend to deal with in the introduction and in each subsequent paragraph.

Jot down the evidence you will use to support your discussion of the issues (cases, statutory authority, quotes, etc.). A useful strategy to adopt is to present the point you intend to make first and then provide the evidence to support your point. Try, where possible, to support all, or most of the points, you are making with some form of evidence. As a law student you are expected to provide evidence and you will gain few marks for not supporting the points you make with authority. At first, it may be a little demoralising to find that you do not need to use all the evidence and materials you have collated. However, it is more important to use only relevant materials than to fill your essay with unnecessary materials just for the sake of it. Be discerning with your materials – there is rarely a need to reproduce large chunks of findings in your essay. Instead, try to use the materials concisely to support the point you want to make. Be aware that you might only need to cite part of a quote in your essay or paraphrase someone else's work. This advice is particularly useful when the essay is subject to a word limit. You should be especially careful when citing cases. In response to an essay question, it would be unlikely that you will need to give details of the facts of the case. What is probably more pertinent is either the *ratio decidendi* (decision) of the case or the dicta of a judge.

So far, you will have made a list of the key points and considered the order in which you will want to make those points, with reference to supporting evidence. Now is the time to double-check that you have organised your ideas in a logical and sequential order and to refer back to the essay title. Ask yourself:

- Are you happy with the material (evidence) you intend to use to support your points in the essay or do you have to undertake further research?
- Will the essay plan help you to stay focussed and develop your answer logically?
- Will you be able to employ your analytical or evaluative skills (depending on the instruction word or phrase) or might you be too 'descriptive?

Writing your Answer

Before beginning the process of writing the essay, it is important first to say a few words about 'writing style'.

Writing style

Some students new to university may have the mistaken belief that there is a particular 'academic writing style' they should adopt for their assessed work. They are not quite sure what the appropriate writing style is and this can cause some students to fret even before they begin to write the answer to the essay. What does writing academically mean? The following quote gives an insight:

> *"Academic style involves the use of precise and objective language to express ideas. It must be grammatically correct, and is more formal than the style used in novels, newspapers, informal correspondence and everyday conversation. This should mean that the language is clear and simple. It does not imply that it is complex, pompous and dry. Above all, academic style is objective, using language techniques that generally maintain an impersonal tone and a vocabulary that is more succinct, rather than involving personal, colloquial, or idiomatic expressions."*[12]

You will see from the definition that you do not have to become someone you are not in terms of your writing style. What you are trying to achieve is to express through writing clearly, your thoughts and ideas on the essay question. There is nothing wrong in using simple and uncomplicated language and indeed this approach to writing is often preferred. What is important is that you write with clarity; that you are concise (try not to ramble on) in what you are saying, and ensure the assessor can follow your arguments. As a law student you should avoid personal pronouns (I/me/one; you/we/us) instead you could write for example, 'The first point to consider is. . . .' and not 'I will consider. . . .' It is perhaps especially important to be objective in your writing and not to use sexist language or slang terms. Always avoid contractions, for example, do not write 'can't' but write in full 'cannot'. These days, there is a trend is to use 'plain English' and none more so than in the legal profession. However, it should be noted that whilst the use of plain English should be promoted when talking to a client or writing a letter to a client, when it comes to academic writing you should try to maintain a writing style that is a little more formal. Try to project a more 'professional' approach in your writing. One thing that should be avoided at all costs, is 'texting speak' – it is becoming more noticeable these days that some students (without realising, I am sure) incorporate inappropriate abbreviations and terms in their writing. Remember your audience; you are not writing to a friend but trying to produce an academic piece of work. To get a feel or sense of academic writing why not read a few of the articles you found as part of your research, not with a view to note the content but more with a view to note the writing style of the author? Can you learn lessons from the author in terms of writing style that you could adapt or adopt in your own writing?

Back to writing the essay . . .

Once you are relatively happy with your essay plan (plans may have to be altered) then you are ready to write the first draft of your essay. I say first draft, as it is more likely than not that you will have to edit what

---
[12] McMillan, K. & Weyers, J. *How to Write Essays and Assignments* (Pearson 2007)

you have written. It might be helpful if you think about your essay as being divided into three parts or stages: the introduction, the main body and the conclusion. This way, you will not feel too overwhelmed when writing the essay and it will assist you with your structure. One important point to make here is, that you should constantly refer back to the essay title as you are writing your essay – this will help keep you on track and make sure you answer the question set.

Introduction

Rather than a lengthy introduction about the topic, the introduction should be short and simple. Merely write in a few sentences a summary of:

- what the essay is about;
- the main issues you intend to deal with; and
- how you intend to deal with them.

This is your brief 'answer' and you can then expand on the points made in the introduction in the main body of your essay. Never write your conclusion in the introduction as it is not possible to know what your final conclusion will be until you have fully reviewed the issues contained in the question. Some of you might prefer to write the introduction after you have written the rest of your essay for fear of missing anything out. This is common when writing an extended essay or a dissertation. Do not stress over your introduction at this stage as you can amend your introduction when you come to edit your essay. It is important, however, at this stage to have some idea of what your introduction will contain as the points you make in your introduction will need to be expanded upon in the main body of the essay. In an examination, you will have to write your introduction first and this is where a good essay plan will help you narrow down the issues you intend to deal with – from the plan you can draft your introduction.

Remember an introduction directs the reader/assessor as to what you intend to address in the essay and will give them an idea of what is to follow. As a general rule an introduction should be less than 10% of your essay and as such will not attract many marks. You will have the opportunity to gain the most marks in the main body of your essay.

Main body

Once you have drafted your introduction or, at least, you have a good idea what the introduction will consist of, the next stage is to give a little more thought to the layout of the main body. One approach to take is for you to start a new paragraph for each new point what you want to make. What is a paragraph? A succinct definition would be as follows:

> "A paragraph is a unit of text usually comprising several sentences. It has a topic that is outlined in the first sentence; the topic is developed further within the paragraph; and the paragraph concludes with a sentence that terminates that topic or, possibly, acts as a link to the topic of the following paragraph."[13]

---

[13] Ibid

Paragraphs are made up of sentences and the sentences should, in the main, be a mixture of short and long. If the sentence is too long, you should attempt to break it down to two shorter sentences. The length of each paragraph will vary and will be dependent, by and large, on the content. Do try to avoid overlong paragraphs. Consider whether you have made more than one point in the paragraph and, if so, could the points be separated into two paragraphs. For each point you make in a paragraph, always try to provide evidence or authority for what you are saying. If you do not provide authority any arguments you make will not have weight or validity. Equally, if you use little authority this may suggest to the assessor that you have not undertaken good quality research or have undertaken very little research. Both of these approaches will mean you do not earn valuable marks.

In addition to authority, the assessor will also be measuring certain skills in your essay. These would include your ability to explain difficult legal concepts; avoid irrelevant material; demonstrate not just knowledge of the subject-matter, but knowledge of relevant policy, social, political, economic issues (if relevant to the question). The assessor will also want to see evidence of you employing analytical and critical skills (refer to the instruction words in the essay) and the ability to evaluate the materials used in the essay. There will be an expectation that you will offer your own insights but these should be considered and convincing. You should refer to the assessment criteria for guidance as to the 'other' skills the assessor will be looking for when assessing your essay.

All paragraphs will normally contain one point (with supporting evidence) and be self-contained. You are essentially building arguments to present in your final conclusion. As such, it is vital that paragraphs flow logically. There should be some transition or link from one paragraph to the next. This not only provides for good structure, but also maintains continuity in the essay. One way to link paragraphs is to use linking words or phrases such as: 'contrastingly' or 'furthermore' or 'consequently'. The transition word or phrase should appear as the first sentence of your next paragraph and thereby you are maintaining continuity and following a consistent pattern in relation to all your paragraphs. It will also demonstrate to the assessor how you are moving on logically from one point to the next. Once you have addressed all the points you want to make in your essay and supported the points you have made with relevant authority, the next stage is to write your conclusion.

Concluding the essay

> *"Your conclusion is the answer to the question in summary form, taking into account everything you have said previously in your essay . . ."*[14]

If appropriate, at the end of each paragraph it might be useful to write a 'mini-conclusion'. There are no hard and fast rules about this. If you do intend to offer a conclusion at the end of each paragraph, then you should link your statement back to the essay question. In any case, you will have to provide a 'final' conclusion.

Your conclusion should summarise the main points as made in each paragraph and, depending on the essay question, you should give a firm answer to the question set. It can be acceptable to give a tentative answer; however, if possible do try to give a definite and reasoned conclusion.

---

[14] Webley, L. *Legal Writing* 2nd Edition (Routledge-Cavendish 2010)

The conclusion should not be long and as a rough guide should be no more than 15% of the total essay. As a general rule, never introduce new material or ideas in the conclusion and ensure that the conclusion is not contradictory to anything said in the main body of the essay. Remember the point of a conclusion is to pull-together points or arguments and to come to a firm conclusion (if possible). Some academics liken the essay writing process to a circle. You start at the top of the circle with your introduction and progress around the circle (with your ideas) and close the circle by answering the question set i.e. by giving your conclusion. This is quite a useful analogy.

Some of you might be forgiven for thinking that this is the end of the essay writing process and you are ready to hand in your work, however, there remain a number of other tasks to do.

Referencing your Essay

"Referencing and citing others' work (along with primary legal sources such as legislation and cases) is one way of demonstrating scholarly research skills. It demonstrates the wealth of material found during the research phrase and provides authority and weight to arguments put forward."[15]

A fundamental part of being a student is that you will be required to do a lot of reading. Much of the materials you will read as part of your studies will include textbooks, journal articles, and cases and so on. One of the skills the assessor will want to measure when setting an essay question, is a student's ability to undertake wide and varied research. It is not only finding relevant materials that is important, you must demonstrate the ability to 'use' and evaluate them. Remember that it is a good thing to rely on other peoples' work. Your writing will be more persuasive when you refer to reliable materials to support your arguments. However, it is not a good thing to submit too many quotes or too many summaries of other people's work (even if correctly referenced) as it will be difficult for the assessor to determine which ideas in the answer are actually your own. Quotes are there to support arguments, not to replace your own arguments. You will not attract many marks for this poor scholarship approach to essay writing.

Every lawyer, whether law student or practitioner, needs to know how to correctly cite or reference every case, statute, statutory instrument, learned article or textbook referred to in any kind of written statement about the law made. Indeed, it is crucial to reference the work or authority used correctly. There are several reasons for this. The purpose of knowing the reference is that someone else (the assessor, for instance) can look up an article or a case cited in your essay and read it in full in its original source. If a student does not reference properly they may be found to have undertaken poor scholarship which will lose marks. The student might be found guilty of plagiarism which has serious penalties attached. By referencing properly, you are attributing the work that belongs to someone else and given them the credit for their thoughts and ideas. It is important not to claim their ideas as your own.

---

[15] Ibid

Whilst there are different methods or approaches to referencing, there is, however, one important rule: be consistent in your approach. There are perhaps two main approaches most commonly used in universities: the Harvard system and since 2000 the Oxford Standard for Citation of Legal Authorities (OSCOLA). If your university uses the OSCOLA guide to citing legal authorities, a quick reference guide can be obtained from www.law.ox.ac.uk/oscola.

It is beyond the scope of this guide to essay writing to go into any detail about how to reference textbooks and legal materials, much will depend on the approach adopted by your Law School. If you are unsure which method your Law School has adopted, ask a tutor or the law librarian.

Editing and Refining your Essay

"Looking critically at your own writing is essential if you want to produce work of the highest quality."[16]

Once you have written the first draft of the essay you should now edit and try to refine what you have written. It may be the case that you have gone over the word limit. You should be aware that some institutions will penalise a student for exceeding the word limit by, for example, deducting marks (depending on by how many words you exceed the word limit). You are advised to check with your Law School to ascertain whether such a penalty will be invoked. In any case, it is not good to exceed the word limit. The assessor will want to measure that you can write within a word constraint and that you have the ability to express yourself succinctly. If you are significantly under the word limit, you are probably missing some vital points or you have under-researched or not used enough authority. If this is the case, now would be the time to enhance your essay by undertaking further research and finding authority for the points you have made.

Editing work is not easy for most students. Everything you say may seem important and relevant to the question set. Almost certainly you will not want to exclude any of the source material you have laboured to find. But edit you must. Editing is not just about reducing the number of words written but also includes reviewing your work objectively and critically. Now is also the time to proof-read your work for spelling, grammatical and other errors.

Perhaps the first stage of editing is to simply walk away from your essay – leave it alone for a day or two. It is necessary to include enough time in your draft timetable to reflect on your essay and make amendments before the final submission. When you return to the essay, you might find it preferable to work from a hard copy of your essay rather than what is written on the computer screen. This is how the assessor will see your work and you might find it easier to annotate a hard copy rather than making changes directly onto the word processor. Go through each part of the essay in a structured way and see where, for example, you can reduce the contents (in terms of the word limit) without being detrimental to the overall essay.

---

[16] McMillan, K. & Weyers, J. *How to Write Essays and Assignments* (Pearson 2007)

Practical Exercise

You might like to ask and answer some of the following questions. You should then consider what remedial action to take.

Question	Remedial action
Is there unnecessary 'padding' in my answer?	
Am I 'waffling' too much?	
Could I be more succinct in what I am saying?	
Do I need to write a quote in full or could I paraphrase or summarise the words of another in a few lines?	
Do I need to recite the facts of a case in detail or is the *ratio* of more importance to the point I want to make?	
Can I summarise some of my points or condense some of the paragraphs?	

Once you are comfortable with the fact that you are within the word limit (or have increased your work to nearer the limit) then you should review the content again. Question whether you have, for example:

- Complied with the instruction word/phrase e.g. have you been critical and/or evaluated . . . ;
- Answered all parts of the question set;
- Demonstrated good knowledge and understanding of the area/topic in question;
- Addressed all the issues (as you see them) in the question;
- Used a variety of sources (and not just relied on a few textbooks);
- Evaluated the materials found – in terms of reliability;
- Used *relevant* legal authority to support your point(s);
- Been objective throughout the essay;
- Correctly and fully referenced all sources referred to and cited.

Next, you should review:

- The clarity or lack of clarity of your argument(s) or points made;
- The coherence and flow of the essay;
- Your writing style – have you used colloquialisms or slang words?
- Whether your conclusion is consistent with the points you made in the main body of the essay;
- The structure of the essay – have you been logical and methodical?

Try to ensure:

- All sentences make sense – are they overly long?
- There are no spelling or grammatical errors;
- There are no typos;
- Your paragraphs do not deal with too many points;
- Your paragraphs are not overly long;
- There is clear transition from one paragraph to the next;
- You have complied with any coursework requirements/conventions;
- You have complied with the word-limit;
- Your overall presentation is of a high standard;
- You have given full and correct citations for *all* materials referred to;
- You have attached a full bibliography, table of cases etc. to the end of your essay
- You have numbered each page;
- You have referred to the assessment criteria or other grading system used within your Law School;
- You have not 'accidently' plagiarised or committed any other academic offences;
- You hand your essay in on time!

Academic Offences in Relation to Assessment

An academic offence in relation to assessment is a collective phrase and may incorporate: collusion; misleading material; cheating and plagiarism.

All universities take all of the above academic offences very seriously and will, as part of the university regulations, be able to impose a range of penalties on a student who is found guilty of an academic offence.

What is collusion?

You collude when you submit work for assessment done in collaboration with another person and you claim the work as entirely your own. Or, you collude with another student that they can submit your work and claim it is their own.

What is meant by 'misleading' material?

This would be where you submit data in your coursework which has been invented or you obtain data by unfair means.

What is cheating?

Cheating would include any irregular behaviour during an examination such as the unauthorised possession of notes; or you copying another candidate's work or the unauthorised obtaining of examination papers.

What is plagiarism?

"Plagiarism is the passing of another person's thoughts, ideas, writings or images as your own. You will commit plagiarism when you incorporate in your own work substantial unacknowledged portions of another's material, or you attempt to pass off such work as original through its inclusion in your work. Here, substantial means more than trivial or minimal."[17]

The list and examples above are not definitive and you are advised to check your university regulations as to what constitutes an academic offence in relation to assessment at your institution.

How do you avoid plagiarism?

You need to take great care that any work you present as your own is in fact your own. Copying a quote from a book or a journal article for instance, without placing the copied extract within quotation marks and attributing it to its source, could land you in serious trouble. To avoid this, do make sure any direct quotes are in quotation marks and include not only the reference of direct quotes (or a summarised text) in your footnotes but also in your bibliography.

Feedback and Reflection

When your essay is returned to you, the assessor will have made comments on your work as well as giving you a mark. It is important to remember that the assessor will have marked your essay against certain criteria. Whilst the criteria used will vary from institution to institution, there is commonality between Law Schools as to the types of skills etc. assessors will be measuring when marking essays (or any assessed work). Some assessors will draft specific criteria in relation to knowledge and communication skills, whilst others may draft criteria in relation to the method of assessment, for example, they may well draft specific

---

[17] University of Lincoln, 2011 statement on plagiarism

criteria in relation to essay writing. Most, if not all assessors, will want to assess your ability to: undertake *legal analysis and reasoning; evaluate* legal rules and the policy of the law; *solve legal problems* and undertake *legal research*. Collectively, these skills could be described as 'legal skills' and the assessor will almost certainly have drafted criteria in relation to these and perhaps other legal skills. Whichever criterion is used, these will have been communicated to you and you will have the confidence in knowing that the assessor will have marked your work against the set criteria.

Upon getting back your essay, probably the only thing that will be of interest to you is the mark you have received. Depending on the mark given, you will be either in a state of euphoria or in a state of disappointment. Whilst it might be tempting to put the essay to one side and never look at it again, this is often a mistake. An important part of the essay writing process is to take note of the feedback you have been given and to reflect on the feedback. It is thus essential that you do read the comments of the assessor – the format or type of the assessor's feedback will vary. Some assessors may present you with typed comments, others handwritten comments on the front sheet of your assignment and some will make comments in the margins of your main text. Some assessors will group their comments under headings, for example, content, structure, expression and style and 'additional' comments. This approach can be helpful to spot quite quickly where your strengths and weaknesses may lay in relation to the essay you submitted. Other assessors may make their comments in continuous prose and, as such, you will have to read very carefully the comments to determine precisely what the assessor's views are on your work.

You should be aware that whilst the feedback you receive *may* appear negative – a catalogue of the things that you have failed to do – the assessor is on your side. They will comment on the good aspects of the essay and may give you some suggestions as to how you could improve in the future. Try to look on the comments as 'constructive' feedback and as an aid to make sure you do not make the same mistakes again or to know where improvements need to made.

After reading the assessor's comments, you are advised to read your essay again. Read the essay with not only the assessor's comments in mind but also with reference to the assessment criteria. Can you see for yourself where you might have gone 'wrong'? If so, this is a fundamental part of your learning process. Hopefully, you will be able to address any weaknesses you may have before you submit any further assessed work. For example, if the assessor has commented on 'poor structure' then perhaps you need to spend more time planning your answer. If they have commented on 'insufficient research' – then you will know that you will need to widen your research and not to rely on, for example, secondary sources of law. Equally, if the assessor has praised you for your 'excellent structure' or 'extensive research' then you should adopt a similar structure in the future and continue to undertake wide and varied research. By referring again to the assessment criteria, you will also be able to gauge for yourself what you need to do in the future in order to raise your mark from say the 2.2 band to the 2.1 band.

Reviewing your essay in this way will make you a reflective learner. Reflection on performance will assist you to do better in the future. Why not ask and answer some of the following questions to help you reflect on your strengths and weaknesses?

- Was the answer too descriptive and not critical enough?
- Did I fail to address the terms of the question?
- Did I fail to address any policy, ethical, social etc. issues which would have enhanced the essay?
- Was the answer clear?

- Was it well structured?
- Was there lack of basic knowledge or fundamental understanding of the topic?
- What were the obvious errors? e.g. a contradictory conclusion
- Were there too many spelling or grammatical errors?
- Was there a lack of primary sources of law?
- Did I fail to produce full and accurate references/citations?
- Was the bibliography organised correctly?
- Was my overall presentation 'sloppy'?
- Did my essay answer the question set?

Depending on the answers to these questions (you might think of other questions to ask) make a note against the relevant ones as to what you need to do to ensure you do not repeat the same mistake again. Try to see this as an objective and positive exercise and not a negative one. Self-reflection allows you to monitor your own learning progress and to know what you need to do in order to continue to improve and achieve better marks in the future. The ultimate goal is that by the final year of your course, you are equipped with the knowledge of what is required of you in terms of assessment, which, in turn, will lead you to achieving the best classification of degree you can.

Further reading

R. Burridge, *et al.*, *Effective Learning and Teaching in Law* (ILT in association with The Times Higher Education Supplement 2002)

T. Buzan, *Speed Reading: Accelerate Your Speed and Understanding for Success*, 3rd Edition (BBC Active 2006)

S. Foster, *How to Write Better Law Essays*, 2nd Edition (Pearson/Longman 2009)

D. French, *How to Cite Legal Authorities* (Blackstone 1996)

H. Frey, *et al.*, *A Handbook for Teaching and Learning in Higher Education*, 3rd Edition (Routledge-Cavendish 2009)

R. Johnstone, *et al.*, *Improving Criteria and Feedback in Student Assessment in Law* (Routledge-Cavendish 1998)

K. McMillan, and J. Weyers *The Smarter Student* (Pearson 2006)

P. Race, *The Lecturer's Toolkit: A Practical Guide to Assessment, Learning and Teaching*, 3rd Edition (Routledge-Cavendish 2007)

S. Strong, *How to Write Law Essays and Exams*, 2nd Edition (Oxford University Press 2006)

9
Finding Cases
Rick Canavan

Introduction

As a student you are frequently encouraged to read cases and not just to rely on a textbook or casebook. As I will try to argue here, there are very good reasons for this and a lot for you to gain personally over time from persevering with reading judgments in the context of the case report – it is and always has been a critical lawyerly skill. In this chapter we will look at the importance of case material and the structure of a case report and strategies and practical advice to ensure you spend as much time as possible reading case law and as little time as possible finding it.

Why do I need to find cases?

It is easy to think when there are so many sources of case law to choose from that actually finding cases (and reading them!) does not really matter anymore. After all, why read fifty pages when the legally important part may be found in just a few paragraphs? Surely all the bits of the case you need to know are in the textbook or at least in the casebook? And, admittedly, when studying law for the first time, cases can be difficult to read too: the older the judgment is, the more archaic and complex the language is likely to be; the more obscure Latin phrases are used and understanding what is really going on can be difficult – it can become hard to separate out the facts, which can seem obscure two hundred years later, from the legally relevant parts. Furthermore, if you are not familiar with a particular area of law, reading a case that rests on the technical terms and principles can be very hard. You may think you do not have the time to read around and develop the necessary understanding just to be able to read a case that may prove not to be especially helpful or relevant. There is no doubt that when you first begin to study law, reading cases particularly is a real challenge, not to mention finding them to begin with.

The problem is that it is in the cases that the law is to be found and in a common law system that is quite literally the case. Decided cases set out new rules, discard old ones, indicate future ones and refine and develop existing ones. The body of decided cases is the primary source of a great deal of the law. Consequently, this means that any textbook, any source that offers a narrative on that body of law is a secondary source.

To really understand the law you have to go back to the primary sources. Furthermore, it is in the reports that the cases come alive. Not only do you get a sense of how counsel structure, assemble and present arguments (and how the judges then dismantle them!) you also see the factual context in which the case had arisen and you see the full picture of the law, not the abridged, filtered, textbook writers account of it. As a result, you will develop a broader, deeper legal knowledge.

Over time this understanding of the factual context that gives rise to the cases will make them much easier to understand and will allow you to develop your analytical and other highly desirable skills such as commercial awareness. Most of all, learning to find, read and digest the contents of cases is a crucial step on the way to learning to work and study independently, which is very important at university and essential in practice. There will not always be someone on hand to tell you what the outline facts of a case are or to indicate the relevant legal points or how it has been subsequently treated or whether or not it is relevant, you will simply be faced with a legal problem and will have to find a solution. If you are confident with finding and reading cases this will present no difficulty whatsoever: your ability to rapidly locate the relevant material and sift the relevant facts and legal issues will ensure you quickly build up a picture of the law and you will soon be well on your way to formulating an effective solution – if you are faced with thousands of cases and have no idea where to begin it may be a very different story!

In this chapter we will look in general at law reports and law reporting, understanding case citations, how you can develop techniques and strategies to search quickly and effectively for case law and the practical skills involved in finding cases in your law library and online. The emphasis will be on finding cases decided in England and Wales but we will also consider how you go about finding European case law.

A few words on law reporting

Law reporting is the process of compiling accurate, detailed accounts of the facts and the decision in a case for publication, usually for a professional legal audience by specialist publishers. While the majority of cases are heard, and judgments given in public and so the judgments are publically available, that does not mean that all judgments will necessarily be reported. Today, law reports are usually based on the text or a transcript of the judgment handed down by the judge. A small number of cases (usually criminal cases) are of interest to the media but the overwhelming majority go unnoticed. Furthermore, mainstream media organisations are seldom interested in the legal content of the case. Media reports therefore are a pretty poor source for lawyers: they tell us very little about the relevant law or the way it has been used by judges and very often fail to even give us a good account of all the facts we might want to know. By contrast, the law reports give us all of this information and therefore must be regarded as *the* source for case reports and to find cases in the law reports you need to know how they work and how to search them effectively.

The first law reports date back to the 13th century, however, before the founding of the Incorporated Council of Law Reporting in 1865, the quality of law reports was not always high, as the reporter simply observed and made notes on the proceedings in court. As a result discrepancies and inaccuracies were commonplace, which can cause problems today when it is necessary to rely on very old case law. Reports from this time tend to be the work of individual authors and are now often referred to as the 'nominate reports'. The founding of the Incorporated Council of Law Reporting in 1865 changed the way in which cases were reported. The reports published by the Council (known simply as the *Law Reports*) were grouped into volumes according to the court in which the case was heard and comprised not a third party narrative, but the actual text of the judgment handed down by the judge with the addition of a summary and other information about the case. In short, the various series of reports published by the Council became universally adopted consigning individual reporters to history. Since the 19th century many new (and equally reliable), often specialist series of law reports have emerged and today there are in the region of fifty printed series of law reports with the vast majority available online.

Until the Practice Direction at [2001] 1 WLR 194, however, there remained a gap between cases that were decided and cases that were reported – it was still for the publishers to determine which cases were likely to be of interest. The Practice Direction provided that all judgments of 'courts of superior record' – all divisions of the High Court, Court of Appeal and at that time the House of Lords – would be prepared in a standard format with paragraph rather than page numbers and given the new 'neutral' citation for publication online. The Practice Direction also encouraged the lower courts to prepare judgments in this way. Lord Woolf, C.J., expressed that the reasons for this were:

> *"to facilitate the publication of judgments on the World Wide Web and their subsequent use by the increasing numbers of those who have access to the Web. The changes should also assist those who use and wish to search judgments stored on electronic databases."*

As you will see from your own work with cases, this Practice Direction has been very helpful. Almost no case is now 'unreported' – even if it is not published in a law report it will be available online. As you will see below, when we discuss BAILII, The Practice Direction was successful in making the text of domestic judgments more easily available to the general public. Having domestic law reports freely available also brought them into line with European cases which had been available for several years through the *Official Journal of the European Union* (OJ). We will now turn to look at where you can find case reports.

Where can I find case reports?

When you want to find and read a case the choice is generally between an online (usually) subscription-only database such as LexisLibrary or Westlaw, or visiting your library and reading the case in hard copy. The law reports that we have just discussed are available both online and in hard copy.

Online databases

Printed case reports have now been, to some extent, superseded by online databases which allow exactly the same case reports to be accessed more quickly and easily from almost anywhere (although you will probably need either a VPN or an ATHENS password to access them off campus – your university IT support service can advise you on how to do this). The online databases feature not only the commercially available series of reports but also what were previously 'unreported' cases – case reports released for public consumption by a judge but which have not been selected for publication in any series of reports. 'Unreported' cases include those from the County Court and various tribunals such as the H.M. Revenue & Customs Tribunal. The online databases are gradually adding more and more unreported cases decided before they came into existence, thereby making a huge range of legal material available for the first time.

As you can imagine, there is real commercial value in law reports and consequently access to them is restricted only to individuals and institutions that subscribe to the databases such as LexisLibrary and Westlaw. These databases cannot be accessed by the public or searched using Google and anything that is returned in Google results or from online encyclopaedias such as Wikipedia cannot be relied upon to be as accurate as the original reports. Not only that, but your lecturers will generally take a dim view of a research process that makes use of these sources in lieu of a proper *legal* research process.

There are some exceptions to this rule, however. Following the Practice Direction at [2001] 1 WLR 194 which made transcripts from all superior courts available for online publication, some courts now have their own websites giving immediate access to their judgments, including the Supreme Court (and its predecessor the Judicial Committee of the House of Lords from 1996–2010) and the Judicial Committee of the Privy Council. Many tribunals such as the Employment Appeals Tribunal, while not bound by the Practice Direction, also format their judgments in the same way and make them available online. They are also working towards making older judgments available in this way. The problem with judgments being spread across numerous websites is that it is very difficult to search across them all or to find a case unless you know the name or citation. It would be really useful if all of this free legal material were brought together onto one searchable, free website... and that is where BAILII comes in. BAILII, a fully searchable website, is operated by a charitable trust dedicated to the dissemination of legal information and collects together all publically available judgments and a range of other primary legal materials and makes them available free of charge, including all cases from the 'courts of superior record'.[1] The free sources of domestic law, however, represent only a tiny amount of the legal material that is available when compared to the big legal databases and, in order to find case law, effectively you need to learn how to search and use these.

In printed volumes

Historically, all case reports were published in print, in your library you will find several series of case reports, which can be divided up into three main types: general, specialist and international, which will include European Union reports and often reports from other common law jurisdictions such as Australia and Canada. The leading 'general' reports, which contain notable cases from all legal disciplines, include the well known *All England Reports* (All E.R.), *Weekly Law Reports* (W.L.R.) and the *Law Reports* which are divided into volumes for *Appeal Cases* (AC), *Chancery Division* (Ch. D), *Queen's Bench Division* (Q.B.D.) and *Family Division* (Fam.). Newspapers such as *The Times* also publish law reports and while these are brief, they are still regularly cited. Public libraries will often hold one or more series of these reports but to research and find case law effectively you really need to use your university library. The specialist reports include series such as *Reports on Patent Cases* (R.P.C.) and the *Lloyd's Reports* (Lloyd's Rep.) and many more. These are usually only found in the libraries of practitioners and universities but the holdings will vary from place to place. In addition, to be able to find cases when you do not know the citation you will need access to a reference work such as the *Current Law Case Citator*.

Reflection Questions

1. Have you read cases in full before? Do you think you are comfortable with reading this sort of legal material?
2. Do you think that you need to read cases in order to really understand the law?
3. Do you think that libraries still need to stock hard copies of law reports?

---

[1] The principles for searching BAILII are the same as those used for searching LexisLibrary and Westlaw, therefore it will not be considered separately in this chapter.

Searching Effectively

To search effectively for case law you need to consider what exactly it is that you are looking for and how you can develop a research strategy to find it. Effective research is almost as much about asking questions about the relevance of the cases you have found, and your familiarity with the resources available and planning and strategising, as it is about working your way through the material you find. In this section we will consider the case reports available, how to develop strategies to find them and how to understand them.

> **Practical Questions**
>
> 1. Do you know how to access your library? Do you know where in the library the law collection can be found?
> 2. Do you know how to get access to a university computer (or to set up your own computer) so that you can use legal databases?

What are you looking for?

This is the first question you need ask before you do any research. The reality is that while a lot of essay related stress can be alleviated by trawling through an online database acquiring a lot of case material, unless you start out with a clear idea about what you want to find, you will probably have to repeat the process or worse, after having read the cases, find you have no time to go back and repeat the process. The best way to avoid this becoming a problem is to think well in advance about the sort of case materials that you will need to locate. For example, will you just need to find case law from the courts of England and Wales or will you need to search case law from the rest of the UK? Will this be a problem? Are there legal issues that relate to this that you will need to familiarise yourself with? Could it be that there is a European dimension to consider also? Do you need to look even further afield? You also need to consider your level of knowledge. Do you have a thorough understanding of this area of law and a good knowledge of the case law? Do you just need to brush up on any recent developments or are you an absolute beginner who is only familiar with a few of the basic principles of this area?

If you are already familiar with an area of law you may find it useful to 'sketch' out the knowledge you already have. Map out the key cases, principles and theories and see if this reveals any as yet unknown lacunae in your knowledge. If not, are you happy that you are on top of less well known and current cases, when did you last do some work to ensure you were up to date?

If you are coming to an area for the first time you need to ensure that, before investigating a specific point or apparently important case, you have a good grasp of the area as a whole. Without experience of working with the law or working in a particular area, there is a real risk that if you do not do this you may get an entirely false impression of the significance (or not) of a case or ideas discussed within it. Whatever your level of knowledge it is well worth building a research vocabulary to ensure that you uncover as much relevant case law as possible as part of a structured, methodical research process.

Developing a research vocabulary

The most effective way to find the material you want and to exclude the material you do not want or that is unlikely to be relevant to your work is by developing and constantly updating a 'research vocabulary' for your project. This will be especially useful where you are coming to a topic for the first time or are searching widely, for example looking at all the applications of a principle as opposed to its application in a particular case. A research vocabulary is comprised of the terms that are most relevant or important in your area of study. It will include words that relate to the basic and most important concepts, words that relate the concept to the question you are trying to answer and words that relate to the most recent or interesting development in that area.

Of course, you can only know the key concepts or the way in which the law is developing if you begin by familiarising yourself with the area. It is wise to do this using recognised, quality texts in conjunction with the syllabus you are following (if available). Once you are familiar with the basics try to map out the key ideas and how they inter-relate with each other, include the leading cases at this point too. Focus your reading on the area relevant to your particular assignment and start to develop your knowledge here. When you feel you have achieved a good working knowledge start working on the detail. Start finding cases you know that you need, using terms you think might be relevant in addition to citations to focus in on specific tracts – as much as anything this will give you the opportunity to experiment with different search terms. Once you have amassed the basic material and digested it, map out where you need to go from here. What are the leading cases, in what direction is the law developing and how does this relate to your assignment? Now you are ready to start assembling and testing your research vocabulary. Search using your search terms, see if they yield apparently useful results. Look at how many results are being returned, if this is more than you think is manageable refer back to your search terms and consider how you can refine them further. Try to read in full as many of your search results as possible, this will be the acid test for the research vocabulary.

Practical Question

1. Thinking about a topic that you are currently studying can you construct a research vocabulary for that topic as a whole and develop it for an area within it that is currently changing?

Which report?

The reality is that most of your case finding will probably be done online using either LexisLibrary or Westlaw. These two services host most of the major series of reports and the text is often very similar if not identical, whichever report you choose.[2] When searching online therefore, there is often no need to target one particular set of reports unless you are looking for cases on a particular subject. As we will see below, a simple search by case name will bring up links to the case as it appears in the various reports – the text of which, as it is usually based largely on the judgment will be identical, except for variations

---

[2] You will find that these services also contain many historical and specialist/unusual law reports.

Table 1 – Brief guide to some of the leading law journals

Title	Cited as	Practice areas covered	Online availability
The Law Reports • Appeal Cases • Chancery • Queen's Bench / King's Bench • Family Division	A.C. Ch. Q.B./K.B. Fam.	Leading series of reports covering all practice areas. Case reports are based upon written judgments and are grouped according to the court in which they were heard rather than subject matter. Over time, the number of courts (and therefore series) has been rationalised from 11 to 4.	Westlaw: 1865 onwards LexisLibrary: 1865 onwards
All England Law Reports	All E.R.	Leading series of reports covering all aspects of law, reports of first instance and appellate judgments.	LexisLibrary: 1936 onwards
All England Law Reports (Commercial)	All E.R. (Comm.)	All aspects of commercial law, including banking, domestic and intl. sale of goods and shipping.	LexisLibrary: 1999 onwards
Butterworths' Company Law Cases	B.C.L.C.	All aspects of company law including cases relating to corporate insolvency.	LexisLibrary: 1983 onwards
Common Market Law Reports	C.M.L.R.	Leading source of European Union law.	Westlaw: 1962 onwards
Criminal Appeal Reports	Cr.A.R.	Leading source of case law exclusively on criminal appeals.	Westlaw: 1909 onwards
English Reports	E.R.	All practice areas and historical cases. Quality and accuracy can vary.	Westlaw: All volumes
Entertainment & Media Law Reports	E.M.L.R.	All aspects of entertainment and media including aspects of contract and intellectual property.	Westlaw: 1993 onwards
European Human Rights Reports	E.H.R.R.	Series dedicated to matters of human rights in the European context.	Westlaw: 1979 onwards
Family Law Reports	F.L.R.	Series dedicated to all aspects of family law.	LexisLibrary: 1984 onwards
Industrial Cases Reports	I.C.R.	Major series of reports dealing with all aspects of employment/labour law.	Westlaw: 1972 onwards
Reports of Patent Cases	R.P.C.	Leading series of reports for intellectual property law.	Westlaw: 1977 onwards LexisLibrary: 1936–1997
Weekly Law Reports	W.L.R.	All areas of practice, all significant cases recorded from all courts.	Westlaw: 1953 onwards

in the headnote or keywords. However, if you are searching through hard copies of the reports you may want to target a particular series, either because you prefer the way that they are indexed or laid out, or because the series tends to report cases from a specialist area of interest to you.

Listed in Table 1 above are some of the main series of reports that you are likely to use as a student (each online database has a list of all the series it has available) and information on where they can be found online (all titles are available in print unless otherwise stated). As you will see, when searching online you can find just about all the domestic and European decisions that you are likely to need, however, if you wanted to search a dedicated European Union law service you can use EUR-Lex and, for decisions of the European Court of Human Rights, the court's own website hosts all its judgments.

Useful Links

- BAILII — www.bailii.org
- LexisLibrary — www.lexisnexis.com
- Westlaw — www.westlaw.co.uk
- EUR-Lex (for European Union law) — http://eur-lex.europa.eu/en/index.htm
- European Court of Human Rights search portal — http://cmiskp.echr.coe.int/tkp197/search.asp

Reading Cases

The 'anatomy' of a case report

Before reading cases it is worthwhile taking a moment to consider what information is contained in a case report and how it is laid out. In addition to the text of the judgment, commercially published case reports contain a lot of additional information, such as the cases considered in the judgment, keywords to help quickly identify the legal issues raised in the case and a headnote which gives a brief summary of the facts and the judgment. Set out below (Fig 1.) is an example of the opening pages of a well known case found in the *All England Law Reports*. A number of features of the report are highlighted on the text and their significance is explained in Table 2 below.

Citations

A citation is a shorthand reference to a case. There is an expectation that in your written work you will provide references for the cases you have referred to and it is crucial that you are comfortable with using them and understand why they are used. Given the sheer volume of case law and the various places where a report might be found, you can immediately see why it is useful to be able to use shorthand notations and necessary to have an agreed system of citations and to use those citations to indicate to a reader precisely

> **CENTRAL LONDON PROPERTY TRUST, LTD.** *v.*
> **HIGH TREES HOUSE, LTD.**
>
> [KING'S BENCH DIVISION (Denning, J.), July 18, 1946.]
>
> *Estoppel—Estoppel in pais—Estoppel by conduct—Lease of flats—Written promise to reduce rent owing to war-time conditions—No consideration—Reduced rent paid—Binding effect of promise—Effect of ending of war-time conditions.*
> *Landlord and Tenant—Rent—Reduction of rent—Lease of flats—Written promise to reduce rent owing to war-time conditions—No consideration—Reduced rent paid—Binding effect of promise—Effect of ending of war-time conditions.*
>
> Landlords let a new block of flats in 1937 to H. Ltd. (called "the tenants"), on a ninety-nine years' lease at a ground rent of £2,500 a year. Few of the flats had been let at the outbreak of war in 1939, and, in view of the tenants' difficulty in paying the rent out of profits in prevailing conditions, the landlords agreed in writing in 1940 to reduce the rent to £1,250. No duration of the reduction of rent was specified and there was no consideration for it. The tenants paid the reduced rent. By early in 1945 the whole block of flats was let. On Sept. 21, 1945, the landlords wrote asking that the full rent of £2,500 should be paid and claiming arrears of £7,916. They subsequently brought a test action to recover the balance of rent for the quarters ending Sept. 29 and Dec. 25, 1945.

K.B.D.   CENTRAL LONDON PTY. *v.* HIGH TREES, LTD. (DENNING, J.)   257

> **Held:** (i) the promise of a reduction of rent, being intended to be legally binding and to be acted on, and having been acted on by the tenants, was binding on the landlords to the extent that they would not be allowed to act inconsistently with it, although it was not the subject of estoppel at common law; but
> (ii) the promise was for a reduction of rent which was temporary and was to endure so long only as the block of flats was not substantially let, and, since the block of flats was substantially let early in 1945, the landlords were entitled to the full rent for the quarters ending Sept. 29 and Dec. 25, 1945.

[As to what conduct gives rise to an estoppel at common law, see 13 HALSBURY'S LAWS (2nd Edn.) 486, para. 555; and for cases on the subject, see 21 DIGEST 292-294, *1041-1051*.

As to the inadmissibility of extrinsic evidence to vary deeds, see 11 HALSBURY'S LAWS (3rd Edn.) 396 et seq; and as to variation by agreement without consideration, see ibid., p. 325, para. 518, text and note (b).]

Cases referred to:
(1) *Berry* v. *Berry*, [1929] 2 K.B. 316; 98 L.J.K.B. 748; 141 L.T. 461; Digest Supp.
(2) *Jorden* v. *Money*, (1854), 5 H.L. Cas. 185; 23 L.J.Ch. 865; 24 L.T.O.S. 160; 10 E.R. 868; 21 Digest 292, *1041*.
(3) *Fenner* v. *Blake*, [1900] 1 Q.B. 426; 69 L.J.Q.B. 257; 82 L.T. 149; 31 Digest (Repl.) 574, *6947*.
(4) *Re Wickham*, (1917), 34 T.L.R. 158; [1917] H.B.R. 272; 21 Digest 299, *1079*.
(5) *Re Porter (William) & Co., Ltd.*, [1937] 2 All E.R. 361; Digest Supp.
(6) *Buttery* v. *Pickard*, (1946), 174 L.T. 144; 31 Digest (Repl.) 247, *3822*.
(7) *Hughes* v. *Metropolitan Ry. Co.*, (1877), 2 App. Cas. 439; 46 L.J.Q.B. 583; 36 L.T. 932; 31 Digest (Repl.) 556, *6757*.
(8) *Birmingham & District Land Co.* v. *London & North Western Ry. Co.*, (1888), 40 Ch.D. 268; 60 L.T. 527; 31 Digest (Repl.) 565, *6856*.
(9) *Salisbury* v. *Gilmore*, [1942] 1 All E.R. 457; [1942] 2 K.B. 38; 111 L.J.K.B. 593; 166 L.T. 329; 31 Digest (Repl.) 378, *5069*.

Action.
> The landlords let a block of flats to the tenants on a ninety-nine years' lease under seal in 1937 at a ground rent of £2,500, which in view of war-time conditions and without consideration they agreed in writing in 1940 to reduce to £1,250. Early in 1945 the flats became fully occupied and in September, 1945, the landlords claimed that rent was payable at the full rate of £2,500 and they also claimed arrears in respect of earlier years. They brought a test action for the recovery of the full rent for the two quarters ending on Sept. 29, 1945, and Dec. 25, 1945. The tenants contended that the reduced rent was payable for the whole term of the lease, or alternatively that it was payable up to September, 1945, on the ground that the landlords were estopped from now claiming the additional rent or alternatively that they were bound by their promise of a reduction in the rent, which was made with the intention that it should be binding and should be acted on and which was, in fact, acted on by the tenants.

Robert Fortune for the landlords.
Ronald Hopkins for the tenants.

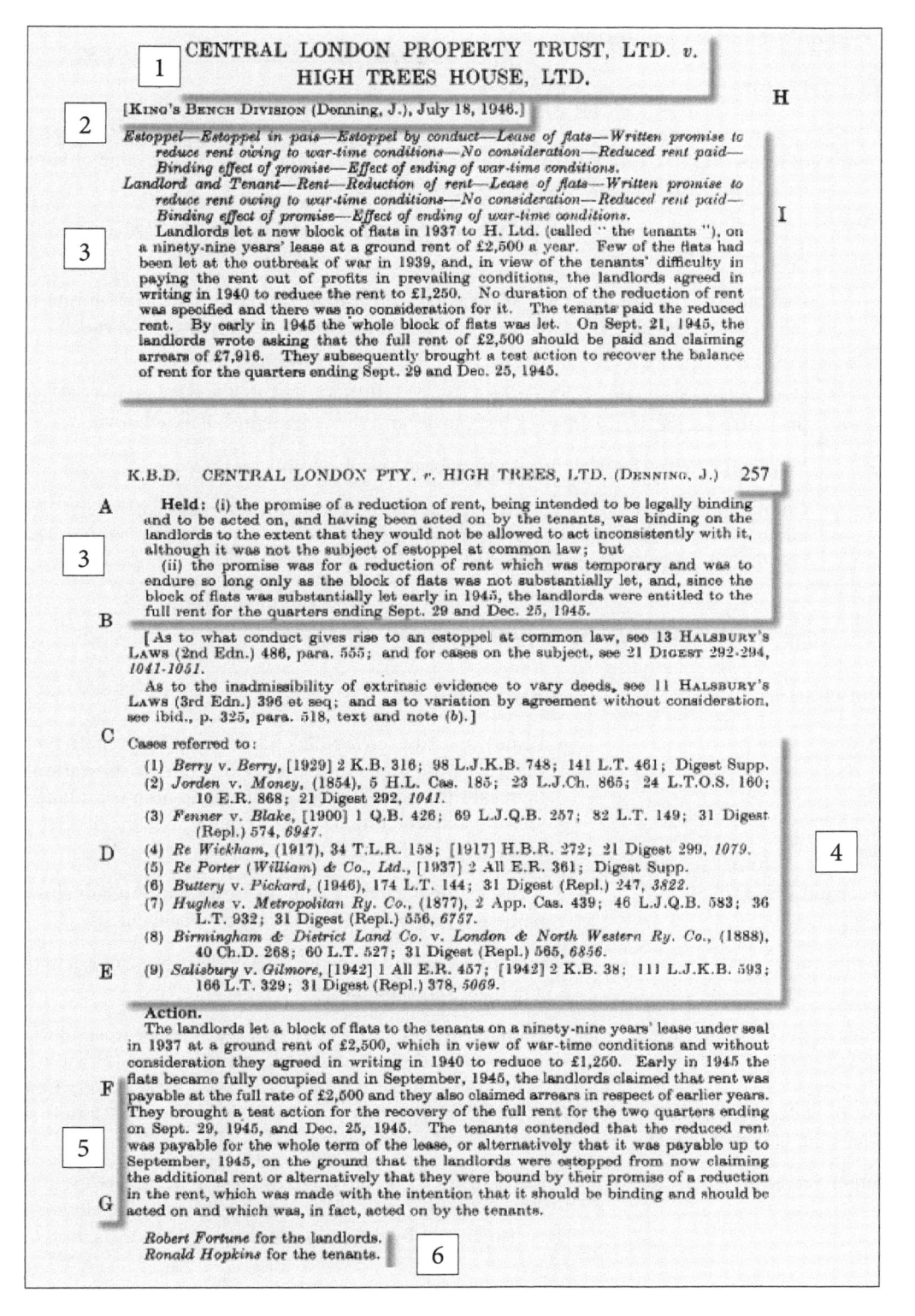

Figure 1: Opening two pages of *Central London Property Trust Ltd. v High Trees House* [1956] 1 All ER 256, pp. 256–257

Table 2 – Features of a case report

Number	Feature
1	Case name – the law report will give the name of the case in full, this will often reveal other parties to the action, or in the case of an appeal other cases on the same or similar facts that are being heard together – conjoined appeals.
2	Information about the hearing – the court and the dates on which the case was heard and the name of the judge(s).
3	Headnote – contains 'catchwords' to assist with searching followed by brief summaries of the facts and the judgment handed down. In appeal cases a summary of the earlier hearing(s) may be given.
4	Cases referred to – this section of the report indicates cases that have been referred to in the course of the arguments put by counsel and the judgment(s) handed down.
5	Marginal letters – these allow you to refer to specific points on the page.
6	Counsel – the names of all counsel who appeared before the court are listed here. The names of the instructing solicitors are usually found at the very end of the report. The text of the judgment begins below this.

Table 3 – Case citations as a guide to practice area

Style of citation	Area of law
A v T	Family law: cases involving children or subject matter where the privacy of adults is essential (for example in relation to medical treatment). Some criminal cases also use a letter to identify a defendant, however in these cases the first letter will always be 'R' e.g. *R v T*.
Re. Spectrum Plus Ltd.	A case name beginning with 'Re' followed by a company name will concern a company that is insolvent.
Re. Swinburne	Usually a case involving wills or probate but can relate to a person who is bankrupt.
R (on the application of Cart) v Upper Tribunal Or R v Sec. of State for Education, ex parte Avon County Council	Both of these citations refer to judicial review cases. Judicial review cases decided since 2001 take the form shown in *Cart*. Before 2001, they take the form shown *Avon County Council*. The words *ex parte* (often abbreviated to (*ex.p.*) simply mean 'on the application of'.
The Super Servant II	Cases involving a ship or an interest in a ship are usually known by the name of the vessel, although officially the case is also known by the names of the parties to the action.[3]

---

[3] For example the *Super Servant II* is also known as *Lauritzen A.S. v Wijsmuller B.V.* [1990] 1 Lloyd's Rep. 1.

which report and case is being referred to. Understanding citations is also important because a citation might be the only thing that you have when you are trying to find a case.

The citation, and particularly the case name, can actually give you some idea what the case might be about. Table 3 above shows the ways in which case names appear in different disputes. It also shows how the case name indicates the area of law from which the case is drawn.

Understanding citations

There are three types of citations – the 'traditional' citations used to refer to cases in the commercially published law reports such as the *Weekly Law Reports*, so called 'neutral citations' used for judgments that are made publically available by the courts and separate systems of citations for European cases. We will now look in turn at what information comprises these citations. Note, however, that English cases will often have both neutral and traditional citations and often more than one of the latter depending on the importance of the case.

'Traditional' citations

An ordinary citation such as the one below for *Karak Rubber Co. Ltd v Burden (No.2)* will look something like this:

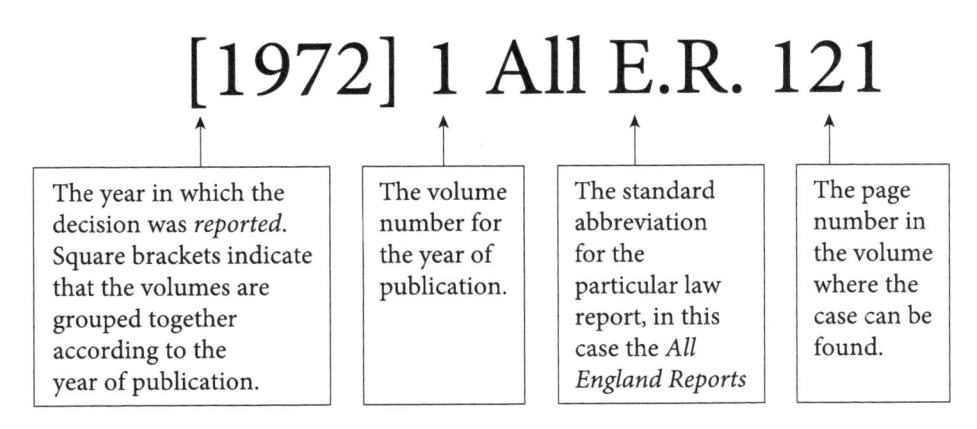

$$[1972] \; 1 \; All \; E.R. \; 121$$

| The year in which the decision was *reported*. Square brackets indicate that the volumes are grouped together according to the year of publication. | The volume number for the year of publication. | The standard abbreviation for the particular law report, in this case the *All England Reports* | The page number in the volume where the case can be found. |

Figure 2: Example of a 'traditional' case citation

A citation might refer you to a specific page in which case, 'at p.122,' (for example) would be added. Where several pages are referred to, 'pp.' is used.

'Neutral' Citations

If we take a more recent case such as *RTS Flexible Systems Ltd v Molkerei Alois Müller* we can see below (Fig. 3) that the citation looks quite different but the information it conveys is more than adequate to find the case online. A decision as important as this one is widely reported and there are several 'traditional' citations for this case.

[2010] UKSC 14

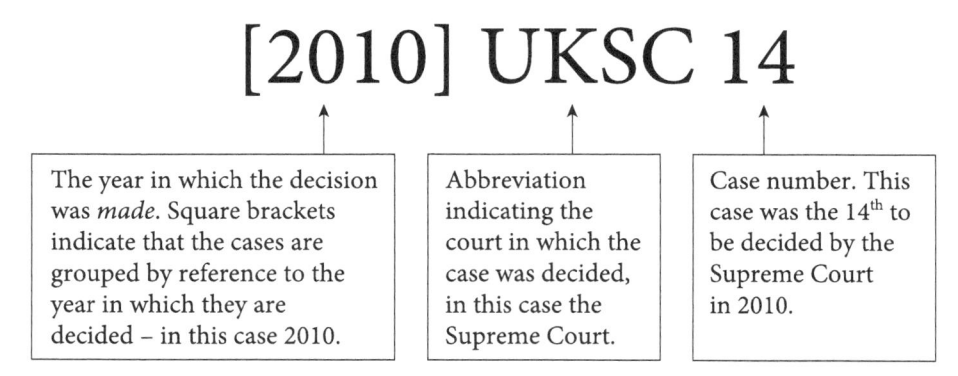

- The year in which the decision was *made*. Square brackets indicate that the cases are grouped by reference to the year in which they are decided – in this case 2010.
- Abbreviation indicating the court in which the case was decided, in this case the Supreme Court.
- Case number. This case was the 14th to be decided by the Supreme Court in 2010.

Figure 3: Example of a neutral citation

The judgments released with neutral citations are given numbered paragraphs rather than page numbers. If a neutral citation is followed by a number it is therefore referring to a specific paragraph in the judgment, e.g. [2010] UKSC 14 at 23.

In the example above we have seen a case decided by the Supreme Court. The system of neutral citations assigns each court a unique abbreviation; these are set out in the table below.

Table 4 – Abbreviations used in neutral citations

Court	Abbreviation
Supreme Court	UKSC
House of Lords	UKHL
Privy Council	UKPC
Court of Appeal – Civil Division	EWCA Civ.
Court of Appeal – Criminal Division	EWCA Crim.
High Court – Administrative Court	EWHC (Admin.)
High Court – Chancery Division	EWHC (Ch.)
High Court – Patents Courts	EWHC (Pat.)
High Court – Queen's Bench Division	EWHC (QB)
High Court – Commercial Court	EWHC (Comm)
High Court – Admiralty Court	EWHC (Amdlty)
High Court – Technology and Construction Court	EWHC (TCC)
High Court – Family Division	EWHC (Fam.)

European Union Citations

Citations of European Union cases (that is to say those decided by either the Court of First Instance (CFI) (now the General Court (EGC)) or cases from the European Court of Justice (ECJ)) are a little more complex than domestic ones as they include both a case serial number and citation. Official judgments are prefixed with either the letter 'T' or the letter 'C'. Cases prefixed with the letter 'T' are judgments of the CFI/EGC while the prefix 'C' indicates a judgment of the ECJ. Below we can see the citation for the judgment of the ECJ in *M v European Medicines Agency*.

C-197/09... [2009] ECR I-12033

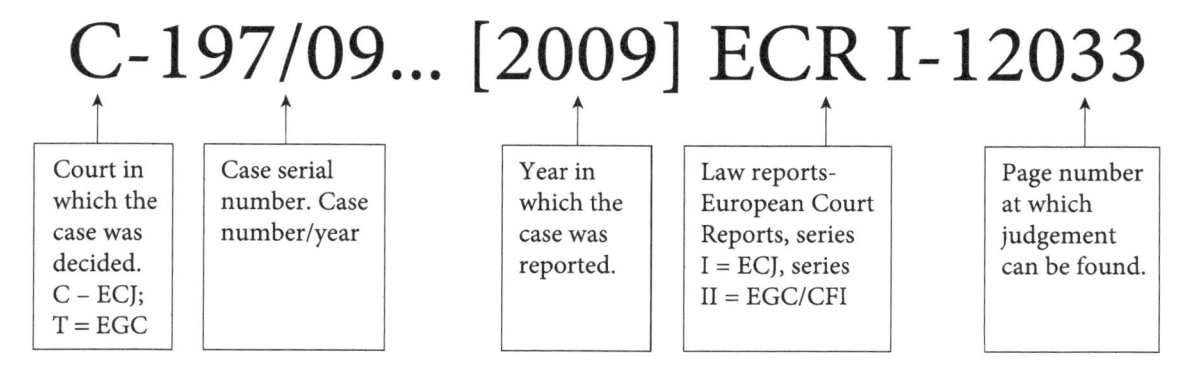

- **C-197/09** — Court in which the case was decided. C – ECJ; T = EGC
- **Case serial number.** Case number/year
- **[2009]** — Year in which the case was reported.
- **ECR** — Law reports- European Court Reports, series I = ECJ, series II = EGC/CFI
- **I-12033** — Page number at which judgement can be found.

Figure 4: Example of a European case citation

Now we have looked at some of the practical skills required to understand and utilise the case material that you are going to find, we will look at how you access case law online before considering how you find case law in print.

Finding Case Law Online

Why find cases online?

Without doubt, the availability of case reports through a variety of online services has dramatically changed the way in which law students and practitioners work. Printed reports had obvious drawbacks: even in the recent past, printed law reports tended to comprise only those cases that were judged by the publisher to be legally noteworthy. Despite being very well compiled, this meant that the reports provided only a snapshot of a court's work and inevitably, more mundane cases dealing with settled law or cases from the lower courts were often excluded and as a result, were almost unobtainable. Printed reports were often not published until many months after cases were decided and reports of the oldest cases were very rare and often kept only by a handful of libraries. Furthermore, while the range of printed reports was extensive, with both general and specialist reports available, most libraries did not subscribe to them all. This could be problematic as while some cases could be found in a range of reports, others may only feature in just one and in any case even a really good library would have only a handful of copies of each volume, and often only single copies of specialist reports.

Nonetheless, finding a case where you knew the citation was straightforward; when you just knew the name, if you knew how to use the correct reference works, then this could be done without too much difficulty, the real problems began when you had to find cases on a particular topic or point of law. Each volume of reports tended to index its contents by topic but this meant trawling through many volumes and skim reading numerous cases to find anything relevant, occasionally helped along by stickers added by the librarians cross-referencing other case law or indicating whether a decision had been subsequently approved or over-turned. Alternatively, the slightly less laborious approach was to use various reference works which listed cases by topic or practice area or simply to read current journals and textbooks to find out about recent or important decisions. Even after spending several hours diligently assembling a list of cases that *may* be relevant that you were going to photocopy then read to see if they were relevant to the essay you were writing, you could almost guarantee that someone would have beaten you to at least some of the elusive volumes.

In the last ten to fifteen years, while printed case reports remain in print and available in law libraries, the launch and subsequent rapid development of a range of online legal databases has made this laborious process of research and reliance on the editorial decision of publishers largely a thing of the past, and there has never been a greater volume of case reports available so easily. Today, the leading legal databases host nearly every decision of every UK court and tribunal and they make these reports available rapidly and sometimes almost immediately. In addition, over the years, the databases have also made available more and more 'historical' reports, ranging from ten to three or four hundred years of age as well as reports from many other jurisdictions and specialised areas of practice – a truly ambitious project of digitisation that makes available a vast amount of knowledge.

As a student or practitioner you can now sift through cases that previously would have been almost undiscoverable and this in itself opens up new avenues for research and debate. The sheer volume of material can, however, be a drawback in itself. Without an editorial team to determine which cases are of real interest (and perhaps without a headnote or keywords to assist) you are often left to make this judgment yourself and it is up to you pluck from the thousands and thousands of decided cases, the one which you actually need. Luckily, the websites offer increasingly powerful search tools allowing you search by name, citation or by reference to other related cases or keywords and more importantly indicating whether a case has been followed, approved, over-ruled, academically commented upon, etc. A recent addition to the databases are features that allow you to save and share searches as part of projects and receive automatic updates based on your previous searches, excellent for keeping right up to date. The result of having access to so much material online is that you can now assemble in a couple of hours or less (and download in seconds), a body of relevant case law drawn from different series of reports, different practice areas and jurisdictions that might previously have taken days to compile. We will now look at the most popular databases and the ways in which they can be effectively searched.

What databases are available?

Depending on the subscriptions taken out by your institution you will have a number of different databases to choose from. Each one offers a different range of materials and can be searched in different ways. The two databases that are likely to be available to you are LexisLibrary and Westlaw. You will be greatly assisted in your studies if you can develop a good working knowledge of the functions of at least one of the databases, not least as they contain a large amount of commentary and professional publications linked to case reports, which you are likely to find very useful.

The decision as to which database you use will probably depend on the sources of law you use most and which database you find easiest to effectively search. It is worth noting that both services offer extensive online training and help and will often hold training events on campus at the start of the academic year where you can get hands-on experience, ask questions and explore the more advanced functions of both services.

Using 'connectors' and 'Boolean' operators

For some searches, particularly keyword searches, you may want to only see results where your keywords (for example case names or practice areas) feature in close proximity to each other, for example in the same sentence or paragraph or together in sequence. You may also be worried that a search might omit some results because of variations in spelling, for example. You can search in this way and overcome these problems using connectors and Boolean operators. The two tables below show you the indicators and Boolean operators that can be used in LexisLibrary and Westlaw.

Table 5 – Connector words for LexisLibrary and Westlaw

Type of search	Connector (LexisLibrary)	Connector (Westlaw)
Proximity – used to find words close to each other. For example to find 'landlord' and 'tenant' within two words of each other or within the same sentence or paragraph.	w/*n* e.g. landlord w/2 tenant w/s e.g. landlord w/s tenant w/p e.g. landlord w/p tenant	/*n*, e.g. duty /5 care /s in the same sentence /p in the same paragraph
Phrase – used to find words that appear together.	No connector needed unless the word 'and' or 'or' feature in the phrase then quotation marks should be used.	Double quotation marks around the phrase, e.g. "duty of care"
Truncated – used to find terms that are different but related e.g. 'liability' and 'liable'.	Exclamation mark (!) e.g. searching for 'liab!' would bring up results for both 'liable' and 'liability'.	Exclamation mark (!)
Wildcard – used to find a word that may be spelled in different ways e.g. 'criticise' and 'criticize'.	Asterisk (*) e.g. if searching for 'critici*e' results with both 's' and 'z' would be returned. More asterisks can be used if necessary.	* for one character ** for two characters etc.

Table 6 – Boolean operators for LexisLibrary and Westlaw

Boolean Operator	LexisLibrary	Westlaw
OR – to *expand* a search, e.g. ship OR vessel OR boat; to search for antonyms, e.g. creditor OR debtor; or spelling variations, e.g. trademark OR trade-mark.	OR	OR
AND – to *restrict* a search, e.g. negligence AND medical; this is generally not a useful search in a long document.	AND	&
NOT – to *exclude* a word from a search, e.g. undertakings NOT contract.	AND NOT	%

Practical Questions

Using connectors and Boolean operators how would you search for the following?

1. A reference to 'refusal to supply' where those words are found in exactly that sequence.
2. Search for a case where within one paragraph they are references to disqualified directors or the disqualification of directors for fraudulent trading under s. 458 of the Companies Act.

Using LexisLibrary

What is on offer?

As we can see from Table 1, LexisLibrary offers a tremendous variety of case reports and in addition to this it can tell you whether a decided case is still 'good law', find cases that refer to or are linked with a case that you are interested in, link you to relevant commentary and also offer a range of journals and practitioner oriented texts.

Searching LexisLibrary

The various sources of case material available through LexisLibrary can be searched easily through the 'cases' search page (shown below in Fig. 5). This is accessed by clicking the 'cases' tab at the top left of the LexisLibrary homepage. From the search page it is possible to search one or all series of law reports, either by citation, complete or partial case name, by reference to keywords or a combination of all of these. The search facility also allows you to further narrow your search by filtering your results by reference: to the date (or approximate date) of the decision, the court from which the judgment was handed down, the presiding judge(s) and the name of counsel. LexisLibrary has powerful and effective search tools, however to harness their full potential you need to know how to compile your search terms correctly, and we will now look in detail at the various searches that you can perform.

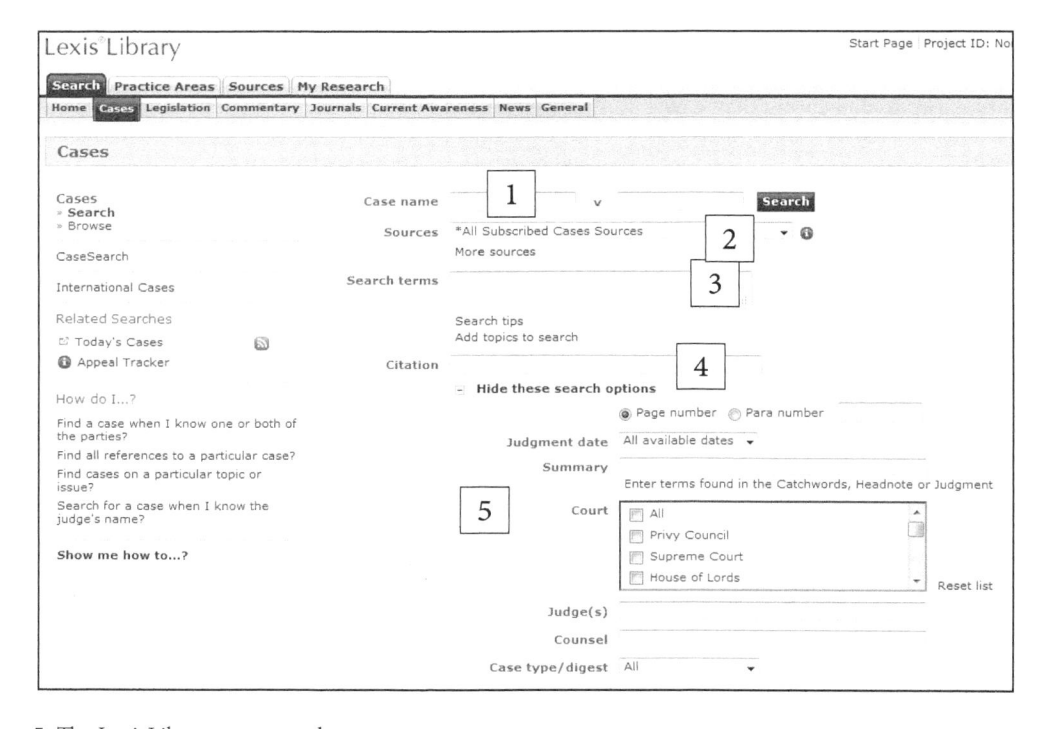

Figure 5: The LexisLibrary case search page

Searching for a case by name

Searching by case name is very simple in LexisLibrary. If you know the full name of the case simply type the name(s) into the boxes (marked '1' on Fig. 5). If you only know part of the case name type that into the box on the left and click 'search'. You will then be taken to the results page. If the case name contains brackets, you should omit these. If you are unsure of the spelling, or only know part of one of the case names, enter the part that you know followed by an asterisk and LexisLibrary will give you all the cases that contain that fragment. A relatively new feature of LexisLibrary is the auto-complete feature. With this as soon as you type a case name it will bring up options and as you continue to type it will narrow them down, allowing you to click straight to the case as soon as you see the correct name. LexisLibrary will return no results if the search terms are spelled incorrectly.

Search a particular series of reports

If you know a case name or want to search by reference to keywords and want to narrow your search to just one series of reports, simply type the full or partial name in the 'Case name' boxes and click the drop down 'Sources' menu (marked '2' on Fig. 5). Select the source you wish to search and click 'search'.

Searching using search terms or keywords

If you are looking for cases on a particular topic, area of law or even more specifically on, for example, a particular type of crime or contract you can search using the 'Search terms function' (marked '3' on Fig. 5). You can use any number of search terms but the more you use or the more specific the terms are, the fewer results your search will return. This is a very useful search when you are not especially familiar with an area of law or where you want to use it to narrow down, for example a name search that is likely to yield a lot of results, for example a case that includes the name *Smith*, or find all mentions of a particular case. From your reading on a topic or from you knowledge of it, certain keywords (and how they might appear together) will no doubt become obvious, all you need to do is to type them into the search box with the appropriate connectors and/or Boolean operators. Tables 5 and 6 above show connectors and operators that can be used in LexisLibrary and their functions.

Searching by citation

Sometimes, all that you have for your search is the citation. With the online databases this is not a problem. All you need to know is how to enter the citation correctly into the 'Citation' search box (marked '4' on Fig. 5). As when searching for a case name you simply type the citation omitting any brackets or punctuation. So if you were searching for case with the citation '[1987] 3 All E.R. 565' you would simply enter '1987 3 All ER 565' in the search box. The search would then return a link to the full text of *Pagnan Sp.A v Tradax Ocean Transportation S.A.* [1987] 3 All E.R. 565. If you only have a partial citation enter what you have, you could combine this search with a (partial) case name.

Advanced search options

The additional search options (marked '5' in Fig. 5) allow you to narrow or refine your searches even further. You can search for the judgments: handed down by a particular judge; in a particular court; by the names of counsel who appeared in the case; or narrow down your search results according to the general type of resource that you are seeking. This is done using the 'Case type/digest' menu and using this tool you can focus your search results solely upon law reports, transcripts, digested/summarised reports or practice directions. The advanced search options also allow you to search by words found in the headnote or judgment again using connectors and Boolean operators if required.

Understanding your search results

As you can see in Fig. 7, unless your search returns only a single result (in which case you will be taken straight to that case) you have a number of search result to choose from. Even then you will still likely have tens of results to sort through. Sometimes the results will be the same case as it appeared in different reports, sometimes the same case as it was heard in different courts but, on occasion and particularly if you have searched by keyword, you will have several results and may want to narrow these down. You can minimise the number of unhelpful search results by using multiple fields in your search.

Let us suppose that we are interested in the way that the Court of Appeal has applied the principles set out in the House of Lords decision *Investors Compensation Scheme v West Bromwich Building Society* [1998]

1 All ER 98 to the interpretation of leases over the last ten years. We can be confident that there will be quite a number of search results but let us assume that we are not concerned about where they have been reported so the search will cover 'all subscribed cases' and we will not discriminate between case reports and digests. Here is how the completed search form might look (the search terms are highlighted):

Figure 6: Sample LexisLibrary search form

Click 'search' and LexisLibrary would then give us these results:

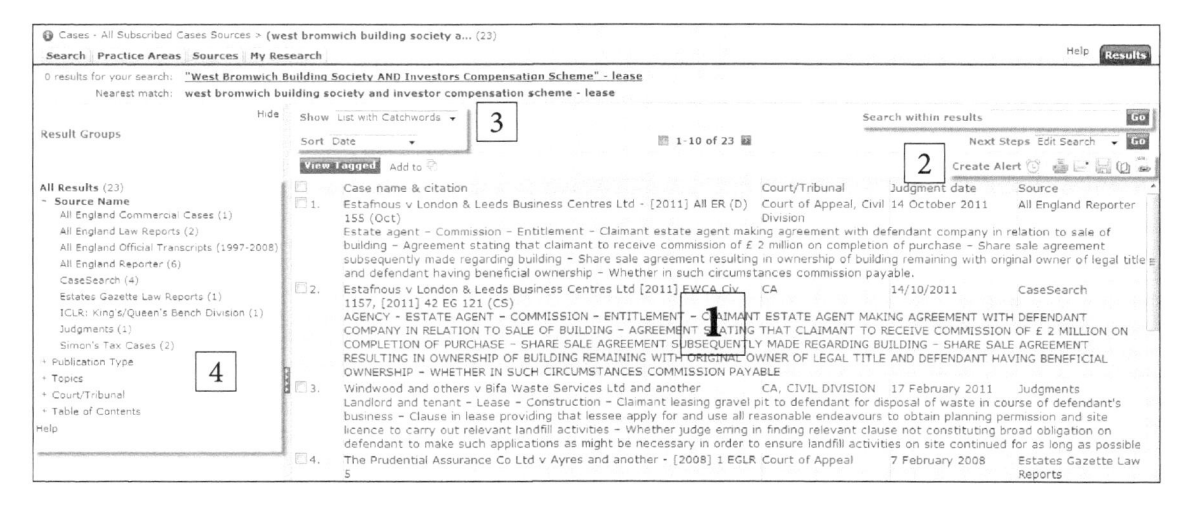

Figure 7: Example of a LexisLibrary search results page

You can see that in the results various features are highlighted, these allow you to further refine a search or deliver one or more of the results. To simply access a case, click on the case name in the main pane (1). If you can see the case(s) that you are looking for at this stage you can download, print or save one or more cases using the buttons at the top right (2). Using these functions you can also forward the search results to someone else, save them as part of a large project and set up alerts to alert you to new cases. To change the order or appearance of the search results use the commands above the results (3). To further refine or focus your search, use the commands on the left of the screen (4), just click on the filter you want to use and the results are amended immediately. This is particularly helpful if we want to look at results from a particular source or decided over a particular period, for example. If we are still not sure which cases might be of interest we can click on a case and LexisLibrary can give us further information. Below we will look in more detail at result 7, *KPMG v Network Rail* [2007] EWCA Civ. 363.

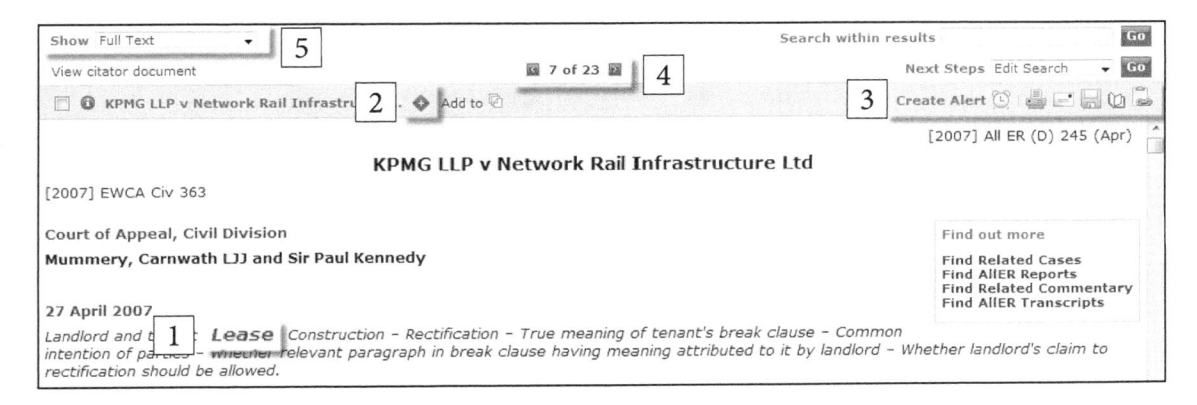

Figure 8: Example of a case report

The key words (1) highlight the word(s) used in the original search and gives us the other catch words for this case – this ought to give us a better sense of what the case is about and whether it might be of use to us. We can also see that we have all the information that we would have in a printed case report. The symbol (2) indicates how the case has been treated. A key to these symbols can be found below in Table 7. Here the symbol indicates positive treatment. If we click on the symbol, LexisLibrary will generate a page indicating the cases where this decision has been cited (we can also do this and more using the options in the 'Find out more' box to the right. If this case is useful we can use the buttons (3) to move to the next case in the results or if we want to print, save or share the case just click the relevant button (4). We can also change the view of the text (5).

Using Westlaw

What is on offer?

As we can see in Table 1, as with LexisLibrary, Westlaw offers a tremendous variety of material and there is some overlap between the two services, although you can see that the Westlaw service is stronger in respect of its holdings in areas such as European law and specialist areas such as employment law, also whereas LexisLibrary has exclusive access to the All England Reports, Westlaw has exclusive access to the Weekly Law Reports. While it is possible, only rarely will you find that Westlaw (or LexisLibrary) has no record of a case. If this does occur the simple solution it to use the other service for that search but the reality is that when you are starting to research law neither service has any obvious or significant flaws, the service that you use more frequently, therefore is likely to be related to whichever database you find easiest to navigate or most intuitive.

Table 7 – Key to LexisLibrary – case treatment symbols

Type	Value	Description
✖	Negative Treatment Icon	This indicates that the decision has been subsequently reversed, disapproved or overruled.
⚠	Cautionary Treatment Icon	This indicates that the decision has had some doubt cast on it.
◆	Positive Treatment Icon	This indicates that the decision has received positive treatment: affirmed, applied, etc.
●	Neutral Treatment Icon	This indicates that the decision has received neutral or ambivalent treatment: considered, explained, etc.
ℹ	Information Icon	This indicates that no treatment has been given—only citation information is available.

As you proceed in your studies you may come to notice that Westlaw, with fewer search options, is a less 'powerful' search tool than LexisLibrary, however, it compensates with outstanding ease of use and a wider range of case reports on the sort of areas you are likely to study. We will now turn to look at the various case law searches that can performed using Westlaw but first, take a moment to look at Fig. 9 which shows the Westlaw cases search page,[4] from where all searches begin. This can be accessed by clicking on the 'Cases' tab at the top of the Westlaw homepage (note the 'help' icons next to each search field).

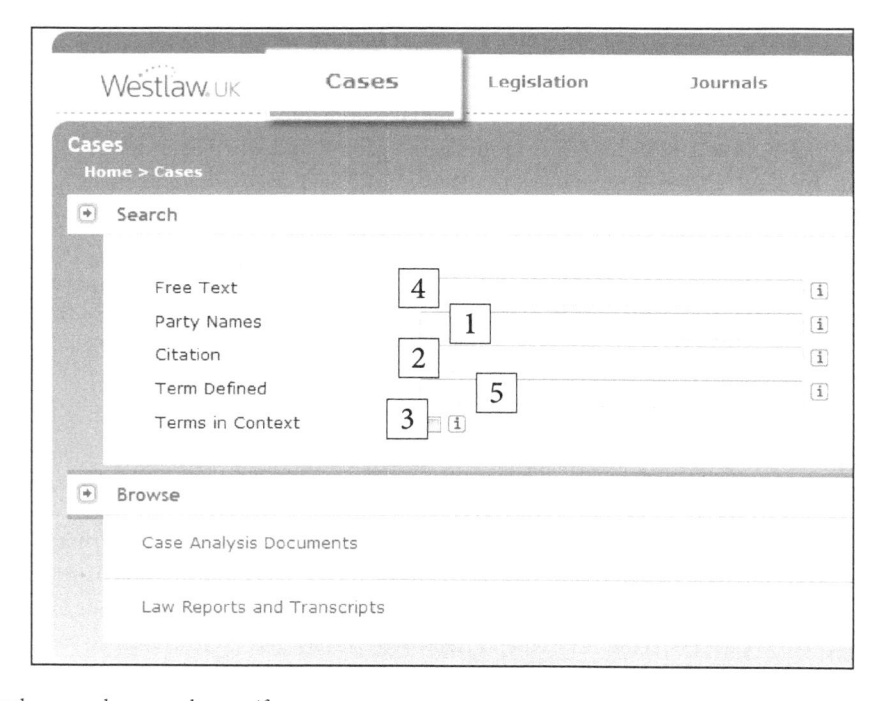

Figure 9: Westlaw case law search page/form

---

[4] Note however that it is possible to search from the Westlaw main page across all types of legal materials including cases.

Searching Westlaw

Searching for a case by name

As with all databases a search by name is usually straightforward and especially so with Westlaw. You can enter one or both names of the parties into the 'Party names' field (marked '1' on Fig. 9), in any order with or without a 'v' inbetween. If you were searching for the case of *Chatterton v Gerson*[5] therefore, you could find it by searching for 'Chatterton', 'Gerson', 'Gerson Chatterton', etc. You can of course also use Boolean operators in this or any other field if you are unsure, for example, of the spelling of the names of the parties.

Searching by citation

Searching by citation is also very simple in Westlaw – just type the citation into the 'Citation' search field (marked '2' on Fig. 9) and hit 'search'. It does not matter if you include brackets or punctuation in your search, the correct case will still be found. If you are unsure of the full citation you can enter a partial citation and all matching results will be shown. The difficulty here is that this may also bring up several unwanted results so you may wish to combine a partial citation with a keyword or phrase.

Search a particular series of reports

Westlaw does not have a specific function that allows you to search a series of case reports. However, you work around this by searching using a part citation and a partial case name, keyword or year. For example, if you if you were aware of a case decided in King's Bench Division on British European Airways you could enter 'KB' in the citation field and British European Airways into the case name field and get the result *Smith v British European Airways* [1951] 2 K.B. 893.

You can also browse the contents of a series of reports much as you would in a library. To browse reports click either 'Case analysis documents' or 'Law reports and transcripts' under the 'Browse' header (marked '3' on Fig. 9). You then select the law report series that you are interest in followed by the year. Westlaw will then give you an alphabetical list of all cases in that series for that year. You can download a copy of the report from that page or click the case name to view the full text on screen.

'Free text' search

A 'Free text' search allows you to search for a case by reference to any terms either in the text, the headnote, the name, etc. You can use connectors and Boolean operators (see Tables 5 and 6) to narrow down or improve the accuracy of your search. Once you have decided on the wording for your free text search enter the words in the 'Free text' search field (marked '1' on Fig. 9). Westlaw will automatically add the 'AND' operator between the words.

To see the text you have searched for in the context of the case report in the results, check the 'Terms in context' box at the foot of the search options this will allow you to quickly get a snapshot of the case without scrolling the entire text.

'Terms Defined' search

If you want to find case law on a particular legal concept, rule or doctrine you should use the 'Terms Defined' search field (marked '5' on Fig. 9). As soon as you begin to type a range of possible options will begin to appear, narrowing down as you continue typing. You can only complete this field with one of the defined search terms. When you have selected your term click 'search' and you will get a chronological list

---

[5] [1981] QB 432

of all cases that have been tagged with that term. As with all the Westlaw search options you can combine it with other terms, citations, names, etc. to narrow your search.

Alerts

If you click on the 'Alerts' tab at the top of the main page you can create personalised alerts that relate to anything from a particular case to a particular area of practice.

Understanding your search results

The basic search features of the Westlaw service are very simple to use indeed. However, as with any database the vast amount of available material inevitably means that even when you have your results – unless you have been able to make a very specific search – you will need to filter them further. We will now look at how Westlaw search results are delivered and how you can use the information supplied to filter them further.

Let us suppose that we are interested in looking for recent cases on the law of hire purchase agreements. To do this either a 'Free Text' or 'Term Defined' search would be appropriate (although for the latter a slightly different term would be used). This search will yield a significant number of results so if in the citation field we enter '2010' this will narrow the search and will mean we can pick up cases that have perhaps now been appealed. The search form therefore looks like this:

Figure 10: Example of a completed Westlaw search form

Our search then yields these results:

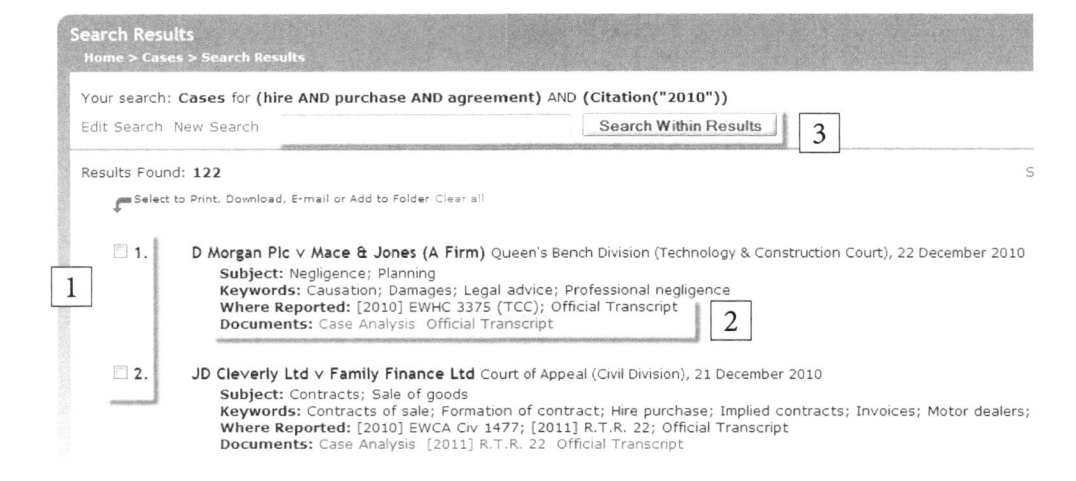

Figure 11: Example of a Westlaw case search results page

The results page offers us a range of options. We can select one or more cases using the numbered check boxes to the left (marked '1' on Fig. 11) and then, using the menu in the top right of the screen (not shown here) choose to print, save or download the cases. If we want to read a case on screen we simply click the desired version of the report listed on the 'Documents' line of the result (marked '2' on Fig. 11). Or, if we want to narrow our search further we can enter additional text into the search bar above the results (marked '3' on Fig. 11).

The treatment a case has received is indicated by a symbol next to the search results and in the 'Status' message at the very top of the full text of the case report (marked '1' in Fig. 12). If we want to link to commentary, cases or legislation cited in the judgment, we must go to the full text:

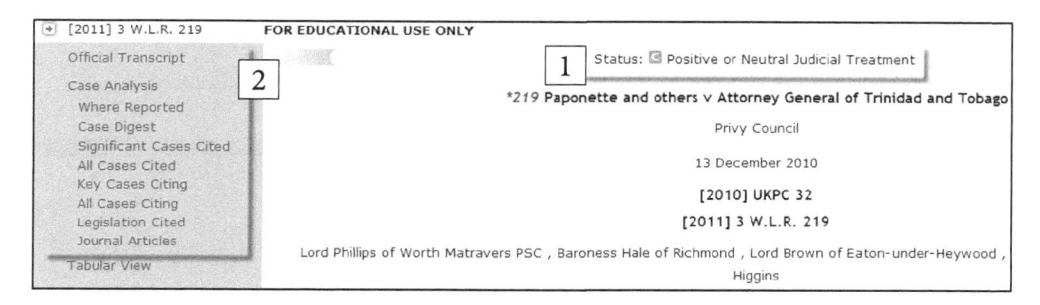

Figure 12: A sample Westlaw search result

When we open the full text of the report we see a new range options in the sidebar to the left (marked '2' in Fig. 12). By clicking on any of these we can explore other versions of the case report, cases that have cited this judgment and cases cited in this judgment and link to any relevant statutory material.

You are now ready to start exploring all the additional features and functions of the two main subscription databases as we turn finally to look at the legal databases that are available without charge.

Practical Questions

Can you find the following cases?

1. Any case concerning the extradition proceedings in respect of Wikileaks founder Julian Assange.

2. A case heard in the 1890s concerning the authority of auctioneers. The report appeared at page 663 but you do not know which series.

3. A case heard in 2010 concerning corporation tax with Stephen Brandon QC and Harriet Brown as counsel for the appellants.

4. A 2001 decision concerning the duty of utmost good faith in insurance law in which *Manifest Shipping Co Ltd v Uni-Polaris Shipping Co Ltd* [2001] 1 All ER 743 was considered and where Longmore L.J., was one of the judges.

BAILII and other free resources

We have looked in some detail at the main commercial legal databases. If you cannot access these for some reason you may find these free legal databases useful. The foremost of these resources is the BAILII website discussed previously. The website brings together a host of case law published under neutral citations[6] including a significant amount of case tribunal case law,[7] all of which is fully searchable using the search page shown in Fig. 13 below. The search techniques that you have encountered previously in respect of LexisLibrary and Westlaw can also be deployed when searching BAILII.

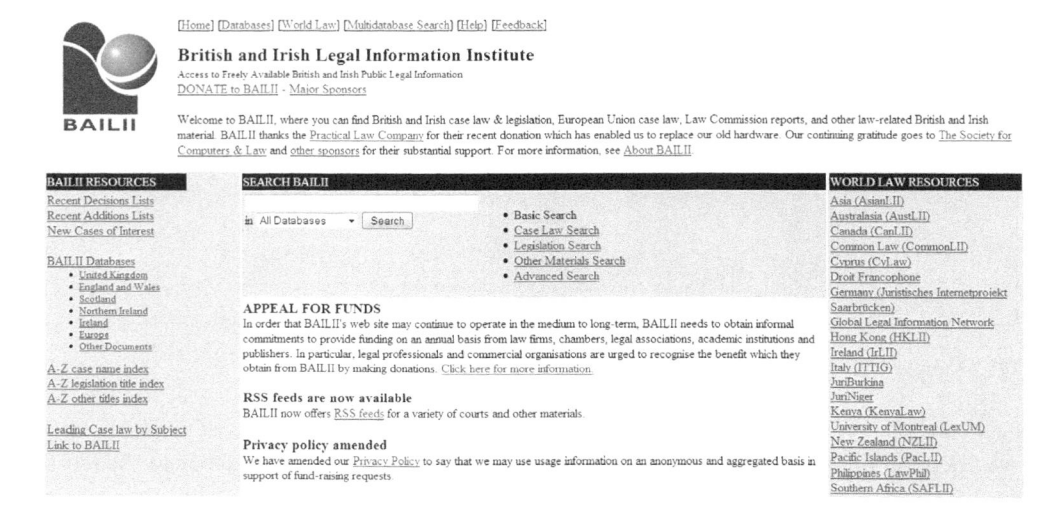

Figure 13: The BAILII home/search page

The Supreme Court

Probably the most well used of the free legal resources is the website of the Supreme Court. The website contains all the judgments of the Court since it began work in September 2010.

Access is completely free and no password or registration is required. The website is easy to navigate. From the main page (see Fig. 14 below), click the 'Decided Cases' link (highlighted in Fig. 14) and you will immediately be given a list of all decided cases with the most recently decided first. You can then download either the full judgment or a short 'press summary' of the case and the decision in PDF format.

---

[6] Full list available at http://www.bailii.org/databases.html#ew
[7] Full list available at http://www.bailii.org/databases.html#uk

Figure 14: The homepage of the Supreme Court website

Once you are on the judgments page, as you can see in Fig. 15, you can also search for a case by neutral citation, case ID or a case name.

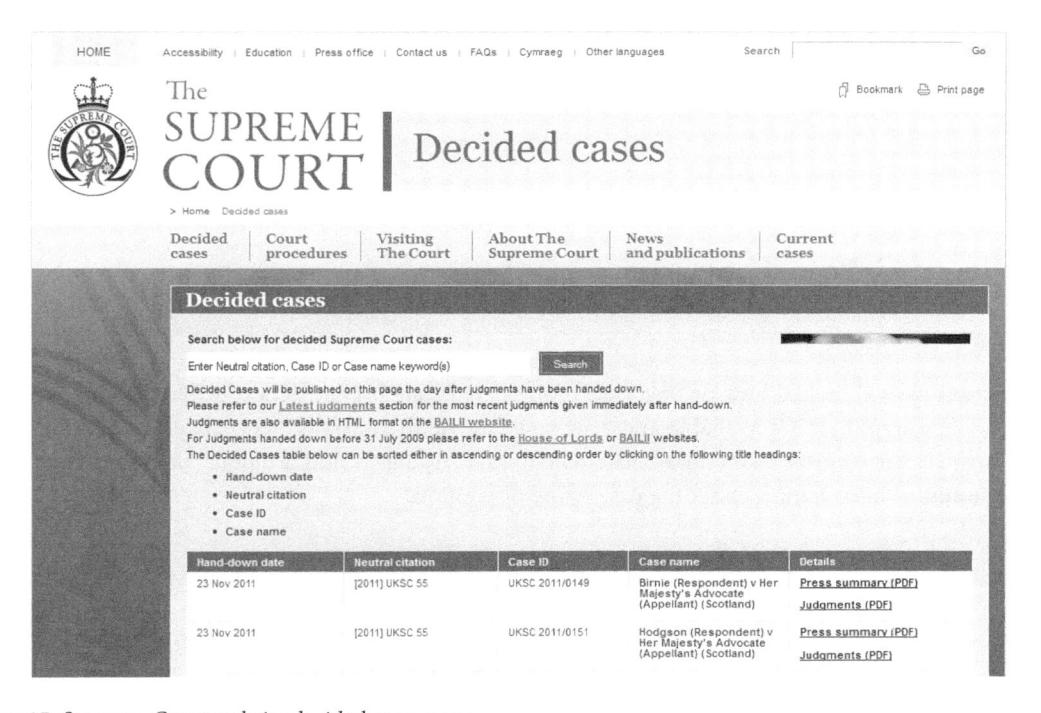

Figure 15: Supreme Court website decided cases page

Reflection Questions

1. Are there any instances when using BAILII or similar resources might be necessary or advantageous?
2. In the course of your studies can you think of instances when using BAILII might be helpful?
3. Are you able to transfer the skills you have learned in relation to LexisLibrary and Westlaw to BAILII?

The Ministry of Justice

The Ministry of Justice oversees the work of all courts and tribunals in England and Wales. It also oversees the appointment and training of judges and the running of the prison system. The website provides links to several courts whose decisions are made available to the public but is particular for exploring the judgments of many tribunals. The tribunal system is divided into the First-tier Tribunals and the Upper Tribunal. The website contains links to all new decided upper tribunal cases from 2003 and varying amounts of searchable case reports for decisions made before then. You will probably find this website particularly useful if you are studying employment law, immigration, asylum or tax law.

> Free sources of law – useful links:
> - British and Irish Legal Information Institute (BAILII): www.bailli.org
> - Judgments of the Supreme Court of the United Kingdom: http://www.supremecourt.gov.uk/decided-cases/index.html
> - Guidance from HM Courts and Tribunals Service: http://www.justice.gov.uk/guidance/courts-and-tribunals/tribunals/index.htm

Finding Case Law in Print

In this section we will look at how printed case reports are located. This section will help you understand the printed resources that are available and how you can use them to find case materials in your library whether you are looking for cases on a particular topic or trying to find a report when you only have a limited amount of information about the case name or citation.

Why find cases in print?

As we have already seen, for centuries, printed case reports were the only way in which a lawyer or student could really gain access to the judgments being handed down by the courts. While the oldest reports varied greatly in quality, by the end of the 19th century they were reliable and plentiful. Until the late 20th century law libraries were, and indeed still are, full of them and they are still a useful and reliable source of the law. Of course the exact same materials can now be accessed online, which is often faster, and online databases give access to a range of materials so vast that only the biggest libraries would ever match it. But it remains the case that not all reports are available online and some might only be available through very specialist services which your institution may not subscribe to, then of course there are the older case reports or reports from other jurisdictions which remain undigitised. Where this is the case, there is no option but to hit the library and find the original report. Finally, you may find that there is some real satisfaction in finding and using the original sources and reading them in their original form.

Finding a case when you only know the name

Finding a case when you only know the name is essentially a process of finding a citation. Clearly the easiest solution to this problem would be a search on one of the online databases, however should you be in a situation where you have only the names of the parties but not the citation you can also find the case using print resources. The most useful are likely to be the *Current Law Case Citator* and indexes published to accompany the various series of law reports. The *Current Law Case Citator* includes all reported cases from 1947 onwards, if you are looking for an older case and do not have a citation you may need to consult *The Digest* or for historic cases, one of the works discussed in the section on finding and using historic case law, below.

Using the current law case citator

The inherent limitation of printed reference works is the speed at which they can be updated. To ensure the most up-to-date information is to hand, this suite is necessarily divided into three parts: the bound volumes, of which each one covers cases reported over the course of the years printed on the spine; of course newly decided cases cannot be found in these so there is an annual paperback edition of the publication which lists all cases decided in the previous year and also a *Monthly Digest*.

Whichever component of the suite you use (you may need to use them all if you have no idea when the case was decided) you will find that inside each volume case names are simply listed alphabetically and for each listed case you will be given all available citation in the law reports and in addition, if available, references to the case in the *Current Law Yearbook* which provides abridged summaries of cases. Once you have found one or more citations for the case you can then find the full report.

Indexes to the law reports

An alternative, although less comprehensive option to the *Current Law Case Citator*, is to consult the various index volumes published to accompany the leading series of law reports. These volumes list every case report and its citation arranged alphabetically. For example the *Consolidated Tables and Index* of the *All England* reports cover the range from 1936–2009 in a single volume, every case reported in this series between those dates can be found arranged alphabetically therein.

Finding a case when you only know the citation

If you have a citation then finding the case to which it relates will be relatively easy. We have looked previously at how citations are formulated and what the various components mean. The key therefore is simply understanding the citation and knowing to which set of reports it refers, how to find them and how to navigate your way through them. In Table 1 above, we saw the abbreviations for some of the most common series of law reports. Over time you will become familiar with the abbreviations of many series and be able to go directly to that series, however, if you encounter an abbreviation that you are not familiar with you will find a key to the abbreviations in your library catalogue or in the *Current Monthly Digest*.[8]

---

[8] You will also find a comprehensive, searchable list of legal abbreviations at: http://www.legalabbrevs.cardiff.ac.uk/

Searching for historic case reports

We discussed previously that before 1865 when the Incorporated Council of Law Reporting was established, case reports were numerous and written and published by individuals who produced reports in varying formats and of very variable quality.[9] The result is that there are several hundred years of 'nominate reports' – series of reports that are identified by the name of the person that published them. The original copies of some of these reports are very rare indeed and the few libraries that have them will make them available for general use. Even the more recent reports tend to be so numerous that no library is likely to carry them all. Luckily, many of these old reports have been gathered together and reprinted in various forms: the *English Reports,* the *Law Journal Reports*, the *Law Times Reports* and the *All England Reports Reprints*. The series most commonly held of these series are the *English Reports*.[10] Many old cases or at least the reprints of them, particularly those that remain relevant today, have been digitised and are available online through the main legal databases. However, if you are looking for a less well known case or do not know the name you may also want to use the HeinOnline service, if your institution subscribes to this, to search the *English Reports* in their entirety. Using this service you will also give you the option of searching by original citation or keyword.

Searching for historic cases by name

A search for a report where you know the name of the case is no more difficult for an historic case than it is for a modern case. All of the cases contained in the *English Reports* are indexed in volumes 177 and 178. All cases are listed alphabetically so you simply locate the case in the relevant volume.

Let us suppose that we are trying to search for the judgment in *Haldenby v Tuke*. Without a citation we know that we cannot just go straight to a particular volume. Volume 177 covers cases beginning with the letters A-K. So we simply leaf through volume 177 until we find 'Haldenby' at page 710. We can then see the case, the original citation and to the right the volume which contains the full case report, along with the page number on which to find the report within that volume. Generally, in your written work, you would use the citation of the original case along with the citation used for the case in the *English Reports*.

Searching for historic cases by citation

If you know the citation of a case but not the name and it was decided before 1865, you can use the *English Reports* to locate the report. The difficulty is that the *English Reports* are arranged according to the full title of the report and not the abbreviated title. To find the report therefore you need to decipher the citation including the abbreviation. You can do this online or by using a text such as the *Index to Legal Citations and Abbreviations*.[11] Once you know the full name of the series of reports you can then identify in which volume that series is to be found using the *Chart to the English Reports*. It is then simply a case of leafing through the volume to find the specific case.

---

[9] For a number of instances of this see A.T.H. Smith, *Glanville Williams: Learning the Law*, 14th Edition, Sweet & Maxwell 2010 at pp 35–6.

[10] You may also want to familiarise yourself with *The Digest* if you are likely to need to find the citations for a large amount of older case law.

[11] D. Raistrick, *Index to Legal Citations and Abbreviations*, 3rd Edition, Sweet & Maxwell 2008.

Practical Questions

Can you find the following cases in print?

1. Hartley v Ponsonby

2. The case cited at (1766) 1 Wm Bl. 593

3. A Court of Appeal libel case from the late 1990s in which one of the parties was 'Al-Fayed'

10
Finding Legislation

Rick Canavan

Introduction

Studying law, particularly if you are coming to law for the first time, requires the study of materials that up until now you had probably never looked at before. As you read this you may be looking at the full text of a case or statute for just about the first time. In this chapter we will try and help you to develop strategies to find and use a range of statutory material (both in print and online) including modern and historic Acts of Parliament, Statutory Instruments (SIs) and European Union legislation.

Why do I need to find statutory materials?

Whether you are looking for a Statutory Instrument that brings into force section 9 of the Consumers, Estate Agents and Redress Act 2007[1] or a piece of legislation as large as the Enterprise Act 2002[2] (281 sections and 26 schedules) you need to have the skills to find and understand the legislation. After all it is in the legislation, one of the primary legal resources (the other main one being case law which often interprets the meaning of legislation) that the law exists. Even if you defer (as we all do) to a textbook for convenience from time to time, if you are not confident and comfortable with the primary legal materials then you will be forever reliant on secondary sources of law and will not be able to broaden, deepen or apply your legal knowledge independently – a skill that will become increasingly useful as you progress through your degree and indispensible if you aspire to practice. While there are many secondary materials that are of a very high quality, rigorously edited and compiled, they simply do not cover everything or may not be available to you and, when this is the case, the only option you have will be to go back to the primary legal sources and construct your own understanding of the law.

---

[1] 2007 c.17
[2] 2002 c.40

What statutory materials are available?

The most prominent form of statutory materials are Acts of Parliament. As we have already identified, these are a primary legal source material and depending on the topic you are studying are likely to be very important – some areas of law (such as land law) are based almost exclusively on statutes and the interpretative case law. Whether you are searching in print or online, Acts of Parliament are readily available to you not only in their original form but also often in annotated form with useful cross-references to Hansard, case law, etc. In addition to statutes, you will also find printed and digital copies of SIs – delegated legislation that is used to bring an Act into force in whole or part or to exercise powers delegated under the Act. In addition to domestic legislation you may also need to consult the original text of European legislation in the course of your studies. The bulk of European legislation comes in the form of Directives and Regulations but you may also want to consult the treaties that define the relationships between memberships and central institutions of the European Union. We will turn first to consider domestic legislation then look at how to find and use European Union legislation.

Where can I find statutory materials?

Online

Given the relatively smaller volume of statutory material that is available by comparison to the volume of case law, it was statutory material that first appeared online. Today, either through subscription services such as LexisLibrary and Westlaw or through free websites such as BAILII and legislation.gov.uk, you can now access nearly 800 years worth of legislative material in seconds. Whichever site you choose you will always be able to find the full text of statutes and SIs as well as European law. In addition, the subscription databases allow you to search for delegated legislation made under a particular statute, offer direct links to cases citing the legislation in whole or part and relevant commentary in the form of the leading legislative reference works such as *Halsbury's Statutes Citator*, and *Halsbury's Statutory Instrument Citator*. These, along with the symbols used in your search results allow you to determine instantly the status of a piece of legislation or even a specific provision of it.

In print

Your law library (and to a great or lesser extent public libraries) will stock a range of legislative materials and the very valuable texts that you need to use in conjunction with that material to ascertain whether it has come into or remains in force, and to assist you with understanding what the text means either by reference to the explicit intention of Parliament or as a result of interpretative decisions made in court. Before exploring the options in detail we will consider the various titles available that we will refer to in the course of this chapter.

Acts of Parliament are published in *Public General Acts and Measures*. There is a volume for each year in which the full text of public Acts of Parliament is printed in chapter number (chronological order) with an index listing statutes in alphabetical order also. Within *Public General Acts and Measures* you will also find the full text of the General Synod Measures of the Church of England and a list of all Local and Private Acts of Parliament for that year. In addition to *Public General Acts and Measures* you can also find original legislation in *Current Law Statutes Annotated*, *Halsbury's Statutes* and *Law Reports: Statutes*, your library is likely to have all of these titles.

Quite often you will know that a piece of legislation is in force and be well aware of a weight of case law that has defined its meaning – there are numerous instances where an entire syllabus may be based around that piece of legislation and its related case law but this will not always be the case. When you need to know whether a piece of legislation is in force or whether it has been amended or repealed you can consult the relevant supplements to *Halsbury's Statutes* and the *Current Law Legislation Citator*. To find and verify whether a statutory instrument is in force you can consult *Halsbury's Statutory Instruments* and *Current Law Statutory Instrument Citator* and we will consider all of these publications in detail in due course.

> ### Reflection Questions
> 1. Have you read statutes or other legislation before? Do you think you are comfortable with reading this sort of legal material?
> 2. Do you agree that you need to actually read primary sources of law such as legislation to understand the law?
> 3. Do you think that libraries still need to stock printed legislation?

Understanding Legislation

If you are going to set about finding and using primary legal sources effectively it is crucial that you are able to understand every aspect of them. While understanding the core legal content will always be the most challenging aspect of working with legislation, this task can be made easier if you know and understand the functions of the other components of legislation and understand how legislation is structured and cited.

The anatomy of legislation

Statutory material comprises many elements in addition to the core of legal material. It is important to be aware of these extra features and the function that they play in understanding the piece of legislation.

Set out below are annotated examples of a statute and statutory instrument the key features of each are numbered and the features explained in accompanying tables.

Table 1 – The component parts of a statute

Number	Feature
1	Short title – this is the name by which the Act is ordinarily known.
2	Official citation – this is the official reference to the Act and the way in which it would be referenced, for example, in an essay.
3	Long title – the full title of the Act which usually gives an indication as to its purpose.
4	Date of Royal Assent – this will ordinarily be the date on which the Act becomes law unless a separate date of commencement is given in the Act or the power to bring the Act into force is to be delegated to a Minister of State.
5	Enacting formula – unless the Parliament Act has been used, this indicates that the bill which preceded the Act has been passed by Parliament.
6	Body of the Act. This contains the legally relevant provisions and is divided into sections, Section 1 (usually written as s.1) can be seen here. The body of the Act is then further divided into sub-sections which are also numbered and paragraphs which are assigned a letter. In Fig. 1 we can see that section 1 has a sub-section (1) and a paragraph (a). If you were referring to this part of the statute you would write it as s.1(1)(a). If you are referring to more than one section of a statute you can refer to it as 'ss.' e.g. ss.17–19. Larger pieces of legislation may also be divided in 'parts' which group together sections on related matters. Some pieces of legislation may also incorporate one or more schedules (abbreviated to sch.).

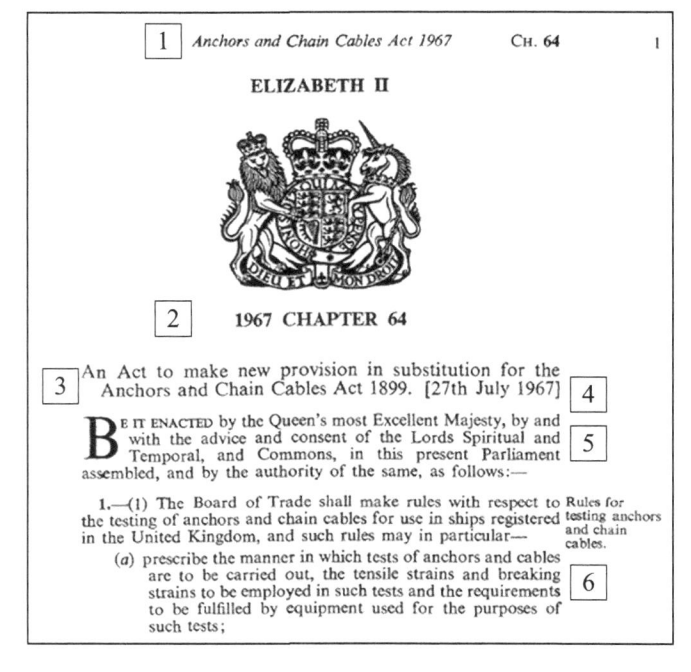

Figure 1: Anchors and Chain Cables Act 1967

Statutory Instrument

Table 2 – The component parts of a SI

Number	Feature
1	Citation
2	Subject matter – this is useful is giving an indication of the area of law with which the provision is concerned without having to read further.
3	Title
4	Date made and date of enactment (this will not indicate if the provision is still in force however).
5	Authority under which the SI is made. In this case powers under the Road Traffic Act 1988
6	Main body of the SI. Each part of the SI is known as a paragraph unless it contains rules or regulations, in which case each section is referred to in this way.
7	The name of the minister who signed the order into force.

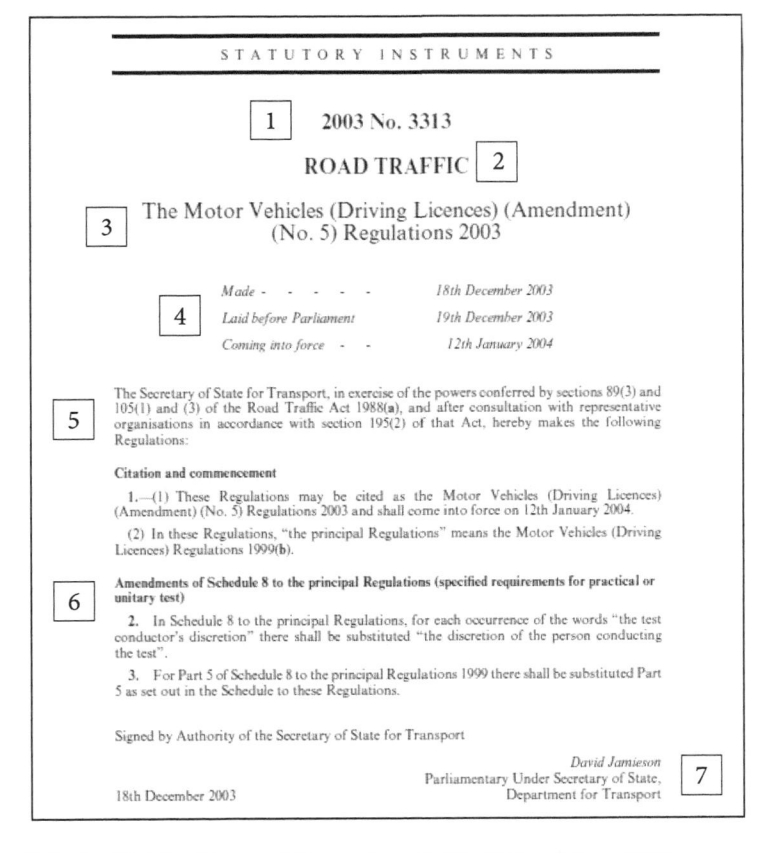

Figure 2: The Motor Vehicles (Driving Licences) (Amendment) (No.5) Regulations 2003

Citations

As with all primary sources of law, lawyers have long adopted agreed forms of shorthand in order to reference the original and legislation is no exception. Citations are used both to assist you in finding law but you should also use them in your work to indicate the source of a provision you are citing.

Act of Parliament

An Act of Parliament is identified by reference to the year in which it was passed and a 'chapter' number which places it in chronological order with all statutes passed in that year. Therefore, the first statute of any given year will be chapter 1. Since 1963 the calendar year is used, prior to this citations were based on regnal years.

The 11th statute passed in 2011 therefore, would be 2011, Chapter 11, which would be cited as 2011 c.11.[3] Statutes cited using the regnal year are not identified by the calendar year in which the Act was passed but by the year in the reign of the monarch in which the Act was passed. For example, the 25th Act passed by Parliament in the year 1849 (the 13th year of Queen Victoria's reign) would be cited as 1849 13 Vict. 25.[4]

Given as this system of citations clearly requires you to have a detailed working knowledge of the years in which various monarchs' reigns[5] began it is clear to see why it was ultimately simplified. Many of the online databases have now gone a step further and applied the modern form of citation to statutes previously identified by regnal year citations, so you could now search instead for 1849 c.25 and find the same (repealed) statute. It is, however, still useful to have a working knowledge of regnal year citations and to help you with this you will see below a table of the abbreviations used to identify the monarch in regnal year citations.

Table 3 – Abbreviations of monarchs and their regnal years

Anne	Ann.
Charles	Car., Chas, Cha.
Edward	Edw., Ed.
Elizabeth	Eliz.
George	Geo.
Henry	Hen.
James	Ja., Jac, Jas.
Mary	Mar., M
Phillip & Mary	Ph.& M., Phil. & Mar.
Richard	Ric., Rich.
Victoria	Vict.
William	Will., Wm., Gul.
William & Mary	Wm. & M., Will. & Mar., Gul. & Mar.

---

[3] *Finance Act 2011*
[4] *Portuguese Deserters Act 1849*
[5] The beginning of the regnal year differs from monarch to monarch and may not have been the same year even within their reign e.g. it may have been the date of a moveable such as Ascension

> **Self-Text Questions**
>
> What regnal year is indicated by the following dates?
>
> 1. 8th February 1902 (A: 2 Geo. V)
> 2. 21st June 1847 (A: 11 Vict.)
> 3. 19th April 1705 (A: 4 Ann.)

Statutory instruments

A citation for a statutory instrument will usually take the form 'year/series', SIs of 2009 therefore begin 2009 followed by the number assigned to the statutory instrument (starting each year with number 1). The 446th statutory instrument of 2009 therefore would be cited as 2009/446.[6]

European legislation

European legislation can be cited either with a short citation or a long citation – there is no fixed rule as to which is to be preferred. The short citation (most usually used) is much like the citation used for domestic SIs and Acts of Parliament for example 'Regulation 2026/95' is the 2026th regulation of 1995. In the case of directives and decisions, the year is followed by the number assigned in series, for example, Directive 71/401/EEC (after 1st November 1993 EEC became EC) refers to the 401st directive or decision of 1971. This citation would be adequate to locate the relevant document in an online search but to search effectively in print you would need to be aware of the location of the document in the *Official Journal of the European Communities* (the *OJ*).

The *OJ* is divided into three series, legislation is found in the 'L' series. The full citation for regulation 2026/95 therefore would be OJ L 198 p.25 of 23.8.95. That is to say that the Regulation would be found at page 25 of the L series, number 198 of 23rd August 1995. Directives and Council decisions would be recorded in the same way.

Finding Legislation Online

In this section we will look at how to effectively search for domestic and European legislation online using both subscription and free databases and the advantages of searching online over searching in print.

Why find statutory material online?

Searching for legislation online is simpler, faster and your results are more likely to be up-to-date than the results you may glean from a search of printed resources. An online search also allows you to focus immediately on a particular section or schedule, to search more easily by reference to key words and to

---

[6] *Official Feed and Food Controls (Scotland) Regulations 2009*

simultaneously search for statutes and SIs and determine instantly whether they are in force using the online versions of the publications used when searching in print.

In short, searching online allows you to search through more material in a moment than you could in hours or even days in the library but speed is not the only advantage. Searching online databases allows you to discover the status of a piece of statutory material more quickly and reliably than you could the print version. Perhaps the greatest advantage of searching online databases for statutory material is the extent to which the material you uncover will be as up to date as possible (making commencement, etc. immediately obvious) and linked to relevant commentary and case law which will expand and deepen your understanding of the statute and enable you to see it in context, which might prove to be very useful indeed.

In this section we will look at the options for finding legislative material online and how you can use online databases to discover not only the original legislation but also its current status, if it is in force, how and when it was brought into force, and material that will help you to explore linked, subordinate legislation and case law.

What databases are available?

Depending on the subscriptions taken out by your institution you will have at least two different databases to choose from. Each one offers a different range of materials and can be searched in different ways. The two databases that are likely to be available to you are LexisLibrary and Westlaw. You will be greatly assisted in your studies if you can develop a good working knowledge of the functions of at least one of the databases, not least as they contain a large amount of commentary and professional publications linked to case reports, which you are likely to find very useful. In addition, you may also want to familiarise yourself at least one of the free services most relevant to your studies or interests: BAILII, EUR-Lex or the legislation.gov.uk website. We will not cover those services in detail here but the skills you will develop in respect of LexisLibrary and Westlaw are for the most part transferrable to these databases and while they offer just the statutory material and not the attendant commentarys they are not in any way inherently inferior, less accurate or up-to-date.

The decision as to which database you use will probably depend on the sources of law you use most and which database you find easiest to effectively search. It is worth noting that both services offer extensive online training and help and will often hold training events on campus at the start of the academic year where you can get hands-on experience, ask questions and explore the more advanced functions of both services.

Using 'connectors' and 'Boolean' operators

For some searches, particularly key word searches, you may want to only see results where your key words (for example case names or practice areas) feature in close proximity to each other, for example in the same sentence or paragraph or together in sequence. You may also be worried that a search might omit some results because of variations in spelling, for example. You can search in this way and overcome these problems using connectors and Boolean operators. The two tables below show you the indicators and Boolean operators that can be used in LexisLibrary and Westlaw.

Table 4 – Connector words for LexisLibrary and Westlaw

Type of search	Connector (LexisLibrary)
Proximity – used to find words close to each other. For example to find 'landlord' and 'tenant' within two words of each other or within the same sentence or paragraph.	w/*n* e.g. landlord w/2 tenant w/s e.g. landlord w/s tenant w/p e.g. landlord w/p tenant
Phrase – used to find words that appear together.	No connector needed unless the words 'and' or 'or' features in the phrase then quotation marks should be used.
Truncated – used to find terms that are different but related e.g. 'liability' and 'liable'.	Exclamation mark (!) e.g. searching for 'liab!' would bring up results for both 'liable' and 'liability'.
Wildcard – used to find a word that may be spelled in different ways e.g. 'criticise' and 'criticize'.	Asterisk (*). e.g. if searching for 'critici*e' results with both 's' and 'z' would be returned. More asterisks can be used if necessary.

Table 5 – Boolean operators for LexisLibrary and Westlaw

Boolean Operator	LexisLibrary	Westlaw
OR – to *expand* a search, e.g. ship OR vessel OR boat; to search for antonyms, e.g. creditor OR debtor; or spelling variations, e.g. trademark OR trade-mark.	OR	OR

Searching with LexisLibrary

What is on offer?

LexisLibrary offers hundreds of years of fully searchable statutory material as well as all SIs from 1786 onwards. In addition to this basic material you can also access the various components of *Halsbury's Statutes* (searchable separately but also helpfully embedded into legislation searches) and other similar specialist publications and the full range of European legal material.

Searching LexisLibrary

Basic searches for legislation (both Acts of Parliament and SIs) can be done very quickly either from the LexisLibrary homepage or the dedicated legislation search page which can be accessed by clicking the 'Legislation' tab in the red navigation bar. The legislation search page is reproduced below (Fig. 3). As an alternative to searching by reference to specific criteria, it is also possible to 'browse' legislation, which may be a useful option if your search criteria are not yet well defined. We will now look at the various searches that can be performed.

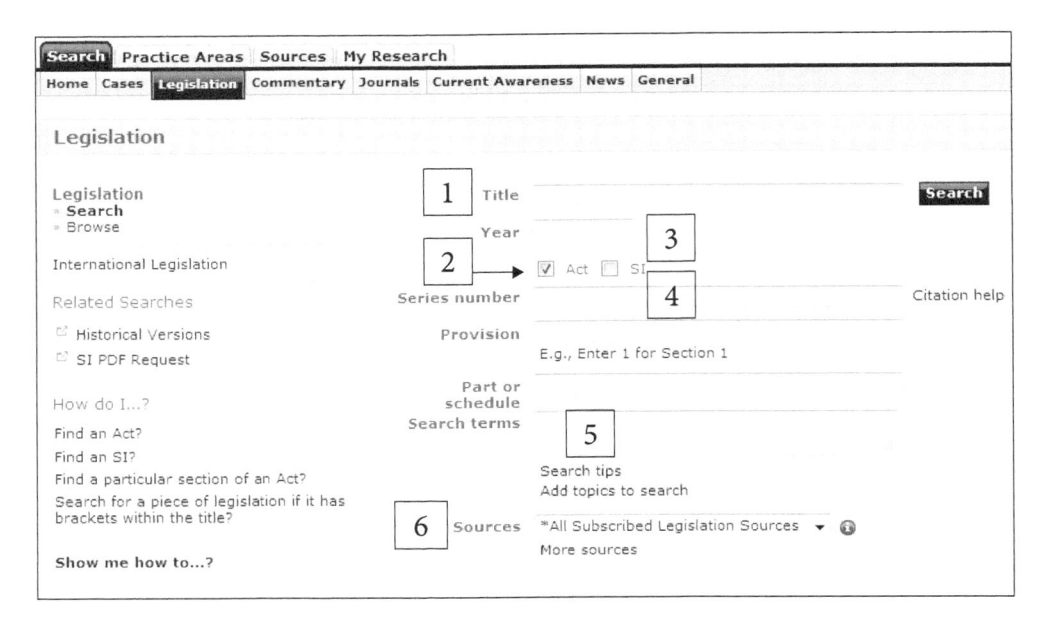

Figure 3: LexisLibrary legislation search pane

Searching for legislation by title

If you know the name or part of the legislation that you are searching for then this search will probably allow you to find it. Simply type the name into the 'Title' search box (marked '1' on Fig. 3) and LexisLibrary will return the results on a new results page. If you know more than one word of the name you can connect your search terms with connectors or Boolean operators. As with all the basic search fields you can search for either Acts of Parliament, SIs or both by selecting the relevant checkbox(es) (marked '2' on Fig. 3 above). The drawback with the LexisLibrary title search is that it relies upon the user entering the words in the sequence that they appear in the title of the legislation, any deviation from this is likely to lead the results returned being of no use or more frequently no results being returned at all. For example if you are looking for the *Supply of Goods and Services Act 1982*[7] and were to search for 'supply services' the database will claim that no results could be returned. While to some extent this difficulty can be alleviated by using the 'Search terms' field (marked '5' on Fig. 3) this may still not prove to be helpful – being as accurate as possible therefore is crucial.

Searching for legislation by year

If you are looking for all legislation passed in a particular year or want to narrow a search in another field down by a year then you would this search field. Simply type in the year for which you want to search into the 'Year' search box (marked '3' on Fig. 3). This search is best used in conjunction with the name or partial name of a statute or keywords.

To search for a statutory instrument or statute by reference to the number assigned to it fill in the 'Series number' field (marked as '4' on Fig. 3) and if possible the year. For example for 1990 c. 18, type '1990' into the 'Year' box and '18' into 'Series number' field.

---

[7] 1994 c.35

Further search options

You can use the LexisLibrary search form to focus your search onto a particular part or schedule using the appropriate boxes on the search form or limit your search results to a particular type of legislation, for example Acts of the Scottish Parliament (ASPs) using the drop down menu (marked '6' on Fig. 3). You can search for European legislation by clicking on the 'international legislation' link on the left of the page. The international legislation search function is in fact a dedicated European law search tool where you can search either by keywords (search terms), title or provision. You may find this search more intuitive and easier to use than EUR-Lex, which is a free service for the purpose of providing public access to European law.

If you already have a piece of legislation in mind, or a component of it and want to ascertain whether it is in force or whether there is any relevant, related case law you can jump straight to the 'commentary' search tool and access entries for the statute or provision from the likes of *Halsbury's Statutes*.

Understanding your search results

The basic search features of LexisLibrary are very simple to use and will suffice for the majority of searches that you will need to undertake, particularly if you are searching for a specific statute or provision with which you are already familiar, however, where this is not the case you may wish to filter your search results further and/or explore them in greater detail using the additional services offered by LexisLibrary. Even if you have only a small number of research results, unless you are familiar with them you may still want to ascertain whether they are in force and determine if there is any relevant, associated case law. We will now look at an example search and at how these tools (which can be used independently) can be used to gain a better understanding and how to filter your search results.

Let us suppose that we are interested in tracing legislation that relates to the regulation of noise from airports. The search form is reproduced below (Fig. 4). As you can see, we have tried to narrow the results as much as possible while attempting to not exclude potentially useful results. In the 'Title' field therefore we have just used a single word and attempted to use a further, general 'Search term' to narrow down the results. We have also chosen to have results that include both primary and secondary legislation as it seems likely that many aspects of aviation policy (particularly local policy) may be given legal effect using the latter.

Figure 4: Sample LexisLibrary legislation search form

This search then returns the results which we can in Fig. 5 below. If some or all of this material is relevant to you in this form you can use the commands highlighted at the top right of Fig. 5 (marked '1') to print or download your results, or you can link them to an existing project that you have set up in LexisLibrary or set up alerts to monitor any changes to the provisions.

If, however, you need to explore or filter your search further you can begin using the commands on the left hand pane (marked '2' on Fig. 5). These allow you to filter results according to their source for example you could exclude statutory instruments, narrow the search to an area of law using the 'topics' or filter by reference to the title of the legislation. There is no particular order or sequence for using the filters it is simply a matter of what seems most appropriate based upon the search results. Let us suppose that we are particularly interested in what legal protections are in place for residents living near an airport. We might narrow our search by reference therefore to a particular topic and decide that 'transport law' is most likely to reveal any such provisions (as opposed to 'commercial law').

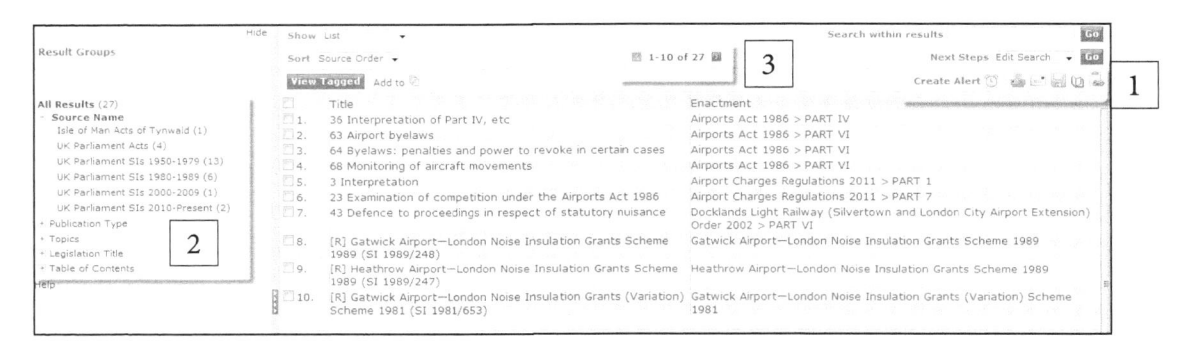

Figure 5: LexisLibrary legislation search result page

Applying this filter narrows the results to just five – a manageable number to review individually. LexisLibrary can help us further however, as we can see by selecting the second result, s.63 of the Airports Act 1986[8] which is reproduced below.

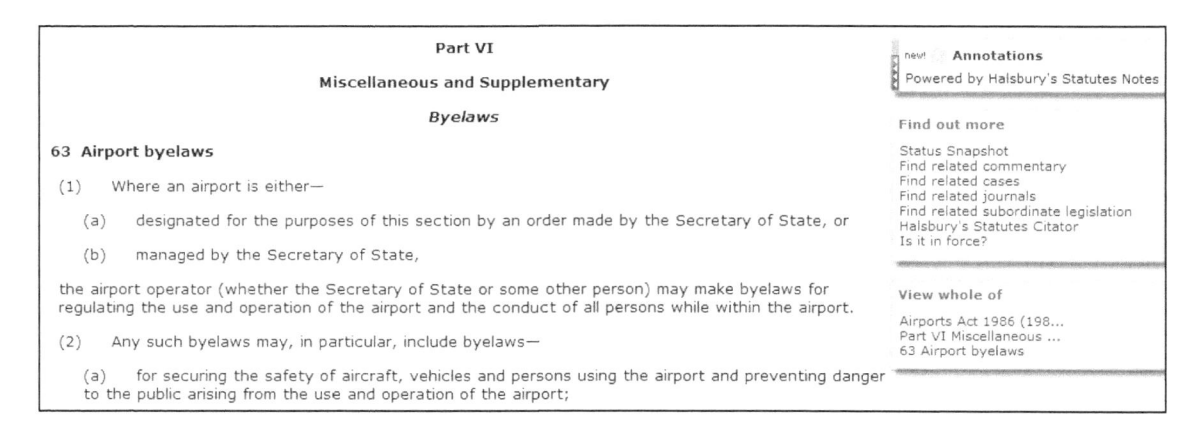

Figure 6: s.63 Airports Act 1986

---

[8] 1986 c.31

In the centre of the pane we can see the text of this particular provision reproduced in full. In the text our key words will be highlighted so that they can be quickly identified and seen in context. While this extract of the statute may be useful in itself we could use the various tools on the right of the pane to learn more and discern absolutely whether this is the case. First we may want to check if this provision is in force. We can do this quickly by clicking the 'status snapshot' link. Using this tool we can identify that the provision entered into force as a result of S.I. 1986/1228, that it remains in force but that s.63(8) was amended by a provision in S.I. 1996/739, which we can view with a single click.

Having identified that the provision is in force we may now want to ascertain more about its meaning and application. For a full analysis of the provision we might first click on the 'Annotation' tab at the top right of the main pane, this will then open a new pane side by side with the body of the text showing a full set of annotations for this provision that can be found in *Halsbury's Statutes*. These annotations will (amongst other things) elaborate the meaning of words or phrases used in the section and provide details of links to sub-ordinate legislation made under the powers created in this section.

At this stage, depending on the underlying reason for our search we are likely to have acquired sufficient information so as to appraise the usefulness of the section for our studies but it may be that what we are really interested in the way in which this section has been interpreted by the courts or received by commentators. To do this we simply click on the appropriate link to the right of the case, although it is worth noting that significant decisions are recorded in *Halsbury's* annotations in any case. Indeed here, the only related case is a minor, Scottish criminal case concerning whether restrictions on the licence held by a taxi are applicable on a road within the perimeter of an airport.[9]

Of course the statute used here is merely illustrative but it should show you the range of information that is available through the LexisLibrary database and how it can be accessed relatively easily, whether you are simply looking for the text of a provision and whether it is in force, legislation on a particular topic or related commentary or case law. We will now go on to look at how you can find legislation on the rival Westlaw database.

Practical Questions

Using LexisLibrary, answer the following questions.

1. 1975 c.56. What is the purpose of the Act and in which section is this set out?
2. Section 1 of the Act is now repealed. By what measure was it repealed and from what date was that repeal effective?
3. What is the most recent case in which the Acquisition of Land (Authorisation Procedure) Act 1946 is mentioned in judgment? Is this also the most recent decision where the Act has been relied upon in judgment?

---

[9] Fulton v Lees 1992 SCCR 923

Searching with Westlaw

What is on offer?

Westlaw offers the full texts of Acts from 1267 to the present and all SIs from 1948 to the present. For every piece of legislation it can show its status at a point in time (i.e. if you wanted to see it before it had been amended or consolidated) and show you how it links to secondary legislation, case law and analysis. It is a very powerful search tool that can be searched with relative ease. A particular benefit of the service is that it will deliver up a snapshot of all related or derived legislation and case law that relates to a particular statute or section of a statute. We will now look at the search forms and how to filter the results of a search.

Searching Westlaw

The Westlaw legislation search page can be accessed by clicking on the 'Legislation' tab on the Westlaw homepage. You will then see the Westlaw 'basic' search form (which is reproduced below at Fig. 7). If you scroll down you can also 'browse' legislation by origin rather than searching through it.

This basic search form ought to suffice for most legislative searches as it allows you to search both Acts of Parliament and SIs on the same form either by reference to the title, key words or by citation. This basic search form also allows you to focus immediately on a particular provision in the legislation using the drop down 'provision number' menu. However, if you want to see a piece of legislation as it previously appeared, or as it will appear once amendments are brought into force, you will need to use the 'advanced search' form (Fig. 8 below) accessed using the link above the basic search form. We will now look at specific searches that can be conducted in Westlaw.

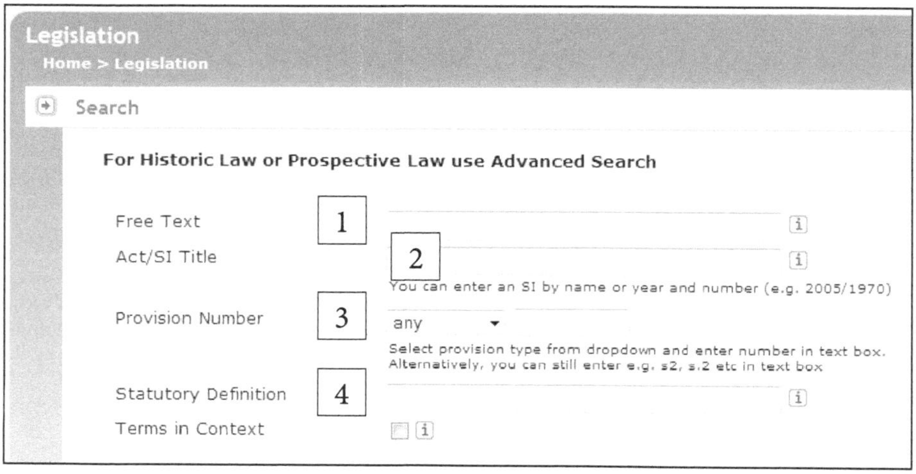

Figure 7: Westlaw legislation search page – basic

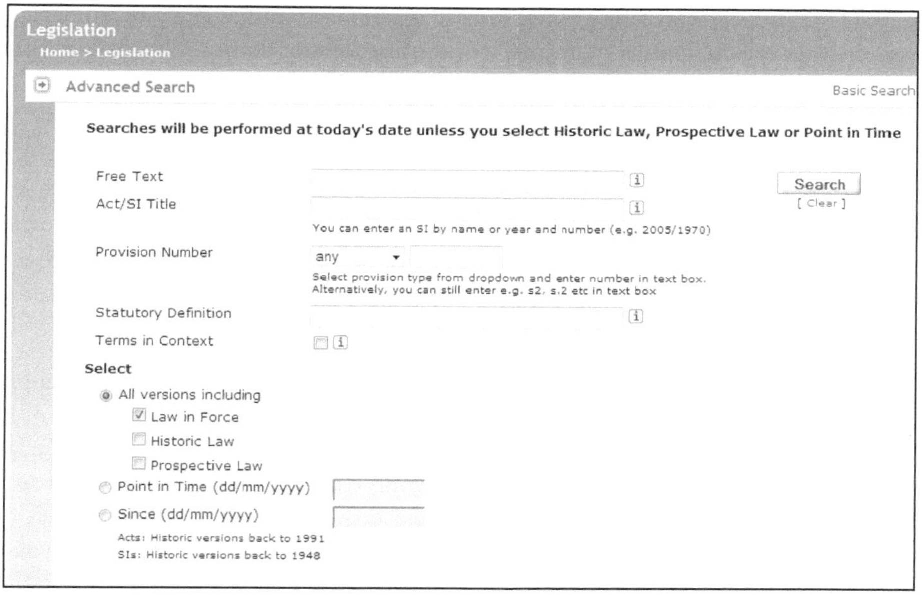

Figure 8: Westlaw legislation search page – advanced

Searching by title

To search for legislation by title you can simply enter the name of the piece of legislation that you are searching for (or part of the name you know) into the 'Act/SI Title' field (marked '2' on Fig. 7) and click 'search'. The Westlaw search is a very flexible one and will likely produce the exact statute you want or a small range of closely related statutes even with a partial title or the words arranged in the incorrect order. You can also add the full or partial date to focus your search at that point. Of course, if you are unsure as to the spelling or order of words you can also use connectors and Boolean operators to overcome this (see tables 4 and 5).

Searching by year

If you are looking for all legislation passed in a particular year or want to narrow a search in another field by a year, then you would type this along with the title or partial title in the 'Act/SI Title' field. You can also use this field to search by citation for both Acts of Parliament and SIs. Once again, you can see that the Westlaw search therefore is a very flexible one.

Further search options

You can use the Westlaw search form to focus your search onto a particular part or schedule using the 'Provision Number' fields (marked '3' on Fig. 7) on the search form. The drop down menu allows you to select the type of provision relevant to the type of legislation you are searching for e.g. article, chapter, section, or schedule. You can also use the 'free text' search (marked '1' on Fig. 7) to find statutory material on a particular subject or to define a search by name. All of the search field can be combined to broaden or focus the search as needed. If you want to know how a term is defined in a statute you can enter the search term in the 'Statutory definition' field (marked '4' on Fig. 7), and the auto complete function of this field will help you to focus in on the available definitions.

238   Legal Context, Skills and Ethics

You can search for European legislation by clicking the 'EU' tab from the Westlaw homepage. This will give you a search form broadly similar to the one we have just seen for domestic legislation with the option to browse cases, legislation, treaties, etc.

Understanding your search results

In common with LexisLibrary, Westlaw allows you to glean further information about the results of your search such as whether the legislation, or a particular provision of it, is in force and whether it has been considered in reported cases. This, as we will see from the example below can be done very easily from the search results.

Let us suppose that we are looking for information on the law relating to the sale and supply of goods. To do this we can simply type 'sale supply goods' into the 'title' search field. The search returns four results, the first of which is the Sale and Supply of Goods Act 1994. If we click on this we can then see the Act laid out section by section and to the left of each section a symbol indicating the status of that section. Fig. 9 below shows the results of an alternative search showing the same symbols in the context of the main search results page. As you can see, some provisions may have more than one symbol. If you hover over the symbol its meaning will appear on screen.

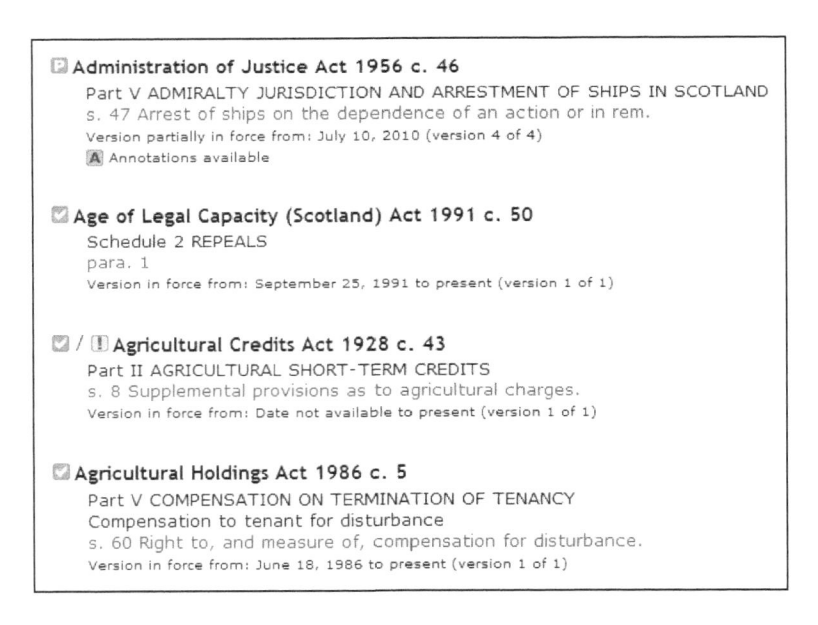

> **Administration of Justice Act 1956 c. 46**
> Part V ADMIRALTY JURISDICTION AND ARRESTMENT OF SHIPS IN SCOTLAND
> s. 47 Arrest of ships on the dependence of an action or in rem.
> Version partially in force from: July 10, 2010 (version 4 of 4)
> A Annotations available
>
> **Age of Legal Capacity (Scotland) Act 1991 c. 50**
> Schedule 2 REPEALS
> para. 1
> Version in force from: September 25, 1991 to present (version 1 of 1)
>
> / **Agricultural Credits Act 1928 c. 43**
> Part II AGRICULTURAL SHORT-TERM CREDITS
> s. 8 Supplemental provisions as to agricultural charges.
> Version in force from: Date not available to present (version 1 of 1)
>
> **Agricultural Holdings Act 1986 c. 5**
> Part V COMPENSATION ON TERMINATION OF TENANCY
> Compensation to tenant for disturbance
> s. 60 Right to, and measure of, compensation for disturbance.
> Version in force from: June 18, 1986 to present (version 1 of 1)

Figure 9: Westlaw search illustrating layout of search results page and status symbols to the left

In addition to the symbols which immediately indicate whether a provision is in force, repealed, about to change, etc. you can find out more specific information about the statute and its links to SIs and case law using the commands to the left of the body of the text (see Fig. 10 below). The 'Overview document' which can be seen in Fig. 10 shows any prospective law, commencement details for the entire Act and details of changes and repeals in the 'Citator' section and links to key definitions in the 'definitions' section. All of this presented on a single page ready for print or download.

Alternatively the statute can be explored in the context of the decided case and journal articles using the 'General Materials' link. Once clicked, a page appears providing links to all of the related case law and commentary.

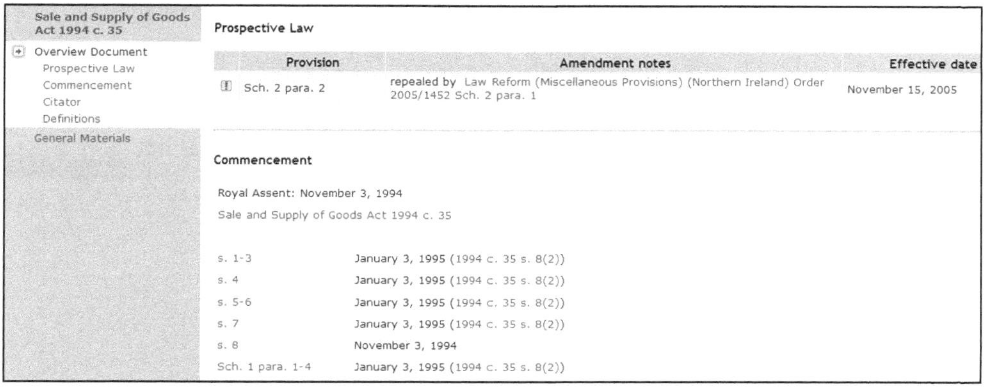

Figure 10: Legislation analysis page – Westlaw

Westlaw provides a fast and simple way of searching a vast amount of legislative material and is particularly helpful when you are covering new ground as its search functions do not require you to distinguish Acts of Parliament and SIs or to have a very carefully crafted set of research terms. Equally, the extent to which it allows you to determine almost immediately whether legislation is in force and the ease with which related material can be found, makes it also a very powerful search tool.

Practical Questions

Using Westlaw can you find the following pieces of legislation?

1. 1979 c. 54 s.20A.
2. Motor Vehicles (Wearing of Seat Belts) (Amendment) Regulations 2006/1892.
3. 2002 c.40 sch.4.

Searching free sources of legislation

BAILII

The not-for-profit organisation BAILII aims to provide access at no cost to the greatest possible quantity of legal material including British and Irish Acts of Parliament and statutory instruments and legislation emanating from the Scottish and Welsh Assemblies and Northern Ireland.

As the legislation search page, which is reproduced in Fig. 11 below, clearly shows, you can search using a wide range of criteria. The search form allows you to search by the title of the legislation, by reference to keywords in a prescribed sequence or within a defined number of words of each other. The search facility is overwhelmingly quick and accurate and in a click from the results page you can access the full text of the legislation and you are usefully assisted by the addition of a number of checkboxes that allow you to search for legislation by reference to its geographic applicability. You can also select the 'advanced search' to undertake a search using connectors. The BAILII site is especially useful for accessing the text of statutes with which you are familiar, for example to verify the wording of a particular section. It is a worthy alternative to the subscription databases when an additional level of detail or commentary is not necessary or if you are unable to access the service.

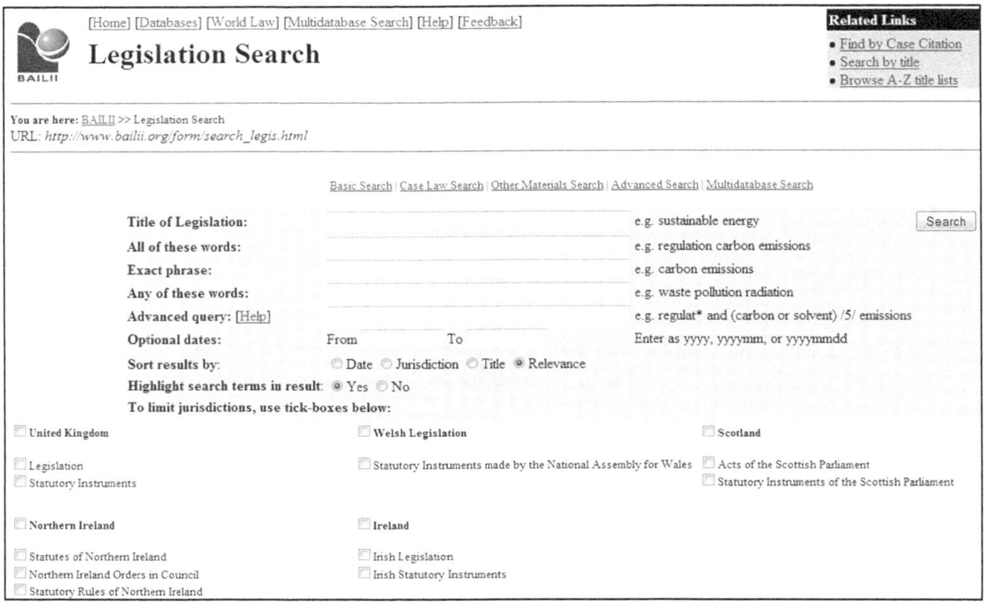

Figure 11: The BAILII legislation search page

Legislation.gov.uk

A relatively new addition (replacing HM Stationery Office website) to the range of free legislative databases that are available via the website legislation.gov.uk. The website, which is extremely easy to navigate, provides an outstanding collection of legislative material. All Acts of Parliament both ancient and modern and those of the former parliaments of Scotland and Ireland and the modern devolved assemblies are present. In addition to primary legislation you can also obtain all sources of secondary legislation here. The only weakness of the service is that it does not feature legislation that is no longer in force, although this is likely to be of interest in only limited circumstances so you can see why its exclusion is a useful feature in that allows you to be certain as to the status of legislation that you do find through the site.

As you can see from Fig. 12 below, the home page provides direct links to commonly searched legislation and legislation affecting a particular region, etc. as well as the search tool that you can see on the right, which allows for both wide and focussed searches based on name, date and number and which can be narrowed by reference to the categories of legislation which you can see on the drop down menu.

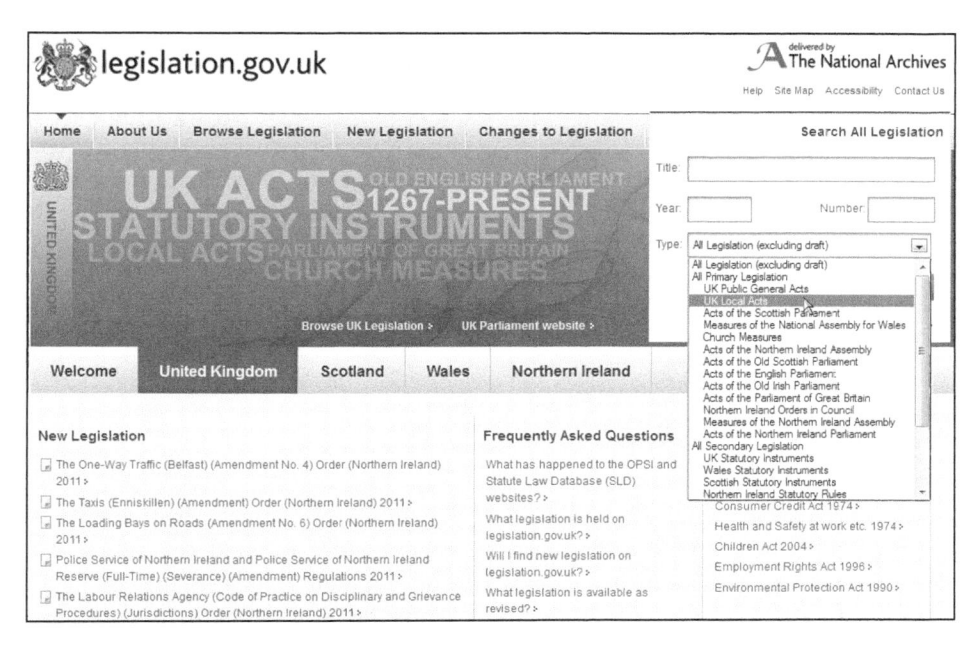

Figure 12: Legislation.gov.uk home/main search page

If you need to immediately narrow your search further, click the 'Advanced Search' button and you will be taken to the screen shown in Fig. 13 below. Using the advanced search tool you can search using keywords, over a range of years and perhaps most usefully by reference to the extent of the geographic applicability of a piece of legislation using the options set to the left of the main search pane. Whichever search you choose the results will often include an option of either the modern digitised text or the text as it originally appeared in portable document format (PDF).

Figure 13: Legislation.gov.uk advanced search screen

Searching for European legislation

Many of the search techniques that we have explored in respect of domestic legislation are equally as applicable when searching for European legislation. As we have already seen, in LexisLibrary, Westlaw and BAILII you are literally a click or two away from European legislation. You can also use the dedicated EUR-Lex service which allows you to search according to a reference in the *OJ* a document number or using textual search terms.

Finding Legislation in Print

Historically, all legislative material, whether Acts of Parliament or statutory instruments, was made available in print. Libraries continue to maintain their historically acquired collections of legislative material and additional material to it. It is almost beyond question to suggest that finding legislative material in print is in any way simpler than finding it online but as a lawyer there is real value in the transferable skills you will learn from finding legislation in print and there are instances where you will no doubt find it very convenient to be able to do so.

In this section we will consider how to find basic legislative materials, namely statutes and SIs in their printed form and how to undertake further research that will reveal when and how the legislation came into force, whether it remains in force and aids that can be used in understanding its meaning.

Acts of Parliament

When looking for Acts of Parliament in print you have a number of options depending on the information you have and/or what exactly you want to find out. If you know the statute that you are looking for you can simply consult the relevant volume of *Public General Acts & Measures*, the governmental publication that groups together the original texts of all public Acts of Parliament. The original text reproduced in these volumes will give you the full text of the legislation and additional information such as the date of Royal Assent, commencement dates, etc. Very often you will want to refer to the text of a particular section or sections in an Act you are already familiar and where this is the case, this is the most appropriate and easiest search that you can do. As an alternative, you may want to use the *Current Law Legislation Citator* which helpfully lists statutes alphabetically making them potentially easier to find. The *Statute Citator*, which is a component of the *Legislation Citator*, can also be referred to ascertain whether the Act that you are searching for has been changed in one of a number of ways including by amendment, addition, consolidation, etc.

If you want to discover more about the legislative history of an Act then you will need to turn to *Current Law Statutes Annotated* which brings together not only the text of the Act but also the relevant passages of Hansard which can give a good (albeit not legally binding) commentary on the meaning (or intended meaning) of the provision(s) you are considering. *Current Law Statutes Annotated* is a loose-leaf publication with each statute arranged alphabetically by year, however, unlike, for example,

Halsbury's Statutes, which we will consider below, there is no series of updates for this publication and so you will need to discern whether or not an Act is in force before you rely on the account of it given here.

If you want to be able to determine the status of a statute and gain access to additional commentary on that statute with a service that is as up to date as it possible, the only option is the series of publications known as *Halsbury's Statutes* which comprises the main volumes containing all current general acts and measures up to the date of publication, the *Cumulative Supplement* which is up to date to the year of publication and the *Noter-Up* which provides more recent updates. While – by comparison to online searches – a cumbersome work by virtue of its volume alone, it is nonetheless compendious and offers outstanding insight into statutory material. Each entry is annotated not only with additional references but actual excerpts of Parliamentary debates, details of amendments and repeals, commencement information, citations of relevant case law and subordinate legislation and definitions of words used in the Act. To use the service to its full potential you need to be familiar with and work methodically through all three parts of it unless you are entirely satisfied that no changes are likely to have been made. You will also need to familiarise yourself with the *Consolidated Index*, a single, annually published volume that will help you to navigate your way through the (substantial) text of the main volumes.

If you are looking for a specific Act, that is to say you know the name, then finding it will prove to be relatively easy using the *Alphabetical List of Statutes* in the *Consolidated Index*. Simply find the Act in the *List* and you will find a reference to the appropriate volume (which contains other Acts according to subject area). The *Index* will then usually refer you to the appropriate volume. Note however, that the volumes are organised according to subject area and as a result some statutes may be split across numerous volumes. The *Index* will indicate how the statute is divided and indicate which sections of the Act are located in which volume. Of course if you do not know which section(s) are relevant to your research you will have to peruse all the relevant volumes in order to understand the statute fully – this is an inherent limitation of searching in print. Once you have found the sections pertinent to your search you will then be able to use the range of information that is published with the text of the statute. Your search should not end there however. You should make sure that no relevant sections have been amended or repealed and ensure that in general this statute does represent the most recent development in this area and that the statute has been brought into force.

To determine whether the Act has been amended or changed you must consult the *Cumulative Supplement* and the *Noter-up* service, in that order. Finally, to determine whether the Act has been brought into force you need to consult the appropriately named *Is it in Force?* volume which lists the commencement dates of all Acts passed since 1960 and which can be a useful standalone volume in itself. Having gone through each stage you can then be sure that the statute you have found is in force and that the section you are going to cite can be reliably cited.

If you are not looking for a specific statute and want to search by reference to a subject area or concept within that area you may find that this is a more rapid and productive process. Using the *Consolidated Index* you can search by subject headings and numerous related sub-headings, which will refer you to the specific volume where you can locate statutory material on that topic. Of course, if you are not familiar with that area of law you may have to read widely across a range of volumes to build up a complete picture and, when you have identified the relevant provisions, ensure that they represent the current state of the law and are in force using the appropriate volumes.

Statutory instruments

Searching for statutory instruments and seeing the nexus to a statute is far easier using an online database, particularly Westlaw, however, you can still search for SIs according to name, year and approximate subject area using paper reference works namely *Halsbury's Statutory Instruments*. While this work does not provide the full text of all SIs it reproduces those of significance and abridged summaries of the remainder. The contents of *Halsbury's Statutory Instruments* is arranged across 22 volumes and grouped together according to broad subject area. Unless you want to simply browse a volume on a particular topic, to navigate through the volumes you will also need the *Service* binder and the *Consolidated Index*.

If you have the name but not the citation of a statutory instrument you will first need to know which broad area of law this is classified into for the purposes of this publication. You can do this by using the Alphabetical List in the *Consolidated Index*. Once you have identified the subject area you can then select the correct volume (each one lists the subject areas that it contains on the cover). At the beginning of the relevant section you will find a chronological list of the contents of that section. If you know the year you can then find the SI easily, if you do not you will have to look over the entire list. When you have found the SI in the list you will then find information on where to find the full or the text relating to it, you may also find information about associated SIs. If you know the citation of the SI that you are looking for you can simply consult the chronological list in the *Service* binder.

To ascertain in print whether a SI is in force or has been subject to amendment you will need to have the year and number of the SI and refer to the *Statutory Instrument Citator* of the *Current Law Legislation Citator*.

European law

The print source of European law is the *Official Journal of the European Communities* – the *OJ*. All legislation is printed in the OJ but that does not mean it is easy to find. The only way to search comprehensively and with any degree of speed is using either the official database of the EU – EUR-Lex or one of the subscription services such as Westlaw. The nature of the *OJ* as a collection of legislation, judgments and other documents and its sheer size (some 30,000 printed pages per year) precludes effective searching as there is no accompanying service to map out its contents. A good starting point therefore is likely to be a quality textbook which will allow you to compile a list of references which you can then use to follow up in the *OJ*, or a reference work such as the loose leaf, *The Law of the European Union*[10] which will allow you to find European legislation according to subject.

> ### Practical Questions
> Using printed sources of legislation find the following
> 1. The most recent Judicial Pensions Act (A: 1981)
> 2. The measure the repealed the Judicial Pensions and Retirement Act 1993 (Addition of Qualifying Judicial Offices) (No. 2) Order 2007/2185 (A: repealed by SI 2008/2833)
> 3. The status of the Ecclesiastical Leasing Act 1842 c.108 (A: in force)

---

[10] Vaughan, D., Q.C., et al, OUP, Oxford 2007 plus supplements.

11
How to Read Primary Sources of Law

Dave Hodgkinson

How to Read Case Law

To read a case is to extract the beauty of the law itself. To take facts, and see them utilised in a manner which creates law is fabulous. When reading a case, what you are actually looking for is its meaning, or, with regards to study skills and learning, you need to learn the point of law from the case.

You should get used to reading cases. It is a fact that you can obtain the points of law and the facts of cases from textbooks or from reading other lecture materials however you should read the cases, or at least as many as you can. It will show you how the judge applies the law to the facts and the facts to the law. It will equip you with knowledge that there are two sides to every story and that in the adversarial system the judge can sometimes be put in a difficult situation when arriving at decisions.

Beyond helping you to understand how the judge interprets law, ensuring you engage with reading cases will also greatly assist your learning: it will open your mind to legal thinking and help you to accommodate and assimilate information in legal manner. All this will improve your understanding and lead to better grades.

There is one other thing which you should be aware of – practice. You will only develop the ability to read cases and other sources, such as statutes, by practice. It is the substance of law that is to be found in the cases and it is only the study of the legal questions that should be important to you at this stage.

The component parts of a law report

If an inferior court is bound by a superior court it is important for the inferior court to know exactly what it is bound by.[1] When a case is decided, a judge will deliver his judgment made up of three distinct parts:

---

[1] A good introduction to the hierarchy of UK courts can be found in chapter 1 of *English Legal System* by Elliott and Quinn (2012, Longman).

1. A statement of **facts** as found by the judge;
2. An account of the judge's **reasoning** and a review of the relevant law;
3. The actual **decision** between the parties.

The second aspect, an account of the judge's reasoning, is the binding element of the decision, and is known by the phrase *ratio decidendi* or, the reason for the decision. The *ratio decidendi* states the law for all persons and, depending on the court in which it is made; it may be binding in later cases.

However, it is not just binding on cases where the facts in dispute are essentially the same. The judges phrase the *ratio decidendi* in such a way that it lays down a principle which is broad enough to be applied across a range of facts.

Besides the *ratio decidendi* there are also groups of words known as **obiter dicta**. These are statements of law which go beyond the limits of the case and are merely persuasive.

When trying to understand how significant a case is, you must check in which court it was decided: if it is a Court of Appeal decision it binds the inferior courts, yet is merely persuasive to the Supreme Court. You must understand judicial precedent in order to understand case law.[2] This should lead you to consider how relevant the case is in your reading; you will find some cases are more 'important' to you in learning the fundamentals of a subject however consider this – if you read some of the less popular and more obscure cases, you might be able to find good relevant law and dictum for your assignments and examinations. This will set you aside from other students using the mainstream authorities and will illustrate research and understanding thereby bringing you higher grades.

You will find your lecturers placing much emphasis on *ratio decidendi*. Indeed, it is very important. However you will find it difficult to analyse so deeply in order to find the *ratio decidendi*. That is not stated to sound derogatory or rude about yours skills. It is stated because it is very difficult to find *ratio decidendi* and students go onto Masters level courses and practitioner courses where they study how to find the *ratio decidendi* and then argue it on a higher level. In appeal cases you could also have the situation where the majority verdict could be comprised of different reasons for the decision. The main thing is to determine the point of law. It is acceptable to understand the reason for the decision as being the basis of facts and the law when applied to those facts. Your lecturers will identify where it might be important to search a little deeper. For now, you should concentrate on how to read a case.

How to read a case

The first thing to take into account is which court the case is held in. This is important because you need to understand a number of different perspectives dependent upon which court the case is held in. If it is being held in a Court of First Instance, you can read the case with the knowledge that counsel will be putting their case, and the judge will be delivering his or her judgment, on the basis that there is a possibility of appeal.

You might question why this is relevant however the fact is that the judgment will be singular and so lacking a certain depth that one would expect to find in the appellate courts, where there are three or five

---

[2] Chapter 1 of Elliott and Quinn's *English Legal System* (op cit) also provides a good introduction to Judicial Precedent.

judges delivering a verdict. Indeed, if the case is in an appellate court then you should look for dissenting judgments to be as important to you as a law student as the majority judgments. This is because you can quite often use a dissenting judgment in order to bring an element of critical evaluation to your assignments and exams. Dissenting judgments are persuasive as well and so will be very handy in mooting competitions.

Whilst the outcome of the case will undoubtedly be interesting and important, and can help you understand the point of law, it is important to keep your thoughts focussed on learning the law from the case. You might have heard your lecturers say things such as 'the facts of this case are irrelevant' or 'the outcome matters little' – what is important is the point of law.

Making notes on the case

Making notes on the case will assist you to get the basics down and keep your mind active with regards to the area of law and what the case is actually about. You can keep the notes simple at this stage. You might like to start by asking:

1. What are the basic facts of this case and how relevant are they?
2. Is there any historical perspective in regard to the case? For example, do you already know that it is an appeal case or a case which you have been told overrules an earlier case?
3. What do you think the point of law to be considered is? You could already have an idea from your lecture or maybe you have a preconceived idea. This is fun because when you read the case you might just be very surprised at the outcome!
4. (*Having read the case . . .*) The actual decision and the reasons for it; were you close in your thoughts before reading the case?
5. What other cases were dealt with in the case? Were they applied, considered, distinguished or dismissed?

The headnote

Here is a good tip for you. Start by reading the headnote. This is the front page of information which you will find before the lead judgment is given. It contains the citation, the facts, the verdict and other information such as the names of counsel involved in the case. The point is that the information delivered is clear, concise and cogent. For you as a law student that is what you want. Some cases are, literally, hundreds of pages long. Well, when we say cases what we mean is the judgment from the court. It is reported in the law reports and printed out. They can be very long and complex. The headnote helps with your understanding and it takes all the salient facts and puts them at the beginning of the case. You will normally find the decision in the case, or the point of law, beginning where it states the word 'HELD'.

So, reading the headnote is a good place to start, and a good habit to develop. However as stated, you should also try to read more in-depth if you can. With regards to written assignments and moot competitions, it will pay dividends to cite some relevant *obiter dicta* from the judge in the case and this can only be found by reading the whole case.

The headnote will also assist you with any other relevant cases, legislation or secondary sources which have been referred to or used in the case before you. This is important for your research trail; it might be the fact that you need to read some of these other cases or research the meanings of the sections in the statutes in order to aid your knowledge and understanding.

If you are using online resources then you will find the headnote information in a tool bar to the side. If you are using a traditional hard copy law report you will find the information about other sources used at the bottom of the headnote, usually in italics but not always. Either way, a little more research never did any harm so you should utilise everything available to you.

Ultimately then, the headnote will set out the legal issue for the court and the judgment. However here is a warning: you must develop further and not simply only read headnotes. You need to think deeper. For example, what is the judge doing?

The role of the judge

The judge in the case you are reading is looking and listening. He is looking at other previously decided cases. It might be that he is bound by judicial precedent. But he is also considering whether or not that law is applicable in the current case before him. Indeed, it might be that he can distinguish previous precedent. He is being persuaded by the lawyers in the case. He is being asked to consider the facts and apply the law to them. Has he applied any principles of which you are already aware?

What the judge is also doing is laying down the *ratio decidendi* for future lawyers to disagree on! There might be some common ground in appellate judgments however by reading a number of cases you will see that the judges do not always agree.

Therefore, the judgment itself makes up a wealth of different avenues and information and you should not set it aside as something which is ill-thought out. It is a fitting emblem to his position of authority.

This is what you must take into account when you are reading a case. You are no doubt reading it because you have an objective of your own, be it an exam of some sort or a mooting competition. Accordingly you need to go through the phases of interpretation and thought which the judge is doing.

Think simply of this: he is working towards a conclusion. That's it. He is delivering a judgment and at the end, nine times out of ten, you will read the judge saying '. . . it is therefore my conclusion that' and so on. This is a conclusion based upon legal principles and argument.

Reading the cases fully and not (always) just the headnote will make you a higher level and more educated lawyer with clearer delivery of thought and understanding. In other words, you'll become a more 'rounded' lawyer and will not only do well in your assessments, but will also be a credit to whichever profession you decide to join.

A logical process

If you think about it, all the judge is doing is listening to the submissions, looking at the facts, interpreting the law and then making a logical decision based on the information before him. The decision is founded on the basis of legal reasoning. The judge must take into account the law, either from statute or previous case law and other principles when arriving at the decision. You can address it by asking yourself 'what is it that truly matters here?'.

It may surprise you to realise, but you can do this as well already. The 'level' of your thinking might not be that of a judge, but you can clearly put forward a rational and logical argument using the law and applying it to the facts. You can, if you like, create your own *ratio decidendi*, just as a judge would in the case. The reason for the decision therefore is something which you can work out logically.

The judge isn't always correct!

We would not have an appeal system if this were the case. Judges are human and have their own thought processes based upon the information put before them. Accordingly, when you read the case, do not always take everything as being exactly correct. This is also something which you should do yourself whilst thinking about law and reading cases. It is quite incorrect to say the outcome will definitely be this or that; you should keep an open and impartial mind, just as the judge must do. You should remain accommodating to the information before you and develop your mind in a legally analytical manner.

Giving a judgment is not a definite science and you can see fallible arguments if you look for them. Think about the issues and whether or not you agree with the judge. Develop your critical thinking ability and evaluate what you think the judge is saying and whether you would decide the case in the same way. Clearly you do not have all the counsel submissions and the smell of the courtroom, but you do have your own knowledge about the area of law and you can evaluate it on your own terms. All of this will be fun and enjoyable whilst deepening your understanding at the same time. Discuss the cases with friends and study partners if you can, it will all assist your knowledge of the law and increase your interest in it as you get 'better' at it.

Exercise

Read the case of **R v Kelly [1999] Q.B. 621**. Try to find the reasons for the decision in your own words; think how the law is applied, question the judicial thinking and consider whether you might have arrived at a different outcome.

> You will find commentary in boxes like this which precede the information.
>
> Think about what is being said and also consider the context of the case and how those meanings might affect your understanding.

Kelly and Lindsay were both charged with the same offence, but were tried in separate courts. Both of them, however, appealed on the same points of law, so the Court of Appeal (Criminal Division) dealt with both of their cases together.

The offence with which they are charged is theft, which is made illegal by the Theft Act 1968. A problem arises because this Act of Parliament uses the words 'property' and 'possession'. These words have been interpreted by the courts as having two different specific meanings in law.

The importance of these meanings is that if the items taken were not capable of being property or being possessed, then the two appellants cannot be found guilty of theft.

This case deals with a historical problem with the nature of the articles stolen, in that traditionally the case law of England (the common law) does not recognise the ownership or possession of bodies or parts of bodies. The court is therefore faced with a problem that is hardly new (people have been snatching bodies for centuries), but are faced with a new legal argument. The court is also aware that changes in society and technological advances may demand a rethink by the courts of this approach, especially in relation to material such as DNA.

The court also had to consider what punishment (sentence) would be appropriate to fit the crime and that would be appropriate for the particular defendants.

Once again, in this novel case, the court has to turn to decisions from other common law jurisdictions (countries with a similar legal system to ours). The court does not have to follow these, but finds them useful in determining the answers to difficult points of law.

> Now consider the following points and then ask yourself if they have made you think more deeply about the case? Could you now answer questions on the case on a deeper and more meaningful basis?

R v Kelly and another

> Virtually all prosecutions for criminal offences are undertaken in the name of the Crown (the Queen [Latin *Regina*] is often abbreviated to *R*).

COURT OF APPEAL, (CRIMINAL DIVISION)

[1999] QB 621, [1998] 3 All ER 741, [1999] 2 WLR 384

HEARING-DATES: 14 May 1998

14 May 1998

> The layout of the Report provides some basic information. The court is named, as are the members of the court. Lord Justice Rose ("Rose LJ"), sitting with Mr Justice Ognall and Mr Justice Sullivan ("Ognall and Sullivan JJ").

CATCHWORDS:
Criminal law – Theft – Property belonging to another – Property – Parts of corpses removed from Royal College of Surgeons – Whether parts of corpse capable of being property – Theft Act 1968 ss.1,4,5

> The first page is not part of the judgment – is not law – but is a summary provided by the editors of the report for quick reference. Do not always rely on the headnote – try to read the whole case.

HEADNOTE:

K, an artist, had privileged access to the Royal College of Surgeons where he was permitted to draw anatomical specimens which were used by doctors training to be surgeons. L was employed at the college as a junior technician, and K asked L to remove a number of body parts. Approximately 35 to 40 body parts were removed, and K made casts of them. Most of the body parts were buried in a field; part of a leg was found in K's attic and the remaining parts were found in the basement of a flat belonging to friends. K and L were charged with theft, contrary to s 1 of the Theft Act 1968. At the trial, the defence submitted at the close of the prosecution case (i) that parts of bodies were not in law capable of being property and therefore could not be stolen, and (ii) that the specimens were not in the lawful possession of the college at the time they were taken because they had been retained beyond the period of two years before burial stipulated in the Anatomy Act 1832, and so did not belong to it. The trial judge rejected those submissions, ruling that there was an exception to the traditional common law rule that there was no property in a corpse, namely that once a human body or body part had undergone a process of skill by a person authorised to perform it, with the object of preserving it for the purpose of medical or scientific examination, or for the benefit of medical science, it became something quite different from an interred corpse and it thereby acquired a usefulness or value and it was capable of becoming property in the usual way, and could be stolen. K and L were convicted, and they appealed against their conviction.

Held – Parts of corpses were capable of being property within the meaning of s 4 of the 1968 Act if they had acquired different attributes by virtue of the application of skill, such as dissection and preservation techniques, for exhibition and teaching purposes. It followed that the trial judge was correct to rule as he did. Further, he was right to hold that the college had sufficient possession for the purposes of s 5(1) of the Act, since such possession was not dependent on the period of possession, whether it be for a limited or indefinite period. Moreover, there was evidence before the jury which illustrated the fact of the college's possession and it was not necessary for the judge to direct the jury further. Accordingly the appeals against conviction would be dismissed.

Doodeward v Spence (1908) 6 CLR 406, R v Turner (No 2) [1971] 2 All ER 441 and Dobson v North Tyneside Health Authority [1996] 4 All ER 474 applied.

NOTES:

For property in general and property belonging to another, see 11(1) Halsbury's Laws (4th edn reissue) paras 544, 548, and for cases on the subject, see 14(2) Digest (2nd reissue) 233–234, 246–252, 7505–7520, 7672–7704.

For the Theft Act 1968, ss 1, 4, 5, see 12 Halsbury's Statutes (4th edn) (1997 reissue) 489, 492, 493.

The cases relied upon in reaching the judgment are also listed, as is the nature of appeal and the counsel (barristers) for both sides.

CASES-REF-TO:

Dobson v North Tyneside Health Authority [1996] 4 All ER 474, [1997] 1 WLR 596, CA.
Doodeward v Spence (1908) 6 CLR 406, Aust HC.
R v Bibi [1980] 1 WLR 1193, (1980) 71 Cr App R 360, CA.
R v Ollerenshaw (1998) Times, 6 May, CA.

R v R (rape: marital exemption) [1991] 4 All ER 481, [1992] 1 AC 599, [1991] 3 WLR 767, HL.
R v Sharpe (1857) Dears & B 160, 169 ER 959, CCR.
R v Turner (No 2) [1971] 2 All ER 441, [1971] 1 WLR 901, CA.
R v W (1992) 14 Cr App R (S) 256, CA.

INTRODUCTION:

Anthony-Noel Kelly and Neil Lindsay appealed against their conviction on 3 April 1998 before Judge Rivlin QC and a jury at the Crown Court at Southwark of theft, contrary to s 1(1) of the Theft Act 1968. They were sentenced respectively to nine months' imprisonment, and six months' imprisonment suspended for two years, and also appealed against their sentence. The facts are set out in the judgment of the court.

COUNSEL:

Terry Munyard for Kelly; Peter Thornton QC for Lindsay; Andrew Campbell-Tiech for the Crown.

JUDGMENT-READ:

14 May 1998. The following judgment of the court was delivered.

PANEL: ROSE LJ, OGNALL AND SULLIVAN JJ

JUDGMENTBY-1: ROSE LJ

JUDGMENT-1:

> Notice that the appeal against the decision and against the sentence of the court of first instance is given with the permission ("leave") of that court. A part of the certificate by the judge granting leave is quoted. The appeal in this case is to clarify a point of law that has not been settled by the courts before, but also to complain against the severity of the sentence.

ROSE LJ: On 3 April 1998 at the Crown Court at Southwark, these appellants were convicted of one offence of theft. Kelly was sentenced to nine months' imprisonment, and Lindsay to six months' imprisonment suspended for two years. They appeal against conviction by certificate of the trial judge, Judge Rivlin QC, in the following terms:

'Whether the trial Judge was correct in ruling as a matter of law that there is an exception to the traditional common law rule that "there is no property in a corpse", namely, that once a human body or body part has undergone a process of skill by a person authorised to perform it, with the object of preserving for the purpose of medical or scientific examination or for the benefit of medical science, it becomes something quite different from an interred corpse. It thereby acquires a usefulness or value. It is capable of becoming property in the usual way, and can be stolen.'

The facts were these. Between 1992 and 1994, the appellant, Kelly, who is an artist, had privileged access to the premises of the Royal College of Surgeons in order to draw anatomical specimens held on display and used for training surgeons. The appellant, Lindsay, was employed by the college during that period as a junior technician. Between 1993 and 1994, Kelly, who was then in his late thirties, asked Lindsay, who was under 21, to remove a number of human body parts from the college. Some 35 to 40 such parts, including three human heads, part of a brain, six arms or parts of an arm, ten legs or feet, and part of three human torsos were removed and taken to Kelly's home. He made casts of the parts, some of which were exhibited in an art gallery. Neither appellant intended to return the body parts, many of which Kelly buried in a field in the grounds of his family home. Part of a leg was kept in the attic of his home. The remaining parts were recovered from the basement of a flat occupied by one of Kelly's friends.

The crucial issue for the jury, when the matter was left for their consideration, was whether the appellants had acted dishonestly or whether, at the time they took the body parts, they acted in the honest belief that they had the right to do so. It was accepted, for the purposes of the hearing, that all the specimens in question antedated in age the Anatomy Act 1984, which had come into force in early 1988. All the specimens taken had been preserved or fixed by college staff or other medical agencies. All were subject to a regular scheme of inspection, preservation, and maintenance and most of them had been the subject of further work, by prosecution, whereby they had been expertly dissected so as to reveal, in highlighted form, the inner workings of the body.

There was evidence that the appellants would not have been permitted to remove body parts from the building under any circumstances. Permission could only be given by a licensed teacher of anatomy for the disposal of the specimens. It was elicited in cross-examination that some of the specimens at the college were no longer in use because of their poor condition due to age, and that other parts had, on occasions, left the college for the purposes of burial or cremation.

There was evidence that the preparation of the specimens by prosecution, to which we have referred, would have involved many hours, sometimes weeks, of skilled work. There was also evidence that the type of dissection indicated that the work was that of a previous generation of anatomists, thereby throwing some light on the age of the parts.

There was evidence that parts kept in the demonstration room would be up to 20 years old, but those in the basement store would be much older. It was not possible to say whether the specimens taken by the appellants had come from the demonstration room or the basement.

There was evidence from the current inspector of anatomy to the effect that the college had full authority to be in possession of these specimens. In cross-examination, he said it was his understanding that the Anatomy Act 1832 did not apply. There was similar evidence from the inspector of anatomy at the time the parts were taken, between 1991 and 1995.

> The Anatomy Act 1832 was repealed by the Anatomy Act 1984 and the judge says that under cross-examination at the Court of First Instance the Inspector of Anatomy for the College said he did not think the 1832 Act applied. This is because the licensing regulations which would have been applicable, and the requirements that body parts should not be taken from the licensed premises, were provided by the 1984 Act. It seems here the judge is setting the 'context' of the appeal; he is setting out what was said at first instance in order to give a legitimate foundation to the judgment of the Court of Appeal. You should think about the whole picture when reading a case: background information will be as important as the information being delivered in the case you are reading.

There was a good deal of material placed before the jury, in the form of a jury bundle, which is before this court, containing letters written by various people, in 1944, on the basis of which arguments were advanced as to the belief as to whether or not the possession of the Royal College of Surgeons was lawfully well founded. We have to say that, for our part, we find no relevance whatever in those documents to any issue which was before the jury.

Kelly was interviewed on a number of occasions by the police. He said he understood the body parts were old, but that they were extremely valuable to the college. He thought that after four years the college required a certificate to retain the parts, which they did not have, and he considered that he was intercepting the parts which were 'on their way to the grave'. Nobody, he agreed, had given him permission to remove the items. He said at first that he had buried all of them but subsequently he gave the address of a friend, to which earlier we referred, where some of the parts were stored. When he was charged with theft and dishonest handling he said he did not intend to commit either such offence.

The appellant, Lindsay, in interview, referred to the age of the anatomical specimens and to the unusual access given to Kelly to the demonstration rooms and basement store. He said that his understanding of the law was that the college was only allowed to keep specimens for a period of three years, after which they had to be buried. He said that Kelly had asked him to remove the items, so that castings could be made in the way which we have described and he, Lindsay, agreed to that on condition that Kelly buried the parts afterwards. Lindsay said he took the items from the anatomy store or the storage tanks which were usually in the demonstration rooms. He removed the identification labels which he threw in a bin. Kelly had paid him £400 for his services but, he said, his main interest was in having the pieces buried.

> The word "submission" means an individual point of argument put forward by counsel. You can see here that a case setting persuasive precedent is introduced.

A submission was made to the learned judge on behalf of the defence at the close of the prosecution. The first part of that submission was that parts of bodies were not in law capable of being property, and therefore could not be stolen. The judge ruled, in favour of the Crown, that the specimens were property, because of an exception to the common law rule, in the terms of the certificate which he has given for the purposes of the appeal to this court, the basis of that exception being a decision of the High Court of Australia in Doodeward v Spence (1908) 6 CLR 406.

The further submission was made that the specimens were not in the lawful possession of the college at the time they were taken, and therefore could not have been stolen. It was, however, accepted that the college was physically in possession of the specimens, but the submission was made at that time that that possession was governed by the provisions of the Anatomy Act 1832 and, in consequence, the college's possession was unlawful because the specimens had been retained beyond the period of two years, referred to in that Act by way of amendment, before burial. The learned judge rejected that submission on the basis that possession and control in the accepted terms of those words for the purposes of the Theft Act, was not in issue. He found that there was certainly no evidence before the court to support the suggestion that the college's possession and control was unlawful. To those submissions, which have been repeated in this court, we shall in a moment return in a little more detail.

The judge having ruled in favour of the Crown, the appellant, Kelly, gave evidence about his work as an artist and his interest in things both living and dead. He described becoming friends with Lindsay and said that he had not sought permission either to remove the pieces from the college's possession, or to do any casting or moulding work in relation to those specimens. He said he had not sought that permission lest it be refused. He said that he may well have convinced his co-accused that the plans for removal and use of these parts were highly important. He had not however wanted to get Lindsay into trouble, and Lindsay had said he would remove them provided he, Kelly, buried them. He accepted that, prior to his arrest, he had concocted and recorded in his diary two stories as to how he had come into possession of the body parts. He said he made up the stories because he had taken the parts without permission. The £400 which he had paid to Lindsay was what he called 'a compensating gesture', not payment for the parts.

Lindsay described taking the specimens. He said that he had never thought that it was wrong to supply them to Kelly. Some of them were in a very bad state. He did not think that he would have been given permission to remove them had he asked. All the parts were from the basement store and, he said, were no longer used for teaching purposes. He said he did not believe that he was doing wrong, or acting dishonestly. He accepted that when he was first questioned by the police, he had lied by saying that he had taken all the parts. That was in order to keep Kelly out of it, and indeed, Kelly himself had said that Lindsay was to say, if asked, that he, Kelly, had taken the parts. He said, in cross-examination, that he felt justified in his actions because he believed the college were keeping the parts illegally.

In the course of his summing up, the learned judge directed the jury that the college was in lawful possession of the parts at the time they were taken. That gives rise to a third complaint, additionally to the two other matters to which summarily we have already referred, on the basis of which it is said that this court should find the convictions of these appellants to be unsafe.

> At this juncture you can see that the judge has very succinctly set out the 'case so far' before turning to considerations of the law; he will then go on to apply the law to the facts and the facts to the law. The 'test' the judge will have to apply is whether the conviction at first instance is 'unsafe'. Indeed, he says that 'before turning to the rival contentions' and these are what he must decide by applying the law to the facts to judge whether the conviction is unsafe or not. In doing so, he separates his judgment into parts and so now he turns to the law. This enables the court to focus on the relevant law and the rest of the judgment will be set in the context of that law; you can also see that the judge is clear, cogent and concise. This is a good skill which you could use in your own studies.

Before turning to the rival contentions, it is convenient to refer to the terms of the Theft Act 1968. Section 1(1) says:

'A person is guilty of theft if he dishonestly appropriates property belonging to another with the intention of permanently depriving the other of it . . .'

Section 4(1) says:

'"Property" includes money and all other property, real or personal, including things in action and other intangible property.'

Section 5(1) provides:

'Property shall be regarded as belonging to any person having possession or control of it, or having in it any proprietary right or interest . . .'
On behalf of the appellant, Lindsay, in submissions adopted by counsel on behalf of Kelly, Mr Thornton QC submits, as we have indicated, that the jury's verdict was unsafe, first, because the body parts were not

property and therefore could not be stolen, secondly, because they did not belong to the Royal College of Surgeons because they were not lawfully in their possession, and thirdly, because the judge's direction that the college was in lawful possession was a prejudicial misdirection of the jury.

In support of those submissions, Mr Thornton advanced eight propositions. First, that the common law rule applies to corpses to be buried but not yet buried. Such, he submits, are not property. Secondly there has been, until this case, no prosecution for theft of a body or body parts, although there do exist in other Acts, in particular the Anatomy Act 1832, certain statutory offences, in relation to corpses and parts of corpses, which are – it is perhaps worth noting in passing – susceptible to a maximum sentence of imprisonment of three months. Thirdly, the common law rule extends to parts of bodies as well as to the entire corpse. Fourthly, the body parts in the present case were not property, they were intended by their donors for burial, and the resolution of that matter, clearly one of fact, was one which could only be favourable to the defence. Fifthly, there is no exception to the general common law rule.

For this part of his submission, it was pertinent for him to take the court, as he did, to do Doodeward v Spence, to which we have already referred. The first of the two majority judgments in that Australian case was given by Griffith CJ. He said ((1908) 6 CLR 406 at 413–414):

'It is idle to contend in these days that the possession of a mummy, or of a prepared skeleton, or of a skull, or other parts of a human body, is necessarily unlawful; if it is, the many valuable collections of anatomical and pathological specimens or preparations formed and maintained by scientific bodies, were formed and are maintained in violation of the law. In my opinion there is no law forbidding the mere possession of a human body, whether born alive or dead, for purposes other than immediate burial. A fortiori such possession is not unlawful if the body possesses attributes of such a nature that its preservation may afford valuable or interesting information or instruction . . . a human body, or a portion of a human body, is capable by law of becoming the subject of property. It is not necessary to give an exhaustive enumeration of the circumstances under which such a right may be acquired, but I entertain no doubt that, when a person has by the lawful exercise of work or skill so dealt with a human body or part of a human body in his lawful possession that it has acquired some attributes differentiating it from a mere corpse awaiting burial, he acquires a right to retain possession of it, at least as against any person not entitled to have it delivered to him for the purpose of burial, but subject, of course, to any positive law which forbids its retention under the particular circumstances.'

Barton J said (at 417):

'I have read the judgment of the Chief Justice, and I entirely agree with the reasons it embodies, which I hold it unnecessary to amplify.'

> A dissenting judgment is important as we have stated previously. The case is decided by a number of judges. They all have different ideas about the context of the facts and the way the law is applicable to them. Also remember – judges are in fact human! This means they have different thoughts about how the law should be applied and this could turn on the basis of how counsel has put it before them. If you read a dissenting judgment it will also bring balance to the case; you can use them in your moot presentations to argue points from a persuasive basis and you can also use them in assessments to show your lecturer that you have researched and also understood the issues on all levels, including theoretical and contextual. You might find that when you read cases you also agree with the dissenting judge and not the majority verdict.

Higgins J (at 417) gave a dissenting judgment. He referred (at 422) to the transformation of a corpse into a mummy, by the skill of an embalmer turning it into something different. He went on (at 423) to say that such traffic as there is in skulls and bones is clandestine. If they come from dissecting rooms, they come in violation of the law. He went on to say that no dead body could be used for dissection except under very stringent conditions and when the dissection was over the body must be decently interred. He said (at 423), which is much relied upon by the appellants in this court:

'... I rather think that sundry contraventions of the strict law as to dead bodies are winked at in the interests of medical science, and also for the practical reasons that no one can identify the bones or parts, and that no one is interested in putting the law in motion.'

At the conclusion of judgment, he said (at 424):

'A right to keep possession of a human corpse seems to me to be just the thing which the British law, and, therefore, the New South Wales law, declines to recognise.'

Mr Thornton draws attention to the fact that that authority, which related to a two headed still born foetus preserved as a curio, arose from a claim in detinue and he relies, as we have said, on the dissenting judgment of Higgins J. The facts of that case, he says, are plainly distinguishable from the present, because the nature of the object there in dispute rendered it something wholly different from a corpse or part of a corpse.

He submitted that there cannot be property for the purposes of the 1968 Act, unless there is a permanent right to possession vested in the person from whom the property is taken. He submitted that the decision of the English Court of Appeal in Dobson v North Tyneside Health Authority [1996] 4 All ER 474, [1997] 1 WLR 596 does not lend succour to the Doodeward v Spence exception. He submitted that no amount of skill expended on a body part can affect its ownership; at the highest, it might affect possessory rights.

His sixth submission was that the body parts in question did not belong to anybody. He further submitted, in his seventh submission, that the Royal College of Surgeons, albeit in control and factual possession, were not in lawful possession because of the expiry of the two-year period under the 1832 Act, and he drew attention to certain sections in that Act.

> You may observe that some of the cases relied upon by Lord Justice Rose do not have very much in common with the facts of the case, but provide useful statements of law which can assist in determining the legal issue at hand. He makes specific reference to the difference in fact with reference to *Reg v Turner (No.2)* [1971] 1 WLR 901 ("the first volume of the Weekly Law Reports for 1971, starting at page nine hundred and one").

He drew the court's attention to R v Turner (No 2) [1971] 2 All ER 441, [1971] 1 WLR 901. In that case, the owner of a car, having taken it to a garage to be repaired, removed it a few hours later without telling the garage proprietor. The learned judge directed the jury, in terms which the Court of Appeal held were proper, that, in order to find the owner guilty of theft, it was essential to prove that he had acted dishonestly and, in weighing his evidence, it was immaterial that he had no basis in law for his belief that he had claim of right to the car. Lord Parker CJ giving the judgment of the court, the other members of which were Widgery LJ and Bridge J said ([1971] 2 All ER 441 at 443, [1971] 1 WLR 901 at 904):

'. . . the sole question was whether Mr Brown had possession or control. This court is quite satisfied that there is no ground whatever for qualifying the words "possession or control", in any way. It is sufficient if it is found that the person from whom the property is taken, or to use the words of the Act, appropriated, was at the time in fact in possession or control. At the trial there was a long argument whether that possession or control must be lawful, it being said that by reason of the fact that this car was subject to a hire-purchase agreement, Mr Brown could never even as against the appellant obtain lawful possession or control. As I have said, this court is quite satisfied that the judge was quite correct in telling the jury that they need not bother about lien, and that they need not bother about hire-purchase agreements. The only question was: was Mr Brown in fact in possession or control?'

Mr Thornton submits that that case has not only been criticised by Professor Sir John Smith QC in an article to which he drew our attention, but it is to be understood as limited to the facts of the particular case and should not be regarded as any authority, for present purposes, as to the construction of s 5(1) of the 1968 Act.

Finally, Mr Thornton referred to the direction given by the learned judge in these terms:

'I direct you that the college was in lawful possession of all of these specimens. In that case the law is that they must be treated as their property. But of course that does not mean that you should ignore the points made by the defence. Far from it. The defendants are, nevertheless, entitled to say, if it is true: "Well, whatever the position may have been, we honestly believed, perhaps mistakenly, but we honestly believed that the parts had been abandoned or didn't belong to anyone," and the defence are entitled to ask you to consider that.'

That direction, submits Mr Thornton, was prejudicial to the defence, because it undermined the defence case on honesty, which depended, in part at least, on the genuineness of the defendant's belief.

It is to be noted that in the summing up, at its inception, the learned judge in the course of directing the jury as to the ingredients of the offences which they must find proved before they could convict, devoted a number of pages to a direction as to dishonesty. In particular, he said:

'. . . in deciding whether the defendants were acting honestly, you are, of course, entitled to take into account everything that they have said to you, about believing these body parts did not belong to anybody; they had been abandoned, and in Lindsay's case, that nobody at the Royal College of Surgeons would have minded if they had known what was going on; if they honestly and genuinely believed these things, even if that honest belief may have been mistaken, that would plainly be evidence that they were not acting dishonestly.'

Mr Munyard, on behalf of Kelly, as we have indicated, adopts the submissions made by Mr Thornton. He took us in further detail to the dissenting judgment of Higgins J, in Doodeward's case. He submitted that in Dobson's case, Peter Gibson LJ was, in the course of his judgment, saying merely that if the Doodeward v Spence exception was arguable, it was not arguable on the facts of that case and therefore no support was given to the Doodeward v Spence exception by the Court of Appeal's decision. As to R v Turner (No 2), he submits that the issue of whether possession was lawful did not arise in that case and, in consequence, the observations of Lord Parker CJ should not afford any assistance to this court.

He also referred to a passage in the summing up in relation to distinguishing dishonesty from motive and the possibility that they could be interrelated. He made a further submission that the learned judge did not, as Mr Munyard submits he should have done, repeat his directions with regard to the burden of proof when, at a later stage in his summing up, he was rehearsing the material matters so far as prosecution and defence were concerned. He submits that that too is a reason for regarding his client's conviction as being unsafe.

> Kelly's barrister runs a particularly clever, if unsuccessful argument that relies upon the European Convention on Human Rights (an International Bill of Rights agreed by many European and Central and Eastern European countries). The argument suggests that if the court finds the two guilty then they will be effectively criminalising an action which was not known to be a crime at the time. This should amount to "retrospective legislation" which is contrary to the Convention. The judge dismisses this argument partly on the basis that the Convention is not in effect in English Law. The Convention was made part of English Law by virtue of the Human Rights Act 1998 on the 2nd October 2000.

His final submission was that the prosecution for the offence of theft was effectively the implementation of retrospective legislation, contrary to the European Convention on Human Rights (the Convention for the Protection of Human Rights and Fundamental Freedoms (Rome, 4 November 1950; TS 71 (1953); Cmd 8969)), and that such a prosecution therefore gave rise to a breach of the appellant's rights under the convention. It is sufficient to say, in relation to that last submission, first, that the convention is not presently part of English law; secondly, that elucidation of the common law cannot, as it seems to us, give rise to retrospective legislation; and thirdly that, to the knowledge of one member of this court, an argument along these lines was rejected, at first instance and not renewed on appeal to this court, in an unreported case tried at the Crown Court at Winchester in 1991, following the House of Lords decision in R v R (rape: marital exemption) [1991] 4 All ER 481, [1992] 1 AC 599, that a husband could be guilty of raping his wife. The appeal against sentence in that case is reported: see R v W (1992) 14 Cr App R (S) 256. Accordingly, we do not accept this submission.

It is convenient to deal with the other subsidiary submissions which Mr Munyard makes. So far as the burden of proof is concerned, that was fully and clearly set out by the learned judge at the beginning of his summing up, as one would expect. We see no reason whatever why subsequently he should have returned to that subject when dealing with the facts of the case. We see nothing in his directions on that matter which could render the verdicts unsafe.

Mr Campbell-Tiech, on behalf of the prosecution, advanced before this court a submission which was not made to the learned trial judge, namely, that a corpse and parts of a corpse are property within s 4 of the 1968 Act; a thing is either property or not. The status of the holder of the thing is irrelevant to determination of whether it is property or not, as is equally irrelevant the intention of the holder of the thing. Section 4 deals with property. Section 5 deals with rights over property. There is no overlap between the two sections. The common law in relation to corpses and parts of corpses deals with rights over things, and that is the province of s 5, not s 4. The common law doctrine as to who has the right to possession or control is irrelevant to whether a thing is property. Parts of a corpse have all the properties of a thing; the common law relates to rights not things. In the 1968 Act, Parliament did not declare that a corpse was not property and could not be stolen. As a matter of statutory construction, a corpse or part of a corpse is within the definition of property in s 4.

We have sought summarily to rehearse Mr Campbell-Tiech's argument lest this matter proceed further. But, as we indicated to him and other counsel in the case, bearing in mind that the submission was not made before the learned trial judge, bearing in mind the way in which the matter proceeded before him and bearing in mind the terms of his certificate to this court, Mr Campbell-Tiech's submission is not one which we shall regard as being in any way determinative of this appeal. We merely comment that the draftsmen of the 1968 Act must presumably have been well aware of the state of the common law for the last 150 years or more, and they do not appear to have made any exception in the 1968 Act by reference to it.

We return to the first question, that is to say whether or not a corpse or part of a corpse is property. We accept that, however questionable the historical origins of the principle, it has now been the common law for 150 years at least that neither a corpse, nor parts of a corpse, are in themselves and without more capable of being property protected by rights (see eg Erle J, delivering the judgment of a powerful Court of Crown Cases Reserved in R v Sharpe (1857) Dears & B 160 at 163, 169 ER 959 at 960, where he said:

'Our law recognises no property in a corpse, and the protection of the grave at common law, as contradistinguished from ecclesiastical protection to consecrated ground, depends upon this form of indictment . . .'

He was there referring to an indictment which charged not theft of a corpse but removal of a corpse from a grave.

> The old rule could have changed if an Act of Parliament had modified or replaced it. Rose believes that the Theft Act 1968 has done so by implication, even though there is no mention of human remains in the Act. The Lord Justice is interpreting the meaning of the Act by assuming that Parliament did not expressly say that body parts could not be stolen, they must have meant that they could be. Reading things into statutes is called statutory interpretation and is one of the most important jobs of the modern judge. Often it is a highly creative process because the judge deals with situations probably never imagined by the person who originally drafted the Act or by Parliament when debating its effects. This next part would seem to form the ***ratio decidendi***. Do you agree?

If that principle is now to be changed, in our view, it must be by Parliament, because it has been express or implicit in all the subsequent authorities and writings to which we have been referred that a corpse or part of it cannot be stolen.

To address the point as it was addressed before the trial judge and to which his certificate relates, in our judgment, parts of a corpse are capable of being property within s 4 of the Theft Act, if they have acquired different attributes by virtue of the application of skill, such as dissection or preservation techniques, for exhibition or teaching purposes: see Doodeward v Spence, in the judgment of Griffith CJ to which we have already referred and Dobson v North Tyneside Health Authority [1996] 4 All ER 474 at 479, [1997] 1 WLR 596 at 601, where this proposition is not dissented from and appears, in the judgment of this court, to have been accepted by Peter Gibson LJ; otherwise, his analysis of the facts of Dobson's case, which appears at that page in the judgment, would have been, as it seems to us, otiose. Accordingly the trial judge was correct to rule as he did.

> Rose observes that "the common law does not stand still". Common law is the law that has evolved out of the decisions of judges over hundreds of years – case law, if you like. The rule in *Reg. v Sharpe* (1857) Dears. & B. 160 is a rule set down by an old appeal court (now replaced by the Court of Appeal (Criminal Division)) and reported in an old collection of law reports named after their compilers (an example of a "nominate report"). Do you think the common law is constantly changing in light of judicial precedent?

Furthermore, the common law does not stand still. It may be that if, on some future occasion, the question arises, the courts will hold that human body parts are capable of being property for the purposes of s 4, even without the acquisition of different attributes, if they have a use or significance beyond their mere existence. This may be so if, for example, they are intended for use in an organ transplant operation, for the extraction of DNA or, for that matter, as an exhibit in a trial. It is to be noted that in Dobson's case, there was no legal or other requirement for the brain, which was then the subject of litigation, to be preserved (see the judgment of Peter Gibson LJ [1996] 4 All ER 474 at 479, [1997] 1 WLR 596 at 601).

So far as the question of possession by the Royal College of Surgeons is concerned, in our judgment the learned judge was correct to rule that the college had possession, sufficiently for the purposes of and within s 5(1) of the Theft Act 1968. We are unable to accept that possession, for the purposes of that section, is in any way dependent on the period of possession, ie whether it is for a limited time, or an indefinite time. In our judgment, the evidence, so far as it was material, before the jury, was to the effect that factually, the parts were in the custody of the Royal College of Surgeons. They were, as it seems to us, in their control and possession within the meaning of s 5(1).

That conclusion is, as it seems to us, reinforced by the judgment of the Court of Appeal in R v Turner (No 2). We do not accept that the passage in Lord Parker CJ's judgment which we have read is to be regarded as limited to the facts of that particular case. In expressing the view that no other word such as 'lawful' was to be read into s 5(1), by reference to possession, that court was construing s 5 entirely consonantly with the construction which we now place upon it for the purposes of this appeal.

There remains the submission as to the judge's direction that the college was in lawful possession of the parts. It is implicit in what we have already said that the lawfulness of the possession was not a matter for necessary inquiry in the trial. There was, as we have said, evidence before the jury as to the fact of possession of these parts, coming from the inspectors of anatomy. Their views as to the law, as we have already indicated, seem to us to be a matter of no relevance or materiality in relation to any issue which the jury had to determine. It follows that it was not necessary for the judge to direct the jury that the college was in lawful possession rather than merely in possession. The question which arises is whether that direction was of a nature to undermine and prejudice the defence of the appellants. We, in the light of the other passages in the summing up in relation to dishonesty which we have already cited, are wholly unpersuaded that that is a tenable view.

It follows that for none of the reasons ably advanced before this court, can the convictions of either of these appellants be regarded as unsafe. Accordingly, the appeals against conviction are dismissed.

Applications for leave to appeal against sentence were referred to the full court, in the case of Kelly by the single judge and, in the case of Lindsay, by the Registrar. We grant both applicants leave to appeal against sentence.

This case presented to the trial judge, and presents to this court, a difficult sentencing exercise, arising, in the first place, from the unique circumstances giving rise to the convictions.

Both appellants are of hitherto good character. Lindsay at the time of the offence, which, it is to be noted, was committed some four or more years ago, was under 21 years of age. The offence in his case gave rise to a breach of trust. The learned judge accepted, that he was motivated not by malice or greed, although he received the not insignificant sum of £400 for doing that which he did. But we accept that financial reward was not his prime reason for doing what he did. His activity was motivated by reasons, however misguided, as to how he thought his employers ought to have been behaving. It is of particular significance in his case that his involvement in these matters came about because he was persuaded to act as he did by a man who was not only considerably older, but who had a considerable force of personality.

So far as Kelly is concerned, as we have said, he too was a man of good character. We are prepared to accept that he had no direct financial motive for doing what he did, and that he was primarily motivated by what he regarded as artistic reasons.

> Rose also considers whether or not Kelly and Lindsay have committed the type of offence that must be punished by imprisonment (a custodial sentence). This is a question about the nature of the crime itself, rather than whether or not it is appropriate to the individuals in the particular circumstances of the case. He concludes that it is a crime that is particularly distasteful and should be punished as such, but also that imprisoning the perpetrators may deter others from doing the same thing.

The first question which arises is whether the circumstances of the case render the offence so serious that only a custodial sentence can be justified, that is, does the offence cross the custody threshold in s 1(2)(a) of the Criminal Justice Act 1991? In our judgment, it does. The theft of a substantial number of body parts, albeit comparatively old body parts is, as it seems to us, something which most members of the general public would view with repugnance. It is, furthermore, an activity which might have a dissuading effect on the mind of someone who was contemplating donating his body for scientific research.

The next question is the length of sentence which the criminality of the particular defendant properly should attract. In R v Ollerenshaw (1998) Times, 6 May this passage appears in the approved transcript of the court's judgment:

'When a court is considering imposing a comparatively short period of custody, that is of about 12 months or less, it should generally ask itself, particularly where the defendant has not previously been sentenced to custody, whether an even shorter period might be equally effective in protecting the interests of the public, and punishing and deterring the criminal. For example, there will be cases where, for these purposes, six months may be just as effective as nine, or two months may be just as effective as four. Such an approach is no less valid, in the light of today's prison overcrowding, than it was at the time of R v Bibi [1980] 1 WLR 1193, 71 Cr App R 360.'

The learned sentencing judge did not have the advantage of those observations before him.

Taking into account the differing roles played by these two appellants, we are of the view that, in the case of Lindsay, a sentence of imprisonment of two months would be appropriate, and in the case of Kelly, who has served already six weeks, a sentence of three months' imprisonment would be appropriate.

So far as Kelly is concerned, we are not able to find that there are exceptional circumstances which would justify the suspension of his sentence. It is true that this was a prosecution which was the first of its kind, but that alone, in our judgment, is not capable of giving rise to exceptional circumstances within the meaning of s 22(2) of the Powers of Criminal Courts Act 1973, as amended by s 5 of the Criminal Justice Act 1991.

So far as Lindsay is concerned, however, because of his age at the time and because his involvement in these matters was due to the pressures brought upon him by the older man, we are with some hesitation, prepared to accept the learned judge's finding, that there were exceptional circumstances in his case, justifying the suspension of the sentence of imprisonment upon him. Accordingly the appeals against sentence in relation to both appellants will be allowed. In relation to Lindsay, the sentence of six months will be quashed. There will be substituted for it a sentence of two months' imprisonment suspended for two years. In the case of Kelly, the sentence of nine months' immediate imprisonment imposed by the learned judge will be quashed and there will be substituted for it a sentence of three months' immediate imprisonment.

> At the end of some cases you will find the following points. It is really just an acknowledgement of the judgment and that the case or proceedings are completed; disposition means the outcome. There is also an acknowledgment of the solicitors' role in the case. Traditionally, only barristers had a 'right of audience' and solicitors would get little recognition in the law reports. The Registrar refers to the administration of solicitors and really the statement of who they are is a mark of respect. It could also be a direction to those using the case report that papers might well be held by the administrative departments which are listed, should they be required at some time in the future.

DISPOSITION:
Appeals against conviction dismissed. Appeals against sentence allowed.

SOLICITORS:
Registrar of Criminal Appeals; Registrar of Criminal Appeals; Crown Prosecution Service.

Reflection Questions

1. Taking into consideration all the facts of the case, do you think what was done by Kelly and Lindsay was wrong?
2. What would have been the broader consequences had they won their appeal (apart from the pair going free)?
3. Do you think this case decides, once and for all, the question of whether you can own or possess part or all of the human body? Why/why not?

How to Read Statute Law

You will now be in the position whereby you are dealing with authorities such as case law and statute law. You should develop your skills in regard to understanding such authorities. One such skill is that of understanding legislation. This requires not only understanding by using an ability to analyse the meanings of the words and phrases, but also an ability to 'interpret' those meanings, just as judges do.

You are probably learning about the rules of interpretation known as the literal rule, the golden rule and the mischief rule. What this chapter does is assist you to apply these particular rules and also look at other sources of interpretation such as intrinsic and extrinsic aids.

Try to think in the context of a judge – what is it that they actually do? They apply the law to the facts and the facts to the law. The advocate will seek to persuade them to a particular view, but it is the judge who must interpret the statute law and determine how it applies in the given situation.

Statutes are primary sources of law. They are known by a number of different names, all meaning the same thing – a statute, an Act of Parliament, an enactment, or the generic term – legislation or legislative provision. The main thing to understand is that they are written law brought into force by Parliament.[3]

Interpreting statutes

Interpreting statutes in the way Parliament intended has difficulties. These are caused by drafting and the nature and complexities of English language. For example, consider the word "bar." You will immediately note that there are a number of obvious different meanings, from a chocolate bar, to a place to get a drink, to being called to the Bar. For these reasons the meaning of a clause or section in a statute and how it applies to a given situation is sometimes unclear. Let's look at s.65A Animal Health Act 1981. You will see is states:

Statute Extract: Animal Health Act 1981

65A Inspection of vehicles
(1) If each of the conditions in subsection (2) is satisfied, an inspector may stop, detain and inspect any vehicle to ascertain whether the provisions of any of the following are being complied with—
    (a) this Act;
    (b) an order made under this Act;
    (c) a regulation of a local authority made in pursuance of such an order.
(2) The conditions are—
    (a) that the vehicle is in a designated area in a designated period;
    (b) that the inspector is accompanied by a constable in uniform.
(3) In subsection (2) "designated" means designated by an order made by the Secretary of State.

---

[3] A good introduction to how Acts of Parliament are passed can be found in chapter 2 of *English Legal System* by Elliott and Quinn (Pearson, 2012).

However, you can see the word 'vehicle' has a certain level of ambiguity to it. To this end, all parts of the section must be read fully. The section might provide some help and guidance as to meanings. This is the case here with s.65A used in the example. Section 65A(4) goes on to state:

> Statute Extract: Animal Health Act 1981
>
> (4) A vehicle includes—
> (a) a trailer, semi-trailer or other thing which is designed or adapted to be towed by another vehicle;
> (b) anything on a vehicle;
> (c) a detachable part of a vehicle;
> (d) a container or other structure designed or adapted to be carried by or on a vehicle.

However, it is still the case that the word 'vehicle' remains ambiguous. For example, does a vehicle have to have an engine? Is it something which is made to carry people from A to B? What if the 'vehicle' is just used to roll along the road without using an engine? Indeed, must a vehicle necessarily travel on a road? You will see these are all questions which arise from the interpretation of the word 'vehicle'.

Approaches to legislation

Judges need to interpret the statutory wording and there are two contrasting schools of thought on how interpretation should be approached –

- **Literal approach:** judge to look solely at the words of the statute and give them their ordinary, literal meaning and make no attempt to look beyond the statute for alternative meaning; and

- **Purposive approach:** allows the judge, in limited circumstances, to look outside the statute itself to find the purpose for which it was enacted and construe the words in accordance with that purpose.

In English law, the literal approach is dominant and the court recognises the limits of its powers by following the wishes of Parliament as expressed in the words of the statute. However, the literal approach in itself is not sufficient and judges use other "rules" to enable them to interpret effectively. There are three primary rules of interpretation which are adopted and a variety of other aids to construction.

This chapter does not aim to teach you the rules themselves; however it would be helpful to remind yourself of the rules as this will form a basis for seeing how the statute can be interpreted in different ways.

The literal rule

In the absence of apparent ambiguity the words in a statute must be given their literal meaning even if this results in absurdity. However, this rule is of little use if the wording is ambiguous or the clause is drafted very broadly.

For example, in the case of *Inland Revenue Commissioners v Hinchy* [1960] AC 748, the Income Tax Act 1952 s.25(3) provided that the defaulting taxpayer should be fined "... *treble the tax which he ought to be charged under this Act*". The question was – did this mean treble unpaid tax or all tax liability for the year? The judge held that phrase was unambiguous and thus the literal meaning of words was that tax payer liable for treble tax payable in that year.

Justification for the literal rule may be that judges are simply following the words of Parliament. Any problems are for Parliament to rectify as Parliament is sovereign not the judiciary. However, this can lead to absurdity and so the judge might look to the golden rule.

The golden rule

Where the ordinary sense of the words leads to a manifest absurdity or repugnancy with the rest of the statute, the apparent grammatical or ordinary sense may be "modified" so as to avoid that absurdity, but no further. Again, the judge must take care. It is not a matter for the judiciary to change meanings of statutes.

For example, *in R v Allen* [1872] LR ICCR 367, Allen, who was already married, married a woman called Harriet Crouch. The OAPA 1861 stated "... *whosoever being married shall marry any other person during the lifetime of his spouse* ... [shall commit bigamy]". Crouch was in fact closely related to Allen and marriage was void on that ground. Allen argued therefore that he had not married Harriet Crouch as in law it was impossible so he had not committed bigamy. The judge interpreted *"shall marry"* as meaning *"going through the ceremony"* because not to do so would have led to an absurd result.

The mischief rule

Where judges experience difficulty with wording in a statute they look at the "mischief" which the statute was intended to remedy. This method is closest to the "purposive" approach. They will look at the facts and make a decision based upon their interpretation of what Parliament actually intended by passing the statute.

For example, *Smith v Hughes* [1960] 1 WLR 830, the Street Offences Act 1959 prohibited soliciting "... *in a public place or street*". A prostitute claimed she was not doing so because she was in her house thus not a public place or street. The judge used the mischief rule and decided the Act was 'intended to stop men being solicited' and that it made no difference from where it took places thus she was convicted.

Reading the statute

Now we have reminded ourselves of the rules of statutory interpretation the first thing to say is that you must look at the statute in two different ways. First, take an overall view and then second, a narrow, more focussed view. The overall view will set the context – what is it that the statute 'says on the tin'?

It is clear that there are many different meanings and also that many different areas of law are covered by similar pieces of legislation so you should try to obtain a basic understanding of the 'nature of the statute'. The second view will assist you to identify which sections are applicable to the problem which has been posed. Ultimately, you must read the whole statute. It is not a question of 'skimming through it', though this might be a good method to isolate the area you need.

The important thing when reading a statute and understanding it is that it is dangerous to only skim and not take account of all the wording and provisions of the statute. So cast your eye over the statute to highlight the main areas for your deeper considerations.

One thing to illustrate is what is known as the Chapter Number. This is usually expressed as the letters 'Ch.' or 'C.' followed by a number. It is used to inform us as to which statute was enacted during the year.

For example, the Appropriation Act 2011 has the Chapter Number 2. This means it was the second statute to be passed in 2011. The Animal Health Act 1981 is Chapter Number 22. This means it is the twenty-second statute to be passed in 1981, and so on. You do not normally have to cite the chapter number when citing the statute in a piece of coursework, though you should check with your lecturer.

It is sometimes difficult to identify which statute you require as the correct authority. To do this, there are a number of intrinsic aids – these are aids to interpretation within the statute itself – such as the short and long title. By reading these you can at least identify the context of the statute and it forms a good initial 'pointer' as to whether you have the correct authority of not. Clearly today using online databases and other electronic sources this is much less problematic than years ago. However, it would still be prudent to 'run your eye over the statute' to ensure you have the correct one.

You should get into the habit of reading all of the statute, where practicable, in order to set context as well as ensuring that you do not miss any important information. The statute may be set out in **Parts** and **Sections**. Parts occur most frequently in large statutes which deal with many different areas however Parliament has determined it fit to put all the areas in one single source[4]. It is then a question of finding which part is the necessary part for your area of law. Then all statutes are set out into sections.

A section is where the wording of Parliament is set out. You might find that the sections break down into sub-sections. The point being made here is that you must read all the relevant sections, including the sub-sections, together as a whole in order to be able to understand the piece of legislation fully. Quite often, you will find that the law is set out in the statute only to find that towards then end there is a section which talks about the jurisdiction.

For example, if you were looking at a factual scenario where you were asked to advise someone living in Belfast about s.65A Animals Act 1981, it would be pointless because this section of the statute does not extend to Northern Ireland. Read it and check.

Should I make notes on the statute?

It can be a good idea to think about the statute and make notes on it, however the problem with this is that it might not assist your understanding or learning and it is also a little 'dangerous' because you should not alter the meanings of the sections.

Therefore, it is a good idea to follow a certain thought process and determine the meaning of the statute by following a set of questions. If you apply these questions to the particular section, you will develop a deeper understanding of it.

Start by asking whether or not this section of the statute is in force. This might not be strictly relevant because if you are doing an academic piece the current position of the section might not matter very much; however if you are reading the statute for a practical or moot exercise then it would be prudent to check whether the section is in force. This can be determined by using the online resource centre or reference to the '*Is It In Force?*' book in the library. Remember that if you use the traditional hard copy library you are required to check with the loose leaf up-daters to see if there have been any amendments to the statute.

---

[4] The Company Act 2006 is a good example of such a huge piece of legislation. Covering the gamut of company law, it contains 1,300 sections within 47 parts, and 16 schedules.

Practical Questions

Once you've found the correct source, keep the following questions in mind:

1. How does the section apply to the situation before me?
2. Are there any words in the section which are or could be ambiguous?
3. Will I be able to ascertain the meanings of the section easily or do I need to look in other areas for assistance such as a dictionary, *Halsbury's Statutes*, a textbook or other cases in which the section was considered?

In following these three questions, you will develop a good and full understanding of the section. This will deepen your learning and assist you to answer questions on the section or put forward information about it in an assignment, examination or other piece of coursework. It will also help you to memorise the basic fundamental points about the section in order that you can recall them more easily at a later date should you be required to do so.

A method of doing this is to consider how the section would be applied in different situations. You might be provided with a number of different scenarios to which you can apply the section however try to think of some yourself. In doing this you will see how the section is interpreted and applied.

Statutory Instruments

Hopefully, you will have heard the term 'statutory instrument'. This is normally a piece of delegated legislation which has been published as a statutory instrument. That is to say, it will have a Parent Act which gives power to a Minister or other body, such as a City Council for example, to 'create' law or, it could be where a section of a particular statute has been drafted by Parliament, however it is not yet in force until the happening of a certain event or the Minster 'see's fit'. Accordingly, it is drafted and enacted as a statutory instrument which has the full force of a primary piece of legislation.

You should take the same approach to reading the statutory instrument as you would with a primary statute itself. They do however, usually differ in their content; you will find that where the provision of a statute sets out the intentions of Parliament and does so with direct wording (which the judge must interpret of course), a statutory instrument might refer to other statutory instruments or provisions of the Parent Act which gave them the power to be brought into force in the first place!

What is the difference then? In general, the statutory instrument is 'limited' and is only capable of being law for a specific purpose i.e. it is not of general application and is only relevant to, for example, road lighting or drinking in a public place, as opposed to the primary statute which would be more concerned with, say, road safety in general or the wider remit of anti-social behaviour and intoxication. You could say that the statutory instrument is a 'small part of a bigger picture'.

Therefore, whilst you should simply read the statutory instrument in the same way as a statute, you should keep in mind that this particular type of provision has a specific application or objective 'as its purpose'.

What this means in practice is that you (generally) need to be aware of the 'wider picture' and other legislation in the particular area of the statutory instrument when reading them in order to understand the context of what you are reading. It is by understanding the context, or the framework of other legislation in the area, that you will be able to understand the statutory instrument.

You will also be able to illustrate that you have researched and considered the wider picture and this is clearly nothing other than good practice and will inform you as to the greater depth of the law. This will help you in tutorials and lectures; it will also inform your knowledge so that you can secure higher grades in assessments.

EU legislation

Do not panic. This is still only a form of legislation. Cleary the contents of the different legislative provisions will have different titles from UK legislation but at the end of the day it is all a similar notion; that of written law.

You can perhaps see quite easily that context will matter here, as well as the fact that EU legislation is applicable in the UK system. But perhaps you can also see that EU law itself (as opposed to UK statute which puts into law Directives to the UK as a member state of the EU) seems to offer a codified and inquisitorial flavour to the contents rather than direct statements about how members of society should conduct themselves or direct indications of the consequences of failure to observe the provisions of a UK statute? This is not always the case of course, but the general terminology of the EU treaty, for example, is different to that of a UK section.

It is simply another style of interpretation and, as with the contextual approach to statutory instruments, you should be aware of the wider remits of EU legislation in order to read it and fully understand it. Indeed, nobody can ignore the legal developments at EU level and as such, you can understand that all member states, and therefore you, must look towards the *purposive approach* of interpretation, most similar to the mischief rule, something which is EU-favoured. The judge will look at the purpose of the law in the statute and not necessarily the literal meanings.

It might also be the case that you should look at the context of the EU provision with sensitivity which is needed to be extended to those additional considerations which are unique to certain member states. For example, driving on the left hand side of the road is a peculiarity of the UK, whilst most other member states drive on the right hand side. This therefore illustrates that there might be a particular member state's idiosyncratic internal values and behaviours and you should be mindful of that fact.

However, in general, the EU legislation, especially EU regulations and Directives, is generally applicable and you should keep an open mind to the purposive approach which will assist your understanding of whichever provision it might be. Indeed, you will find that Directives in particular have a wide impact on domestic legislation and develop new frontiers of law within the member states and the EU as a whole.

But think about this important tip: you can use the same methods of construction and interpretation that we have been investigating for UK legislation as you can for EU legislation.

> **EU legislationn extract: Regulation (EU) No 1169/2011 of the European Parliament**
> (20) Food information law should prohibit the use of information that would mislead the consumer in particular as to the characteristics of the food, food effects or properties, or attribute medicinal properties to foods. To be effective, that prohibition should also apply to the advertising and presentation of foods.

It might appear to be easy to apply and interpret because the Regulation is setting out the definitions. However, ask yourself this – is the standard or type of presentation of foods in the UK the same as you might find, for example, in Spain? Do you also consider that advertising might be a little more, shall we say, "relaxed," in some member states than it is in the UK? The answers could be yes or no, but the point here is that you should interpret the provision in light of the context of application for which you need to apply the law.

The bottom line would most likely be that a Spanish judge would interpret this in a different way than a judge sitting in the UK. What you must ask yourself however is how do you read the provision and interpret its meanings? You simply apply your own values, methodology and purposive approach to achieve the meaning. Does the UK food information law prohibit such things as are stated? Of course it does.

Other Aids to Interpretation

Fortunately, the judge is also able to call into assistance some common sense rules and so can you. These are known as *canons*. They provide help where the interpretation of the statute requires more guidance. There are quite a number of them and you might find more research into this area very interesting. However for our main purposes we will look at three textual canons and the way they will help you to understand the subtle methods by which a statute can be understood.

Ejusdem generis

"Of the same kind/nature". This is applied where a list of specific items is followed in Act by general words. The rule is that the general words should be interpreted as having a similar meaning to those going before. Thus, a statute applying to, for example ". . . *lions and tigers and bears and other animals* . . ." would not apply to domestic cats because the specific items are indicative of *wild* animals.

Expressio unius est exclusion alterius

'The mention of one word in itself rules out a contrary meaning'. This means, for example, if a statute imposed rates on occupiers of "*coalmines*" it would exclude mines which excavated anything other than coal, such as gold mines and lead mines.

Noscitur a sociis

"A thing known by its companions". It means a word must be translated in context. For example, if the wording of a statute stated an offence committed where the defendant "... *stabbed, cut or wounded another*" if the defendant bit the victim, they would not commit the offence because the words "*stabbed*" and "*cut*" implied the use of an implement and, by implication, the word "*wounded*" carries a similar requirement – it is known by the company it keeps.

Human Rights Act 1998

This Act has a persuasion over the whole spectrum of statutory interpretation and you should be aware of it when reading a statute. The Act brought into force the rights contained in the European Convention on Human Rights so that those rights could be enforced in the UK courts. This means that when the judge is interpreting a statute he must do so in "so far as is possible" with those ECHR rights in mind. He will interpret the statute and what you should really focus on here is that he will be thinking about the words of the statute and whether they can be interpreted in a manner which upholds the ECHR.

You can see that this is another "task" for the judge and might make the already potentially difficult task of interpretation even trickier. For your purposes, you should just ask yourself if the words of the statute are "in keeping" with what you consider to be human rights, such as the right to life or freedom of expression and so forth.

If you do this every time you interpret a statute, and make a conscious effort to ask yourself if the words of the statute can be read with ECHR rights in mind, then it will soon become a natural ability for you.

You must note however that even though the wording of a statute can be pulled in all directions to keep in line with the ECHR, the judge must still abide by the language of the statute and if he cannot do so, he will make what is called a "*declaration of incompatibility*" with the ECHR. Parliament might then decide to legislate to bring the statute in line with ECHR rights.

External aids

- **Parliamentary debates:** you refer to Hansard to interpret Parliament's intention. This is a method of looking 'behind the statute' and thinking about what Parliament actually wished to do by the enactment. It is closest linked to the mischief rule.
- **Earlier statutes:** if it is the same subject matter the words in earlier statutes can be used as an aid to interpret new statutes. These may no longer be in force yet they can assist with the interpretation of a current statute.
- **Interpretation Act 1978:** a general statute which provides rules of construction and definitions. It has some very general information and provides a foundation to try to make concepts 'simpler'. Have a look at it and you will see that it aims to set definitions. It is the case that if everybody works to the same general definitions then law might be easier to interpret and apply.
- **Dictionaries:** these will help you just as they do judges. You can use a legal dictionary however the use of dictionaries here really refers to an English language dictionary. After all, it is the word in the statute which you must interpret and understand. The English language is so rich and complex and leads to subtle differences. For example, do you know the difference between the words 'giving' and 'donating'?[5]

---

[5] It's generally fair to say that "giving" would mean presenting something to someone with no expectations for compensation, nor what they elect to do with the gift, whereas "donating" would imply that you expect the recipient to put the gift to a specific (most likely charitable) use.

272 LEGAL CONTEXT, SKILLS AND ETHICS

- **Books of authority:** more than textbooks, these books refer to books used by the court.
- **Government publications:** these will assist you to understand the context of the statute; you can search online and will more than likely find materials which explain statutes or discuss issues in the lead up to the statute being passed.

Internal aids

These are aids to interpretation which you will find contained in the statute itself. Long and short title, Introductory Text (formally known as the preamble), Headings, Side-notes. All these 'aids to interpretation' can be found in the statute itself. You will also find help if you use online resources or Halsbury's Statutes because there might be included a section below called 'annotations' in which you will find information relevant to the section you are reading, including case citations and other materials. This section also contains very useful explanatory notes which will allow you to understand each section in greater detail.

Practical example

We'll now look at an actual piece of legislation. The statute we'll look at is quite brief but will hopefully help you get an understanding of the complexities involved with reading and understanding a piece of statutory legislation. As with the case example above, commentary on this statute is provided in boxes preceding the part of the statute we'll look at.

Once you've read through the Act, answer the questions which follow below.

The first part of the Act gives its short title, followed by its official citation.

Below the citation are the copyright lines.

Then comes the long title, which explains the purpose of the Act. The date in square brackets just below indicates when the Act received Royal Assent.

Finally comes the standard "enacting formula" which is a set of words that tell us that the Bill has become an Act.

Some older Acts also have a preamble before the long title, but this is rare in more recent statutes.

Horses (Protective Headgear for Young Riders) Act 1990

1990 CHAPTER 25

Thomson Reuters (Legal) Limited.

UK Statutes Crown Copyright. Reproduced by permission of the Controller of Her Majesty's Stationery Office

An Act to secure the wearing of protective headgear by children while horse riding; to prescribe offences and penalties; and for connected purposes.

[13th July 1990]

BE IT ENACTED by the Queen's most Excellent Majesty, by and with the advice and consent of the Lords Spiritual and Temporal, and Commons, in this present Parliament assembled, and by the authority of the same, as follows: –

> Next follow the sections of the Act. Larger pieces of legislation may also be divided into parts, with a number of related sections in each. You'll notice that there are many subsections (and sub, sub sections) in the Act. The first section here outlines the offence and already provides some clues as to how the statute should be interpreted. For example, it provides us with the age of the child, along with a steer towards the meaning of "child" by reference to further legislation.
>
> **Note:** Section 1(2)(a)(ii) contains an amendment made to this Act by a later Act [indicated by square brackets]. These crop up frequently in statutes as subsequent legislation regularly affects previously passed Acts. The amending statue is always cited but you should be aware that sometimes an amendment is pending and hasn't been made to the Act in question yet. As such, you should always check to see if there are any amendments outstanding. Fortunately, if there are any, they are clearly indicated on the legislation.gov.uk website at the top of the Act you're looking at.

1. – Causing or permitting child under 14 to ride on road without protective headgear.

(1) Except as provided by regulations, it is an offence for any person to whom this subsection applies to cause or permit a child under the age of 14 years to ride a horse on a road unless the child is wearing protective headgear, of such description as may be specified in regulations, in such manner as may be so specified.

(2) Subsection (1) above applies to the following persons –
  (a) any person who
    (i) for the purposes of Part I of the Children and Young Persons Act 1933, has responsibility for the child; or
    (ii) for the purposes of Part II of the Children and Yong Persons (Scotland) Act 1937, has [parental responsibilities (within the meaning given by section 1(3) of the Children (Scotland) Act 1995) in relation to, or has][1] charge or care of the child;
  (b) any owner of the horse;
  (c) any person other than its owner who has custody of or is in possession of the horse immediately before the child rides it; and
  (d) where the child is employed, his employer and any other person to whose orders the child is subject in the course of his employment.

(3) A person guilty of an offence under subsection (1) above is liable on summary conviction to a fine not exceeding level 1 on the standard scale.

(4) Until the coming into force of paragraph 5 of Schedule 13 to the Children Act 1989, subsection (2)(a)(i) above shall have effect as if for "responsibility for the child" there were substituted "custody, charge or care of the child".

> Section 2 provides details of the scope for providing further delegated legislation.

---

[1] Words substituted by Children (Scotland) Act 1995 c.36 Sch.4 para 51 (November 1, 1996)

2. – Regulations.

(1) The Secretary of State may by regulations made by statutory instrument –
(a) provide that section 1 of this Act shall not apply in relation to children of any prescribed description, or in relation to the riding of horses in such circumstances as may be prescribed;
(b) prescribe for the purposes of that section (by reference to shape, construction or any other quality) the descriptions of protective headgear to be worn by children o any prescribed description in prescribed circumstances; and
(c) prescribe for those purposes the manner in which such headgear is to be worn.

(2) Before making any regulations under this section the Secretary of State shall consult such representative organisations as he thinks fit.

(3) Any statutory instrument containing regulations under this section shall be subject to annulment in pursuance of a resolution of either House of Parliament.

> Section 3 provides some "in-statue" guidance as to interpretation as discussed earlier in this chapter. Again, some definitions are provided by reference to other pieces of legislation.

3. – Interpretation.

(1) In this Act –
"horse" includes pony, mule, donkey or other equine animal;
"regulations" means regulations under section 2 of this Act; and
"road" does not include a footpath or bridleway but, subject to that, has –
(a) in England and Wales the meaning given by section 192(1) of the Road Traffic Act 1988; and
(b) in Scotland the meaning given by section 151(1) of the Roads (Scotland) Act 1984.

(2) For the purposes of the definition of "road" in subsection (1) above –
(a) "footpath" means a way –
(i) over which the public have a right of way or, in Scotland, of passage on foot only; and
(ii) which is not associated with a carriageway;

and

(b) "bridleway" means a way over which the public have the following, but no other, rights of way: a right of way on foot and a right of way on horseback or leading a horse, with or without a right to drive animals of any description along the way.

4. – Corresponding provision for Northern Ireland.

An Order in Council under paragraph 1a(1)(b) of Schedule 1 to the Northern Ireland Act 1974 (legislation for Northern Ireland in the interim period) which states that it is made only for purposes corresponding to those of this Act –
(a) shall not be subject to paragraph 1(4) and (5) of that Schedule (affirmative resolution of both Houses of Parliament); but
(b) shall be subject to annulment in pursuance of a resolution of either House of Parliament.

5. – Short title, commencement and extent.

(1) This Act may be cited as the Horses (Protective Headgear for Young Riders) Act 1990.

(2) This Act, apart from section 4 and this section, shall not come into force until such day as the Secretary of State may by order made by statutory instrument appoint.

(3) Section 4 and this section extend to Northern Ireland, but otherwise this Act does not extend there.

Self-Test Questions

1. How many pieces of legislation were passed before this Act in 1990?
2. Identify which other statutes you'd need to refer to in relation to this Act. Find the relevant statutes at www.legislation.gov.uk
3. Identify the potential defendants who can commit the offence outlined in s.1(1).
4. Under what (if any) circumstances does the Act allow a child under 14 to ride a horse on a road without protective headgear?
5. Which interpretive aid is used in s.3(1)?
   (a) *Ejusdem Generis*
   (b) *Expressio unius est exclusion alterius*
   (c) *Noscitur a sociss*

12
Using Secondary Sources

Stephen Bunbury

Beginning your Research

It is a well known fact that all law students have to undertake legal research using both primary and secondary sources. At first it may seem daunting; however it is a skill that successful law students must develop throughout their studies in order to do well. It is a requirement in assignments to use evidence which is derived from primary and secondary sources. You may find that you spend hours in the library trying to locate relevant secondary sources. This is the norm which requires dedication and patience. Whilst conducting research the library should become your second home even though some of the research can be completed online.

The terminology you encounter may seem difficult at first but once you start undertaking research it becomes easier. Understanding the terminology is crucial in understanding the research process. There are many sources available in the library which make reference to both primary and secondary sources. It is therefore important to understand the difference between the two. This chapter will consider the various types of secondary sources you are likely to encounter whilst conducting research. It will also consider the benefits of starting your research with a secondary source. It should be remembered that the skill of research is not only important whilst studying, but is also a crucial requirement if you intend to practise as a lawyer. Lawyers have to research on a daily basis to keep up to date with the ever increasing changes and developments in the law. Such research will very often involve the consideration and use of secondary sources which means that if you are to practise as a lawyer you will have to be able to research effectively.

What are secondary sources?

Law students must understand the difference between different legal sources and in particular appreciate the difference between primary and secondary sources. A primary source is a term used to describe source material in its raw form without interpretation or commentary. For example, statutory legislation and law reports are considered primary sources in law since there is no interpretation or commentary. In contrast, secondary sources are sources which consist of or include some commentary or interpretation. The commentary or interpretation may or may not be about a primary source. For example an article which discusses the legal issues under the Sale of Goods Act 1979 may contain the actual wording of the Act, or contain certain sections of the Act, but it is the commentary – the author's views and interpretation of the Act – which make the article a secondary source. It must be noted that secondary sources are not 'the law' as such. These sources may include the law, as in the above example, but contain the author's interpretation and commentary. Whilst undertaking research law students will have to make use of both primary and secondary sources.

Secondary sources may also be referred to as 'literary sources'. Holland and Webb have highlighted that:

"The term 'literary sources' is used to describe books about law, as opposed to books of law, which contain 'official' copies of legislation or case reports. Literary sources are sometimes referred to as secondary sources to distinguish them from books of law, which are primary sources. Be careful that you do not confuse the term secondary meaning literary with other uses of the term, particularly in relation to secondary legislation."[1]

Literary sources can therefore include legal encyclopaedias, textbooks, and journals. Accordingly, the difference between a primary and secondary source can be summarised as:

"A primary source is 'the thing' itself, and not someone's interpretation of 'the thing'. Secondary sources (there are tertiary, etc., too) are sources through which others give their opinion or their interpretation of something."[2]

Imagine you are in the first year of your degree and you are asked to write an essay about the advantages and disadvantages of having a jury. You have little knowledge of juries but you decide to start your research by looking at a primary source which is the Juries Act 1974 or the Criminal Justice Act 2003. Will you find any further information by just looking at the statutory legislation? Or for that matter would you even understand the statutes? Would you know which other sources to locate, or be able to appreciate what the contentious issues are? It will be very difficult. It is thus, not only common practice, but indeed advisable to start with a secondary source and then go to the primary source. Approaching the matter in this way will enable you to find background information and put the source into context. It will also make the research process much easier since secondary sources generally give background information to the subject area and may include history or other relevant background material.

In contrast, primary sources will very rarely refer you to other sources unless this is in the form of a law report where some reference may be given to other cases. As such, starting off with primary sources may well limit your research and in turn limit your understanding of a topic. As a result, in order to get the best out of your research, you should start with secondary sources and once you are comfortable with the sources you can then consider the primary source.

---

[1] J. Holland and J. Webb, *Learning Legal Rules* 7th Edition (Oxford University Press 2010) p.39.
[2] L. Webley, *Legal Writing* 2nd Edition (Routledge-Cavendish) p.69.

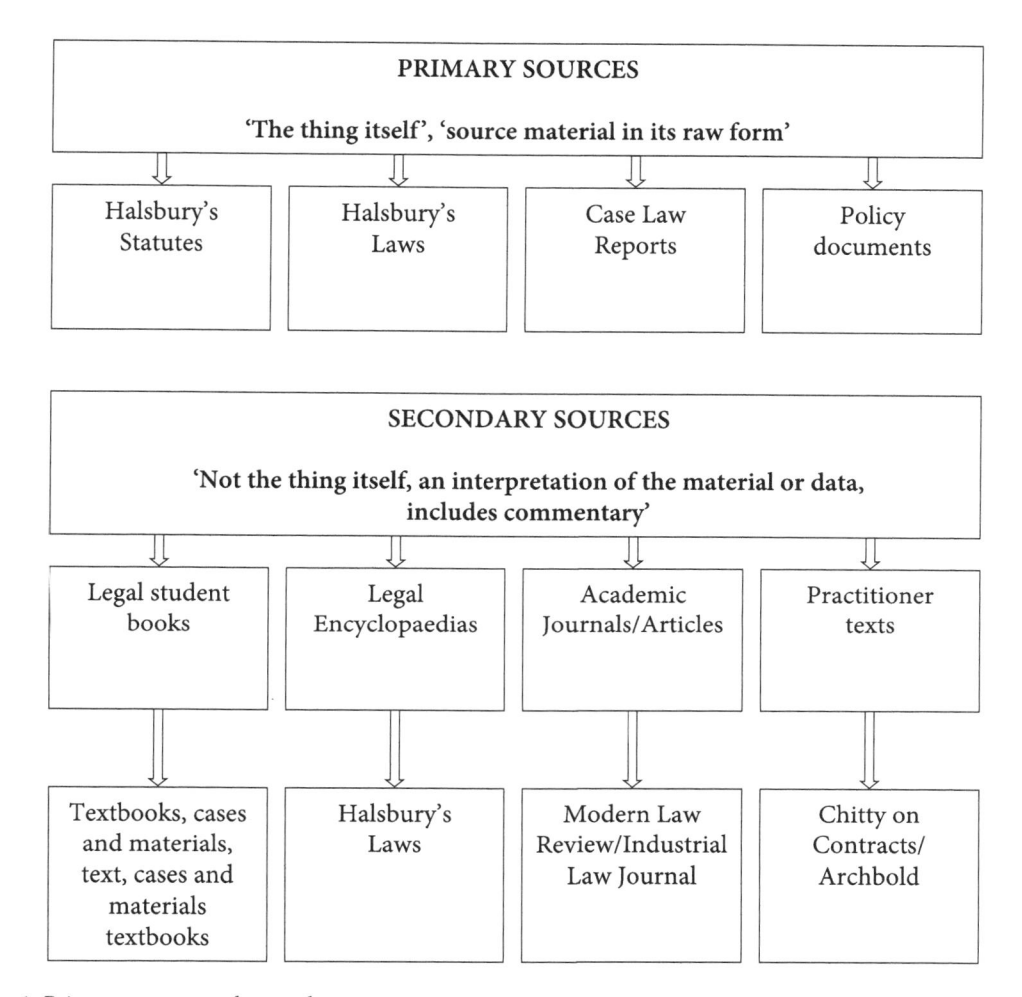

```
┌─────────────────────────────────────────────────────────────┐
│                      PRIMARY SOURCES                        │
│                                                             │
│     'The thing itself', 'source material in its raw form'   │
└─────────────────────────────────────────────────────────────┘
       ⇓              ⇓              ⇓              ⇓
┌────────────┐ ┌────────────┐ ┌────────────┐ ┌────────────┐
│ Halsbury's │ │ Halsbury's │ │  Case Law  │ │   Policy   │
│  Statutes  │ │    Laws    │ │   Reports  │ │ documents  │
└────────────┘ └────────────┘ └────────────┘ └────────────┘


┌─────────────────────────────────────────────────────────────┐
│                     SECONDARY SOURCES                       │
│                                                             │
│  'Not the thing itself, an interpretation of the material   │
│             or data, includes commentary'                   │
└─────────────────────────────────────────────────────────────┘
       ⇓              ⇓              ⇓              ⇓
┌────────────┐ ┌────────────┐ ┌────────────┐ ┌────────────┐
│Legal student│ │   Legal   │ │  Academic  │ │Practitioner│
│   books    │ │Encyclopaedias│ │Journals/Articles│ │   texts   │
└────────────┘ └────────────┘ └────────────┘ └────────────┘
       ⇓              ⇓              ⇓              ⇓
┌────────────┐ ┌────────────┐ ┌────────────┐ ┌────────────┐
│Textbooks,  │ │ Halsbury's │ │ Modern Law │ │ Chitty on  │
│cases and   │ │    Laws    │ │Review/Industrial│ │ Contracts/ │
│materials,  │ │            │ │Law Journal │ │  Archbold  │
│text, cases │ │            │ │            │ │            │
│and materials│ │            │ │            │ │            │
│ textbooks  │ │            │ │            │ │            │
└────────────┘ └────────────┘ └────────────┘ └────────────┘
```

Figure 1: Primary sources and secondary sources

Why use secondary sources?

Secondary sources are not generally regarded as 'authorities' in the strict sense, since they tend to describe or explain the law and consist of academic opinion of the subject area whilst making reference to other materials. However, the use of secondary sources when commencing research will enable you to locate other research material which may include primary and other secondary sources. In some instances secondary sources may be persuasive in court proceedings so using them whilst undertaking legal research is vital.

If you start your research with a primary source it is highly likely that you may get lost whilst researching especially if you have little knowledge of the subject area. To obtain a proper understanding you will need to use more than one secondary source. If undertaking extensive research it may sometimes be a good idea to locate older editions of the secondary sources and then locate the most recent source – this will give you background information on the subject area that may not be included in the latest version of the secondary source. However, you need to be careful when using 'latest editions' since such books may be 1 or 2 years old and the law on a particular issue may have changed since the book was published. Nevertheless, by using a variety of up-to-date (latest edition) secondary sources, the potential for such issues arising should be minimal, since most authors will indicate, where relevant, the possibility of a change in the law after the book has been published. Importantly, having a variety of sources enables you to compare and contrast, which will not only aid your understanding, but will also assist you when deciding whether any of the information is worth using in your research. It is also useful to cross-check these sources against others to ensure the information is correct or accurate. It is thus abundantly clear, that if used properly, secondary sources provide a good basis upon which further research can be built.

However, as a law student you need to realise that because secondary information includes commentary, normally the views of an academic or legal practitioner, this does not necessarily mean that the information is incorrect or outdated; it may just be another view on the subject area. This is where you, as a law student, must decide whether to include such information by weighing up the differing views and deciding whether one particular view carries more weight than the others.

Types of secondary sources

Legal textbooks

It is essential to not only understand the different types of secondary sources but to also understand when to use each source. There are various types of secondary sources which have been illustrated in the diagram above. These include; legal text books for students, legal encyclopaedias, and practitioner texts. It is also necessary to be able to distinguish between the different types of books available since they serve different purposes. Most courses or modules refer students to a reading list or guide which may contain various books. It is therefore important to familiarise yourself with the different types of texts available. There are some texts that have been combined into a textbook and casebook. If you use one of these there is generally no need to purchase a separate casebook.[3] A discussion of the most common types of books you are likely to come across in your studies is set out below.

Law textbooks

Law textbooks are a good source of information but go out of date as soon as they are published. This is why authors produce various editions of textbooks throughout the year. When researching you need to make sure you are using the latest edition of the text. You also need to be aware of when the book was published since the law changes rapidly. Purchasing textbooks can be very expensive and because of this you may be tempted to buy older editions. However you must be careful since the latest versions of textbooks contain the latest legal developments at the time of print. In some cases the law may have changed and therefore using an outdated textbook or casebook may be detrimental since you may be referring to law that is out of date. This is even more important if you qualify as a lawyer as giving the wrong legal advice could result in you being sued for professional negligence.

Textbooks generally give you a structure or framework of a topic area. Depending upon how advanced and detailed a textbook is will determine how critical it is. Some textbooks merely describe the law whilst others go into considerable detail dealing with the criticisms or contentious issues on a particular

---

[3] An example of this is L. Webley and H. Samuels, *Public Law: Text Cases and Materials* and E. McKendrick *Contract Law Text: Cases and Materials*.

subject. You must remember that material in a textbook is an academic opinion on the state of the law and hence why it is regarded as secondary source. Although using a textbook as a basis for your research is recommended, most textbooks will refer you to other sources which may include both primary and secondary sources. This will enable you to research more widely and locate other material which may be relevant to the topic you are researching. A good starting point is to make notes of other sources the textbook may refer you to and read these sources also. Textbooks often refer the reader to articles which is an excellent source of research. Using 'journal articles' will be discussed later in the chapter.

Whilst studying core modules there are numerous textbooks available. However the module team for a particular subject area will provide a recommended reading list. Relying on one textbook throughout your studies is not advisable and will, in most cases, limit your understanding of the subject area. It is good practice to use a variety of sources especially when undertaking research for an assignment which involves in-depth research. There may be textbooks which are highlighted on your module as recommended reading or included in the module reading list and it is one of these that you should generally purchase. It is a good idea to visit the library or bookshop before you purchase a textbook to get a feel for the author's style of writing. By doing this you may find that you are not comfortable with, or understand the author's style of writing. In such a case, it may be advisable, after consulting with your lecturer, to purchase a different textbook.

Casebooks/Cases and materials

Casebooks, which are also referred to as cases and materials, are predominantly used by law students. Casebooks are very useful for reading cases and highlighting the main parts of judgments or statutes. They should however be used in conjunction with a textbook since the casebook will only give you a limited amount of background and structure of the topic as a whole. In some cases certain authors will have a textbook which is published alongside the casebook. Some casebooks may contain article extracts and some may not. Thus, it is not advisable to rely wholly on any casebook for in-depth research, although they can cut down the amount of reading time since they tend to provide the most important parts of a judgment which eliminates having to read the judgment it in its entirety. Be that as it may, when undertaking in-depth research for an assignment it is advisable to read the full judgment.

Legal encyclopaedias

Legal encyclopaedias are another form of texts which are regularly used by both practitioners and law students. There are subject specific encyclopaedias which deal with certain aspects of law and are usually available online or in hard copy. Legal encyclopaedias contain detailed information about a certain legal topic. One of the main legal encyclopaedias you will come across and be required to use is Halsbury's Laws of England and Wales which covers the whole spectrum of English law. It is the only comprehensive narrative statement of the law of England and Wales containing law derived from every source. It is written by or in consultation with leading lawyers, both practitioners and academics. It covers every proposition of English law and is divided into alphabetically arranged titles. It has a monthly and annual updating service and is available in both hard copy in your institution's library and online.

You should be familiar with this encyclopaedia since you may need to use it to undertake research on an unfamiliar area, or on a novel point of law. It contains a plethora of footnotes and additional supplements, which refer to, amongst other things, primary sources and other useful references for further research.

Dictionaries

Legal dictionaries provide definitions of certain terms and can be very useful. There are various legal dictionaries which are available, and it is advisable to have one since these help define not only complex legal terms, but also Latin terms and phrases which are used heavily in law. Some of the legal terms may seem difficult to grasp, however once you know the meaning it provides a platform which aids understanding. The advanced legal dictionaries such as *Black's Law Dictionary* contain various tables which may include further definitions as well as abbreviations of terms. They may also make reference to particular cases or statutes and sometimes give specific examples of the phrase or phrases in use.[4]

As you will come to realise, law books are often written in a rather forbidding style – perhaps an inevitable consequence of the subject matter or of the particular style of writing of the author. As a result, every law student will need to be equipped with at least 1 comprehensive conventional dictionary. Conventional dictionaries offer an excellent introduction into the 'world of words' and their different meanings and uses. After all, understanding and applying the law rests upon an understanding and appreciation of the words that make up the law. You will find, unless you happen to blessed with an encyclopaedic knowledge of words and their different meaning and uses, that a conventional dictionary will become the most used book throughout your studies. Your law library will have a copy of the *Oxford Shorter English Dictionary* – the standard reference work for modern English and its history. It is unlikely that you will come across a word which cannot be found in the *Oxford Shorter*. There are of course other excellent dictionaries, including; the standard *Oxford Reference Dictionary*, the *Chambers Reference Dictionary*, and the *Collins Dictionary* any of which will serve all law students equally well.

Study aids

There are various study aids available. However you should not rely on them heavily. In order to get a proper understanding of the subject you should use the materials recommended in your course or module handbook. Study aids and revision guides are only helpful for consolidating your knowledge in a subject area – if a core module could contain the content of that found in a revision guide or study aid why are the textbooks so detailed? It is clear that these aids do not have enough detail to be used as your main reading material and even worse as a main textbook, although it is acknowledged that they can provide an overall structure of the subject area. So if you do choose to use them, use them with caution. There are various study aids available such as Law Express, Law Cards and Questions and Answers.

Monographs

It is important to distinguish between monographs and textbooks. A textbook discusses and criticises general areas of a subject area. However a monograph covers a subject area but goes into particular detail about a certain topic. For example in criminal law a specific topic such as theft could be covered in great detail. The detail which a monograph may cover may be that expected of a PhD thesis.

Journals

There are various types of journals available in a law library. Journals are also often referred to as periodicals and are published weekly, monthly or at various points in the year. Journals have editorial boards which assess each article and most reputable journals will have a peer review process which scrutinises each article

---

[4] There are also judicial dictionaries which are available. These dictionaries contain words or phrases that judges have interpreted in a particular way.

submission. Most journals contain a synopsis of the articles which means you can find out whether any of the articles will be relevant for your purposes without having to read each article in full.

There are broadly two categories of journals available; professional journals and academic journals. Professional journals provide information and updates for practitioners on current legal issues and may be related to a specific legal area such as Criminal Law, or Housing Law or more general with articles on topical legal issues across a range of different subject areas. They are published regularly and the articles tend to be shorter than those found in academic journals. Examples of professional journals include; *The Lawyer*; *The Law Society Gazette*, and the *New Law Journal*.

Academic journals, which are generally directed at students and academics, contain articles which discuss particular legal issues in-depth and provide critical commentary and analysis. These types of journals provide an excellent source of research and are particularly useful when undertaking research for assignments or coursework. An example of a popular academic journal is *The Modern Law Review*. The use of academic journals also demonstrates that you have undertaken broad research, and if used properly further demonstrates that you have reached reasoned conclusions based on evidence. Once you have used the journal articles in your piece of work it is important to weigh up the evidence and reach a reasoned conclusion. It may be that your conclusion suggests that the law is in a complete mess or is unclear. However, this must be evidenced by the academic opinion you get from academic articles. It is important to have your own views; however you need to be aware that it must be backed up by reliable sources. Academic journal articles can serve this purpose.

Journals may also include case notes on particular cases. Case notes provide you with detailed discussion about a case and gives analysis or viewpoints which may be worth including in your work. Using journal articles gives you a broad understanding of the subject and may include other issues that would not have been apparent without reading the article. When using an idea from an article it is sometimes a good idea to paraphrase.[5] Even though quotes may be useful in a piece of work, in some cases, it may not add any value to the work – therefore use quotes when you need to. A typical use of a quote in a piece of work is to use it as evidence for a particular proposition or assertion. However, using a string of quotes throughout your piece of work will not add much value to you assignment. An important part of the marks in an assignment is for the use of your analytical skills – relying heavily on quotes without analysis does not demonstrate this skill. So if you use a quote make sure you explains its purpose, and more importantly make sure it relates to the question and has not been used to simply make up the word count or because you are trying to impress the person who is marking your work. They will know whether this is the case since they see many pieces of work and will have extensive experience of marking. It is also advisable to use a variety of academic journals since this will demonstrate extensive research.

It is good practice to read a journal in full but whilst researching it is not advisable to read every journal you locate that you think may help you during your research. You should become familiar with the structure of an article as this enable you quickly decide whether the article is relevant for the research you are undertaking. The diagram below illustrates the structure of an article. It must be noted that the journals themselves are not the law but can be used as evidence. Moreover, journal articles include authoritative material which consists of primary sources. Reading both the abstract and conclusion can help you decide whether to read a particular article in full.

---

[5] Paraphrasing is *'reading what someone else has written. Putting the source to one side (so that you do not inadvertently copy it) and then summarising the essence of what they have said entirely in your own words. Then providing a reference to the original source.'* L. Webley, *Legal Writing* 2nd Edition (Routledge-Cavendish 2010) p.81.

Name of journal/volume/date/page number/publishers This usually appears on the top of the first page and may appear on every page depending on the journal. It can be either printed on the top of the page or at the bottom. It is important to make a record of this information for referencing and citation purposes. It may be useful if you have to locate the source again.
Title of article This usually gives you an idea about the content. However in some cases the article may contain other relevant information which may not be in the title.
Name of author This gives you the name of the authors and usually some reference to their academic position and where they teach or practice. Some articles have a footnote detailing the author affiliation, but others may include the lecturer's details in the main text.
Abstract This usually provides a brief synopsis in relation to the content of the article and may include reference to the relevant statutory material or cases which the article considers. However this is normally a summary but please note that not all abstracts are short. Some journals may include abstract as part of their house style and others may not. There may also be a key words section.
Body 1. **Introduction:** This section introduces the topic and may give some background material about the topic. It highlights the main theme that will be discussed throughout the article. The introduction prepares the reader as to what will be discussed throughout the article. 2. **Main body:** The main body discusses the main themes, arguments or contentious points throughout the article. The main body usually makes reference to other research materials. 3. **Conclusion:** The conclusion in an article normally summarises the main points discussed in the main body of the article. It may include proposals for reform. It can be used if you don't want to read the whole article, however if you are not familiar with the subject matter or area reading the conclusion first may be confusing. 4. **Bibliography/references:** This section includes sources the author has used throughout the article. However again the referencing style may differ according to the journal.
Referencing and citation Journal house styles differ depending on the journal. Some journals may prefer endnotes or footnotes. These normally give you the reference of a particular source an author has used or further reading. It may also include further information.

Figure 2: Structure of article (structure may vary depending on the journal)

Practitioner texts

Another form of text book you are likely to encounter is the practitioner text. As the name suggests, this is a book that is used principally by practising lawyers. As with student textbooks there is a corresponding major practitioner text for each legal area. However, in contrast to student textbooks, practitioner texts contain comprehensive coverage of the particular subject area (very often including the rules of the court and procedure) rather than selected topics which are likely to be found on most law degrees. They also contain a multiplicity of decisions – in some cases first instance decisions – as well as frequent updating supplements. It is unlikely that you will be regularly referred to a practitioner text, but it is important to

Table 1 – Subject area and types of journals

Subject area	Journal name	Frequency
Tort (Obligations 2)	Journal of Personal Injury	4 issues per year
Public Law	Administrative Court Digest	6 issues per year
Criminal Law	Criminal Law Review	Monthly
	Criminal Law Week	46 issues per year
European Union Law	European Law Review	6 issues per year
	European Current Law	Monthly
	European Human Rights Law Review	6 issues per year
Land Law	Conveyancer and Property Lawyer	6 issues per year
	Landlord and Tenant Reports	Quarterly

appreciate the differences if you come across them when researching. You should also note that practitioner texts rarely contain detailed theoretical discussion on novel or obscure points of law, or of different academic debates about a decision of the court. For this you will need to refer to the student textbooks and relevant journal articles. Some examples of major practitioner texts include; *Chitty on Contracts, Clerk & Lindsell on Torts*, and *Goff & Jones The Law of Restitution*.

Keeping up to date

As a law student it is crucial to keep up to date with current legal affairs. This can be achieved by regularly listening to the news on television or by listening to the radio. Similarly, reading the newspaper (a broadsheet such as *The Times* or *The Guardian*) is another way of keeping up to date with current legal affairs. Some broadsheets will have sections dedicated to legal affairs, as well as reports and commentary on certain decisions of the courts as found in *The Times*. Though newspapers are a very good source of secondary information, it should be remembered that they are, more often than not, writing about the law from a particular perspective with different aims and objectives to those of a textbook or a journal article. Moreover, it is not usual practice to cite newspaper articles in assignments or coursework, unless perhaps there is a current issue that may not have been reported in a journal – in this case it may be appropriate to cite the newspaper article.[6] Nevertheless, your research should predominantly include legal textbooks and academic articles.

The Internet contains a vast amount of material, much of which is not checked. For this reason carrying out a Google search as your principal research method is inadvisable. Such a search may locate material which is outdated, or inaccurate, or it may contain information that is only relevant to a particular country. It is also difficult to confirm the reliability of information, especially information that is found in articles on the Internet. If you were to try and confirm the reliability of such information, you would arguably have to embark on a further research campaign to confirm the accuracy of the information which is likely to result in an unnecessary waste of your time. For instance Wikipedia provides a vast amount of

---

[6] It must be noted that newspapers may report in a way which contains political bias, therefore you need to be aware of this if you are using them in your piece of work.

information on all topics but it is not edited or updated and anyone can upload content to the website. Therefore any material obtained from a site like Wikipedia has to be treated with absolute caution. As discussed earlier the best way to start your research is by using textbooks and then using an online database such as LexisNexis, Westlaw, or HeinOnline, all of which contain both primary and secondary sources. You will therefore need to be aware of the legal databases your institution has subscribed to. If you do use Google to carry out research the most effective method is a Google scholar search.

It should be pointed out that there are in fact many websites which give access to various materials free of charge, an example of this is the Equality and Human Rights Commission. Similarly government policy reports from academic or political commentators are also freely available online.

How do I check the credibility of a secondary source?
- Check the author's affiliation and standing in the legal field.
- Does the author include any analyses or conclusions in the document?
- Do they contribute something original or discuss a particular contentious issue in detail which adds value to a particular area of law?
- Does the author provide evidence for their points and is the evidence based on other academic or practitioners' views from publications or reports?
- Does the content of the article include an interpretation of a primary source and include in-depth research?
- Is the source up-to-date and reflect the current state of law?

Advantages and disadvantages using secondary sources
Legal textbooks are usually used by undergraduate and postgraduate students. They are very rarely used in court. There are advantages and disadvantages with using student textbooks. Firstly they are quite expensive to buy however they can form the basis for your research which may make it much easier later on during the research process. Student textbooks also refer you to other sources, therefore doing some of the research for you, which in turn saves you time. Using the latest editions of textbooks normally keeps you abreast of the most recent developments relating to the subject area. Textbooks undergo a review process which asks specialists in the area to comment on content, relevance and accuracy of the law. This is useful for the author when they are publishing another edition since they are able to incorporate any necessary amendments or additions identified. This reason alone justifies the purchase of the latest edition of a textbook.

Self-Test Questions
1. Define a secondary source.
2. List three different types of secondary sources.
3. Is Halsbury's Law a primary or secondary source? Give reasons for your answer.
4. What are the main differences between a casebook and a textbook?
5. Are secondary sources authoritative?

Practical Questions

1. Do you know the difference between a biography and autobiography? If not, look up these terms in a conventional dictionary and distinguish between the two. Are these primary or secondary sources?

2. Have a look at the abstract in the article below and see if you can summarise the main points the article is going to consider.

3. How would you be able to identify whether this article (below) was worth reading for an assignment?

4. Imagine you were asked to write an essay on whether the police have too many powers. How would you start your research?

5. What does the abstract tell you about the content of the article?

6. Does this article contain footnotes or endnotes?

Example: Extract from International Journal of Discrimination and the Law, 2009, Vol. 10, pp. 111–131

International Journal of Discrimination and the Law, 2009, Vol. 10, pp. 111–131
1358-2291/2009 $10
© 2009 A B Academic Publishers. Printed in Great Britain

THE EMPLOYER'S DUTY TO MAKE REASONABLE ADJUSTMENTS. WHEN IS A REASONABLE ADJUSTMENT, NOT REASONABLE?
STEPHEN BUNBURY
Lecturer in Law, University of Westminster Law School

ABSTRACT

This article considers the impact of the reasonable adjustments duty imposed upon employers in section 4A of the Disability Discrimination Act (1995) where a provision, criterion, practice, or physical feature of the premises of the employer places the disabled person at a substantial disadvantage in comparison with persons who are not disabled. It considers that while the duty to make reasonable adjustments has contributed to the rising rates of employment among disabled people, an examination of the Employment Tribunal and EAT Statistics (GB) conversely reveals that there has been a steady increase in cases of disability discrimination in recent years. It is argued that the complexity of section 4A and the ensuing case law have contributed to the rising tide of cases in this field and is a trend which is likely to continue for the foreseeable future.

1. INTRODUCTION
Research findings in the United Kingdom had long established that disabled people, whom account for nearly one fifth of the working age population[1], face discrimination and barriers to equal participation and opportunity in employment.[2] Yet until the introduction of the Disability

Discrimination Act ("the Act") in 1995, disabled people were afforded no protection whatsoever from disability discrimination. The passing of the Act therefore marked a major milestone in the development towards the full protection of disabled people's rights in the employment context. The broad aim of the Act is to provide comprehensive anti-discrimination legislation for disabled people, throughout all stages of the employment relationship (recruitment to dismissal).[3] It may also apply after employment has ended.[4] Insofar as employment is concerned, Part 2 of the Act is based on the principle that disabled people should not be discriminated against in employment or when seeking employment.[5]

5. CONCLUSION

The decision in *Archibald* and its complex interpretation of 'arrangements' leaves the precise limits of the notion unclear. Taken together with the existing well-known legal technicalities and difficulties in bringing a successful claim under the Act, not least the need for an individual to show a disability within the meaning of the Act, claimants now face the 125 additional hurdle of needing to show that their employer or potential employer was aware of their disability. Having done so, they must then make their claim fit within the framework of the section 4A duty to make reasonable adjustments.

Moreover, the personal nature of the duty to make reasonable adjustments means that employers are left with no legal incentive to be proactive in removing barriers to the full participation of disabled people in the workplace. The requirement of knowledge reinforces the reactive nature of the reasonable adjustment duty and likewise places no obligation on employers to consider adjustments until they are confronted either by an applicant, or employee whom they know, or ought to know, to be disabled and to be exposed to a substantial disadvantage as a result of their provisions, criteria, practices or physical features.

What is more, as mentioned above, an interpretation of knowledge in line with the case of *Ridout* would not give proper effect to the Equality Directive, the purpose of which is to ensure equality of opportunity and participation in the workplace for disabled persons. Unfortunately, it seems there is still some considerable way to go before such ambitions are fully realised.

ACKNOWLEDGEMENTS

I would like to thank Professor Andy Boon and Dr Lisa Webley who commented on drafts of this article, as well as Leroy Bunbury for his suggestions on a later draft.

NOTES

1. Evans, S. *"Disability, Skills and Work: Raising our ambitions"*. (2007), The Social Market Foundation, page 3.
2. As well as in education, health and social services, housing and transport, leisure and social activities and civic rights.
3. Discrimination in other areas such as Goods, Facilities and Services are regulated under Part III. Discrimination in Education is regulated under Part IV and Discrimination in respect of Public Transport is regulated under Part V.
4. DRC. *"Code of Practice Employment and Occupation"* para 5.5.
5. *Ibid* at 4 para 1.1.
6. *Ibid* at 4 para 2.2. For a discussion see Barnes, C. *"A Case for Anti-Discrimination Legislation"* 2nd edition, C, Hurst & Co (Publishers) Ltd, page 1.

Practical Questions

Read the extract from Wilson, *Criminal Law*, 4th edition and answer the following questions:

1. Imagine you were given an essay title that required you to compare subjective and objective fault for a Criminal Law essay. How would you use this text to help you research further?
2. Does this textbook contain enough material to produce an essay?
3. Look at footnote nine. What is the purpose of this footnote?
4. How would you use the information in footnote nine to conduct further research? Locate the information in footnote nine. How easy was it to locate?
5. What does the abbreviation mean in the footnote? If you were unsure how would you find out?
6. Look at the article and extract from the textbook? What are the main differences between them? Are they both authoritative?

Example: Extract from *Criminal Law*, Wilson, 4th edition (Pearson Education Limited, 2011); pp. 124–6

6.3 Subjective and objective fault

If freely choosing to do wrong is the basis for desert in punishment then one would expect liability to be predicated upon the prosecution proving the existence of some form of mental state, for example intention, knowledge, or awareness, on the part of the wrongdoer. This mental state or attitude accompanying wrongdoing is termed subjective fault. The accused is at fault in having this state of mind. If bad character is the basis for desert in punishment, proof of an accompanying mental attitude is not so crucial. People can show bad character through their actions both by thinking and by *not* thinking of the wrongfulness of their action. So, A shows subjective fault by directing his car at his enemy in order to kill him. His mental state is that of intention. A shows objective fault by driving his car in such a way that ordinary reasonable people would realise, although he did not, that he was subjecting other road users and pedestrians to the unjustified risk of harm. We term this type of fault negligence. Negligent conduct is blameworthy not on account of the actor choosing to do wrong but on account of the fact that he fails to behave like ordinary people.

It is not universally accepted that criminal responsibility should depend upon proof of subjective fault.[9] On the one hand, it will usually be difficult to prove what was in a person's mind at the time of acting. They may not even know themselves. On the other, requiring subjective fault ignores the fact that sometimes we feel justified in blaming people lacking a criminal 'intent'. People who fail to consider the ways in which their conduct may affect others distance themselves morally from reasonable people. They exhibit a dangerous and perhaps frightening character defect. It is perhaps not surprising that criminal doctrine reflects an uneasy tension between these two forms of fault.

Increasingly, statutes comprise fault elements which do not require proof of a subjective mental element. A recent example in which objective fault suffices for criminal liability is the (statutory) offence of rape. Under the common law the fault element of rape was recklessness, which was defined so as to require subjective fault. The prosecution bore the burden of proving that the accused did not honestly believe the victim to be consenting, that is, of proving an attitude of mind. Under the new definition the prosecution task is easier since the accused's belief in the fact of consent must now be a reasonable one. The jury are entitled to discount the accused's honest belief, in other words, if the circumstances are such that reasonable people would not have formed such a belief. People who do not take care to ensure others are consenting to their sexual advances or harbour unrealistic ideas about 'what women want' are blameworthy precisely because they are inexcusably out of step with society's core values of respect for others.

It is important, therefore, when analysing individual crimes, to interpret whether the fault required by the offence is subjective or objective. As a rule of thumb, the more serious the crime the more likely it is that subjective fault will be required although, in truth, the difference between subjective and objective fault may be more apparent than real.

Case 1 Adam is observed to drive his car at full tilt towards Eve while she is crossing the road. As she moves to avoid the impending crash Adam is seen also to change direction. He hits and kills Eve. Adam claims that he did not intend to kill Eve but only to frighten her. He did not even think she might get hurt.

If Adam's claim is to be believed he cannot be guilty of murder, which is a crime of intention (subjective fault). However, can we believe him? The evidence stacks up against him. Not only was he driving at full tilt towards Eve, he changed direction just before hitting her. The prosecution may think that this is good enough evidence to show an intention to kill. The facts seem to speak for themselves. The prosecution might well therefore charge with murder, relying on the jury's good sense to infer a subjective state of mind (intention) from objective facts (manner of driving). In other words Adam may well be found guilty of murder whether the fault element in murder is objective or subjective. We tend to ignore what people say they intended or foresaw, when this is out of step with our experience.

It should be noted that the vast majority of criminal offences do not require proof of fault, objective or subjective. Many traffic offences, say, are constituted simply upon proof of the relevant conduct, for example parking in the wrong place or failing to display a tax disc. This is out of step with the ethic discussed earlier that censure and punishment should be deserved and should be limited to those who are blameworthy. Indeed it may serve to undermine this ethic. The position is complicated by the fact that Parliament often will not indicate one way or the other whether an offence is one of strict liability or requires proof of fault. In such circumstances, as will be seen in the next chapter, the courts may nevertheless interpret the provision as requiring a fault element. So, in *B v DPP*, the accused was charged under section 1 Indecency with Children Act 1960 with inciting a girl under 14 to commit an act of gross indecency. The accused claimed that he believed the girl to be over 14. Although there is no mention in the Act of any fault element he argued that, given the gravity of the offence, the Act should be interpreted to require one. The House of Lords, quashing the conviction, agreed that Parliament should be presumed to have intended a fault element in the absence of words to the contrary. It should be noted that the (implied) fault element was subjective fault. His belief that the girl was over 14 did not have to be a reasonable one.

---

[9] For an example of judicial scepticism as to its merits see the judgment of Lord Diplock in *Caldwell* [1981] 1 All ER 961.

Using Secondary Sources: Further reading

A. Bradney, F. Cownie, A. Neal, and D. Newell, *How to Study Law*, 6th Edition (Sweet & Maxwell 2010)

H. Carr, S. Carter, and K. Horsey, *Skills for Law Students* (Oxford University Press 2009)

S. Cottrell, *The Study Skills Handbook*, 3rd Edition (Palgrave Macmillan 2008)

S. Cottrell, *Critical Thinking Skills* (Palgrave Macmillan 2005)

P. Clinch, *Using a Law Library*, 2nd Edition (Oxford University Press 2001)

E. Finch and S. Fafinski, *Legal Skills*, 3rd Edition (Oxford University Press 2010)

E. Higgins and L. Tatham, *Successful Legal Writing* (Sweet & Maxwell 2006)

J. Holland and J. Webb, *Learning Legal Rules*, 7th Edition (Oxford University Press 2010)

R. Huxley-Binnd, L. Riley and C. Turner, *Unlocking Legal Learning*, 2nd Edition (Hodder Education 2008)

J. Knowles and P. Thomas, *Effective Legal Research*, 1st Edition (Sweet & Maxwell 2006)

A. Smith, *Glanville Williams: Learning the Law*, 14th Edition (Sweet & Maxwell 2010)

L. Webley, *Legal Writing*, 2nd Edition (Routledge-Cavendish 2010)

13
Finding Secondary Sources
Stephen Bunbury

The nature and importance of secondary sources

Secondary legal sources are materials which outline the law, but are not the *actual* law in and of themselves, and which generally comment on legislation or case law. Secondary sources include textbooks, cases and materials books, monographs, practitioners' texts, legal encyclopaedias, dictionaries, revision guides, and academic and professional journals. Many of these types of materials can be accessed both as hard copies and online.

Using secondary sources is an essential element of your studies and fully engaging with these (along with the primary sources of law) is the only way to achieve the highest grades. As such, the ability to find, understand and utilise secondary sources are crucial skills you must develop. This chapter will deal with the former: how to effectively find relevant secondary sources.

Given the huge volume of literature concerned with law, the idea of tracking down the secondary sources you need may sound like a hard task at first. However, as with any skill, the key to mastering it is practice: the more you do it, the easier it will get. It's often the case that many students' first attempt at independently finding secondary sources will be when they need to research around a formal assignment such as an essay. However, the first tip is to start practising the skills we'll discuss here right away, when there are no assessments looming. By beginning to develop this skill early, your ability to find relevant materials will be that much better than they would if you waited for the first assessment period to come along. This will, in turn, save you a lot of time and, just as importantly, stress at assessment time!

Where to start

As mentioned, the amount of secondary legal source material available to law students, academics and practitioners is vast – frighteningly vast. However, you will be presented with numerous starting points when it comes to finding relevant secondary materials for your studies. The first of these will be your module guide. Among the details of what the module will cover, learning outcomes and so on, the module guide will also provide reading lists. It's likely that the module leader will have selected one or two course textbooks that s/he suggests you might want to use throughout the duration of the module, along with further reading, which may include journal articles or monographs, pertinent to each of the topics that will be covered throughout the course.

Course textbooks are essential secondary sources which provide an initial point of reference and which introduce you to the key elements of the subject you're about to study. Often, the name of the subject area the module covers will feature in the textbook title, but they are generally referred to by the author's last name. For example, *Law of Contract* by Paul Richards, might simply be referred to as "Richards." Textbooks are your first port of call (in terms of secondary sources) when dealing with a given topic. Your lecturer may well instruct you to read a chapter which covers a certain aspect of a module before a lecture or seminar on that area, so that you've got a sense of what's what ahead of more detailed analysis or discussion in the classroom.

Owing to the constraints around textbook extent, they simply cannot cover *everything* that you'll need to know about a given subject, however, the textbook(s) that you decide to use will provide you with numerous pointers as to further secondary resources that will develop your understanding of that subject. They might take the form of footnotes in the text where, for example, the author identifies another resource which examines the point they've looked at in more detail.[1] Other secondary sources may be referenced directly in the main body of the textbook itself, for example:

> *"One of the leading proponents of this view is Richard Abel, Professor of Law at the University of California. His book on the legal profession in England and Wales (1988) describes in great detail how solicitors and barristers have controlled who become lawyers, how they operate and what they sell. He suggests that they have done this in their own interests to keep the price of legal services high."*[2]

Increasingly, student textbooks have a detailed further reading section at the end of each chapter which list yet more secondary sources that will help you research around, or increase your understanding of, the subject matter that particular chapter deals with.

So imagine that as part of your contract law module you've been set an essay around the formation of a contract, which asks you to focus on offer and acceptance in particular. Your first step would be to identify the keywords the essay has asked you to consider (in this case, "contract," "formation," "offer" and "acceptance"). You'd then want to find the relevant section or chapter in your course textbook by using the extended table of contents and also the index. Then read what the chapter has to say around those areas, making a note of any references to journal articles etc listed that are pertinent to the question you've been asked. Already, you're finding secondary sources (or at least their titles) – now it's going to be a case of getting your hands on them.

The library

There are numerous secondary sources available in the library and remotely. Some libraries are now referred to as Learning Resource Centres but don't let the terminology put you off – a Learning Resource

---

[1] Of course, footnotes will also regularly refer you to the key cases and legislation around a particular area of law, but this chapter is just dealing with secondary sources, so I've not mentioned them in the main body.
[2] C. Elliott and F. Quinn: *English Legal System* 12th edition (Pearson 2011) p.214.

Centre serves the same purpose as a traditional library: that is to assist individuals whilst conducting research and studying. The law library is invaluable in helping you conduct legal research so the first thing to do is to get to grips with the physical layout of the library building. Just about all university libraries will run some training or orientation programmes around this that you'll be expected to attend, but if not just ask and someone will undoubtedly help.

The library catalogue

The library catalogue is the best place to start when locating secondary sources. It is, essentially, a database which holds details of all the legal materials available within a particular institution and will contain textbooks, journals and other reference material. It is advisable to get used to using the catalogue as soon as you're able and to use it regularly to ensure you're familiar with the way it works and the search functions within it. The library catalogue, depending on the institution, may also tell you where you can locate materials that are not held in that particular library.

Most university libraries have remote access via the internet which enables you to access library information whilst not actually in the library itself. You can access this at any time of day which is convenient and enables you to search for materials at your leisure. It may be that some materials will only be available in hard copy so, clearly, it will be necessary to visit the library to pick them up. That said, however, the catalogue should also indicate whether copies of a particular title have already be loaned out, so accessing the catalogue from home could save you an unnecessary trip if you find that the title you want is currently unavailable for loan. If you're looking for a textbook you should be aware that the library catalogue or the library search may include various earlier editions of that particular textbook so it is important to ensure you pick the latest edition which will be the most up to date in terms of any pertinent legal developments.

A library catalogue search will likely operate much like the kinds of search engine you're probably already familiar with when using the internet. The interface may look slightly different and the search terms might differ but you'll (hopefully) be pleasantly surprised at how similar these can be.

Bibliographic data

Before getting on to searches, it's important to briefly cover the way that the catalogues hold data on the titles available. Essentially, the catalogue is just a database and each record has information about it stored in various "fields". Some common fields might be as follows:

- Title – quite simply, the title of the book/article/paper etc
- Author – the author name
- Keywords – a collection of terms which broadly outline what the title examines
- ISBN – International Standard Book Number, a unique number which identifies a particular title
- ISSN – International Standard Serial Number, as for ISBN but for journal articles
- Subject – the subject area that the title deals with
- Journal title – the title of the journal a given article appears in
- Type – many libraries hold all sorts of resources (including tapes, CDs, CD-ROMs)
- Publication year – the year in which the title published

Basic and advanced searches

When you bring up a library catalogue page you'll probably be given a "basic" search option by default. This, just like a basic search on an internet search engine will take the terms you enter and look for anything within the library containing those specific words somewhere within their bibliographic data. If you know precisely the resource you're looking for then this is often the easiest search to use. For example, if you were looking for the book *Human Rights and Civil Liberties* by Steve Foster then simply typing "human rights civil liberties foster" into the basic search should return a manageable handful of results for you to look through and quickly identify the title you want.

It's also likely that the catalogue will have an advanced search functionality, just like those on regular search internet engines, which allows you to break your query up using various parameters. These would most likely be the same fields as the titles' bibliographic data are organised (author, title, etc).

Substitution and truncation

Let's say you're researching around the historical legal rights of women. It may be that you wish to search for both "woman" and "women" at the same time. Of course, you could enter both terms but most catalogues will allow you to use a "wildcard" – a symbol which represents any letter. In this instance, we'll say it's a question mark. As such, entering "wom?n" would recall records which contained both *woman* and *women* in the relevant field.

Similarly, you should be able to use truncation to find many types of word with the same stem. For example, using the hash key to represent our truncation function, "libert#" would return any instances of words which begin with "libert" (liberty, libertarian, liberties etc).

Operators

Many catalogue searches will also allow you to indicate operational relationships between words to help refine your search further. The terms or symbols used to identify such operators may vary from catalogue to catalogue, but I'd strongly urge you to ask your library if they provide a guide to all the functions (or failing that, read through the catalogue's help pages) as these can be very powerful tools in helping you search.

Boolean operators

These locate records in one of the specified bibliographic fields, all of them, or only one of them. Some common Boolean operators include AND, OR, or NOT. A **keyword** search of "offer" and "acceptance" with these operators would work as outlined below:

- "Offer AND acceptance" would locate records with both these terms in their keywords
- "Offer OR acceptance" would locate records with one or the other of these terms in the keywords
- "Offer NOT acceptance" would locate records which contained "offer" but did not contain "acceptance"

Positional operators

These help identify terms within specified bibliographic fields depending on their position. Some common positional operators include SAME, WITH, NEAR and ADJ. A **title** search of "legal" and "history" with these operators would work as outlined below:

- "Legal SAME history" would retrieve only records which had the words "legal" and "history" somewhere within its title (WITH also works in this way).

- "Legal NEAR history" would retrieve records where the terms occur next to each other in the title, but not necessarily in the order in which they were entered in the search.
- "Legal ADJ history" would retrieve records where the terms occur next to each other in the title, in the exact order as entered in the search.

Relational operators

These allow you to specify numerical values to your searches. The syntax for these can vary considerably from catalogue to catalogue but I'd advise you to find out how these work as they can help you refine your searches by, for example, date (e.g. discounting any titles published before a certain date).

> ### Self-Test Question
>
> So, if we go back to our Foster example. Let's say we can't quite remember the name of the book we're looking for but we're pretty sure it does have the word "human" in it and we're sure it has a word like "liberty" in it somewhere. We also can't remember whether the author's name is Foster or Forster. How would you find the right title?

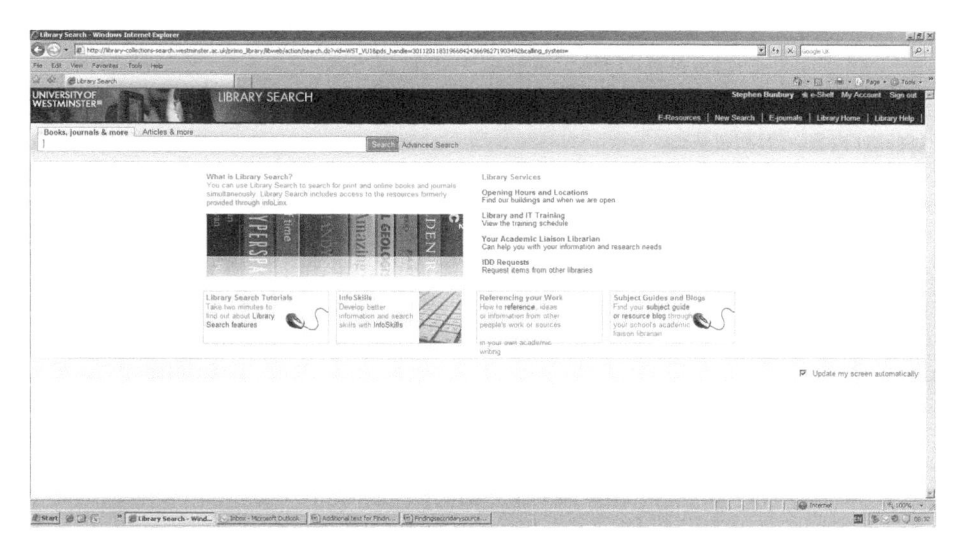

Figure 1: Example University of Westminster library search[3]

Finding books

As mentioned, the library catalogue is the best way to start your research. As we touched on above, if you know the book you're looking for, it should be very easy to find in the library catalogue. If you have

---
[3] http://library-collections-search.westminster.ac.uk/primo_library/libweb/action/search.do?vid=WST_VU1&pds_handle= 3011201183196684243669627190349&calling_system= Accessed 30/11/11

the ISBN then all the better (it's the *only* title with that unique identifier) but failing that the title and author surname should suffice. It is important to make sure you have found the very latest edition of any given textbook. You will soon come to realise that textbooks go out of date very quickly and, indeed, even the very latest edition might be a little out of date. Therefore, in some cases, you will also have to use other sources, such as legal encyclopaedias, to cross-check and ensure you have the most up to date information.

In some cases you may be asked to carry out research in an unfamiliar area of law. Using the library catalogue or a library search will assist you in locating different textbooks and casebooks about that particular subject area. It should also be noted that textbooks can assist you in generating keywords for further research. The importance of keywords cannot be over-emphasised as, when you're researching a brand new area of law (without guidance from your lecturer/module guide) then the art of finding relevant key terms will make your life much easier when beginning your search for further material. This will also be helpful if you are searching material from online databases or using hard copy materials such as *Halsbury's Laws of England*. The best way to identify keywords is, yet again, practice. The more you do this, the easier it will be for you to recognise which keywords will help you. Let's say for example that you were given an essay asking you to critically evaluate the Homicide Act 2005. You'd of course add the title of the Act to your search, but adding terms like "criticism," "critique," "analysis," "evaluation" and so on into your keyword search will help uncover books or monographs which are critically examining the act, rather than just outlining it, and which will be much more useful to your essay.

Finding journal articles

An academic article will generally examine a very specific area in considerable detail. Unlike a textbook (which, for the most part try to provide a neutral overview of the law) the author will generally argue their own point based on the research they have done. As such, articles are an invaluable secondary source that you should get used to reading and using in your own studies. They are written by academics and will be peer reviewed by other academics so you should be able to trust that the arguments or findings presented are sound and firmly based on valid evidence. They are, for the most part, examples of the kind of work you should aspire to be producing yourself.

Journals are edited collections of academic articles. Some journals will concern themselves with a particular area of law, for example, *The Criminal Law Review* includes, unsurprisingly, scholarly articles pertaining to the area of criminal law. Other journals will include articles from a range of legal subject areas. Journals are generally published several times each year (often monthly or quarterly) in volumes. As you can imagine, there can be a great number of articles published in any given year so it is very important that you get used to using and understanding citations. Essentially, citations provide information about the article, it's title and author and, crucially, in which volume of which journal it appears. This makes it much easier for you to trace a particular article (or indeed, for any article you cite in your work to be traced).

> International Journal of Discrimination and the Law, 2009, Vol. 10, pp. 111–131
> 1358-2291/2009 $10
>
> © 2009 A B Academic Publishers. Printed in Great Britain
>
> **THE EMPLOYER'S DUTY TO MAKE REASONABLE ADJUSTMENTS. WHEN IS A REASONABLE ADJUSTMENT, NOT REASONABLE?**
>
> STEPHEN BUNBURY
> *Lecturer in Law, University of Westminster Law School*
>
> **ABSTRACT**
>
> This article considers the impact of the reasonable adjustments duty imposed upon employers in section 4A of the Disability Discrimination Act (1995) where a provision, criterion, practice, or physical feature of the premises of the employer places the disabled person at a substantial disadvantage in comparison with persons who are not disabled. It considers that while the duty to make reasonable adjustments has contributed to the rising rates of employment among disabled people, an examination of the Employment Tribunal and EAT Statistics (GB) conversely reveals that there has been a steady increase in cases of disability discrimination in recent years. It is argued that the complexity of section 4A and the ensuing case law have contributed to the rising tide of cases in this field and is a trend which is likely to continue for the foreseeable future.

Figure 2: Journal extract

The figure above is a reproduction of the beginning of a journal article. When citing from an article you need to supply the following information (shaded in the figure): the author name, the title of the article, the title of the journal it was published in (often you can abbreviate this to an acronym of the journal title), the volume number, the year, and the pages within the journal where the article can be found. There are different styles of citation but generally this information is present. Although most UK law schools seem to favour the Harvard style, you should make sure you're aware of which method your institution requires you to use.

> **Example: some examples of citation styles**
>
> Harvard
> Bunbury, S (2009) "The employer's duty to make reasonable adjustments: when is a reasonable adjustment not reasonable?" *International Journal of Discrimination and the Law* vol. 10 pp. 111–131
>
> OSCOLA
> Stephen Bunbury, 'The employer's duty to make reasonable adjustments: when is reasonable adjustment not reasonable?' [2009] 10 International Journal of Discrimination and the Law 111
>
> Chicago
> Stephen Bunbury "The employer's duty to make reasonable adjustments: when is a reasonable adjustment not reasonable?" *International Journal of Discrimination and the Law* 10 (2009): 111–131
>
> MLA
> Bunbury, S "The employer's duty to make reasonable adjustments: when is a reasonable adjustment not reasonable?" International Journal of Discrimination and the Law 10 (2009): 111–131

Most libraries will contain information about the journals they subscribe to but will not have a central list of the articles that they hold. Therefore you will need to become proficient in searching for articles relevant to your research. As with searching for textbooks, the process will be much easier if you have the details of an article and you can simply search the library catalogue in a similar way as if you knew the title of a book you were looking for. However, when you do not know which article you will need you can find some initial details of journals in indexes, the library catalogue or various other databases. Again, as with books you can use the library catalogue by searching for keywords pertinent to your research brief. Many catalogues will allow you to filter your search results to journal articles, which will help eliminate textbooks from your search results.

Indexes are arranged by title, author, bibliographic detail and a summary of the article (which is usually quite brief). The summary will be very important as you will be able to quickly scan this to get a sense of the subject matter of a given article and thus assess whether or not it will be relevant to your research. The index will also contain details of where to locate the full text, so if you believe it is worth investigating you can easily get your hands on a copy. Whilst many indexes are no longer in print (owing to the wealth of journals now available online – more on this below) there are some indexes that are still available in hard-copy format, such as the Current Law Monthly Digest and the Index to Legal Periodicals which is based in the US. The Legal Journals Index which is published by Sweet and Maxwell is by far the best possible way to search UK law articles whether they are in print or online (via Westlaw). It includes the key points in the article and the online version provides you with links to various sources such as cases and legislation. It is advisable if you are carrying out research to use this as your starting point. Finally, you may find that your library does not stock a particular journal. If this is the case make use of other libraries and check their library catalogue.

Below is a list of indexes to assist you when searching for journals.

Table 1 – Adapted from indexing Service given by LawLinks[4]

Index Title	Details
IBSS	Bibliographical information from an international selection of publications (including over 2,600 journals) in the field of economics, political science, sociology and anthropology.
Index to Foreign Legal Periodicals	Access to legal literature worldwide including all forms of non Anglo-American law.
Index to Legal Periodicals	Bibliographic data for articles from legal periodicals and law books.
Index to Articles Related to Law	Includes details of substantial English language articles published throughout the world that are of research value. Reproduction of a printed index.
Journals Index on LNB	Covers c.120 journals from legal and business publishers.
Legal Journals Index on Westlaw	Covers legal journals published in the UK and Europe and journals covering topics related to the laws of the European Community and its member states.

---

[4] http://www.kent.ac.uk/lawlinks/researching-the-law/articles.html Accessed 28/11/11

Finding journals online

It is now common practice to use electronic sources to conduct legal research although you should be aware that not all research can be conducted online. However it is true to say that the majority of research can be conducted through legal databases. There are many databases that students use, though it should be recognised that in order to use these facilities your institution has to subscribe to them. You should avoid relying on just one database and instead use a variety to ensure you do not miss anything and have researched thoroughly.

There are a number of databases that universities or colleges will subscribe to. Two of the most popular such online resources are LexisNexis and Westlaw[5] and you will no doubt become very familiar with these throughout the course of your studies. These will be discussed below as well as other online databases. Electronic databases will only be effective if you know how to search them properly. As such, getting used to using different search terms, or different methods of searching the various databases is crucial. Searching the databases normally involves use of the same search methods as with hard copy searches. In order to search effectively you will need to have specific search terms. If you know the particular article you are trying to locate an advanced search may assist. All the databases have online search engines which may differ slightly. As with textbooks, you should always be aware of the dates when searching journals to ensure that they're current enough to be of use to your research.

Westlaw UK

Westlaw is a database that contains various articles which can assist you whilst undertaking research. It also has links to international law. The majority of articles in Westlaw are published by Westlaw UK, although they do have other journals which are owned by other publishers. If you cannot find a journal you are looking for in Westlaw UK it may be worthwhile searching in LexisLibrary.

HeinOnline

HeinOnline is another online resource your institution may subscribe to. It is owned by American publishers and contains various articles from the UK and America. It also stores the articles in their original format. Therefore when you print or view the article it displays the text as it would in its original hard copy format. Using HeinOnline in conjunction with other online databases is advisable as it may not include some of the popular or important journals you may wish to use for your research. It does however have the added benefit of being able to archive old information which may be useful for your research.

LexisLibrary

LexisLibrary is a huge database which includes, a wealth of primary and secondary sources. It is used by law students and practitioners to research areas of law. LexisLibrary does not hold every legal journal. Other online databases such as Westlaw may hold the journals that LexisLibrary do not have and may also provide online access to the content which is in hard copy. It also includes a series of law reports. For the purposes of this chapter we are concentrating on the latter which is commentary (*Halsbury's Laws* – more on this below) and journals.

---

[5] Both of these databases also hold primary sources of law but as this chapter focuses on secondary sources we will not cover this here.

Even though practitioners' texts are a source of secondary material it is unlikely that you will be asked to use these to carry out academic research as these texts are practice focused. If you do have to use these sources you will often find they have an update facility. The updating process is similar to that discussed above as with all other online databases and hard copy sources.

How to search secondary sources effectively using online databases

Step 1
Identify any keywords. These can be referred to as synonyms. These are words that mean the same thing or nearly have the same meaning as the term(s) you've identified as being important to your search

Step 2
If you have all the details of the article it may be an idea to search using the author and title details. (for example if you are using LexisLibrary select the journals from the tab button on the top of the screen)

Step 3
Search for a particular phrase or phrases. Use quotation marks at the beginning and ending of the phrase (" ")

Step 4
There may be other advanced searches you may wish to use but this will depend on the specific databases e.g. truncation or substitution

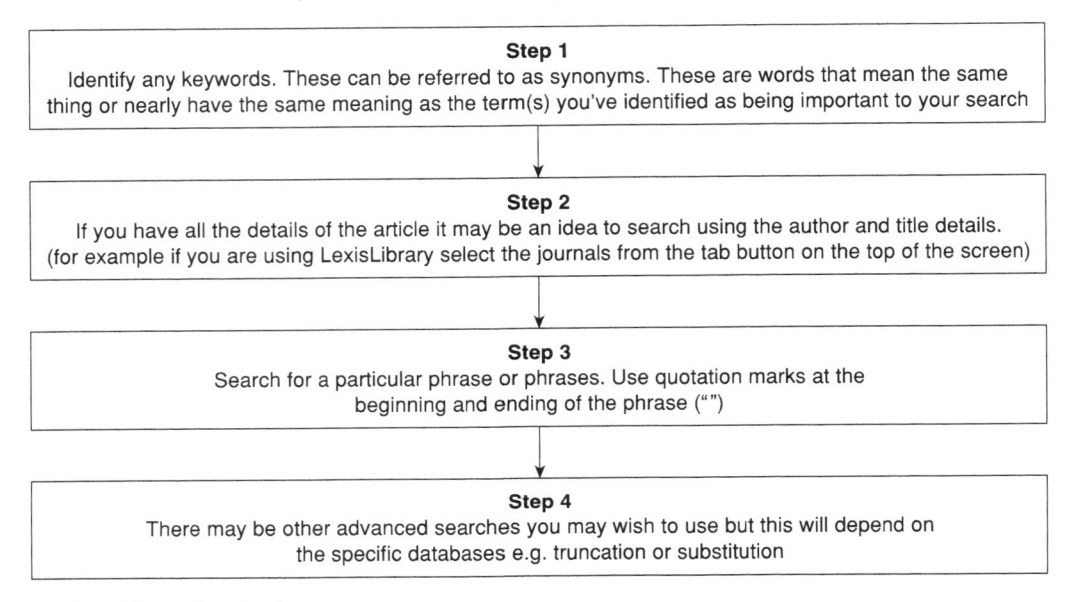

Figure 3: Searching online databases

Halsbury's Laws of England

Halsbury's Laws of England is a general legal encyclopaedia which is an essential tool for all law students embarking on legal study. It is the most comprehensive general encyclopaedia which contains a wealth of information on various areas of law. It not only contains secondary material, but also contains information about how and where to locate the primary sources. It is therefore an invaluable source of information for any law student. *Halsbury's Laws* provides you with an overview of the subject area and is an excellent starting point for any type of research. It is highly likely that your institution has subscribed to a number of online databases but most institutions will subscribe to *Halsbury's Laws* online and may also have the hard copy still available.

Using a hard copy of Halsbury's Laws

Using *Halsbury's Laws* in hard copy is a good place to start your research. It can be very helpful if you are finding it difficult to start any piece of legal research. For example, if you are having difficulties with trying to find search terms or keywords the hard copy of *Halsbury's Laws* index may assist you in trying to come up with such terms. Halsburys is arranged into alphabetical order and there is also the added benefit of being able to look through the index and tackle the area from a different perspective or look at other areas of law you may think will be helpful. Research using the in print version also has the benefit of each volume detailing the issue date. Another advantage of using the hard copy is that you have access to a *Consolidated Table of Cases* and *Consolidated Table of Statutes/Statutory Instruments* which may be of use to you.

You should keep in mind that there can be a great demand for these materials – especially at busy assessment periods and therefore there may not be enough copies for you to use at a particular time. As with any hard copy text that will likely be in high demand around such periods, if you think you're going to need it, don't leave your research until the last minute!

It is important to understand the difference between the online database (see below) and the hard copy. Updating differs from the electronic source in that the hard copy *Halsbury's Laws* has a loose-leaf annual *Cumulative Supplement* and monthly *Noter-Up-Service*. It is important to understand the two and these are illustrated in the table below:

Table 2 – Updating difference between Noter-Up Service *and* Cumulative Supplement

	Frequency	**Purpose**	**How to update?**
Noter-Up Service	Monthly	A more frequent update. For e.g. a development in the law may have affected a particular area of law, which may in turn overhaul the previous law relating to that area. Or there may be new cases, statutes or statutory instruments which may be of use. Updates in between the Cumulative Supplement. Serves the same purpose as the Cumulative Supplement but is more frequent.	**Step 1:** Look up volume and paragraph number **Step 2:** Look for the paragraph number **Step 3:** Check to see if there have been any amendments.
Cumulative Supplement	Annually	To update yearly to make sure the law is up-to date. Updates each volume to a particular date. Part 1 of the cumulative supplement will detail the date.	Same process as above.

Practical Question

Imagine that you have been asked to write an essay on contract formation which includes the rules around offer and acceptance in contract formation specific to auctions. Work through the example below with a hard copy of *Halsbury's Laws* . . .

Step 1: Consolidated index –

Search the index for some keywords. It is divided into headings and subheadings.

Keywords: Contract, auction

Results: Contract, auction

Results: Auction → offer and invitation to treat

Note: this section of the index from Halsbury's Laws has been shortened for ease of replication.

> ATTORNMENT
>   bailee, by, 4th (5th), 231
>   equitable assignment distinguished, 9(1) (4th), 743n⁵
>   receiver, to, 39(2) (4th), 375
>   stamp duty on, 44(1) (4th), 1057
>   tenancy created by, 27(1) (4th), 3
>
> AU PAIR
>   leave to enter United Kingdom, 4(2) (4th), 108
>
> AUCTION
>   *The title* AUCTION *is contained in vol* 4 (5th), *para 1 et seq*
>   Meaning, 4 (5th), 50
>   advertisement of, 4 (5th), 41
>   auctioneer. *See* AUCTIONEER
>   bidding, 4 (5th), 50
>   firearms, sale of, 4 (5th), 1
>   livestock, of, 4 (5th), 40
>   offer and invitation to treat, 9(1) (4th), 636
>   postal, 4 (5th), 56
>   reserve price–
>   notification of, 4 (5th), 48
>   private sale at, 4 (5th), 8
>   sale below, 4 (5th), 9
>   withdrawal of property from, 4 (5th), 55

Step 2: Volume

Locate the volume number

Results: offer and invitation to treat 9(1) (4th), 636. Details the law relating to auctions. Find this section in the relevant volume. As you can see from the first paragraph of this extract, we've found the area we're looking for in terms of offer and acceptance:

> **636. Auctions** At auction sales, it is a long-established rule that prima facie the auctioneer's request for bids is a mere invitation to treat[1], and that each bid constitutes an offer[2] which is accepted on behalf of the seller by the auctioneer when signifies his acceptance in the usual manner[3]. It would seem, moreover, that each bid lapses as soon as a higher bid is made[4], and that any bid may be withdrawn before the auctioneer's acceptance of it[5]. Generally, the sale of an interest in land can only be made in writing[6], but this rule does not apply when the sale is conducted by public auction[7].

Step 3: Update using the Cumulative Supplement Results: There is only one entry in this case, as below:

---

636 Auctions

NOTES-Certain functions under provisions mentioned in this paragraph are 'relevant functions' for the purposes of the Regulatory Enforcement and Sanctions Act 2008 s.4, Sch 3: see LOCAL GOVERNMENT vol 69 (2009) PARA 733.

639-640 Offers to the world at large, Options

Certain functions under . . .

Step 4: Update using Noter-up Results: In this instance, there are no entries in the Noter-up.

Using Halsbury's Laws online

Whilst there are some advantages in using the hard copy of *Halsbury's Laws* . . . as identified above, there are also many benefits from using the online version. The clearest being that the information is available at the click of a button and updating is much easier as there are links which allow you to update the source. This combines both the Cumulative Supplement and Noter-up.

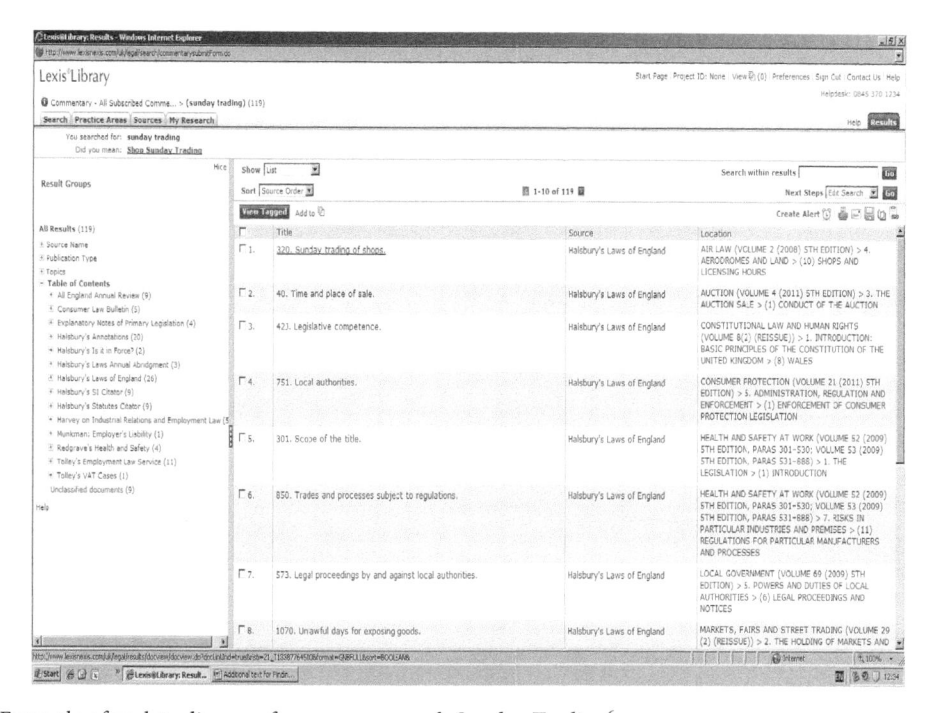

Figure 4: Example of update diagram from screen search Sunday Trading[6]

---

[6] http://www.lexisnexis.com/uk/legal/results/docview/docview.do?docLinkInd=true&risb=21_T13373949570&format=GNBFULL&sort=BOOLEAN&startDocNo=1&resultsUrlKey=29_T13373949574&cisb=22_T13373949573&treeMax=true&treeWidth=0&csi=274661&docNo=1 Accessed 28/11/11

In order to use *Halsburys Laws* online version effectively you need, which should be no surprise by now, to search keywords. You will then need to click the red search button to search for the terms you have entered. The search screen will display the results. You may also wish to organise your search results in a particular order such as by date, or by relevance. The screen also contains the location details of the source and may be of assistance when footnoting or referencing the material, so it is a good idea to make a note of the location as this will save you time when it comes to referencing and writing a bibliography.

Once you have found the relevant information you wish to use, you will need to access the material. In order to do this you click on the title and then the text will appear. This will provide the full text which is identical to the hard copy. The text will then contain information relevant to your search or subject matter and will include what *Halsbury's Laws* has to say on that particular subject. Footnotes will be included which may contain information on where to locate the primary source i.e. cases or statutory legislation. The update icon may also include links to various legislation or cases which may be of relevance. **It is vitally important to click on the update tab** since this will make sure the law you cite in your work will be the most current, thus ensuring that the law you are using is not outdated.

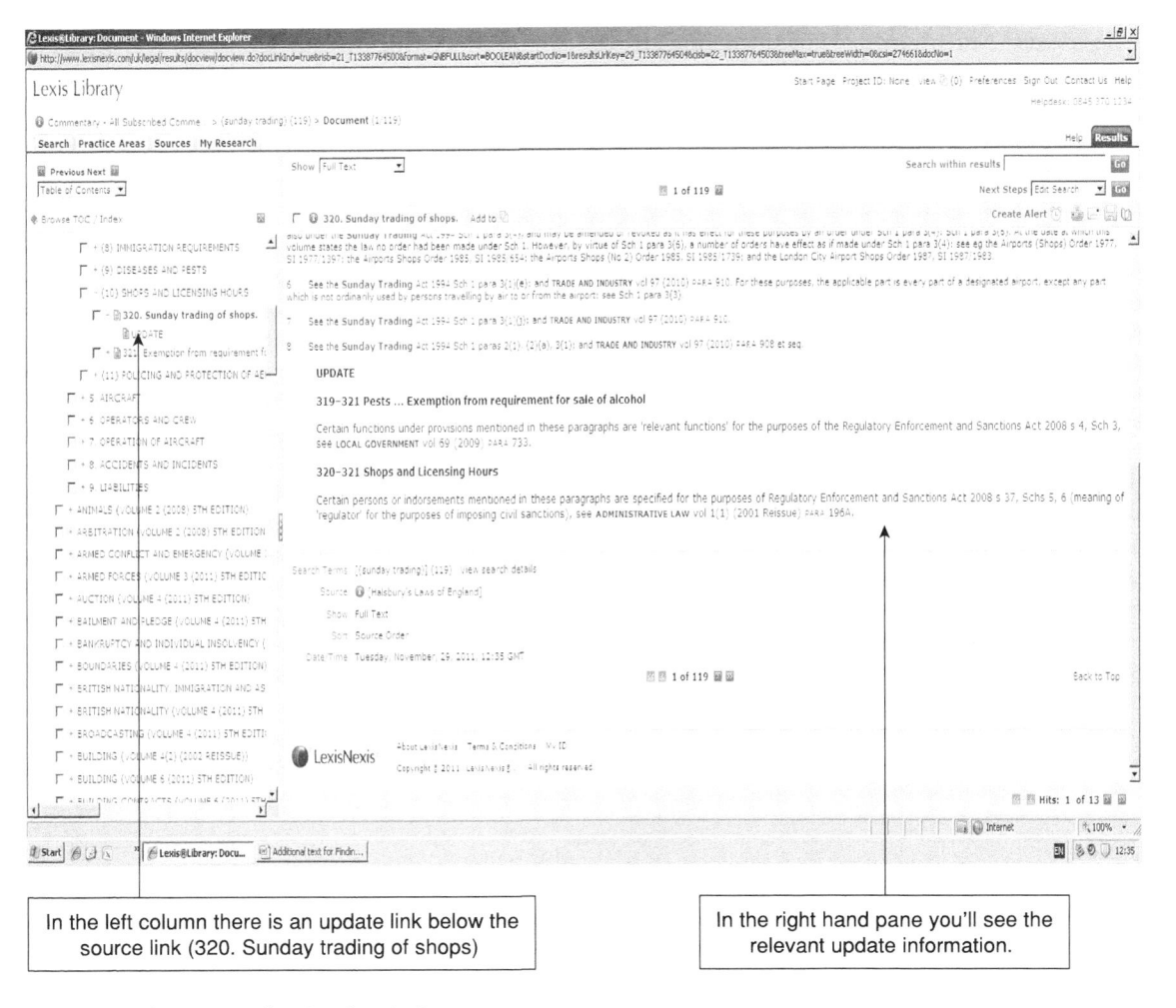

Figure 5: Update screen shot Sunday Trading

How to search Halsbury's Laws online

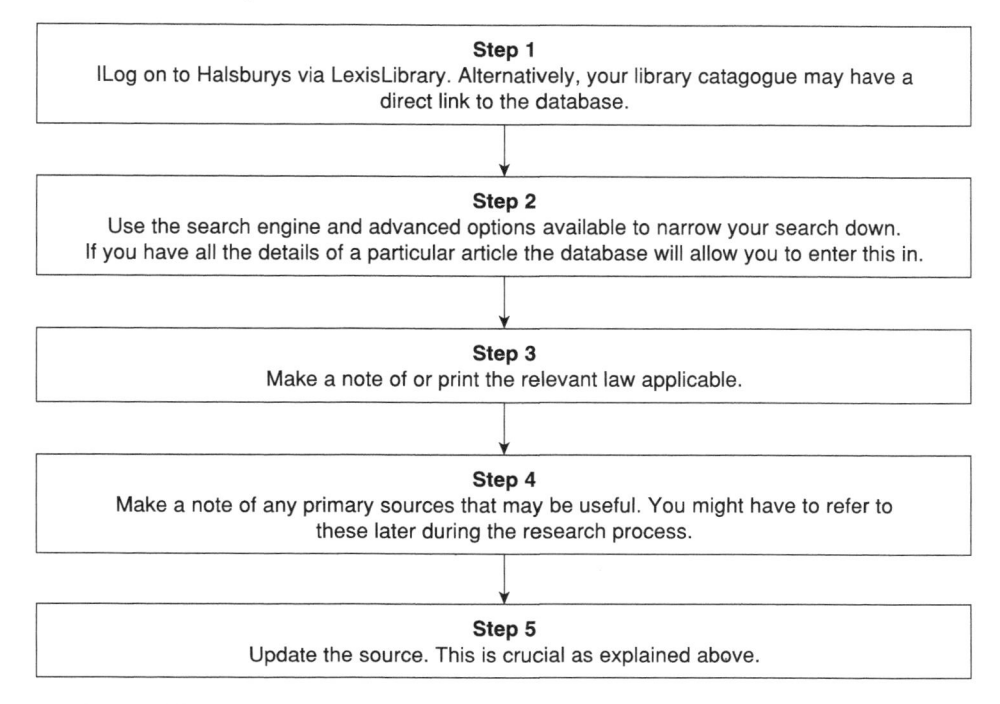

Step 1
ILog on to Halsburys via LexisLibrary. Alternatively, your library catagogue may have a direct link to the database.

Step 2
Use the search engine and advanced options available to narrow your search down. If you have all the details of a particular article the database will allow you to enter this in.

Step 3
Make a note of or print the relevant law applicable.

Step 4
Make a note of any primary sources that may be useful. You might have to refer to these later during the research process.

Step 5
Update the source. This is crucial as explained above.

Figure 6: Searching *Halsburys Laws*

Other secondary sources

Use of the Internet

It has been stated that:

> "some material on the internet will not have been reviewed or edited. Indeed, some of it will be misleading or possibly incorrect. Many lecturers will consider open-access sources that can be freely edited by anyone, such as Wikipedia, as unreliable in view of this fact. Some entries will be written to a very high standard and others will not. On that basis it is probably safer not to rely on them, but to find a more readily authoritative source that you can use instead."[7]

Therefore it is never a good idea to start any legal research using internet sources such as Wikipedia. Whilst the internet provides a wealth of secondary material it is often the case that, at best, the material is outdated, and at worst, inaccurate, inconsistent, and unverified. That said, the internet can provide information that may be of use, if you know where to look and what sources to disregard.

---

[7] L. Webley, *Legal Writing* 2nd edition (Routledge-Cavendish 2010).

Perhaps the best advice to offer here is to ask your lecturer which websites they use and trust when they're researching in the area they're teaching you. For example, if you're studying human rights, your lecturer might refer you to the European Court of Human Rights (ECHR) website which does hold a lot of valuable secondary information (such as codes of practice).

If you are going to use the internet to search for secondary sources a Google Scholar search may be beneficial. A Google Scholar search will locate various secondary sources and may assist you in trying to locate journal articles. JustCite is another search engine which may be helpful to use whilst undertaking research on a particular area. It is a search engine which provides links to case law, legislation and legal journals. However, and I cannot stress this strongly enough, it really is best to start your research with online databases that your institution subscribes to such as LexisLibrary and Westlaw UK.

Newspapers

Newspapers are another type of secondary source which may be useful. However you need to be careful with newspapers and understand that they often contain bias. It is quite simple to locate a good quality newspaper. Regional and international newspapers are available in any local newsagent or alternatively available online. For older editions LexisLibrary is useful. The *Guardian, Independent and Times* have legal sections on Lawtel and are regarded as good quality newspapers. The coverage of newspaper reports is extensive therefore you will have to be clever when searching for certain material. There are options on the databases to narrow your search down to legal material in particular newspapers.

Practical Questions

1. Using Halsbury's Law hard copy find out whether there is any legislation that restricts trading hours on a Sunday?
2. Using Halsbury's Laws online find out the legal requirements for having a Pit bull Terrier Dog in the United Kingdom? Is it illegal to have this type of dog as a pet?

Reflection Questions

1. Which search did you find more time consuming?
2. Which one would you use in future?

Self-Test Questions

1. Name two major online databases which can be used for searching online material.
2. What is the purpose of updating *Halsbury's Laws* hard copy and online?
3. What are the differences between updating *Halsbury's Laws* hard copy and *Halsbury's Laws* online database?
4. Why is it good to use a variety of online electronic sources when searching for journal articles?
5. What are the advantages and disadvantages of using textbooks?
6. Imagine you were asked to write an essay on the reform of the House of Lords. What key words would you use? How would you search for articles relating to the subject matter?

Further reading

A. Bradney, F. Cownie, A. Neal and D. Newell, *How to Study Law*, 6th edition (Sweet and Maxwell, 2010)
H. Carr, S. Carter and K. Horsey, *Skills for Law Students* (Oxford University Press, 2009)
P. Clinch, *Using A Law Library*, 2nd edition (Oxford University Press, 2001)
S. Cottrell, *The Study Skills Handbook*, 3rd edition (Palgrave Macmillan, 2008)
S. Cottrell, *Critical Thinking Skills* (Palgrave Macmillan, 2005)
E. Finch and S. Fafinski, *Legal Skills*, 3rd edition (Oxford University Press, 2010)
E. Higgins and L. Tatham, *Successful Legal Writing* (Sweet and Maxwell, 2006)
J. Holland and J. Webb, *Learning Legal Rules*, 7th edition (Oxford University Press, 2010)
R. Huxley-Binnd, L. Riley and C. Turner, *Unlocking Legal Learning*, 2nd edition (Hodder Education, 2008)
J. Knowles and P. Thomas, *Effective Legal Research,* 1st edition (Sweet and Maxwell, 2006)
A. Smith, *Glanville Williams: Learning the Law*, 14th edition (Sweet and Maxwell, 2010)
L. Webley, *Legal Writing*, 2nd edition (Routledge-Cavendish 2010)